ANTI-BLACK THOUGHT

THOUGHT

1863 - 1925

"THE NEGRO PROBLEM"

AN ELEVEN –VOLUME ANTHOLOGY OF RACIST WRITINGS

edited and introduced by

JOHN DAVID SMITH

Alumni Distinguished Professor of History at North Carolina State University

A GARLAND SERIES

VOLUME FIVE

THE "ARIEL" CONTROVERSY

RELIGION AND "THE NEGRO PROBLEM"
PART I

edited with introductions by

JOHN DAVID SMITH

GARLAND PUBLISHING, INC.
NEW YORK & LONDON
1993

Library of Congress Cataloging-In-Publication Data

The "Ariel" controversy : religion and "the Negro problem" / edited by John David
Smith.
    p.   cm. — (Anti-Black thought, 1863–1925 ; v. 5)
    Includes bibliographical references.
    ISBN 0-8153-0977-5 (alk. paper)
    1. Racism—United States—History—19th century. 2. Afro-Americans—History—
1863–1877. 3. Racism—Religious aspects. 4. United States—Race relations.
5. White supremacy movements—United States—History—19th century. I. Smith,
John David, 1949– . II. Series.
E185.2.A75 1993
241'.675'0973—dc20   92-32358
                                               CIP

FOR ALEX, LISA, AND LORENZ

CONTENTS

THE "ARIEL" CONTROVERSY

ACKNOWLEDGMENTS

Anti-Black Thought 1863–1925 began in 1989 when Professor Paul Finkelman suggested to Leo F. Balk, Vice President of Garland Publishing, Inc., that I undertake an anthology of texts that documented late nineteenth-century American racism. I am grateful to Professor Finkelman for his endorsement and to Mr. Balk for his commitment to and enthusiasm for the project. My editors at Garland, Anita Vanca and Jonathan Oestreich, have been most helpful in locating texts, obtaining permissions to publish, and hammering out details. I very much appreciate their labors.

At North Carolina State University, I benefited from the research assistance of graduate students Eric Jackson, Paul Peterson, Michelle Justice, and Jo Frost. Eric and Paul helped me compile a data base of possible texts and verified citations. Michelle and Jo joined me in the appraisal process and Jo played an important role in deciding upon the final arrangement of the texts. Much of this work was tedious, and I value the care and precision with which these graduate students performed their tasks.

Professor Randall M. Miller offered keen advice regarding my use of the American Colonization Society texts. Dr. Jeffrey J. Crow and Professors David P. Gilmartin, William Kimler, and Linda O. McMurry subjected the "General Introduction" and the volume introductions to thoughtful criticism and thereby strengthened the entire project. I am especially indebted to Will Kimler for his painstaking analysis of the introductory section on "science" and race in Volumes V and VI, and for his help in revising this section. I hold in high regard the judgments of each of these colleagues and thank them for the time and effort they devoted to evaluating various drafts of my essay.

As the project neared completion, Alex Andrusyszyn assisted me in managing the extensive files. And finally, over the course of editing *Anti-Black Thought 1863–1925*, Sylvia A. Smith provided valuable insights into the nature of racial and sexual oppression and the role of law in social change.

When a man attempts to discuss the negro problem at the South, he may begin with the negro, but he really touches, with however light a hand, the whole bewildering problem of a civilization.

—*Edgar Gardner Murphy (1904)*[1]

The most formidable of all the ills which threaten the future existence of the Union arises from the presence of a black population upon its territory; and in contemplating the cause of the present embarrassments or of the future dangers of the United States, the observer is invariably led to consider this as a primary fact.

—*Alexis de Tocqueville (1835)*[2]

GENERAL INTRODUCTION

Writing in 1903, more than a half-century after Alexis de Tocqueville, W.E.B. Du Bois, the brilliant black historian, sociologist, and polemicist, viewed America's "ills" from a radically different perspective. Nonetheless, the two men concurred on the role that race played in defining America's character and destiny. Du Bois wrote in the shadow of Jim Crow race relations, American imperialism, and emerging Progressivism. As he looked back toward the nineteenth century, Du Bois found a legacy of slavery and racial oppression. He branded it a blot on the United States, which was then an emerging industrial and world power.

"The problem of the twentieth century," wrote Du Bois in *The Souls of Black Folk*, was "the problem of the color-line,—the relation of the darker to the lighter races of men in Asia and Africa, in America and the islands of the sea." Summarizing the history and cultural lives of African Americans, Du Bois underscored a question that ran as a leitmotif through white racial thought from the age of emancipation to the age of segregation. "What," he asked, "shall be *done* with Negroes?"[3] In his many writings Du Bois pounded away at the passive roles whites had always assigned to blacks— first as slaves—and later as freedmen, all too often caught in the web of neoslavery. From years of observing racial conditions in the North and South, Du Bois concluded that blacks and whites lived worlds and cultures apart—separated by a veil of racism. Years later, reflecting on the emancipation experience, Du Bois lamented that the freedman shared little of the progress and optimism that had marked white Victorian America. He wrote with elegant pathos: "The slave went free; stood a brief moment in the sun; then moved back again toward slavery."[4]

Though a propagandist for black rights, Du Bois in no way overstated the case. Most white Americans in the nineteenth century, north and south, before and after emancipation, did in fact view blacks as inferior "others." Though their attitudes toward blacks varied from place to place and over time, the vast majority of whites nevertheless held blacks, as a people and as a class, in contempt. To be sure there were exceptions. Whites always could identify "good Negroes," persons who conformed to their definition of acceptable behavior—deferential blacks who knew their "place." In the main, however, whites treated blacks as persons who differed in pejorative ways from themselves.

As so often in American history, whites defined "different" to mean "inferior." Not only their skin color, but their temperament, culture, and community, allegedly marked African Americans as "different." Such variances from the "normal"—the white ideal—were interpreted by the dominant caste as immutable characteristics. Yet, in what constituted just one of many contradictions in the ideology of white racism, whites lived in seemingly constant fear of racial mixing. If black "traits" were unalterable, why then were whites so apprehensive of miscegenation? The Old South's large mulatto population stood as a silent reminder that racial fears had not prevented racial mixing under slavery. After slavery whites continued to perceive blacks as marginal men and women—persons who mattered little, whose alleged childlike behavior and intellects deserved minimal respect. Blacks were to be acted upon. Decisions were to be made for them, not by them. During slavery's long history, various schools of racists trotted out a broad range of arguments—biblical, "scientific," historical, social, and economic—to bolster the idea of keeping blacks in chains.[5]

Following emancipation in 1865, whites, notably southerners, continued to describe blacks as degraded, certainly unprepared for the responsibilities and challenges of freedom. Many whites predicted that blacks could not survive as freedmen and women. Without the alleged paternalism of slavery, they reasoned, blacks would fall by the wayside, unable to compete in the class and racial struggle with whites. Some extreme racists even continued to define blacks as subhuman "beings," whose reported separate creation destined them to a perpetual servitude regardless of laws and legislation passed by civil authorities.

There was a direct relationship, of course, between the end of slavery and the determined search by whites for other means to regulate blacks. By the post-Civil War years, explains historian George M. Fredrickson, an "explicit or ideological racism" had taken root in the South. Social forces—"selfishness, greed, and the pursuit of privilege"—exacerbated the notion that blacks were natural inferiors. By the end of the century, social and economic tensions—as well as an upsurge of racism worldwide—led whites to campaign for the legal segregation and disfranchisement of their former slaves.[6]

At first white southerners settled on the Black Codes passed and then overthrown during Presidential Reconstruction. When other forms of racial control failed, post-Civil War whites eventually resorted to violent means.

From 1882, when statistics began to be collected systematically, until 1903, white mobs lynched 1,941 blacks.[7] Many other lynchings no doubt went unreported. Those blacks who were spared the barbarities of white racial "justice" faced a labyrinth of legal and extralegal barriers: *de jure* segregation under the Jim Crow laws and *de facto* segregation imposed by custom. Turn-of-the-century blacks had to fight to gain the most basic constitutional rights, minimally adequate schools, medical care, housing, and economic opportunities. As historian Nell Irvin Painter has delineated:

> At the turn of the twentieth century nine out of ten blacks lived in the South, and three-quarters of black farmers were tenants or sharecroppers. In the generation since emancipation, blacks, who constituted about 40 percent of the southern population, had bought one-eight [sic] of the region's farms. Even so, nearly all Afro-Americans, even the landowning minority, were poor. The most oppressed lived as peons, tied to planters by long-term contracts that deprived them of the right to change employers for as much as ten years, or as convicts, whom the states leased to planters and industrialists. In either situation, employers, who cared only about extracting a maximum of work from actual or virtual prisoners, provided wretched living and working conditions. These southern blacks, who earned bare subsistence and often died before earning their freedom, represented the worst-paid workers in this country.

Though African Americans never stood passively by acquiescing to white hegemony, theirs was a constant uphill struggle. Again, as before Appomattox, blacks confronted a maze of white arguments determined to keep them locked into inferior social, political, and economic status.[8]

Writing in 1908, the reform journalist Ray Stannard Baker analyzed the causes and consequences of America's race "problem," what whites generally termed "The Negro Problem." In *Following the Color Line* Baker identified "the most sinister phase of the race problem" as "instinctive race repulsion and competitive jealousy." Race relations, marred by "mutual fear and suspicion," led to the segregation of blacks and whites, what Baker described as "the rapid flying apart of the races." "More and more," he noted, "they are becoming a people wholly apart—separate in their churches, separate in their schools, separate in cars, conveyances, hotels, restaurants, with separate professional men. In short, we discover tendencies in this country toward the development of a caste system."[9]

This system of American apartheid marred the burgeoning industrial complex of the North as well as the agricultural South. Black northerners experienced *de facto* segregation while competing for jobs, housing, and social services with the "new" immigrants who populated the urban North. Racial violence often erupted in the North as persons with different cultural and ethnic backgrounds clashed. Race riots, for example, occurred in Springfield, Ohio, in March, 1904, and in August, 1906; in Springfield, Illinois, in August, 1908; in East St. Louis, Illinois, in July, 1917; and in

Chicago in July, 1919. To be sure, the northward migration of blacks after the turn of the century added diversity, texture, and power to the northern black community. Blacks challenged white discrimination at every turn. While Baker observed "comparatively little social and political prejudice" in the North, he nevertheless admitted that in the North "the Negro has a hard fight to get anything but the most subservient place in the economic machine." Black workers, in East St. Louis, for example, "had separate washrooms and dressing rooms, usually worked in segregated labor gangs, and ate meals in 'the colored section' of the lunchrooms." The African Americans lived in black ghettoes and their children attended "Negro schools."[10]

In the South, post-Civil War whites drew upon a two-hundred-year history of perceiving blacks as passive extensions of the master class. The old proslavery argument remained very much alive long after General Robert E. Lee's men stacked their guns at Appomattox, becoming a permanent fixture in the intellectual life and economic and legal world of the New South.[11] While few whites dreamed of reviving chattel slavery, conditions of neoslavery—modified serfdom, economic peonage, enticement laws, emigrant agent restrictions, contract laws, vagrancy statutes, the criminal-surety and convict labor systems—ensnared African Americans. After 1890 Jim Crow laws in one southern state after another locked blacks into a truly separate and unequal world.[12] Frightened by the thought of "social equality" and economic competition with blacks, white southerners employed all manner of racial violence to keep African Americans generally landless, undereducated, and powerless. Whites even conjured up the notion of black men as rapists of white women, thereby projecting their racial fantasies upon the sons of their ex-slaves. "Racial purity" became a catch-all phrase in the lexicon of the Jim Crow South. White southerners' determination to maintain absolute control over blacks amounted to what historian Joel Williamson has termed a "rage for order." "Uppity" blacks— men and women who demanded respect, fair treatment, and equal opportunities—threatened the very fabric of the South's biracial system.

Determined to maintain racial control, white Americans after the Civil War published widely on the causes and consequences of what they defined to be "The Negro Problem." As they struggled to find answers to the race question, whites flooded popular magazines, newspapers, scholarly journals, polemical tracts, monographs, and "scientific" treatises with writings on racial themes. Conferences, symposia, and public lectures underscored the sense of immediacy whites felt about the "race problem." By the turn of the century discussion of the "The Negro Problem" had virtually become a cottage industry. "Race thinkers" aplenty satisfied the seemingly insatiable demand in the white community for "experts" on just how to deal with the Negro.[13]

This eleven-volume anthology of writings on "The Negro Problem," written with only one exception by white authors, documents the various strains of racist thought in America from 1863 to 1925. The collection reproduces in facsimile format eighty-six texts that espoused a broad range of racist ideas—from relatively mild paternalistic remarks to extreme racialist diatribes—prevalent over the course of the post-emancipation age. It contains a microcosm of the various negative images whites held of blacks, including vulgar racist caricatures, genteel but condescending suggestions for black "uplift," and endorsements of black colonization. Many of the eighty-six texts are obscure racist pamphlets and speeches. To round out the collection, and to provide context, I have included several hard-to-find books, conference proceedings, and Ku Klux Klan items. The texts are drawn from the holdings of nineteen research libraries, and from the collections of the editor and the publisher.

In order to provide researchers with convenient topical access, the volumes are arranged thematically. Some themes (for example, the alleged backwardness of Africans, innate inferiority of blacks, slavery's "civilizing" influence, the horrors of emancipation and Reconstruction, fear of miscegenation among whites, the crucial importance of maintaining white supremacy, and the advantages of racial segregation) appear again and again throughout the collection. The topical format has eliminated much redundancy from volume to volume and serves to illustrate the breadth and depth of racist thought. Within the topical arrangement, each volume is arranged chronologically, suggesting the continuity and evolution of thought, as well as the subtle shift of racial themes over time. With no illusions of being "comprehensive" (the difficulties of locating texts and then gaining permission to publish them have been staggering), this edition is by design selective and eclectic. Nonetheless, it is hoped that *Anti-Black Thought 1863-1925* provides a representative sampling of conservative and reactionary racial thought from the era of the Civil War until the 1920s.

To be sure, these volumes tell only one side of the story—the white side of the discourse on race during the age of Jim Crow. They document the hurtful racial stereotypes and unfortunate images of blacks associated with that period. They illustrate how whites viewed the black presence as a "problem"—a menace—and how whites defined sources of the "problem" and identified solutions to it. For almost twenty years I have worked with these and similar materials and I am cognizant of just how painful and disturbing this sort of material is to African Americans. It is my determination, however, that the process of bringing such historical texts to light—and making them readily available for students and a general audience—will play some small role in battling racial injustice, bigotry, and class rule. An understanding of the pervasiveness and intensity of white racism is a key to comprehending the obstacles to true black freedom and equality.

This is not to suggest that blacks were passive and stood aimlessly by as whites acted upon them. Fortunately recent historical scholarship has uncovered how blacks actively fought slavery and the Jim Crow system that replaced it—a system with the cards consistently stacked against African

Americans. Blacks resisted nonetheless.[14] In different ways W.E.B. Du Bois, Booker T. Washington, Charles W. Chesnutt, Kelly Miller, and hundreds of other black leaders forcefully engaged their white critics and demanded racial justice throughout the period. With eloquent outrage they protested lynching, limited industrial education, disfranchisement, and segregation in every avenue of American life. Along with such white reformers as George Washington Cable, Lewis H. Blair, Albion W. Tourgée, and Franz Boas they challenged Jim Crow America. The overwhelming scale of the white racist barrage, however, had the effect of keeping blacks on the defensive. Just as whites controlled American society, so too did their racist dogma dominate the popular press. As a result, all too often blacks were forced to respond to whites on their terms. In other words, whites dictated the contours of the turn-of-the-century discourse on race. One of the tragedies of white racism is that the talents of many black scholars were diverted from more useful pursuits to defending what should have been obvious—the humanity of African Americans.

Even so, Du Bois and other African Americans remained ever hopeful that "out of the shame and oppression of the past" that "a new and broader humanity" might succor suffering blacks. As Frederick Douglass explained in 1886, the phrase "the negro problem" was itself "a misnomer." Eight years later Douglass referred to the "so-called but mis-called Negro problem." Responding to the common assumption among whites that they were civilized and blacks were uncivilized, Douglass charged "that there is nothing in the history of savages to surpass the blood-chilling horrors and fiendish excesses perpetrated against the coloured people of this country, by the so-called enlightened and Christian people of the South." "The Negro Problem" was, as Tocqueville, Du Bois, and Douglass had known all along, the white man's problem after all.[15]

Endnotes

[1]Murphy, *Problems of the Present South: A Discussion of Certain of the Educational, Industrial and Political Issues in the Southern States* (New York: Macmillan Company, 1904), 158.

[2]Tocqueville, *Democracy in America,* 2 vols. (1835; New York: Schocken Books, 1974), 1:424.

[3]Du Bois, *The Souls of Black Folk: Essays and Sketches* (1903; Greenwich: Fawcett Publications, 1961), 23, second quotation, emphasis added.

[4]Du Bois, *Black Reconstruction in America* (1934; New York: Atheneum, 1973), 30.

[5]George M. Fredrickson, *The Black Image in the White Mind: The Debate on Afro-American Character and Destiny, 1817–1914* (New York: Harper and

Row, 1971); Larry E. Tise, *Proslavery: A History of the Defense of Slavery in America, 1701–1840* (Athens: University of Georgia Press, 1987).

[6]Fredrickson, "Toward a Social Interpretation of the Development of American Racism," in Nathan I. Huggins, Martin Kilson, and Daniel M. Fox, eds., *Key Issues in the Afro-American Experience*, 2 vols. (New York: Harcourt Brace Jovanovich, 1971), 1:241, 254.

[7]Robert L. Zangranado, *The NAACP Crusade Against Lynching, 1909–1950* (Philadelphia: Temple University Press, 1980), 6. On the recent literature on racial violence, see W. Fitzhugh Brundage, "Mob Violence North and South, 1865–1940," *Georgia Historical Quarterly*, 75 (Winter, 1991): 748–770.

[8]I.A. Newby, *Jim Crow's Defense: Anti-Negro Thought in America, 1900–1930* (Baton Rouge: Louisiana State University Press, 1965); Lawrence J. Friedman, *The White Savage: Racial Fantasies in the Postbellum South* (Englewood Cliffs: Prentice-Hall, 1970); Joel Williamson, *The Crucible of Race: Black-White Relations in the American South Since Emancipation* (New York: Oxford University Press, 1984); Painter, *Standing at Armageddon: The United States, 1877–1919* (New York: W.W. Norton, 1987), xxi.

[9]Baker, *Following the Color Line: American Negro Citizenship in the Progressive Era* (New York: Doubleday, Page & Company, 1908), 298, 299, 300.

[10]Baker, *Following the Color Line*, 129; Elliott Rudwick, *Race Riot at East St. Louis, July 2, 1917* (New York: Atheneum, 1972), 6.

[11]John David Smith, *An Old Creed for the New South: Proslavery Ideology and Historiography, 1865–1918* (1985; Athens: University of Georgia Press, 1991).

[12]Pete Daniel, *The Shadow of Slavery: Peonage in the South, 1901–1969* (1972; New York: Oxford University Press, 1973); Daniel A. Novak, *The Wheel of Servitude: Black Forced Labor After Slavery* (Lexington: University Press of Kentucky, 1978); William Cohen, *At Freedom's Edge: Black Mobility and the Southern White Quest for Racial Control, 1861–1915* (Baton Rouge: Louisiana State University Press, 1991).

[13]See Alfred Holt Stone, "More Race Problem Literature," *Publications of the Southern History Association*, 10 (July, 1906): 218–227. "The great salient feature of the problem of race relations to-day," concluded Stone, "is the steadily increasing uniformity of ideas among white men all over the world,—as they come face to face with the negro." See p. 227.

[14]See, for example, Arnold H. Taylor, *Travail and Triumph: Black Life and Culture in the South Since the Civil War* (Westport: Greenwood Press, 1976); Leon F. Litwack, *Been in the Storm So Long: The Aftermath of Slavery* (New York: Alfred A. Knopf, 1979); Vincent Harding, *There Is a*

River: The Black Struggle for Freedom in America (New York: Harcourt Brace Jovanovich, 1981); Mary Frances Berry and John W. Blassingame, *Long Memory: The Black Experience in America* (New York: Oxford University Press, 1982); John Hope Franklin and August Meier, eds., *Black Leaders of the Twentieth Century* (Urbana: University of Illinois Press, 1982); Howard N. Rabinowitz, ed., *Southern Black Leaders of the Reconstruction Era* (Urbana: University of Illinois Press, 1982); Eric Foner, *Nothing But Freedom: Emancipation and Its Legacy* (Baton Rouge: Louisiana State University Press, 1983); Armstead L. Robinson, "The Difference Freedom Made: The Emancipation of Afro-Americans," in Darlene Clark Hine, ed., *The State of Afro-American History: Past, Present, Future* (Baton Rouge: Louisiana State University Press, 1986), 51–75; Leon Litwack and August Meier, eds., *Black Leaders of the Nineteenth Century* (Urbana: University of Illinois Press, 1988).

[15]Du Bois, "The Negro South and North," *Bibliotheca Sacra*, 62 (July, 1905), in Herbert Aptheker, ed., *The Complete Published Works of W.E.B. Du Bois: Volume I, 1891–1909* (Millwood, NY: Kraus-Thompson Organization, 1982), 256; Douglass to W.H. Thomas, July 16, 1886, Frederick Douglass Papers, Manuscript Division, Library of Congress; Douglass, *The Lessons of the Hour* (1894), in Philip S. Foner, ed., *The Life and Writings of Frederick Douglass*, 4 vols. (1955; New York International Publishers, 1975), 4:491, 492–493.

FURTHER READINGS[1]

Anderson, Eric. *Race and Politics in North Carolina, 1872–1901: The Black Second.* Baton Rouge: Louisiana State University Press, 1981.

Bauman, Mark K. "Race and Mastery: The Debate of 1903." In *From the Old South to the New: Essays on the Transitional South.* Edited by Walter J. Fraser, Jr., and Winfred B. Moore, Jr. Westport: Greenwood Press, 1981.

Berry, Mary Frances. "Repression of Blacks in the South, 1890–1945: Enforcing the System of Segregation." In *The Age of Segregation: Race Relations in the South, 1890–1945.* Edited by Robert Haws. Jackson: University Press of Mississippi, 1978.

Boskin, Joseph. *Sambo: The Rise & Demise of an American Jester.* New York: Oxford University Press, 1986.

Bowler, Peter J. *The Eclipse of Darwinism: Anti-Darwinian Evolution Theories in the Decades Around 1900.* Baltimore: The Johns Hopkins University Press, 1983.

———. *Theories of Human Evolution: A Century of Debate, 1844–1944.* Baltimore: The Johns Hopkins University Press, 1986.

Bruce, Dickson D., Jr. *Black American Writing From the Nadir: The Evolution of a Literary Tradition, 1877–1915.* Baton Rouge: Louisiana State University Press, 1989.

Burton, Orville Vernon. "'The Black Squint of the Law': Racism in South Carolina." In *The Meaning of South Carolina History: Essays in Honor of George C. Rogers, Jr.* Edited by David R. Chesnutt and Clyde N. Wilson. Columbia: University of South Carolina Press, 1991.

Cartwright, Joseph H. *The Triumph of Jim Crow: Tennessee Race Relations in the 1880s.* Knoxville: University of Tennessee Press, 1976.

Cassity, Michael J., editor. *Chains of Fear: American Race Relations Since Reconstruction.* Westport: Greenwood Press, 1984.

_____ , editor. *Legacy of Fear: American Race Relations to 1900*. Westport: Greenwood Press, 1985.

Cell, John W. *The Highest Stage of White Supremacy: The Origins of Segregation in South Africa and the American South*. Cambridge: Cambridge University Press, 1982.

Clayton, Bruce. *The Savage Ideal: Intolerance and Intellectual Leadership in the South, 1890–1914*. Baltimore: Johns Hopkins University Press, 1972.

Cooper, William J., Jr. *The Conservative Regime: South Carolina, 1877–1890*. Baltimore: The Johns Hopkins University Press, 1968.

Cortner, Richard C. *A Mob Intent on Death: The NAACP and the Arkansas Riot Cases*. Middletown: Wesleyan University Press, 1988.

Crow, Jeffrey J. "An Apartheid for the South: Clarence Poe's Crusade for Rural Segregation." In *Race, Class, and Politics in Southern History: Essays in Honor of Robert F. Durden*. Edited by Jeffrey J. Crow, Paul D. Escott, and Charles L. Flynn, Jr. Baton Rouge: Louisiana State University Press, 1989.

Dittmer, John. *Black Georgia in the Progressive Era, 1900–1920*. Urbana: University of Illinois Press, 1977.

Drago, Edmund L. *Initiative, Paternalism, and Race Relations: Charleston's Avery Normal Institute*. Athens: University of Georgia Press, 1990.

Ellsworth, Scott. *Death in a Promised Land: The Tulsa Race Riot of 1921*. Baton Rouge: Louisiana State University Press, 1982.

Fields, Barbara J. "Ideology and Race in American History." In *Region, Race, and Reconstruction: Essays in Honor of C. Vann Woodward*. New York: Oxford University Press, 1982.

Fischer, Roger A. *The Segregation Struggle in Louisiana, 1862–77*. Urbana: University of Illinois Press, 1974.

Flynn, Charles L., Jr. *White Land, Black Labor: Caste and Class in Late Nineteenth-Century Georgia*. Baton Rouge: Louisiana State University Press, 1983.

Fredrickson, George M. *The Arrogance of Race: Historical Perspectives on Slavery, Racism, and Social Inequality*. Middletown: Wesleyan University Press, 1988.

————."Black-White Relations Since Emancipation: The Search for a Comparative Perspective." In *What Made the South Different? Essays and Comments*. Edited by Kees Gispen. Jackson: University Press of Mississippi, 1990.

Gerber, David A. *Black Ohio and the Color Line, 1860–1915*. Urbana: University of Illinois Press, 1976.

Gossett, Thomas F. *Race: The History of an Idea in America*. Dallas: Southern Methodist University Press, 1963.

Graves, John William. *Town and Country: Race Relations in an Urban-Rural Context, Arkansas, 1865–1905*. Fayetteville: University of Arkansas Press, 1990.

Gutman, Herbert G. *The Black Family in Slavery and Freedom, 1750–1925*. New York: Pantheon Books, 1976.

Hair, William Ivy. *Carnival of Fury: Robert Charles and the New Orleans Race Riot of 1900*. Baton Rouge: Louisiana State University Press, 1976.

Harlan, Louis R. *Booker T. Washington: The Making of a Black Leader, 1856–1901*. New York: Oxford University Press, 1972.

———. *Booker T. Washington: The Wizard of Tuskegee, 1901–1915*. New York: Oxford University Press, 1983.

———. *Separate and Unequal: Public School Campaigns and Racism in the Southern Seaboard States, 1901–1915*. Chapel Hill: University of North Carolina Press, 1958.

Harrison, Alferdteen, editor. *Black Exodus: The Great Migration from the American South*. Jackson: University Press of Mississippi, 1991.

Hartzell, Lawrence L. "The Exploration of Freedom in Black Petersburg, Virginia, 1865–1902." In *The Edge of the South: Life in Nineteenth-Century Virginia*. Edited by Edward L. Ayers and John C. Willis. Charlottesville: University Press of Virginia, 1991.

Haynes, Robert V. *A Night of Violence: The Houston Riot of 1917*. Baton Rouge: Louisiana State University Press, 1976.

Horsman, Reginald. *Josiah Nott of Mobile: Southerner, Physician, and Racial Theorist*. Baton Rouge: Louisiana State University Press, 1987.

Ingalls, Robert P. *Urban Vigilantes in the New South: Tampa, 1882–1936*. Knoxville: University of Tennessee Press, 1988.

Lofgren, Charles A. *The Plessy Case: A Legal-Historical Interpretation*. New York: Oxford University Press, 1987.

Luker, Ralph E. "In Slavery's Shadow: North Carolina Methodism and Race Relations, 1885–1920." In *Methodism Alive in North Carolina*. Edited by O. Kelly Ingram. Durham: Duke Divinity School, 1976.

———. *The Social Gospel in Black & White: American Racial Reform, 1885–1912*. Chapel Hill: University of North Carolina Press, 1991.

McGovern, James R. *Anatomy of a Lynching: The Killing of Claude Neal*. Baton Rouge: Louisiana State University Press, 1982.

McMillen, Neil R. *Dark Journey: Black Mississippians in the Age of Jim Crow*. Urbana: University of Illinois Press, 1989.

Mandle, Jay R. *Not Slave, Not Free: The African American Experience Since the Civil War*. Durham: Duke University Press, 1992.

Newby, I. A., editor. *The Development of Segregationist Thought*. Homewood: The Dorsey Press, 1968.

Nieman, Donald G. *Promises to Keep: African–Americans and the Constitutional Order, 1776 to the Present*. New York: Oxford University Press, 1991.

Olsen, Otto H., editor. *The Negro Question: From Slavery to Caste, 1863–1910*. New York: Pitman Publishing Corporation, 1971.

———, editor. *The Thin Disguise: Turning Point in Negro History, Plessy v. Ferguson, A Documentary Presentation (1864–1896)*. New York: Humanities Press, 1967.

Painter, Nell Irvin. "'Social Equality,' Miscegenation, Labor, and Power." In *The Evolution of Southern Culture*. Edited by Numan V. Bartley. Athens: University of Georgia Press, 1988.

Perman, Michael. "Counter Reconstruction: The Role of Violence in Southern Redemption." In *The Facts of Reconstruction: Essays in Honor of John Hope Franklin*. Edited by Eric Anderson and Alfred A. Moss, Jr. Baton Rouge: Louisiana State University Press, 1991.

Rabinowitz, Howard N. "A Comparative Perspective on Race Relations in Southern and Northern Cities, 1860–1900, with Special Emphasis on Raleigh." In *Black Americans in North Carolina and the South*. Edited by Jeffrey J. Crow and Flora J. Hatley. Chapel Hill: University of North Carolina Press, 1984.

———. *Race Relations in the Urban South, 1865–1890*. New York: Oxford University Press, 1978.

———. "Segregation and Reconstruction." In *The Facts of Reconstruction: Essays in Honor of John Hope Franklin*. Edited by Eric Anderson and Alfred A. Moss, Jr. Baton Rouge: Louisiana State University Press, 1991.

———. "The Weight of the Past Versus the Promise of the Future: Southern Race Relations in Historical Perspective." In *The Future South: A Historical Perspective for the Twenty-first Century*. Edited by Joe P. Dunn and Howard L. Preston. Urbana: University of Illinois Press, 1991.

Rable, George C. *But There Was No Peace: The Role of Violence in the Politics of Reconstruction.* Athens: University of Georgia Press, 1984.

Rogers, William Warren and Robert David Ward. *August Reckoning: Jack Turner and Racism in Post-Civil War Alabama.* Baton Rouge: Louisiana State University Press, 1973.

Shapiro, Herbert. *White Violence and Black Response: From Reconstruction to Montgomery.* Amherst: University of Massachusetts Press, 1988.

Smith, H. Shelton. *In His Image, But . . . Racism in Southern Religion, 1780–1910.* Durham: Duke University Press, 1972.

Stanfield, John H. *Philanthropy and Jim Crow in American Social Science.* Westport: Greenwood Press, 1985.

Takaki, Ronald T. *Iron Cages: Race and Culture in 19th-Century America.* New York: Alfred A. Knopf, 1979.

Toll, Robert C. *Blacking Up: The Minstrel Show in Nineteenth-Century America.* New York: Oxford University Press, 1974.

Tuttle, William M., Jr. *Race Riot: Chicago in the Red Summer of 1919.* New York: Atheneum, 1970.

Wayne, Michael. *The Reshaping of Plantation Society: The Natchez District, 1860–1880.* Baton Rouge: Louisiana State University Press, 1983.

Weaver, John D. *The Brownsville Raid.* New York: W.W. Norton, 1970.

Westin, Richard B. "Blacks, Educational Reform, and Politics in North Carolina, 1897–1898." In *The Southern Enigma: Essays on Race, Class, and Folk Culture.* Edited by Walter J. Fraser, Jr., and Winfred B. Moore, Jr. Westport: Greenwood Press, 1983.

Wheeler, Joanne. "Together in Egypt: A Pattern of Race Relations in Cairo, Illinois, 1865–1915." In *Toward a New South? Studies in Post-Civil War Southern Communities.* Edited by Orville Vernon Burton and Robert C. McMath, Jr. Westport: Greenwood Press, 1982.

Wilson, Charles Reagan. *Baptized in Blood: The Religion of the Lost Cause, 1865–1920.* Athens: University of Georgia Press, 1980.

Wright, George C. *Life Behind a Veil: Blacks in Louisville, Kentucky, 1865–1930.* Baton Rouge: Louisiana State University Press, 1985.

———. *Racial Violence in Kentucky, 1865–1940: Lynchings, Mob Rule, and "Legal Lynchings."* Baton Rouge: Louisiana State University Press, 1990.

[1]These citations develop themes suggested in the "General Introduction" and are designed to supplement the works cited in the Endnotes. In no sense comprehensive, the references are drawn heavily from the historical literature published since 1980, and reflect the ongoing reassessment of white racism in late nineteenth-century America.

INTRODUCTION

Volumes V and VI present texts illustrating the central role that religion played in bolstering white resistance to emancipation during the post-Appomattox decades. Biblical interpretations, of course, had provided a major pillar for the old proslavery argument and, not surprisingly, white racists trotted out many of the old arguments anew. In 1867 "Ariel," Nashville publisher and clergyman Buckner H. Payne, published *The Negro: What is His Ethnological Status?*—a pamphlet grounded in antebellum pre-Adamite and polygenist theories. At the very moment, then, when the Reconstruction amendments were being passed, Payne charged that blacks and whites were members of different species. His pamphlet sparked considerable debate, the contours of which appear in Volume V.

Payne argued that blacks had not descended from Ham and, accordingly, were not human beings. In his opinion, God frowned upon attempts to equalize the races. Payne assumed "That the negro being created before Adam, consequently . . . is a *beast* in God's nomenclature." The author asserted that calamities in the Bible were God's punishments for miscegenation between white descendants of Adam and Eve and blacks. Payne charged that because blacks lacked souls and could not be saved, they could not worship God. And whereas blacks allegedly were beasts, not men, God disapproved of attempts to equalize the races. To "elevate a *beast* to the level of a son of God," explained Payne, was analogous to insulting the Creator. As a result, "the states or people that favor this equality and amalgamation of the white and black races, *God will exterminate.*" Before emancipation, slaveholders had acted as God's agents to prevent this calamity. But now, Payne argued, only two alternatives remained for the African American: "You *must send him back to Africa or re-enslave him.*"[1]

"A Minister," D.G. Phillips of Louisville, Georgia, agreed with Payne that God had created blacks before the rest of mankind. In *Nachash: What Is It?*, Phillips argued that the serpent who deceived Eve had been a black, thereby dooming all blacks "to perpetual menial crouching slavery." Phillips's postwar biblical defense of slavery was strongly influenced by Dr. Samuel A. Cartwright, one of the Old South's foremost "scientific" apologists for slavery. Convinced that blacks could live only as slaves or perish, Phillips denounced emancipation as being against God's will, "and," he warned that, "the consequences must be direful in the end."[2] Similarly, the works by "Prospero" and "Sister Sallie" generally supported Payne. In addition, the editor has included Payne's *Ariel's Reply* to his critics in Volume V, and, in Volume VI, A. Hoyle Lester's *The Pre-Adamite, or Who Tempted Eve?* and Charles Carroll's *The Tempter of Eve* to suggest the persistence of the "Ariel" debate as late as 1902.

The controversy generated by "Ariel" not only provides insights into the post-Civil War race question but also offers glimpses into the contemporary discourse on race. Significantly, most racists, as historian Forrest G. Wood suggests, rejected Payne's arguments as "utter nonsense." To accept Payne's biblical thesis would have undercut "a sacrosanct white supremacy dogma—namely, the curse-of-Canaan notion." For example, in *Speculum for Looking Into the Pamphlet Entitled "The Negro,"* included in Volume V, "Optician" attacked Payne and denied that slaveholders had ever viewed their blacks as beasts and had in fact treated them humanely. Another critic, Nashville's Robert A. Young, identified numerous errors in Payne's pamphlet and declared: "We do not believe in the social equality of the Negro. We do not believe he knows how to handle a vote. We are disfranchised. Still, we believe *the Negro is a descendant of Adam and Eve; that he is the progeny of Ham; that he is a human being, and has an immortal soul.*" "M.S." lashed out not only against Payne but against Young as well, concluding "that the negro is not a *beast*, but has a soul, but [was] not created after the image of God; that he was created and placed upon the earth *anterior* to Adam, together with all the other inferior races . . . ."[3] Harrison Berry, who described himself as "A Full Blooded Cushite," ridiculed Payne on several counts, especially for denying that blacks were part of the human family. Berry, who as a slave reportedly defended the enslavement of his own race, denounced Payne's pamphlet as "the last effort of the great diabolical aristocratic slave power." Berry's case is just the most curious instance in the bizarre debate over the alleged biblical sanctions of a racial hierarchy.[4] According to Wood, "The Ariel controversy was most revealing as a reflection of the widespread belief in, and the preposterous extremes of, religious fundamentalism, at least when it involved racial matters."[5]

Just as polygenist theology bolstered nineteenth-century theories of white supremacy, so too did the burgeoning disciplines of anthropometry, craniometry, and ethnology. After the Civil War, polygenist theories remained alive, thanks largely to Dr. Josiah C. Nott of Mobile, Alabama. In the most important development for the scientific study of humanity, Charles Darwin's evolutionary theory stressed man's basic unity, while allowing for varieties and inequality. "Darwin," explains historian Paul F. Boller, Jr., "rejected the notion . . . that species of plants and animals (including man) originated in a special act of creation which fixed their forms for all time. Evolutionary change, . . . not immutability, is the law of life; living organisms are the products of gradual, minute changes taking place over vast periods of time, and their origins can be traced back to ancient species that are quite different in form from those prevailing in modern times." In other words, Darwin argued that all human races belong to a single species, but that some races were superior to others. Organisms competed in a struggle for existence through a process that Darwin termed "natural selection."[6]

As historian Carl N. Degler points out, Darwin's theory of evolution was based upon "hereditarianism, not racism, because it lacked the invidious comparison among races that is the essential and distinguishing element in the concept of racism." Others, however, developed the theory of racist evolution from his work. Darwin actually wrote little about the issue of human origins, other than to argue for a primate link and against polygenist notions of separate creations. The number of shared physical characteristics among all humans made them one species, Darwin said. Nonetheless, he accepted the standard social hierarchy of the races, as seen by Europeans. That allowed racial theorists to call themselves "Darwinian" while connecting the social ladder of the races to a biologically determined hierarchy of superiority and inferiority. Evolutionists in general arranged the different races along a linear path of progress, with the "lower" races showing the remnants of primitive stages. Drawing upon anthropometrics and ethnology, anthropologists and other "race thinkers" defined a hierarchy of stages in evolution with the European as the goal.[7]

Invoking Darwin's name to gain the legitimacy of "science," they recast polygenist creationism into a biological theory of the separate nature of the races, or a racist evolutionism. These writers argued that differences between the races stemmed from different species of mankind, *not*, as Darwin insisted, from varieties within the human family. By the end of the century, when white racism in America was rampant, the "science" of race had "proven" beyond a doubt the immutable inferior mental and physical capacity of blacks. Discounting the roles of culture or environment, racists employed "science" to establish an elaborate explanation for the retrogression of African Americans. Lacking the "protection" of slavery, post-Civil War blacks were allegedly falling by the wayside in direct competition with whites. They also reportedly succumbed to innate degenerative tendencies and were dying off. According to scientists and pseudo-scientists, mulattoes were especially prone to deteriorate physiologically. "While the Anglo-Saxon," notes historian John S. Haller, Jr., "reaped the benefits of a man-centered evolutionary process, the so-called 'inferior races' and 'stocks' remained outcasts from the evolutionary struggle, restricted from participation because of innate racial characteristics that were unresponsive to environmental influences."[8]

In 1896, after compiling data on black mortality, statistician Frederick L. Hoffman of the Prudential Insurance Company of America advised his firm that African Americans posed "a bad actuarial risk." "With an inordinate rate of mortality," he said, "with an excessive degree of immorality, with a greater tendency to crime and pauperism than the whites, the negro race has also . . . a far lower degree of economic activity and inclination towards accumulation of capital and other material wealth." According to Hoffman, "education, philanthropy and religion" for blacks "have failed to develop a higher appreciation of the stern and uncompromising virtues of the Aryan race." Exuding pessimism, Hoffman predicted that "gradual extinction is only a question of time." In 1910, however, Hoffman revised his earlier forecast, concluding "that the [Negro] race will reach a stationary condition, very much as is the case with the Gypsies in Europe, and to a certain extent with our Indian population."[9]

Endnotes

[1]"Ariel," *The Negro: What Is His Ethnological Status?* (second edition; Cincinnati: n.p., 1867), 45, 48, 46, 48; Wood, *Black Scare: The Racist Response to Emancipation and Reconstruction* (Berkeley: University of California Press, 1968), 6-7.

[2]A Minister, *Nachash: What Is It? or An Answer to the Question, "Who and What is the Negro?" Drawn From Revelation* (Augusta: James L. Gow, 1868), 42, 43, 44; D.G. Phillips to W.R. Hemphill, December 31, 1868, Hemphill Family Papers, Duke University.

[3]Wood, *Black Scare*, 6; "Optician," *Speculum for Looking Into the Pamphlet Entitled "The Negro"* (Charleston: Joseph Walker, 1867), 6, 20; Young, *The Negro: A Reply to Ariel* (Nashville: J.W. M'Ferrin & Co., 1867), 4-5; "M.S.," *The Adamic Race. Reply to "Ariel." Drs. Young and Blackie, on the Negro* (New York: Russell Bros., 1868), 67.

[4]Berry, *A Reply to Ariel* (Macon: American Union Book and Job Office Print, 1869), 36, 34. In 1861 Berry published *Slavery and Abolitionism, as Viewed by a Georgia Slave* (Atlanta: Franklin Printing House, 1861), in which he described himself as the slave of S.W. Price of Covington, Georgia. Berry defended slavery as the product of God's will and maligned the Abolitionists as "the worst of all enemies of the Slave." See pp. 31-32, 40. As Maxwell Whiteman suggests, Berry's authorship of this anti-abolition tract is "highly suspect." If Berry did indeed write *Slavery and Abolitionism*, explains Whiteman, "the ideas were the ideas of his master." According to Whiteman, Berry's 1882 pamphlet, *The Foundation of Atheism Examined, With an Answer to the Question, "Why Don't God Kill the Devil?"* "showed him as a semi-literate man not even equal to the logic of apologetics of his first literary venture, giving credence to the likelihood that the work was not his own." See Whiteman, "Harrison Berry: A Georgia Slave Defends Slavery, A Bibliographical Note," [introduction to] Berry, *Slavery and Abolitionism, as Viewed by a Georgia Slave* (reprint edition; Wilmington: Scholarly Resources, 1977), [1-2]. In his authoritative *A Bibliography of*

the Negro in Africa and America (1928; New York: Argosy-Antiquarian, 1965), 314, 576, Monroe N. Work failed to identify Berry as a Negro author, again raising questions as to the legitimacy of his writings.

[5]Wood, Black Scare, 7. See also I. A. Newby, Jim Crow's Defense: Anti-Negro Thought in America, 1900-1930 (Baton Rouge: Louisiana State University Press, 1965), 93-98.

[6]William Stanton, The Leopard's Spots: Scientific Attitudes Toward Race in America, 1815-59 (Chicago: University of Chicago Press, 1960); Jacques Barzun, Race: A Study in Superstition (1937; New York: Harper and Row, 1965), 47-48; Boller, American Thought in Transition: The Impact of Evolutionary Naturalism, 1865-1900 (Chicago: Rand McNally, 1969), 1-2; Stephen Jay Gould, The Mismeasure of Man (New York: W.W. Norton, 1981), 71-72; Glenn C. Altschuler, Race, Ethnicity, and Class in American Social Thought, 1865-1919 (Arlington Heights, IL: Harlan Davidson, 1982), 3-4.

[7]Degler, In Search of Human Nature: The Decline and Revival of Darwinism in American Social Thought (New York: Oxford University Press, 1991), 14.

[8]Haller, Outcasts From Evolution: Scientific Attitudes of Racial Inferiority, 1859-1900 (1971; New York: McGraw-Hill, 1975), 187.

[9]Altschuler, Race, Ethnicity, and Class in American Social Thought, 1865-1919, 5; Hoffman, "Race Traits and Tendencies of the American Negro," Publications of the American Economic Association, 11 (August, 1896): 308, 329; Hoffman to Edward Eggleston, August 17, 1910, in Edward Eggleston, The Ultimate Solution of the American Negro Problem (Boston: Gorham Press, 1913), 273.

THE NEGRO:

WHAT IS HIS ETHNOLOGICAL STATUS?

IS HE THE PROGENY OF HAM? IS HE A DESCENDANT OF
ADAM AND EVE? HAS HE A SOUL? OR IS HE A
BEAST IN GOD'S NOMENCLATURE? WHAT
IS HIS STATUS AS FIXED BY GOD IN
CREATION? WHAT IS HIS RELA-
TION TO THE WHITE RACE?

By ARIEL.

"Truth, though sometimes slow in its power, is like itself, always consistent; and
like its AUTHOR, will always be triumphant.
The Bible is true."

SECOND EDITION.

CINCINNATI:
PUBLISHED FOR THE PROPRIETOR.
1867.

1

THE NEGRO.

What is his Ethnological Status? Is he the progeny of Ham? Is he a descendant of Adam and Eve? Has he a Soul? or is he a Beast, in God's nomenclature? What is his Status as fixed by God in creation? What is his relation to the White race?

THE intelligent will see at once, that the question of *slavery*, either right or wrong, is not involved in this caption for examination: nor is that question discussed. The points are purely ethnological and Biblical, and are to be settled alone by the Bible and by concurrent history, and by facts existing outside of the Bible and of admitted truth. We simply say in regard to ourself, in this day of partisan strife, religious and political, that we take no part in any such party strife, and that it is many years since we cast our last vote. This much, to prevent evil surmises.

With this understood independence of all parties, we begin by saying, that the errors and mistakes, in understanding the true position of the negro, as God intended it to be in his order of creation, are all traceable to, and arise out of two assumptions. The learned men of the past and present age, the clergy and others have assumed as true:

1. That the negro is a descendant of Ham, the youngest son of Noah. This is false and untrue.

2. That the negro is a descendant of, or the progeny of, Adam and Eve. This is also false and untrue.

These questions, or rather these assumptions, of the learned and unlearned world, are Biblical, and are to be settled by the Bible alone, whether they be true or false, and by outside concurrent history—and of facts known to exist, and admitted to be true by the intelligent, and as they may serve to elucidate any statement or account given in the Bible.

We shall have frequent use of the term, "logic of facts," and now explain what we mean by it. It is this: If one sees another with a gun in his hands, and that he shoots a man and kills him, and the bullet is found afterward in the dead man's body, that although we did not see the bullet

(3)

put into the gun, yet we *know* by this "logic of facts," that it was in the gun. It is the strongest evidence of what is true, of any testimony that can be offered.

It will be admitted by all, and contradicted by none, that we now have existing on earth, two races of men, the *white* and the *black*. We beg here to remind our readers, that when they see the word men, or man, *italicised*, we do not use it as applying to Adam and his race. But we may sometimes use these words in the general and accepted sense of them, but it is only for the purpose of getting before the minds of our readers, the propositions of the learned of this age, exactly as they would wish them to be stated. We will now describe, ethnologically, the prominent characteristics and differences of these two races as we now find them.

The white race have long, straight hair, high foreheads, high noses, thin lips, and white skins: the olive and sunburnt color, where the other characteristics are found, belong equally to the white race.

The negro or black race, are woolly or kinky-headed, low foreheads, flat noses, thick-lipped, and have a black skin.

This description of the two races is (though not all their differences), full enough for the fair discussion of their respective stations in God's order of creation, and will be admitted to be just and true, as far as it goes, by all candid and learned men. Therefore the reader will observe, that when either of the terms, *white, black* or *negro*, is used, referring to race, that we refer to the one or the other, as the case may be, as is here set forth in describing the two races.

In God's nomenclature of the creation, his order stands thus: 1. Birds; 2. Fowls; 3. Creeping things; 4. Cattle; 5. Beasts; 6. Adam and Eve. We shall use this, but without any *intended* disparagement to any, as it is the *best* and *highest authority*.

Before proceeding with the examination of the subjects involved in the caption to this paper, we will for a moment, notice the prevailing errors, now existing in all their strength, and held by the clergy, and many learned men, to be true, which are: 1. Ham's name, which they allege, in Hebrew, means black; 2. The curse denounced against him, that a servant of servants should he be unto his brethren; and that *this* curse, was denounced against Ham, for the accidental seeing of his father Noah naked—that this curse was to do so, and did change him, so that instead of being long, straight-haired, high forehead, high nose, thin lips and white, as he then was, and like his brothers Shem and Japheth, he was from that day forth, to be kinky-headed, low forehead, thick lipped and black skinned; and that his *name*, and this *curse*, effected all this.   And truly, to answer their assumptions, it must have done so, or the case would not fit the negro, as we now find him.   And they adduce in proof, that Ham's name in Hebrew (tCHam), means *black*, the present color of the negro, and that therefore Ham is the progenitor of the black race.   They seem to forget, or rather, they ignore the fact, that the Bible nowhere says, that such a curse, or that any curse whatever, was denounced against Ham by his father Noah; but that this curse, with whatever it carried with it, was hurled at Canaan, the youngest son of Ham.   But it is of little consequence, in the settlement of these great questions, *which* was intended, whether Ham or his youngest son Canaan.   But if it be of any value in supporting their theory, this meaning of Ham's name in Hebrew, in designating *his* color to be black, and *black* it must be, to answer the color of the negro, then the names of Shem and Japheth should be of equal value, in determining *their* color; for each of the brothers received their respective names a hundred years or more before the flood, and were all the children of the same father and same mother.   Now, if Shem and Japheth's names do not describe their color (which they do not), upon what principles of logical philology or grammar, can Ham's *name* determine his color?   How many of this day are there who are called, black, white, brown, and olive, all of whom are white, and without the slightest suspicion, that the *name* indicated the color of their respective owners.   Is it not strange, that intelligent and learned men, should be compelled to rely on such puerilities, as arguments and truly supporting such tremendous conclusions?   But they say it was his name in conjunction with the curse, that made him and his descendants the negro we now find on earth.   It is an axiom in logic, that, that which is not in the constituent, can not be in the constituted.   We have seen, that the making of Ham a negro, is not *in* the name, which is one of the constituents, now let us see, if it is in the other constituent, the *curse*. Now the *curse* and *name* changed Ham, if their theory be true, from a white man, to a black negro.   If the curse, were capable of effecting such results, it is to be found in the word *curse*, and not in the words, that a servant of servants should he be, as he and his descendants could, as readily be servants,

5

white as black, and he was already white, and no necessity
to make him black, to be a servant. If *this* effect on *Ham*,
is to be found in the word *curse*, it will then be necessary,
for the advocates of the assumption, to show, that such were
its *usual* results, whenever that word was used; for unless
such were its common effects, when used by God himself, by
men of God, by patriarchs and by prophets, then we ask, on
what grounds, if any there be, it is, that they assert, that
it did produce this effect, in *this instance*, by Noah on Ham
and his descendants? We do not question or doubt, that
Canaan, was denounced in the curse, pronounced by Noah,
that *he* should be a servant of servants; but whether Ham
or Canaan *alone* is meant, is not material to the questions at
issue, except in this view; but the advocates of such being
its effect, must show, that such, at least was its effect previous to, and after Noah used it; and if they fail in this,
that necessarily, this .part of their argument is also a total
failure. Let us look into the Bible. God cursed our first
parents. Did this curse kink their hair, flatten their skulls,
blacken their skin and flatten their nose? If it did, then
Noah was sadly mistaken and these gentlemen too, in supposing that it was Noah's curse, that accomplished all this,
for it was already done for the whole race—and long before,
by God himself. God cursed the serpent. Did the curse
produce this effect on him? He cursed Cain—did it affect
his skin, his hair, his forehead, his nose or his lips? These
curses were all pronounced by God himself and produced no
such effects. But we proceed and take up the holy men of
God, the patriarchs and prophets, and see what their curses
produced. Did the curse of Jacob, produce this effect on
Simeon and Levi? did it produce this effect on the man who
would make a graven image? did it produce this effect on
the man who would rebuild Jericho? did it produce this effect
on those, who maketh the blind to wander out of the way?
did it produce this effect on those, who perverteth the judgment of the stranger, the fatherless and the widow? *Cum
multis aliis.* It did not. But if it did produce this effect in
these cases, then when we read, that Christ died to redeem
us from the curse, are we to understand, that he died to redeem us from a kinky head, flat nose, thick lips and a black
skin? But such curses, never having produced *such* effects,
when pronounced by God, by patriarch, by prophet, or by
any holy man of God before or since, then we inquire to
know, on what principles of interpretation, grammar or logic

it is, that it can so mean in this case of Noah? There are no words in the curse, that express, or even *imply* such effects. Then in the absence of all such effects, following such curses, and as they are narrated in the Bible, whether pronounced by God or man; and there being nothing in the language beside to sustain it, and if true, Ham's posterity must be shown now, as its truthful witnesses, from this, our day, back to the flood or to Ham; and which can not be done— and if this can not be done, then all arguments and assertions, based on such assumptions, that Ham was the father of the negro or black race, are false; and if false, then the negro is in *no sense*, the descendant of Ham; and therefore, he must have been in the ark, and as he was not one of Noah's family, that he *must* have entered it in some capacity, or relation to the other beasts or cattle. For that he did enter the ark is plain from the fact, that he is now here, and not of the family or progeny of Ham. And no one has ever suspicioned either Shem or Japheth of being the father of the negro; therefore he must have come out of the ark, and he could not come out, unless he had previously entered it; and if he entered it, that he must have *existed* before the flood, and that, too, just such negro as we have now, and consequently not as a descendant of Adam and Eve; and if not the progeny of Adam and Eve, that he is inevitably a beast, and *as such*, entered the ark, though having the *form* of man, and *man* he is, being so *named* by Adam. Such is the logic, and such are the conclusions to which their premises lead, if legitimately carried out; and by which it is plainly seen, that the position assumed by the learned of the present and past ages—that the present negroes are the descendants of Ham, and were *made so* by his *name*, or by the *curse* of his father—is false in fact, and but an unwarranted assumption at best. But while this conclusion is inevitable, it also reveals to us another sad fact, that the good men of our own race (the white), though learned and philanthropic, exhibit a weakness, alas! *too* common in this our day, that anything they wish to believe or think will be popular, that it is very easy to convert the greatest *improbabilities* into the *best* grounds of their *faith*. The word used by God, used by patriarch and by prophet, is the *same* word used by Noah. If the word thus used by God, and by holy men, did not produce the effect as is charged by these men, how can the *same* word, when used by Noah, do it? And yet, on these assumptions, the faith of more than half the world seems to be now based. To expose these cobweb fabrics, called by *some* reason, on this subject, and *Christian* philanthropy by others, in which are involved, such tremendous conclusions, for weal or for wo, of so large a portion of the biped creation, that we feel like apologizing to our readers, for answering such *learned* ignorance, blindness or weakness. But the meaning of Ham's name in Hebrew is not *primarily* black. Its primary meaning is : 1. Sunburnt; 2. swarthy ; 3. dark ; 4. black—and its most *unusual* meaning.

Having now disposed of these *fancies*, for they are nothing better, of the effects of Ham's name, and Noah's curse, in making him a negro; and having examined them, for the purpose of showing on what flimsy grounds this mightiest of structures of air-built theories rests, and for *this* purpose *only*, as what we have said about them is not connected with, nor germain to the way we intend to pursue, in investigating the questions forming the caption to this paper. But having now disposed of them, we take up our own subject. The reader will bear in mind the description we have given respectively of the white and black races.

The first question to which we now invite attention is: Do the characteristics which we have given of the white race, belong equally, to all three of the sons of Noah—Shem, Ham and Japheth, and their descendants? If they do, then the black race, belong to, and have since the flood at least, belonged to another and totally different race of *men*.

Now to our question: Do the characteristics, which we have given of the white race, belong equally to the three sons of Noah and their descendants alike? We will begin with Noah himself first. The Bible says of Noah, that he was perfect in his generation. We will not stop to criticise the Hebrew translated " generation," for any English scholar on reading the verse in which it occurs, will see at once, that to make sense, it should have been *genealogy*. Then Noah was perfect in his genealogy—he was a preacher of righteousness—he was the husband of one wife, who was also perfect in her genealogy; by this one wife, he had three sons, all born about one hundred years before the flood, and all three of them married, before the flood, to women who were perfect also in their genealogies. Ordinarily speaking, this little statement of facts, undenied by all, and undeniable, would settle at least *this* question, that whatever the color of *one* might be, the others would be the same color—if one were black, all would be black—if one were white, all would be white. Out of this arises the question, what was the color of these three brothers—were they and their descendants black or white?

We will begin with Shem, so as to find his race *now* on earth, to see if they are white or black. The Bible tells us where he went, and where his descendants settled, and what countries they occupied, until the days of our Saviour, who was of Shem's lineage after the flesh. From the days of the Saviour down to the present day, we see the Jews, the descendants of Shem, in every country, and see they belong to the white race, which none will pretend to deny—that they were so before, and after the flood, and have continued to be so to the present time, is unquestionably true. We know then, on Biblical authority, with mathematical certainty, that they are not negroes, either before, at, nor since the flood, but white.

We next take up Japheth. We know where he went, and what countries his descendants peopled, with equal certainty and on equal authority—and all outside concurrent history, equally clearly prove, that Japheth's descendants peopled Europe, whence they have spread over all the world. That they too belong to the white race, is also unquestioned, nor doubted by any that have eyes to see. That they were so before, and at the flood, and not negroes then, nor since, is equally undoubted and indisputable. We have not taken the trouble of showing step by step, where those two brothers went, and what countries they peopled *seriatim*, because they are admitted by all, learned and unlearned, to be and to have done just what is here stated in spreading over the world. It was, therefore, unnecessary to incumber this paper, by proving that which none disputes. This being so, then two of the three brothers, are known certainly, to be of the white race, and not of the negro, either before or after the flood.

We now take up the youngest brother, Ham. The evidence establishing the fact, that he too, and *his descendants* belong to the white race, with long, straight hair, high forehead, high noses and thin lips, is if *possible still stronger*, than that of either of his brothers; if indeed anything can, in human conception, be *stronger* than that, which is of perfect strength, and if this is true, then Ham can not be the father of the negro. As in the cases of the other two brothers, the Bible tells us where Ham, and his descendants went, and what countries they peopled, and where his race

may be found at this day; and which likewise, all contemporaneous history abundantly testifies, and shows that they are
of the white race, and were so before the flood, and from the
flood continued so, and yet continue so to the *present time*;
and that not one of them, is of the negro race of this day.
We will, in establishing the truths of the above declarations,
take up two of Ham's sons and trace them and their descendants, from the flood to the present time, and show what they
were, and what they are down to this day. These two sons
of Ham, whose posterity we propose to trace, and show that
they *now* belong to the white race, are Mizraim and Canaan,
the second and the youngest of his sons. The families of all
of the sons can be traced from the flood to the present day,
but we presume two are sufficient, and that they be white; and
we have selected Canaan *intentionally* and for a purpose that
will be seen hereafter. Canaan *was* denounced by Noah, that
he should be a servant of servants to his brethren, and if it turns
out, in this investigation, as we *know* it will, that they belong
to the *white race*, it will satisfactorily settle this question, that
the *curse* of Noah did not make *him* and his descendants the
black negro we now find on earth, much less Ham, who was
not so cursed. The Bible plainly tells us, that the country
now called Egypt, was settled by Mizraim, the second son
of Ham, and was peopled by his descendants; that Mizraim,
the second son of Ham, and grandson of Noah, gave his
name to the country; that they called it the land of Mizraim, and by which name it is still known, to the present
day, by the descendants of its ancient inhabitants; that they
built many magnificent cities on the Nile—among them, the
city of Thebes, one of the largest and most magnificent in
its architecture, and the grandeur of its monuments and
temples, the world ever saw. Its ruins at the present day,
are of surpassing magnificence and grandeur. The city was
named Thebes, to commemorate the Ark, that saved Noah,
the grandfather of Mizraim, from the flood; the name of the
Ark in Hebrew, being *Theba*. Then we take it for granted,
all will admit, that what is now called Egypt, was settled by
Mizraim, the son of Ham, and grandson of Noah. The Bible, and outside concurrent history, abundantly prove that
he and his descendants, held, occupied and ruled over Egypt,
and continued in the possession and the occupancy of the
country as such, until long after the Exodus of the Hebrews,
under Moses and Aaron; that Ham's descendants, through
Canaan, in the persons of his sons Sidon and Heth, settled

Sidon, Tyre and Carthage. This will not be denied by any intelligent Biblical student or historian. Sidon itself was named after Canaan's oldest son.

From Egypt in Africa, Mizraim's descendants passed over to Asia, and settled India, whence they spread over that continent; that great commerce sprung up between India, etc., and Egypt and connecting countries, which was carried on by caravans; that Greece and Rome subsequently, shared largely in this commerce, especially after the march of Alexander the Great to India, by the caravan route, three hundred and thirty-two years before our Saviour's birth. This commerce has continued to our day. All these facts are undeniable, and will be denied by none acquainted with the Bible and past history. These descendants, of this maligned Ham, were at, and after the flood, and continue to be, *to this day*, of the white race, all having long, straight hair, high foreheads, high noses and thin lips; that they are so, and as much so as the descendants of the other two brothers, and possessing all of the same general lineaments—lineaments that so long as the race shall exist, will be an eternal protest against their being of the negro race that we now have. But as we intend to show conclusively that Ham and his descendants were and are white, long, straight hair, etc., from Noah to the present time, so *plainly* and so *positively* that no fair or candid man can have the least doubt of its truth, we proceed to state: That we will now give the names of the country, now called Egypt, beginning with its first settlement by Mizraim, in regular order down, to enable the Biblical and historical student to refer readily to the histories of the different epochs, to detect any error, if we should make one, in tracing Ham's descendants, down to the present day. In Hebrew it is called Mizraim, in Coptic and Arabic (the former being now the name of its ancient or first inhabitants), it is called Misr or Mezr, being spelled in both these ways by the Arabian and Coptic writers. In Syro-Chaldaic and Helenic Greek it is called Aiguptos—and in Latin, Ægyptus. In many of the ancient Egyptian and Coptic writings it is called *Chimi*, that is, the land of Ham, and is so called in the Bible, see Psalms cv, 23; cvi, 22, and other places. The ancient inhabitants now in Egypt, the Copts, are called the *posterity of Pharaoh*, by the Turks of the *present day*. The ancient *Hyksos*, or shepherd kings (patriarchs) of the Hebrews, are sometimes confounded in ancient history, with the descendants of Ham, being of the same original stock.

Egypt has not had a ruler of *its own* since the battle of Actium, fought by Augustus Caesar, thirty years before our Saviour, as God by his prophet had foretold that their own kings would cease forever to reign over that country. After the battle of Actium, it became a Roman province, and since that time, it has been under *foreign* rule. It now is, and has been governed by the Turks since 1517.

It appears (see Asiatic Miscel., p. 148, 4to), that Mizraim, the son of Ham, and his sons (descendants), after settling Egypt, a portion went to Asia, which was settled by them, and that they gave their names to the different parts of the country where they settled, and which they *retain yet.* The names of these sons of Mizraim as given in history are as follows: Hind, Sind, Zeng, Nuba, Kanaan, Kush, Kopt, Berber and Hebesh, or Abash. From these children of Ham, we not only readily trace the present names of the countries, but that of the people also to this day; that they founded the nations of the Indus, Hindoos, Nubians, Koptos, Zanzebar, Barbary, Abysinia, the present Turks, is unquestioned and undoubted, by any intelligent scholar. That they are the white race, with long, straight hair, etc., is equally unquestionable, and are so *this day*, and as positively as that Shem and Japheth's descendants are now white. They first commenced to settle on the Nile in Africa, they then passed into Asia; and these two continents were principally settled by them. A portion of Europe (Turkey) is occupied by them—these, too, have long, straight hair, etc.

A portion of Ham's descendants, through Canaan's sons, Sidon and Heth, settled Sidon, Tyre, and later, Carthage. Tyre became a great power, and a city of much wealth and commerce, as we learn by the Bible and other history. Tyre was eventually overthrown, and her Queen and people fled. They subsequently built the great city of Carthage, near to where Tunis, in Africa, is now situated. They were again overthrown and their city destroyed by Scipio Africanus Secundus, after the battle of Zama. But, during one of the sieges, the city being invested by the Romans, the people became hard pressed for provisions, to supply which, they resolved on building some ships, to run the blockade for provisions. But after their ships were built, they had no ropes to rig them, nor anything within the city to make them. In this dilemma, the ladies, the women of Carthage, to their eternal honor be it spoken, patriotically stepped forward, and tendered their hair, *their long* and *beautiful tresses,* to make the much needed ropes, which was accepted, and a supply of provisions obtained. Now *how many*, and what *sort* of ropes would the kinky-headed negro have furnished, had the inhabitants been negroes? This noble act of the women of Carthage, is mentioned to their honor, by Babylonian, Persian, Egyptian, Grecian, Roman and Carthagenian writers and historians; and yet, we have seen it stated, and stated by learned modern writers, and who ought to have known better, that Hannibal, Hamilcar, Asdrubal, etc., the great Carthagenian Generals, were kinky-headed negroes—that Carthage itself, was a negro city. Why, the annals of fame do not present such an array of great names, whether in arts and sciences, and all that serves to elevate and make man noble on earth, or in the senate, or the field, by any other race of people, as will compare with those of Ham's descendants. These Carthagenians were all long and straight haired people. After the fall of Carthage, in the last Punic War, many of its people passed over subsequently into Spain, which they held and occupied for centuries, and are known in history as Saracens. A part of Spain, they held and occupied, until the reign of Ferdinand and Isabella, when they were expelled. These, too, had long and straight hair, etc. But to return to that portion of Ham's descendants through Mizraim. These settled Egypt, India, China, and most all of Oriental Asia, where they have *continued to live*, and where *they yet live*, and not one of them is a negro. They all have long, straight hair, etc., peculiar *only* to the white race. Not one negro belongs to *their race*. That this is their history, none will deny.

Ham, the maligned and slandered Ham—Ham who is falsely charged as being the father of the negro—Ham, the son of the white man Noah—this Ham, and his descendants, the long and straight haired race, it appears from history—from *unquestioned* history—*governed* and *ruled the world* from the earliest ages after the flood and for many centuries—and gave to it, all the arts and sciences, manufactures and commerce, geometry, astronomy, geography, architecture, letters, painting, music, etc., etc.—and that they thus governed the world, as it were, from the flood, until they came in contact with the Roman people, and then their power was broken in a contest for the mastery of the world, at Carthage, one hundred and forty-seven years before A. D., and Carthage fell—but fell, not for lack of talents in her people, not for lack of orators, statesmen and generals of the most consummate abilities, but *because* God had long before determined, that the Japhethic race should govern the world; and the Roman people were Japheth's children. When Hannibal, the most consummate general the world ever saw to his day, fought the battle of Zama, he met a fate similar to that which befel another equally consummate commander at a later day, on the field of Waterloo—both became exiles. That Ham's talents, abilities, genius, power, grandeur, glory, should now be attempted to be *stolen*, and to be stolen, not by the negro, for he has neither genius or capacity for *such* a theft, but stolen by the learned men of this and the past ages, and thrust upon the negro, who has not capacity to understand, when, where, or how, he had ever performed such feats of legislation, statesmanship, government, arts of war and in science. The negro has been upon the earth, coeval with the white race. We defy any historian, any learned man, to put his finger on the *history*, the *page*, or even *paragraph* of history, showing he has ever done one of these things, thus done by the children of Ham; or that he has shown, in this long range of time, a capacity for self-government, such as Ham, Shem and Japheth. If he has done *anything* on earth, in *any age* of the world, since he has been here, as has been done by the three sons of Noah, in arts and sciences, government, etc., it surely can be shown; and shown equally as clear and *unequivocally, when* and *where he did it*, as that of Shem, Ham and Japheth can. But such a showing can never be made; that page of history has never yet been written that records it. On these subjects, *his history* is as blank as that of the horse or the beaver. But we are not yet done with Ham's descendants. The great Turko-Tartar generals, Timour, Ghenghis Kahn and Tamerlane, the latter called in history, the scourge of God—the Saracenic general, the gallant, the daring, the chivalrous, the noble Saladin, he who led the Paynim forces of Mahomet, against the lion-hearted Richard, in the war of the Crusades, all, all these were children of Ham. Mahomet himself, the founder of an empire, and the head of a new religion, made his kingdom of Ham's descendants, as *all Turks are:* and these all have straight, long hair, etc. Those who have read the various histories of the crusades of the eleventh and twelfth centuries, know that the Turkish forces then, had long, straight hair, etc., and that it is so yet with their descendants none doubt—and these were children of Ham.

It will be seen now, how we have taken up one of Ham's

sons; that we have traced him and his descendants from the flood to Egypt, *where they are still;* that we have traced them across the continent of Africa into Asia, settling countries as they went; and to the countries still bearing their names, where they settled, and where they *are yet;* that we have taken up another son, and traced him and his descendants to Sidon, Tyre, Carthage, and Spain, and shown that they, too, *without exception,* were long, straight haired, high foreheads, high noses, thin lips, and belong to the white race. Not a kinky-headed negro among them. We have shown that Ham's descendants have led and governed the world, for twenty-three centuries after the flood to the battle of Actium; that they gave it, also, the arts and sciences, manufactures and commerce, etc., etc. There is one discovery, one dye, as old as Tyre itself, and yet eminently noted—the *Tyrian Purple*—consecrated exclusively to imperial use. Imperial purple is the synonym of a king, in ancient and modern history; that we have found these children of the slandered Ham, and have traced them step by step, as it were, from country to country, from the days of the flood down to the present day; that *wherever* we found them, and *whenever* found, in any day, of any century from Noah down to this day, we have found them white, and of the *white race only.* And we now challenge the production of a single history, or a single paragraph of history, showing *one* nation— *one single nation* or *kingdom*—of kinky-headed, flat-nosed, thick-lipped and black-skinned negroes, that made such discoveries in arts and sciences, built such cities, had such rulers, kings, and legislators, such generals, such commerce, and such manufactures, as Mizraim's people on the Nile, or as Ham's children in Tyre, in Carthage, in Spain, show that they had—we defy its production. But we are not yet done with our proofs about Ham and his descendants being white.

It seems as if God, foreseeing the slander that would, in after ages, be put, or attempted to be put, on *his son Ham,* by ignorant or designing men attempting to show that he was the progenitor of the negro race, directed Mizraim, the second son of Ham, by an interposition of his power and providence, or by direct inspiration, to put away his dead, by a process of embalming, the details of which, for the accomplishment of the object, can be regarded as little, if anything, short of being miraculous; and by which, we can *now* look into the faces of the children of Mizraim, male and female, even at this day, in succeeding generations, and from the flood; and which *can not be done* with the children of Shem and Japheth, about whose identity with the white race no controversy has ever existed. It was this fact that caused us to say, that the testimony establishing Ham's identity, as belonging to the white race, was *stronger,* if possible, than that of either of his brothers. God foreseeing, as we have said, this atrocious slander, that would be put on Ham and his posterity, so directed Mizraim, and at once inspired his mind, that from the first, he appeared to be fully acquainted with all the necessary ingredients, and how to use them, and in what proportions, and how many days were to be consumed to perfect the corpse, that it would be incorruptible, and thereby become and be *forever* a testimony of God for Ham, that should speak to the eyes and senses of all men, in after ages, and proclaiming as they do, to this day, and from the very time of the flood, and *through each successive generation from the flood,* that their ancestor, Ham, and they, his descendants, were like the children of the other brothers, their equal, in all the lineaments that stamp the race of Adam with the image and likeness of the Almighty, and belonging to the white race. That these mummied witnesses of Ham, his dead children, speaking from the tombs of ages for their father, and proclaiming from the days of the flood as they do, by each succeeding generation of his buried ones, down to the present day, and protesting by their long, straight hair, by their high foreheads, by their high noses, and by their thin lips, now hushed in silence forever, that the slander, that their father was the progenitor of the negro, was a *slander most foul*—a slander most *infamous.* Well might their indignant bodies be so aroused—well might Ham's children, who have been slumbering for centuries, be so electrified by these foul aspersions, as to burst their sarcophagii, and tear the cerements of the grave, and this foul calumny, from their faces at one and the same time and forever. It looks as if God *intended,* by this overruling or inspiring of Mizraim, so to embalm his dead, to teach *us* a lesson, that there was an *importance,* in being of the white race, *to be attached to it,* of grander proportions, and of nobler value, than any earthly, filial or paternal affections that could be symbolized by it. Millions of these mummied bodies have been exhumed this century, but *not one* negro has been found among them. What does this teach? What value do you place on this testimony prepared and ordained by God himself, as *his testimony to the worth* of the *white race?* The writer of this has seen many of these mummies, but never a negro. He has assisted in unrolling some, and all had straight, long hair. It was his fortune, as it happened, to assist in unrolling the body of one possessing peculiar interest. From the hieroglyphic inscription on the sarcophagus, it proved to be the body of a young lady, who died in her seventeenth year, that she was the daughter of the High Priest of On (the temple of On was situated six miles northeast from the present Cairo), and that she was an attendant of the princesses of the court of King Thothmes 3d. This king is recognized and believed to be that Pharoah under whom Moses and Aaron brought out the children of Israel from Egypt. This mummy we assisted in unrolling. The inner wrapping next to the skin was of what we now call *fine linen cambric*. When this was removed, the hair on the head looked as though it had but recently been done up. It was in hundreds of very small plaits, three-ply, and each from a yard to a yard and a quarter long; and although she had then been buried 3,338 years, her hair had the *apparent* freshness as if she had been dead only a few days or weeks. The face, ears, neck and bosom were guilded; and so were her hands to above the wrists, and her feet to above the ankles. Such had been the perfect manner of her embalmment, that the flesh retained its roundness and fullness remarkably, with fine teeth, beautiful mouth, and every mark by which we could, at this day, recognize her as a beautiful lady of the white race. Without disparagement to our fair country-women, we can say, that a more beautiful hand, foot and ankle, we never beheld.

Now, what have we proven by this recitement of Bible history—of that of contemporaneous and concurrent history outside of the Bible—of facts, facts now existing in the mummied remains of Ham's descendants, commencing with Mizraim and coming down through centuries since the flood —of the *yet living nations*, comprised *unquestionably* of his descendants, and who, like the descendants of Shem and Japheth, have the distinctive marks of the white race *alone*, and as clear as either Shem or Japheth, and that, too, as they *exist now on earth*, and running back as such from this our day to Noah; and as *distinct* from the negro race as that race is now distinct from the children of Japheth? Of that miraculous intervention of divine power, in causing Mizraim so to embalm his children, that they should speak from the grave, in attestation of their being of the white,

2

17

and not of the negro, race. Why did God require that *only* the children of Ham should be embalmed, of all then on earth? No other nation, as such, then or *since*, embalmed their dead. Why was it, that the children of Ham alone did this? Except but for the reason that God, foreseeing the disputes to arise about the negro, and that Ham would be slandered and held to be the progenitor of the negro; that, therefore, in vindication of him, as belonging to the white race, and as an *immortal* being, and not of the beasts that perish, God caused these descendants of Ham to embalm their dead, and to *continue* doing so for many centuries. No other valid reason can be assigned, why these people of Mizraim, *alone* of all the nations of the earth, did so. There may have been, and doubtless there were, many reasons with the people, of a private and personal character, inciting them to do so; but *this* was *God's reason,* and he chose these personal considerations of the people, as *his* means of accomplishing it.

We have shown conclusively: 1. That Ham's descendants now on earth, in Egypt, in India, all over Asia, a portion of Africa and Europe respectively, have, *this day,* long, straight hair, high foreheads, high noses and thin lips—that they have ever *been* so; this, all history in the Bible, and all history outside of the Bible, fully attest. 2. While, on the other hand, all history tells us (when it says anything about them), that the negro race is kinky-headed, low forehead, flat nose, thick lip and black skin; that he has *always* been so, and the negro of this day attests that he is so yet; and that, consequently, he is in *no way* related to Ham, even by a *curse,* for he is black, and Ham is white. 3. That the descendants of Shem and Japheth are white, and have always been white, none dispute. 4. That, having established, then, that Shem, Ham and Japheth were perfect in their genealogies from Adam and Eve; that they were the children of one father and one mother; that they were born about a hundred years before the flood; that their wives, like themselves, were perfect in their genealogies; that these brothers and their descendants, as regards their genealogy, were the perfect equals of each other; that the curse of Noah, even if directed against Ham, and which it is not, that it is *impossible* that that curse could, in any way, make him the father or progenitor of the present negroes—as no curse denounced by God himself, by patriarch or by prophet, had ever done so before or since, and there is nothing in the language used by Noah that covers that idea; that, on the contrary, the *exact word* used by Noah, had been before used by God and by patriarchs, without the slightest suspicion being excited that such was its effect on the person so cursed; that it was not found in Ham's name, and that the effort to connect the color of the negro with the meaning of Ham's name in Hebrew, is a mere *fancy*, not of the strength even of a cobweb. Now, reader, are these things true? Look into your Bible—look into contemporaneous and concurrent history—look at existing facts outside of the Bible, and running from the flood down to the present day, and hear the prophet of God defiantly ask, Can the Ethiopian change his skin, or the leopard his spots?—both beasts; and when you have so looked, you will say, *true*, every word, *indubitably* true! Then, what? One word more, before we proceed further. The embalming of Ham's dead and the Jewish genealogical tables *ceased* at about the same time, and by God's interposing power. Each were permitted by God to continue as *national records*—the one to show the genealogy of Jesus of Nazareth to be the Messiah, the other to show that Ham was *white*, and *not* the progenitor of the negro; and each having accomplished the end designed, God permitted them to cease, and both ceased about the same time. Is not this embalming, then, in effect, the direct testimony of God himself, that Ham and his children were of the white race, and that there is an *importance in being of the white race*, and which we will see by and by, and beyond any appreciation ever given to it heretofore? And is it not equally God's testimony, *ipso facto*, that the negro race have always existed as we have it now, and as have those of the three brothers equally always existed, and as we have *them* now?

But, reader, suppose we admit, for the sake of the argument, that Ham was black, and that he was made so by the curse of his father Noah—we say, suppose we were to admit this, then what follows? Ham would have been just *such a negro* as we now find on earth—admitted; but then he would have been the *only* negro on earth. Where was his negro wife to be had? He could not propagate the negro race, by a cross with the white woman; for that would have produced a *mulatto*, and not the negro, such as we now have. To propagate the negro that we now have on earth, the *man* and the *woman* must both be negroes. Now, where did Ham's negro wife come from? She did not come out of the ark? She was not on earth? Do we not see clearly from this statement of facts, that the assumption of the learned world even admitting it, destroys itself the moment that we bring it to the test of facts. Under *no* view of their *assumptions* can the negro we now have on earth be accounted for.

These things being so, now what? We proceed with our subject. It being shown to be incontestibly true, that the three brothers, Shem, Ham and Japheth, when they came out of the ark, were *each* of the white race, and that they have continued so to the *present day* in their posterity—this is incontestible, and being true, it settles *the question, that Ham is not the progenitor of the negro*, and we must now look to some other quarter for the negro's origin. As the negro is not the progeny of Ham, as has been demonstrated, and knowing that he is of neither family of Shem or Japheth, who are white, straight haired, etc., and the negro we have now on earth, is kinky-headed and black, by this logic of facts we *know, that he came out of the ark*, and is a totally different race of men from the three brothers. How did he get in there, and in what station or capacity? We answer, that he went into the ark by *command of God*; and as he was neither Noah, nor one of his sons, all of whom were white, then, by the logic of facts, *he could only enter it as a beast, and along with the beasts*. This logic of *facts* will not allow this position to be questioned. But we will state it in another way equally true, from which the same result must necessarily follow, that the negro entered the ark *only as a beast*. All candid or uncandid men will admit that the negro of the *present day*, have kinky heads, flat nose, thick lip and black skin, and which we have shown is *not* true of either Shem, Ham or Japheth's progeny of *this day*, and consequently *it is impossible* that either of them could be, or could have been, the progenitor of the negro, at or since the flood, for each race exists now, the one white and the other black; and then, as it is impossible to believe that the negro was created at or since the flood, therefore, he must have been in the ark. This being so, now let us see what God said to Noah in proof of this position. He told Noah that he intended to destroy the world by a flood, but that he intended to *save* him and his wife, and his three sons and their wives. These were all God intended to *save*, for *they* had *souls* and *beasts have not*. God told him he must prepare an ark, into which besides his family, he must also take of *every beast* after his kind, and all cattle after their kind, and of every creeping thing that creepeth on the earth, and every fowl after his kind, and every bird after his sort, and food for their support.   Thus did Noah, and thus by God's command he entered the Ark with his family.   God promised Noah to *save* him and his family—but God did not promise to *save* the *beasts*, etc., although he preserved them in the ark; but, *besides this preservation*, Noah and his family were to be *saved*—why, we will see presently.   Then, Ham, not being the father of the negro, the negro must have come out of the ark with the beasts, and *as one*, for he was *not one of Noah's family* that entered it.   This is inevitable, and can not be shaken by all the reasonings of men on earth to the contrary.   Now, unless it can be shown that, from Noah back to Adam and Eve, that in some way this kinky-headed and black-skinned negro is the progeny of Adam and Eve, and which we know can not be done, then *again* it follows, indubitably, that the negro is not a *human* being—not being of Adam's race.   This point we will now examine and settle, and then account for the negro being here.

Noah was the tenth in generation from Adam and Eve. We have before shown that the descendants of Shem, Ham and Japheth, at this day, are white—have been so from the flood, with long, straight hair, etc.   This fact establishes another fact, viz: that Noah was also white, with long, straight hair, etc.   The Bible tells us that Noah was perfect in his genealogy, and the tenth in descent from Adam and Eve; that, consequently, Adam and Eve were white—with long, straight hair, high foreheads, high noses and thin lips.   Our Saviour was also white, and his genealogy is traced, family by family, back to Adam and Eve—which *again* establishes the fact that Adam and Eve were white.   We have also shown that the negro did not descend from either of the sons of Noah.   That he is now here on earth, none will deny; and being here now, this logic of facts proves that he was in the ark, and came out of the ark after the flood; and that it indubitably follows, from the necessities of the case, that he entered the ark as a *beast*, and *only* as a beast.   Now, it is very plain, from this statement, that as he came out of the Ark, the negro, *as we now know him*, existed anterior to the flood, and *just such a negro as we have now*, with his kinky head, flat nose, black skin, etc.; and that, Noah and his wife being white, and perfect in their genealogy, it establishes that Adam and Eve were white; and no *mesalliance* having taken place from Adam to Noah, by which the negro could be produced, that, therefore, as neither of the sons of Noah, nor Noah himself, nor Adam and Eve, ever could by any possibility be, either of them, the progenitor of the negro, that, therefore, it follows, from this logic of facts, that the negro is a *separate* and *distinct* species of the *genus homo* from Adam and Eve, and being distinct from them, that it *unquestionably* follows that *the negro was created before Adam and Eve.* Created before them? Yes. How do we know this? Because the Bible plainly tells us that Adam and Eve were the last beings of God's creation on earth, and bei*r ʒ the last,* that the negro must have existed before they were created; for he is here now, and not being their offspring, it follows, from this logic of facts, that he was on the earth before them, and if on the earth before Adam, that he is inevitably a beast, and as a beast, entered the ark. Let us recapitulate our points. We have shown that the assumption of the learned world, that Ham is the progenitor of the negro, is a mistake, philanthropically and innocently made, we have no doubt, but nevertheless a mistake, and a very great one. As Ham is not the father of the negro, and no one asserts that either Shem or Japheth is, then the negro belongs to another race of people, and that he came out of the ark, is a demonstrated fact; and not being of Noah's family, who are white, and Adam and Eve being likewise white, therefore, *they* could not be the progenitors of the negro; and as neither the *name* or *curse* did make Ham a negro, or the father of negroes (and this covers the space of time from now back to the flood and to Noah), and no *mesalliance* ever having taken place from the flood or Noah, back to Adam and Eve, by which the negro can be accounted for, and Adam and Eve being white, that they could never be the father or mother of the kinky-headed, low forehead, flat nose, thick lip and black-skinned negro; and as Adam and Eve were the last beings created by God on earth, therefore, all beasts, cattle, etc., were consequently made *before* Adam and Eve were created; and the negro being now here on earth, and not Adam's progeny, it follows, beyond all the reasonings of men on earth to controvert, that he was created *before* Adam, and with the other beasts or cattle, and being created *before* Adam, that, like all beasts and cattle, they have no souls. This can not be gainsaid, and being true, let us see if it is in philosophic harmony with God's order among animals in their creation. Not to be prolix on this point, we will take a few cases. We will begin with the cat. The cat, as a genera of a species of animals, we trace in his order of *creation* through various grades—cougar, panther, leopard, tiger, up to the lion, improving in each gradation from the small cat up to the lion, a noble beast. Again, we take the ass, and we trace through the intervening animals of the same species up to the horse, another noble animal. Again, we take up the monkey, and trace him likewise through his upward and advancing orders—baboon, ourang-outang and gorilla, up to the negro, another noble animal, the noblest of the beast creation.

The difference between these higher orders of the monkey and the negro, is very slight, and consists mainly in this one thing: the negro can utter sounds that can be imitated; hence he could talk with Adam and Eve, for they could imitate his sounds. This is the foundation of language. The gorilla, orang-outang, baboon, etc., have languages peculiar to themselves, and which they understand, because they can imitate each other's sounds. But man can not imitate them, and hence can not converse with them. The negro's main superiority over them is, that he utters sounds that could be imitated by Adam; hence, conversation ensued between them. Again, the baboon is thickly clothed with hair, and goes erect a *part* of his time. Advancing still higher in the scale, the ourang-outang is less thickly covered with hair, and goes erect most altogether. Still advancing higher in the scale, the gorilla has still less hair, and is of a black skin, and goes erect when moving about. A recent traveler in Africa, states that the gorilla frequently steals the negro women and girls, and carry them off for wives. It is thus seen that the gradation, from the monkey up to the negro, is in philosophical juxtaposition, in God's order of creation. The step from the negro to Adam, is still progressive, and consists of change of color, hair, forehead, nose, lips, etc., and *immortality.* That the negro existed on earth before Adam was created, is so positively plain from the preceding facts, no intelligent, candid man can doubt; and that he so existed before Adam, and *as a man* (for he was so *named* by Adam), we now proceed to show.

We read in the Bible, and God said, let us make man *in* our own image and after *our* likeness; which is equivalent to saying, we have *man* already, but *not in our* image; for if the negro was already in God's image, *God could not have said,* now let us make man *in our* image. But God did say, after he had created every thing else on earth *but Adam,* that he *then* said, let us make man *in our* image, and after *our likeness,* and let him, so created now, have dominion. God so formed *this* man, out of the dust of the earth, and breathed into his nostrils the breath of life, and he became a living soul, and endowed with immortality. Now, it is indisputably plain, and so shown from the Bible in this paper, that *this* BEING, thus created by God, had long, straight hair, high forehead, high nose, thin lips, and white skin, and which the negro has not; and it is equally clearly shown that the negro is not the progeny of Adam. Therefore the negro must have existed before Adam. But another fact: Adam was to have *dominion* over all the earth. There must, of *necessity*, be an established boundary to that dominion, as betwixt God and himself, in order that Adam should rule only in his allotted dominion. In settling this domain, the Bible is full and exact. That which was to be, and to continue under *God's* dominion, rule and control, God named himself. He called the light, day; the darkness he called night; the dry land he called earth; and the gathering together of the waters, he called seas; and the firmament he called heaven, etc. And what was to be under Adam's dominion, rule and control, Adam named himself, but by God's direction and authority. But mark: *Adam did not name himself*—for no child ever names himself. But God named *him and his race*, but he did not call or name him *man* after he created him. Adam's dominion, starting *from* himself, went *downward* in the scale of creation; while God's dominion, starting *with* Adam, went upward. God, foreseeing that Adam would call the negro by the name *man*, when he said, let us make man, therefore so used the term; for by such *name* "man," the negro, was known by to the flood, but not *the* man.

Whenever Adam is personally spoken of in the Hebrew scriptures, invariably his name has the prefix, *the* man, to contradistinguish him from the negro, who is called *man* simply, and was so *named* by Adam. By inattention to this distinction, made by God himself, the world is indebted for the confusion that exists regarding Adam and his race, and the negro. Adam and his race were to be *under God's dominion, rule and government*, and was, therefore, *named* by God, "and he called *their* name Adam," in reference to his *race*, and *the man*, to contradistinguish *him* from the negro, whom Adam named "*man.*" *But God did not call Adam man after he created him*—he called their name Adam—while Adam named the negro *man*. But some may say, again, as many have already said, that the negro might be the offspring of Adam by some other woman, or of Eve by some one other than Adam. Have such reasoners thought of the destruction, the *certain* destruction, to their own theory, this assumption would entail upon them? Can they not see that, in either case, by Adam or by Eve, the progeny would be a *mulatto*, and not a kinky-headed, flat nose, black negro, and that we should be at as much loss as before, to account for the negro as we now have him on earth, as ever. And if such miscegenating and crossing continued, that now we would have *no kinky heads* nor *black skins* among us. But this amalgamation of the whites and blacks was never consummated until a later day, and then we shall see what God thought of its practice. But while on this point, just here let us remark, that God in the creating of Adam, to be the head of creation, intended to distinguish, and did distinguish, him with eminent grandeur and notableness in his creation, over and above everything else that had preceded it. But when creating the negro and other beasts and animals, he made the male and female—each out of the ground. Not so with Adam and his female, for God expressly tells us that he made Adam's wife out of himself, thus securing the *unity* of immortality *in his race alone*, and hence he called *their* name Adam, not *man*. The black *man* was the *back ground* of the picture, to show the white man to the world, in his dominion over the earth, as the *darkness* was the back ground of the picture of creation, before and over which light, *God's light*, should forever be seen.

The discussion and practice of the social and political equality of the white and black races, heretofore, have always carried along with them their kindred error of the equality of *rights* of the *two* sexes, in all things pertaining to human affairs and government. But both end in destruction, *entire* destruction and extermination, as we shall see in the further prosecution of our subject, and as the Bible plainly teaches. The conclusion, then, that the negro which we now have on earth was created *before* Adam, is inevitable, from the logic of facts, and the divine testimony of the Bible, and can not be resisted by all the reasonings of men on earth.

How is it that we say that the horse was created before Adam? The Bible does not tell us so in so many words, yet we *know* that it is true. How do we know it? Simply because we know that the Bible plainly tells us that Adam and Eve were the last of God's creation on earth, and by the fact that we have the horse *now*, and know that he must have been created, and Adam being the last created, that, consequently, by this logic of facts, we *know* that the horse was made *before*

3

Adam. The horse has his distinctive characteristics, and by which he has been known in all ages of the world, and he has been described in all languages by those characteristics, so as to be recognized in all ages of the world. His characteristics are not more distinct from some other animals than that of the white race is distinct from that of the negro, or of the negro from the white. We can trace all the beasts, etc., now on earth, back to the flood, and from the flood back to the creation of the world, and just *such animals* as we find them now. Why not the negro? We know we can that of the white man. Then we ask, again, why not the negro as readily as the white man or the horse? Has *any* animal so changed from their creation that we can not recognize them now? Certainly not. Then, why say that the negro has? Has God ever changed any beings from the *order* in which he created them since he made the world? Most certainly he has not. Has he ever intimated in any way that he would do so? Certainly not. Has he created any beings since he made Adam? No. How, then, can any man *assert that he did make or change a white man* into a black *negro*, and say not *one word* about it? Such a position is untenable, it is preposterous.

But, to go on with our subject: We read in the Bible that it came to pass when *men* began to multiply, etc., that the sons of God saw the daughters of *men*, that they were fair, and they took themselves wives of all which they chose. A word or two of criticism before we proceed. In this quotation the word *men* is correctly translated from the Hebrew, and as it applies to the negro, it is not in the original applied to Adam, for then it would be *the* men, Adam and his race being so distinguished by God himself, when Adam was created. Again, the *daughters* of *men* were *fair*. The word *fair* is not a correct rendering of the original, except as it covers simply the *idea*, captivating, enticing, seductive.

With this explanation we proceed, and in proceeding we will show these criticisms to be just and proper.

Who were these sons of God? Were they from heaven? If they were, then their morals were sadly out of order. Were they angels? Then it is very plain they never got back to heaven: nor are wicked angels ever sent to earth from heaven. And they are not on earth; for the angels that sinned, are confined where there is certainly no water; and these were all *drowned*. And angels can not be drowned. Angels belong to heaven, and if they do anything wrong there, they are sent, not to earth, but to—tophet.   They are not the sons of men from *below*, nor its angels; for these could not be called sons of God. Who were they then ? We answer, without the fear of successful contradiction, that they were the sons of Adam and Eve, thus denominated by *pre-eminence;* and as they truly were, the sons of God, to show the horrible *crime* of their criminal association with *beasts.*   Immortal beings allying themselves with the beasts of the earth.   These daughters of *men* were *negroes,* and these sons of God, were the children of Adam and Eve, as we shall see presently, and beyond a shade of doubt.

God told Adam and Eve to multiply and replenish the earth.   Then it is plain, God could have no objection to their taking themselves wives of whom they chose, of their own race, in obeying this injunction ; for they could not do otherwise in obeying it. But God *did* object to their taking wives of *these daughters of men.*   Then it is plain that these daughters of *men,* whatever else they may have been, *could not be the daughters* of Adam and Eve ; for, had they been, God would certainly not have objected, as they would have been exactly fulfilling his command, to take them wives and multiply.   But our Saviour settles these points beyond any doubt, when he taught his disciples how to pray—to say, *Our Father,* who art in heaven.   His disciples were white, and the lineal and pure descendants of Adam and Eve.   This being so, then, when he told such to say, "Our Father, who art in heaven," equally and at the same time told them that, as God was their father, *they were the sons of God;* and as God did object to the "sons of God" taking them wives of these daughters of *men,* that it is *ipso facto* God's testimony that these daughters of *men* were negroes, and *not his children.* This settles the question that it was Adam's pure descendants who are here called the *sons of God,* and that these daughters of men were negroes.

By this logic of facts we see, then, who these sons of God were, and who these daughters of *men* were ; and that the crime they were committing, could not be, or ever will be, *propitiated;* for God neither *could* or *would forgive it,* as we shall see.   He determined to destroy them, and with them the world, by a flood, and for the crime of *amalgamation* or *miscegenation* of *the white race* with that of *the black*—*mere beasts of the earth.*   We can now form an opinion of the awful nature of this crime, in *the eyes of God,* when we know that he destroyed the world by a flood, on account of its perpetration. But it is probable that we should not, in this our day, have been so long in the dark in regard to the sin, the *particular* sin, that brought the flood upon the earth, had not our translators rejected the rendering of some of the oldest manuscripts—the Chaldean, Ethiopic, Arabic, *et al.*—of the Jewish or Hebrew scriptures, in which *that sin* is plainly set forth; our translators believing it *impossible* that brute beasts could corrupt themselves with mankind, and then, not thinking, or regarding, that the *negro* was the *very beast* referred to. But even after this rejection, such were the number and authenticity of manuscripts in which that *idea* was still presented, that they felt constrained to admit it, covertly as it were, as may be seen on reading Gen. vi: 12–13, in our common version.

It will be admitted by all Biblical scholars, and doubted by none, that immediately after the fall of Adam in the garden of Eden, God then (perhaps on the same day), instituted and ordained sacrifices and offerings, as the media through which Adam and his race should approach God and call upon his name. That Adam did so—that Cain and Abel did so; and that Seth, through whom our Saviour descended after the flesh, did so, none can or will doubt, who believe in the Bible. Now, Seth's first-born son, Enos (Adam's first grandson), was born when Adam was two hundred and thirty-five years old. Upon the happening of the birth of this grandson, the sacred historian fixes the time, the *particular time*, immediately after the birth of Enos, as the period when a certain important matter *then first* took place; that important event was: that "*Then* men *began* to call on the name of the Lord," as translated in our Bible. Who are *these men* that *then began* to call on the Lord? It was not Adam; it was not Cain; it was not Abel; it was not Seth; And these were all the men that were of Adam's race that were upon the earth at that time, or that had been, up to the birth of Enos; and these had been calling on the name of the Lord ever since the fall in the garden. Who were they, then? What *men* were they, then on earth, that *then began* to call on the name of the Lord? There is but one answer between earth and skies, that can be given in truth to this question. This logic of facts, this logic of Bible facts, plainly tells us that these *men* who *then began* (A. M. 235), to call upon the name of the Lord, were negroes—the *men* so named by Adam when he named the other beasts and cattle. This can not be questioned. Any other view would make the Bible statements false, and we know the Bible to be true. If our translators (indeed all translators whose works we have examined), had not had their minds confused by the *idea* that all who are, in the Bible, called *men* were *Adam's* progeny; or had they recognized the simple fact, that the term *man* was the *name* bestowed on the *negro* by Adam, and that this *name* was never applied to Adam and his race till long after the flood, they would have made a very different translation of this sentence from the original Hebrew. The logic of facts existing *before* and at the time the sacred historian said that "Then *men* began to call," would, in conjunction with the original Hebrew text, have compelled them to a different rendering from the one they adopted. But, believing as they did, that it was some of *Adam's race*, then called *men*, they stumbled on a translation that *not one* of them has been satisfied with since they made it. The propriety of this assertion in regard to antecedents *controlling* the proper rendering, will be readily admitted by all scholars. The rendering, therefore, of the exact *idea* of the sacred historian, would be this: "Then *men* began to profane the Lord by calling on his name." This is required by the *Hebrew*, and the antecedent facts certainly demand it; otherwise we would falsify the Bible, as Adam and his sons had been calling on the Lord ever since the fall; therefore, the men referred to, that then *began* to call, could not be Adam, nor any of his sons. This logic of facts compels us to say that it was the negro, created before Adam and by him *named man*, for there were no other *men* on the earth. That the calling was profane, is admitted by all of our ablest commentators and Biblical scholars, as may be seen by reference to their works. See Adam Clark, *et al.* The Jews translate it thus: "Then men began to profane the name of the Lord."

But we have this singular expression in the Bible, occurring about the flood: That it repented the Lord that he had made *man* on the earth, and that it *grieved him at his heart.* Now, it is clear that God could not refer, in these expressions, to Adam as the man whom it repented and grieved him that he had made; for Adam was a part of himself, and became so when God breathed into his nostrils the breath of life and he became a living soul, immortal, and must exist, *ex consequentia*, as long as God exists. God can not hate any part of himself, for that would be perfection hating perfection, and Adam did partake of the divine nature to some extent; and therefore the *man* here referred to could not have been Adam's posterity; and must have been, from the same logic of facts, the *man*, negro, the beast, called by God, *man before he created Adam.* Now, it must have been some awful crime, some terrible corruption, that could and did cause God to repent, to be grieved at his heart, that he had made man. What was this crime? what this corruption? Was it moral crimes confined to Adam's race? Let us see. It was not the eating of the forbidden fruit; for that had been done long before. It was not murder; for Cain had murdered his brother. It was not drunkenness; for Noah, though a preacher of righteousness, did get drunk. It was not incest; for Lot, another preacher of righteousness, committed that. It was not that of one brother selling his own brother as a slave, to be taken to a strange land; for Joseph's brethren did that, and lied about it, too. It was not—, but we may go through the whole catalogue of moral sins and crimes of *human* turpitude, and take them up separately, and then compound them together, until the whole catalogue of *human* iniquity and infamy is exhausted, and then suppose them all to be perpetrated every day by *Adam's race,* and as they have been *before* and *since* the flood, still we would have but one answer, and that answer would be, It *is none of these, nor all of them combined,* that thus caused God to repent and be grieved at his heart, that he had made *man;* but add one more—nay not *add,* but take one crime alone and by itself— one *only,* and that crime Adam's children, the sons of God, amalgamating, miscegenating, with the *negro—man—beast, without soul—without the endowment of immortality,* and you have the reason, *why* God repented and drowned the world, because of its commission. It is a crime, *in the sight of God,* that can not be *propitiated* by any sacrifice, or by any obla- tion, and can not be forgiven by God—*never* has been for- given on earth, and never will be. Death—death inexorable, is declared by God's judgments on the *world* and *on nations;* and he has declared death as its punishment by his law— death to both male and female, without pardon or reprieve, and beyond the power of *any* sacrifice to expiate.

That Adam was especially endowed by his Creator, and by him commissioned with authority to rule and have dominion over everything created on earth, is unquestioned; that to mark the extent of his dominion, everything *named by him* was included in his right to rule them. His wife was the last thing named by him, and consequently under his rule, government and dominion. But a being called *man* existed before Adam was created, and was *named man* by Adam, and was to be under his rule and dominion, as all other beasts and animals. But did God call Adam *man*, after he had created him? Most certainly he did not. This fact relieves us of all doubt as to *who* was meant as the *men* of whose daughters the sons of God took their wives, independent of the preceding irrefragible proofs, that it was the negro; and the crime of amalgamation thus committed, brought the flood upon the earth. There is no possibility of avoiding this conviction.

But this will be fully sustained as we advance. Cush was Ham's oldest son, and the father of Nimrod. It appears from the Bible, that this Nimrod was not entirely cured, by the flood, of this antediluvian love for and miscegenation with negroes. Nimrod was the first on earth who began to monopolize power and play the despot: its objects we will see presently. *Kingly power* had its origin in love for and association with the negro. Beware! Nimrod's hunting was not only of wild animals, but also of *men*—the negro—to subdue them under his power and dominion; and for the purposes of rebellion against God, and in defiance of his power and judgment in destroying the world, and for the *same sin*. This view of Nimrod as a *mighty* hunter, will be sustained, not only by the facts narrated in our Bible, of what he did, but to the mind of every Hebrew scholar, it will appear doubly strong by the sense of the original. We see that God, by his prophets, gives the name *hunter* to *all tyrants*, with manifest reference to Nimrod as its originator. In the Latin Vulgate, Ezekiel xxxii: 30, plainly shows it. It was Nimrod that directed and managed—ruled, if you please—the great multitude that assembled on the Plain of Shinar. This multitude, thus assembled by his arbitrary power, and other inducements, we shall see presently, were mostly *negroes*; and with them he undertook the building of the tower of Babel—a building vainly intended, by him and them, should reach heaven, and thereby they would escape such a flood as had so recently destroyed the earth; and for the *same sin*. Else why build such a tower? They knew the sin that had caused the flood, for Noah was yet living; and unless they were again committing the *same* offense, there would be no necessity for such a tower. That the great multitude, gathered thus by Nimrod, were mostly negroes, appears from the facts stated in the Bible. God told Noah, after the flood, to subdue the earth, "for all beasts, cattle," etc., "are delivered into thy hands." The negro, as already shown, was put into the ark with the beasts, and came out of it along with them, as one. If they went into the ark by sevens, as is probable they did, from being the head of the beasts, cattle, etc., then their populating power would be in proportion to the whites—as seven is to three, or as fourteen is to six; and Nimrod *must* have resorted to them to get the multitude that he assembled on the Plain of Shinar; for the Bible plainly tells us where the other descendants of Noah's children went, including those of Nimrod's *immediate* relations; and from the Bible account where they *did* go to, it is evident *that they did not go with Nimrod* to Shinar. This logic of facts, therefore, proves that they were negroes, and explains why Nimrod is called the *mighty* hunter before, or *against* the Lord, as it should have been translated in this place. David stood *before* Goliah, but evidently *against him.* The whole tenor of the Bible account shows these views to be correct, whether the negro entered the ark by sevens or only a pair. For, when we read further, that they now were all of one speech and one language, they proposed, besides the tower, to build them a city, where their power could be *concentrated;* and if this were accomplished, and they kept together, and acting in *concert,* under such a man as the Bible shows Nimrod to have been, it would be impossible for Noah's descendants to *subdue* the earth, as God had charged they should do. It was, therefore, to prevent this *concentration* of power and numbers, that God confounded their language, broke them into bands, overthrew their tower, stopped the building of their city, and scattered or dispersed them over the earth.

Let us now ask: Was not their tower an *intended* offense to, and defiance of, God? Most certainly. If not, why did God destroy it? Did God ever, *before* or *after,* destroy any *other* tower of the many built about this time, or in any subsequent age of the world, made by any *other* people? No. Why did he not destroy the towers, obelisks and pyramids, built by Mizraim and his descendants, on the banks of the Nile? And why prevent *them* from building a city, but for the purpose of destroying concentrated power, to the injury of Noah's children, and their *right* from God to rule the earth? The Bible nowhere tells us where any of the beasts of earth went at any time: hence, the negro being one, it says not one word about where any of them went. But we are at no loss to find them, when we know their habits. The negro, we know from his habits, when unrestrained, never inhabits mountainous districts or countries; and, therefore, we readily find him in the level Plain of Shinar. The whole facts narrated in the Bible, of what was *said* and *done*, go to show that the positions here assumed, warrant the correctness of the conclusion that the main body of these people were negroes, subdued by and under the rule and direction of Nimrod; that the language used by them, why they would build them a tower, shows they were daily practicing the *same sin* that caused God to destroy the earth by a flood; and that, actuated by the fear of a similar fate, springing from a *like cause*, they hoped to avoid it by a tower, which should reach heaven; that their confusion and dispersion, and the stopping of the building of *their* city by God—all, all go to show what sort of people they were, and what sin it was that caused God to deal with them so *totally* different from his treatment of *any other* people. The very language used by them, on the occasion, goes plainly to prove that those Babel-builders knew that they were *but beasts*, and knew what the effect of that sin would be, that was being committed daily. They knew it was the very *nature* of beasts to be scattered over the earth, and that they had *no name* (from God, as Adam had); therefore they said, "one to another, let us make brick, and let us build *us* a *city*, and a *tower* whose top may reach heaven; and let us make *us a name* (as God gave us none), lest we be *scattered abroad.*" *Name*, in the Hebrew scriptures, signified "power, authority, rule," as may be readily seen by consulting the Bible. And God said: "And *this* they will begin to do, and nothing will *be restrained from them* which they have *imagined to do;* let us, therefore, confound their language, that they might not understand one another." This language is *very peculiar*—used as it is by God—and there is more in it than appears on the surface, or to a superficial reader; but we will not pause to consider it now. The confusion of language *was confined to those there assembled.* Why should God object to *their* building a city, if they were the descendants of Adam and Eve? But it is plain he did object to *their* building one. Did God object to Cain's building a city?—although a fratricidal murderer. Did he object to Mizraim and his descendants building those immense cities which they built on the Nile? No. In short, did God ever object to any of the known descendants of Adam and Eve building a city, or as many as they might choose to build? Never. But, from some cause or other, *God did object to those* people building *that* city and *that* tower. The objection could not be in regard to its locality, nor to the ground on which it was proposed to build them; for the great City of Babylon, and with higher towers, too, was afterward built on the same spot—*but by another people*—Shem's descendants. Then, what could be the reason that could cause God to come down from heaven to prevent *these* people from building it? It must be some great cause that would bring God down to overthrow and prevent it. He allowed the people of Shem, afterward, to build the City of Babylon at the same place.

Reader, candid or uncandid, carefully read and reflect on the facts described in this whole affair. Then remember that, on one other occasion, God came down from heaven; that he talked with Noah; that he told him he was going to destroy the world; that he told him the reason why he intended to destroy it. Reader, do not the facts here detailed, of the objects and purposes of these people, and this *logic of facts*, force our minds, in spite of all opposing reasons to the contrary, to the conviction that *the sin* of these people was the identical sin, and consequent *corruption* of the race, as that which caused the destruction of the world by the flood; and that sin, the amalgamation or miscegenation of Nimrod and his kindred with beasts—the daughters of *men*—negroes. But, this view of who it was that attempted the building of the tower and city of Babel, and their reasons for doing so, will be confirmed by what is to follow.

The Bible informs us that Canaan, the youngest son of Ham, settled Canaan; and that it was from him the land took its name, as did the land of Mizraim, Ham's second son take its name from him, of what is now called Egypt. It was against this Canaan (not Ham) that the curse of Noah was directed, that a servant of servants should he be to his brethren. There is something of marked curiosity in the Bible account of this Canaan and his family. The language is singular, and differs from the Bible account of every other family in the Bible, where it proposes to give and does give the genealogy of any particular family. Why is this, there must be some reason, and some valid reason too, or there would be no variation in the particulars we refer to from that of any other family? The account in the Bible reads thus—"And Canaan begat Sidon his first born, and Heth." So far so good. And why not continue on giving the names of his other sons as in all other genealogies? But it does not read so. It reads, "And Canaan begat Sidon his first born, and Heth, *and the Jebusite,* and the *Amorite,* and the *Girgasite,* and the *Hivite,* and the *Arkite,* and the *Sinite,* and the *Arvidite,* and the *Zemarite,* and the *Hamathite,* and who afterward were the *families* of the *Canaanite* spread abroad." With all *other* families the Divine Record goes on as this commenced, giving the names of all the sons. But in this family of Canaan, after naming the two sons Sidon and Heth (who settled Sidon, Tyre and Carthage, and were *white* as is plainly shown) it breaks off abruptly to these *ites.* Why this suffix of *ite* to *their* names? It is extraordinary and unusual; there must be some reason, a *peculiar* reason for this departure from the usual mode or rule, of which *this* is the only exception. What does *it mean?* The reason is plain. The progeny of the horse and ass species is never *classed* with either its father or mother, but is called a *mule* and represents neither. So the progeny of a son of God, a descendant of Adam and Eve with the negro a beast, is not classed with or called by the name of either its father or mother, but is an *ite,* a *"class"*—*"bonded class,"* not race, God intending by *this distinguishment* to show to all future ages what will become of *all such ites,* by placing in bold relief before our eyes the *terrible end of these* as we shall see presently. Reader, bear in mind the end of these *ites* when we come to narrate them. These *ites,* the progeny of Canaan and the negro, inhabited the land of Canaan; with other places, they occupied what was then the beautiful plain and vale of Siddim, where they built the notorious cities of Sodom, Gomorrah, Admah and Zeboim. Like all *counterfeits,* they were ambitious of appearing as the genuine descendants of Adam, whose name they knew or had heard meant "red and fair" in Hebrew; they, therefore, called one of their cities *Admah,* to represent this "red and fair" man, and at the same time it should mean in negro "Ethiopic" "beautiful"—that kind of beauty that once seduced the sons of God, and brought the flood upon the earth. About the time we are now referring to, Abraham, a descendant of Shem was sojourning in Canaan. He had a nephew named Lot who had located himself in the vale of Siddim, and at this time was living in Sodom. One day three men were seen by Abraham passing his tent; it was summer time, Abraham ran to them and entreated that they should abide under the tree, while he would have refreshments prepared for them; they did so, and when about to depart one of them said, "shall we keep from Abraham that thing which I do (God come down again), seeing he shall surely become a great and mighty nation, *for I know he will command his children and his household* after him, *and they shall keep the way of the Lord;"* that is, keeping Adam's race pure—a mission the Jews are to this day fulfilling. And they told Abraham of the impending fate of these cities. Abraham interceded for them, and pleaded that the righteous should not be destroyed with the wicked. God ultimately promised him, that if there were ten righteous in all these cities that he would not destroy them. What strong foundation have we people of the United States in God's mercy and *forbearance* in this incident? Will we prove worthy? The angels went to Sodom and brought out *all* the righteous, being only Lot and his two daughters (and their righteousness was not in their morality), his wife being turned into a pillar of salt. This done, God rained fire upon these cities and literally burnt up their inhabitants alive, and everything they had, and then sunk the very ground upon which their cities stood more than a thousand feet beneath, not the pure waters of the deluge, but beneath the bitter, salt, and slimy waters of Asphaltites, wherein no living thing can exist. An awful judgment! But it was for the most awful crime that man can commit in the sight of God, of which the punishment *is on earth.* Exhaust the catalogue of human depravity—name every crime human turpitude can possibly perpetrate, and which has been perpetrated on earth since the fall of Adam, and no such judgment of God on any people has ever before fallen, on their commission. But one crime, one *other* crime, and that crime the same for which he had destroyed every living thing on earth, save what was in the ark. But now he destroys by fire, not by water, but by fire, men, women and children, old and young, for the crime of miscegenating of *Adam's race with the negroes.* Noah was a preacher of righteousness to the antediluvians, yet he got drunk after the flood. Lot too was a preacher of righteousness to the cities of the plain, and he too not only got drunk but did so repeatedly, and committed a double crime of incest besides. Then we ask, what *righteousness,* what *kind* of righteousness was it that was thus preached by such men? We speak with entire reverence when we say that the logic of facts shows but little of morality—but it does show, as it *was intended to be shown by God,* that, though frail and sinful in a *moral sense* as they were, yet, being *perfect* in their genealogies from Adam and Eve, *they* could still be *his* preachers of righteousness, they themselves being *right* in keeping from beastly alliances.

But the Bible evidence to the truth of these views does not stop here. God appeared unto Abraham at another time, while sojourning in the land of Canaan, and told him that all *that* land he would give to him and to his seed after him forever. But the land was already inhabited and owned by these *ites*. If they were the natural descendants of Adam and Eve, would they not have been as much entitled to hold, occupy and enjoy it as Abraham or any other? Most certainly. If these *ites* were God's children by Adam and Eve, it is impossible to suppose that God would turn one child out of house and land and give them to another, without right and without justice; and which he would be doing, were he to act so. Nay! but the Lord of the whole earth will do right. But God did make such a promise to Abraham, and he made it in righteousness, truth and justice. When the time came for Abraham's seed to enter upon it and to possess it, God sent Moses and Aaron to bring them up out of Egypt, where they had long been in bondage, and they did so. But now mark what follows: God explicitly enjoins upon them, (1.) that they *shall not* take, of the daughters of the land, wives for their sons; nor give their daughters in marriage to them. Strange conflict of God with himself, if indeed these Canaanites were *his* children! To multiply and replenish the earth, is God's *command* to Adam; but his command to Moses is, that Israel, known to be the children of Adam, shall not take wives of these Canaanites for their sons—nor shall they give their daughters to them. Why this conflict of the one great lawgiver, if these Canaanites were God's children through Adam? It could not be to identify the Messiah, for that required only the lineage of one family. But mark, (2.) "But of the *cities* and *people* of the land which the Lord thy God giveth thee for an inheritance, thou shalt save alive *nothing that breathes*, but thou shalt *utterly destroy* them, namely the Hittites, Canaanites," etc., naming all the *ites*—this is their end. Why this terrible order of extermination given? and given by God himself? Will not the Lord of the whole earth do right? Yes, verily. Then, we ask, what is that great and terrible reason for God ordering this entire extermination of these *ites*, if indeed they were his children and the pure descendants of Adam and Eve? What crimes had they committed, that had not been before committed by the pure descendants of

Noah? What iniquity had the little children and nursing infants been guilty of, that such a terrible fate should overwhelm them? There must have been some good cause for such entire destruction; for the Lord of the whole earth does right, and only right. Let us see how God deals with *Adam's* children, *how bad soever they may be, in a moral sense,* in contrast with this order to exterminate. The Bible tells us, that when the Hebrews approached the border of Sier (which is in Canaan), God told them not to touch *that* land nor its people, for he had given it to Esau for a possession. Yet this Esau had sold his birthright for a mess of pottage, and he and his people were idolaters, and treated the children of Israel with acts of hostility which some of these *ites* had not. Again, they were not to touch the land of Ammon, nor that of Moab, although *they* were the offspring of incestuous intercourse, and were, with the people of Sier, as much given to idolatry and all other moral crimes, and as much so as any of these Canaanites whom God directed Moses to exterminate. Why except those, and doom these to extermination? Was not Canaan, the father of these *ites,* a grandson of Noah, and as much related to the Hebrews as were the children of Esau, Moab and Ammon? Certainly. Then, their destruction was not for want of kinship; nor was it because they were idolaters more than these, or were greater *moral* criminals in the sight of Heaven; but *simply because they were the progeny of amalgamation or miscegenation between Canaan, a son of Adam and Eve, and the negro;* and were *neither* man nor *beast.* For this crime God had destroyed the world, sown confusion broad-cast at Babel, burnt up the inhabitants of the vale of Siddim, and for it would now exterminate the Canaanite. It is a crime that God has never forgiven, *never will forgive,* nor can it be propitiated by all the sacrifices earth can make or give. God has shown himself, in regard to it, *long-suffering and of* great forbearance. However much our minds may seek and desire to seek other reasons for this order of extermination of God, yet we look in vain, even to the Hebrews themselves, for reasons to be found, in their superior *moral* conduct toward God; but we look in vain. The very people for whom they were exterminated were, in their moral conduct and obedience to God, no better, save in that sin of amalgamation. The exterminator and the exterminated were bad, equally alike in every moral or religious sense—save one thing, and *one* thing only—one had not brutalized himself by amalgamating with negroes, the other had. This logic of facts, forces our minds, compels our judgment, and presses all our reasoning faculties back, in spite of ourselves or our wishes, to the conclusion that it was this one crime, and *one crime only*, that was the originating cause of this terrible and inexorable fate of the Canaanite; being, as they were, the *corrupt* seed of Canaan, God destroyed them. For, if these Canaanites had been the full children of Adam and Eve, they would have been as much entitled to the land, under the grant by God, of the whole earth, to Adam and his posterity, with the right of dominion, and their right to it as perfect as that of Abraham could possibly be; but, being partly *beasts* and partly *human*, God not only dispossessed them of it, but also ordered their *entire* extermination, *for he had given no part of the earth to such beings.* This judgment of God on these people has been harped upon by every deistical and atheistical writer, from the days of Celsus down to Thomas Paine of the present age, but without understanding it. This crime must be unspeakably great, when we read, as we do in the Bible, that it caused God to repent and to be grieved at his heart that he had made *man.* For, the debasing idolatry of the world, the murder of the good and noble of earth, the forswearing of the apostle Peter in denying his Lord and Saviour—all, all the crimsoned crimes of earth, or within the power of man's infamy and turpitude to commit and blacken his soul—are as nothing on earth, as compared with this. Death by the flood, death by the scorching fire of God burning alive the inhabitants of Sodom and Gomorrah, death to man, woman and child, flocks and herds, remorseless, relentless and exterminating death—is the *just judgment* of an *all-merciful God, for this offense.* The seed of Adam, which is the seed of God, must be kept pure; it *shall be kept pure, is the fiat of the Almighty.* Man perils his existence, nations peril their existence and destruction, if they support, countenance, or permit it. Such have been God's dealings with it heretofore, and such will be his dealings with it hereafter.

But we have said before, that we intentionally selected Canaan, the youngest son of Ham, and for a purpose. This we will now explain. Had Noah named Ham instead of Canaan, when he declared that he should be a servant of servants to his brethren, the learned world are of the opinion that it would have forever, and *satisfactorily* settled the question, in conjunction with the meaning of his name in Hebrew, *that Ham was the father* of the present negro race—that if *this curse* had been *specifically* and personally directed against Ham, instead of his youngest son Canaan, then, no doubt could exist on earth, but that Ham was, and is the father of the negro. This is the opinion of the learned. But, why so? Could not the curse affect Canaan as readily? If it could affect Ham in changing his color, kinking his hair, crushing his forehead down and flattening his nose, why would it not be equally potent in producing those effects on Canaan? Surely its effects would be as great on one person as another? It was to relieve our learned men from this dilemma, among others, that we took up Canaan, to show, that although this *curse* was hurled specifically and personally at Canaan, by Noah, that a servant of servants should he be, yet it carried *no such effects* with it on Canaan or his posterity. Then, if it did not make the black negro of Canaan, how could it have produced *that effect* on Ham, Canaan's father? Canaan had two *white* sons, with long, straight hair, etc., peculiar alone to the white race, and not belonging to the negro race at all, which is proof that the curse did not affect his hair or the color of his skin, nor that of his posterity. Canaan had two white sons by his first wife, Sidon and Heth. They settled Phœnicia, Sidon, Tyre, Carthage, etc. The city of Sidon took its name from the elder. That they were white, and belong to the white race *alone*, we have before proven, unquestionably. But we will do so again, for the purpose of showing what that curse was, and what it did effect, and why this order of extermination. Canaan was the father of all these *ites*. Nine are first specifically named, and then it is added, "and who afterward, were the families of the Canaanite spread abroad." Was not Canaan as much and no more the father of these *ites*, than he was of Sidon and Heth? Certainly. Then why doom them and their flocks and herds to extermination, and except the families of Sidon and Heth, his two other sons? Were they morally any better, except as to their not being the progeny of amalgamation with negroes? They were not. Then why save one and doom the other? If these *ites* were no worse *morally* than the children of Sidon and Heth, then it is plain, that we must seek the reason for their destruction, in something *besides moral delinquency?* Let us see if we can find *that* something? The Bible tells us, that God in one of his interviews with Abraham, informed him that all that land (including all these ites) should be his and his seed's after him—

" that his seed shall be strangers in a land not theirs, and be afflicted four hundred years, and thou shalt go to thy fathers in peace; but *in the fourth generation* they shall come hither again, *for the iniquity* of the *Amorites*" (these representing all the ites), " *is not yet full.*"

In the fourth generation their cup of iniquity would *then* be full—in the fourth generation God gave this order to exterminate these ites, and to leave nothing alive that breathes. If this filling of their cup, referred to *moral* crimes to be committed, or to moral obliquity as such, then it is *very strange*. If this be its reference, then these people were, at *that* time (four generations previous to this order for their extermination), *worse* than the very devil himself, as it was not long before they did fill *their cup*, and the devil's cup is not full yet. If this filling up of iniquity, referred to their *moral conduct* in the sight of God, how was Moses or Joshua to *see* that it was full, or *when* it was full? Yet, they must *know* it, or they would not know when to commence exterminating, as God intended. How were they to know it? As in the case of Sodom they had a few Lots among them, and the *color* would soon tell when their iniquity was full, and neither Moses nor Joshua would be at any loss when to begin, or who to exterminate. Consummated amalgamation would tell *when* their cup of iniquity was full. The iniquity of the Amorites (these representing all), is not *yet* full, is the language of God—in the fourth generation it will be full, and *then* Abraham's seed should possess the land, and these *ites* be exterminated. Let us inquire? Does not each *generation*, morally stand before God, on their own responsibility in regard to sin? Certainly they do. How then, could the cumulative sins of one generation be passed to the next succeeding one, to their *moral* injury or detriment? Impossible! But *the iniquity* here spoken of, *could be so transmitted*; and at the time when God said it, he tells us that it required *four generations* to make the iniquity full. What crime but the amalgamation of Adam's sons, the children of God, with the negro—beasts—called by Adam *men*, could require four generations to fill up their iniquity, but this crime of amalgamation? None. Then we *know the iniquity*, and what God then thought and yet thinks of it.

Nor is this all the evidence the Bible furnishes, of God's utter abhorrence of this crime, and his decided *disapprobation of the negro*, in those various attempts to *elevate* him to *social, political* and *religious equality* with the white race. In the laws delivered by God, to Moses, for the children of Israel, he expressly enacts and charges, "that no *man* having a *flat nose*, shall approach unto his altar." This includes the *whole negro race*; and expressly *excludes* them from coming to his altar, for *any act of worship*. God would not have their worship then, nor accept *their* sacrifices or oblations—*they* should not approach his altar; but all of Adam's race could. For Adam's children God set up his altar, and for their benefit ordained the sacrifices; but not for the race of *flat-nosed men*, and such the *negro race is*. And who shall gainsay, or *who dare* gainsay, that what God does is not right? The first attempt at the social equality of the negro, with Adam's race, brought the flood upon the world—the second, brought confusion and dispersion—the third, the fire of God's wrath, upon the cities of the plain—the fourth, the order from God, to exterminate the *nations* of the Canaanites—the fifth, the inhibition and exclusion, by express law of

4

God, of the *flat-nosed* negro from his altar. Will the people of the United States, now furnish the sixth? *Nous verrons.*

There remains now but one other point to prove, and that is—That the negro has no soul. This can only be done by the express word of God. Any authority short of this, will not do. But if God says so, then all the men, and all the reasonings of men on earth, can not change it; for it is not in man's power to *give* a soul to any being on earth, where God has given none.

It will be borne in mind that we have shown, beyond the power of contradiction, that the descendants of Shem and Japheth, from the present day back to the days of our Saviour, and from our Saviour's time back to Noah, their father, that they were all long, straight-haired, high foreheads, high noses, and belong to the white race of Adam. In the case of Ham, the other brother, there is, or has been, a dispute. It is contended, generally, by the learned world, that Ham is the progenitor of the negro race of this our day, and that, such being the case, the negro is our social, political and religious equal—*brother;* and which he would be, certainly, if this were true. The learned world, however, sees the difficulty of how Ham could be the progenitor of a race so distinct from that of Ham's family; and proceed upon their own assumptions, but without one particle of Bible authority for doing so, to account why Ham's descendants should now have kinky heads, low foreheads, flat noses, thick lips, and black skin (not to mention the exceptions to his leg and foot), which they charge to the *curse* denounced by Noah, not against Ham, but against Ham's youngest son—Canaan. But, to sustain their theory, they further assume that this curse was *intended* for Ham, and not Canaan; and they do this right in the teeth of the Bible and its express assertions to the contrary. Forgetting or overlooking the fact that, confining its application to Canaan, as the Bible expressly says, yet they ignore the fact that Canaan had two white sons—Sidon and Heth—and that it was impossible for the *curse* to have made a negro such as we now have, or to have exerted any influence upon either color, hair, etc.; as these two sons of Canaan, and their posterity, are shown, unequivocally, to have been, and yet are, in their descendants, white. The learned world, seeing the difficulties of the position, and the weakness of their foundation for such a tremendous superstructure as they were rearing on this supposed curse of Ham, by his father, undertake to prop it up by saying that Ham's name means black in Hebrew; and, as the negro is *black,* therefore it is that the *name* and the *curse* together made the negro, such as we now have on earth. And, although the Bible nowhere *says,* and nowhere charges, or even intimates, that Ham is or was the progenitor of the negro; and in defiance of the fact that *no such* curse was ever denounced against Ham, as they allege—nor can it be found in the Bible; yet they boldly, on these *assumptions* and contradictions, go on to say that Ham *is* the father of the negro of the present day. Contradicting the Bible; contradicting the *whole order of nature* as ordained by God himself—that like will produce its like; contradicting the effect of every curse narrated in the Bible, whether pronounced by God, or by patriarch, or by prophet; and assuming that it did that, in this case of Noah, which it had never done before nor since——that it did change Ham from a white man to a black negro. Forgetting or setting aside the declaration of the Bible, that Ham and his brothers were the children of one father and one mother, who were perfect in their genealogies from Adam, and that they were white, they assume again, that the Bible forgot to tell us that Ham was turned into a negro for accidentally seeing his father naked in his tent. Tremendous judgment, for so slight an offense! We do not ask if this is probable; but we do ask, if it is within the bounds *of possibility* to believe it? Did not the daughters of Lot see the nakedness of their father in a much more unseemly manner? Ham seeing his father so, seems altogether accidental; theirs deliberately sought. And on this flimsy, self-stultifying theory, the learned of the world build their faith—that Ham *is* the progenitor of the negro! While, on the other hand, by simply taking Ham's descendants—those *known to be his descendants now*, and known as much so and as *positively* as that we know the descendants, at the present day, of Shem and Japheth—that by thus taking up Ham's descendants of this day, we find them like his brothers' children—with long, straight hair, high foreheads, high noses, thin lips, and, indeed, every lineament that marks the white race of his brothers, Shem and Japheth; that we can trace him, with history in hand, from this day back, step by step, to the Bible record, with as much positive certainty as we can the descendants of his brothers; that, with the Bible record after, we can trace him back to his father, Noah, with equal absolute certainty, no one will deny, nor *dare* deny, who regards outside concurrent history, of admitted authenticity and the Bible, as competent witnesses in the case; that the testimony in regard to Ham and his descendants being of the white race, is more overwhelming and convincing than that of Japheth—and none doubt Japheth's being of the white race; that God himself, foreseeing the slander that after ages would attempt to throw on Ham, as being the father of the kinky-headed, flat-nosed and black-skinned negro, caused a whole nation to do one thing, and that *one* thing had never been done before, nor by any other nation since, and that he caused them to continue doing that one thing for centuries, and for no other purpose in God's providence, that we can see, but for the *alone* purpose of proving the identity of Ham's children, from the flood downward, for more than twenty-three centuries, and that they, thus identified, were of the white race; and that this embalmment of Ham's children was so intended, as evidence by God; that like, as the Jewish genealogical tables served to identify Jesus of Nazareth as the Messiah, so this embalming of the children of Mizraim, the second son of Ham, serves to identify his descendants as belonging to the white race; and that, like the Jewish tables of genealogy, when they had accomplished the end designed by God, they both ceased, and at one and the same time.

Mizraim settled what is now called Egypt. He embalmed his dead. Where did he get the idea from? No nation or people had ever done it before; none have done it since. It was a very difficult thing to accomplish, to preserve human bodies after death; and to preserve them to last for thousands of years, was still more difficult. How did Mizraim come to a knowledge of the ingredients to be used, and how to use them? Yet he did it, and did it at once. The only satisfactory answer to these questions, is, that God *inspired him.* Then, it is God's testimony, vindicating *his son Ham* from the aspersions of men—that he was a negro, or the father of negroes.

Ye learned men of this age—you who have contributed, by your learned efforts, and by your noble but mistaken philanthropy, innocently, honestly and sincerely as they were made, but wrongfully done— to fix and fasten on Ham this gross slander, that he is the father of the present race of negroes, must re-examine your grounds for so believing heretofore, and now set yourselves right. God's Bible is against your views; concurrent history is against them; the existing race of Ham is against them; *God's living testimony* is against them, in the *dead* children of Mizraim, embalmed ever since the flood, but now brought forth into the light of day, and testifying for Ham, that he and his descendants were, and yet are, of the white race. You must now come forth and abandon your fortress of *assumptions*, for *here that citadel falls; for, if Ham is not the father of the negro* (which is shown *to be an impossibility*) then the negro came out of the ark, *and as we now find him;* and if he came out of the ark, *then he must have been in the ark;* and if he was in the ark, which, by the logic of facts, *we know* he was—now let us read the Bible, the divine record, and see whether or not the negro has a soul. It reads thus: "When the long-suffering of God waited, in the days of Noah, while the ark was preparing, wherein few, that is *eight souls*, were saved;" the negro being in the ark, was not one of those eight souls, and consequently he has *no soul to be saved*—the Bible and God's inspiration being judge. Carping *is* vain, against God. His order *will stand*, whether pleasing or displeasing to any on earth. But God only promised to *save eight*—Noah and his wife, and his three sons and their wives. These *had souls*, as the apostle (Peter) testifies, and *all that were in the ark that did have souls. The negro was in the ark; and God thus testifies that he has no soul.*

One point more. God has set a line of demarcation so ineffaceable, so indelible besides color, and so *plain*, between the children of Adam and Eve whom he endowed with immortality, and the negro who is of this earth only, that none can efface, and none so blind as not to see it. And this line of demarcation is, that Adam and his race being endowed by God *with souls*, that a *sense of immortality* ever inspires them and sets them to work; and the one race builds what he hopes is to last for ages, his houses, his palaces, his temples, his towers, his monuments, and from the earliest ages after the flood. Not so the other, the negro; as left to himself, as Mizraim was, he builds nothing for ages to come; but like any other beast or animal of earth, his building is *only for the day*. The one starts his building on earth, and builds for immortality, reaching toward Heaven, the abode of his God; the other also starting his building on earth, builds nothing durable, nothing permanent—*only* for present *necessity*, and which goes down, *down*, as everything merely animal must forever do. Such are the actions of the two races, when left to themselves, as all their works attest. Subdue the negro as we do the other animals, and like them, teach them all we can; then turn them loose, free them entirely from the restraints and control of the white race, and, just like all other animals or beasts so treated, back to his native nature and wildness and barbarism and the worship of dæmons, he *will go*. Not so with Adam's children: Starting from the flood, they began to build for Etérnity. Ham, the slandered Ham, settled on the Nile, in the person of his son Mizraim, and built cities, monuments, temples and towers of surpassing magnificence and *endurance;* and here, too, with them, he started all the arts and sciences that have since covered Europe and America with grandeur and glory. Even Solomon, whose name is a synonym for wisdom, when about to build the Temple, instructed as he was by his father David, as to how God had told him the Temple was to be built; yet he, notwithstanding his wisdom, was warned of God, and he sent to Hiram, King of Tyre, for a workman skilled in all the science of architecture and cunning in all its devices and ornaments, to raise and build that structure, designed for the visible glory of God on earth.

And Hiram, King of Tyre, sent him a widow's son, named Hiram Abiff; and who was Grand Master of the workmen. He built the Temple and adorned it, and was killed a few months before Solomon consecrated it. This Hiram, King of Tyre, and this Hiram Abiff, although the mother of the latter was a Jewess, were descendants of *this slandered Ham.* Now, we ask, is it reasonable to suppose that God would call, or would suffer to be called, a descendant of Ham to superintend and build his Temple, and erect therein his altar, if Hiram Abiff had been a negro?—a *flat-nosed negro,* whom he had expressly forbidden to approach his altar? The idea is entirely inconsistent with God's dealings with men. God thus, then, testifying, in calling this son of Ham to build his Temple, his appreciation of Ham and his race.

Now, let us sum up what is written in this paper: We have shown. (1.) That Ham was not made a negro, neither by his name, nor the curse (or the supposed curse) of his father Noah. (2.) We have shown that the people of India, China, Turkey, Egypt (Copts), now have long, straight hair, high foreheads, high noses and every lineament of the white race; and that these are the descendants of Ham. (3.) That, therefore, it is *impossible* that Ham could be the father of the present race of Negroes. (4.) That this is sustained by God himself causing Mizraim to embalm his dead, from directly after the flood and to continue it for twenty-three centuries; and that these mummies now show Ham's children to have long, straight hair, etc., and the lineaments alone of the white race. (5.) That Shem, Ham and Japheth being white, proves that their father and mother were white. (6.) That Noah and his wife being white and perfect in their genealogy, proves that Adam and Eve were white, and therefore *impossible* that *they* could be the progenitors of the kinky-headed, black-skinned negroes of this day. (7.) That, therefore, as neither Adam nor Ham was the progenitor of the negro, and the negro being now on earth, consequently we *know* that he was created before Adam, as *certainly* and as *positively* as we *know* that the horse and every other animal were created before him; as Adam and Eve were the last beings created by God. (8.) That the negro being created before Adam, consequently he is a *beast* in God's nomenclature; and being a beast, was under Adam's rule and dominion, and, like all other beasts or animals, nas no soul. (9.) That God destroyed the world by a flood, for the crime of the amalgamation, or miscegenation of the white race (whom he had endowed with souls and immortality), with negroes, mere beasts without souls and without immortality, and producing thereby a *class* (not race), but a *class* of beings that were neither *human* nor *beasts.* (10.) That this was a crime against God that could not be expiated, and consequently could not be forgiven by God, and never would be; and that its punishment in the progeny is on earth, and by death. (11.) That this was shown at Babel, Sodom and Gomorrah, and the extermination of the nations of the Canaanites, and by God's law to Moses. (12.) That God will not accept religious worship from the negro, as he has expressly ordered that no man having a *flat nose,* shall approach his altar; and the negroes have flat noses. (13.) That the negro has no soul, is shown by express authority of God, speaking through the Apostle Peter by divine inspiration.

The intelligent can not fail to discover who was the tempter in the garden of Eden. It was a *beast,* a *talking* beast—a beast that talked *naturally*—if it required a *miracle* to make it talk (as our *learned* men

suppose, and as no one could then perform a miracle but God only
and if he performed *this* miracle to make a snake, a serpent, talk, and
to talk only with Eve, and that as soon as the serpent (?) seduced Eve
into eating the forbidden fruit, God then performed another miracle to
stop his speaking afterward, that if this be true), then it follows beyond
contradiction, *that God is the immediate and direct author* or cause
of sin : an idea that can not be admitted for one moment, by *any* believer in the Bible. *God called it a beast—"more subtile than all the
beasts the Lord God had made."*   As Adam was the federal head of
all his posterity, as well as the real head, so was this beast, the negro,
the federal head of all beasts and cattle, etc., down to creeping things—
to things that go upon the belly and eat dust all the days of their life.
If all the beasts, cattle, etc., were not involved in the sin of their federal head, why did God destroy them at the flood?   If the crime that
brought destruction on the world was the sin of Adam's race alone, why
destroy the *innocent* beasts, cattle, etc.?   When all things were created,
God not only pronounced them good, but "very good;" then why destroy
these innocent (?) beasts, cattle, etc., for Adam's sin or wrong-doing?
But, that these beasts, etc., were involved in the *same* sin with Adam, is
positively plain, from *one fact alone*, among others, and that fact is: That
before the fall of Adam in the garden, all was peace and harmony among
and between all created beings and things.   After the fall, strife, con-
tention and war ensued, as much among the beasts, cattle, etc., as with
the posterity of Adam; and continues so to the present time.   Why
should God thus afflict *them* for another's crime, if they were free and
innocent of that crime?   God told Adam, on the day of his creation,
"to have dominion over everything living that moveth upon the earth;"
but to Noah, after the flood, he uses *very* different language; for, while he
told Noah to be fruitful and multiply and replenish the earth, the same
as he said to Adam, yet he adds, "and the fear of *you* and the *dread*
of you *shall* be upon every beast of the earth, etc., and all that moveth
upon the earth, etc.; into *thy* hands are they delivered."   If these had
continued in their "*primeval* goodness," wholly unconnected with
Adam's sin, is it reasonable to suppose that God would have used the
language toward *them*, that he did in his *instructions* to Noah?   It is
impossible!   The intelligent can also see the judgments of God on this
"*unforgivable*" sin, at the flood, at Babel, at Sodom and Gomorrah,
and on the Canaanites, and in his law; and they may profit by the
example.   They can see the exact time (A. M. 235), *when men*—the
negro—erected the *first* altar on earth; *they* had seen Adam, Cain,
Abel, and Seth, erect altars and call on the name of the Lord.   They,
too, could *imitate* them; they *did* then *imitate;* they then built *their*
altars; they *then* called on the name of the Lord; they are yet *imi-
tating;* they are *yet profaning* the name of the Lord, by calling on his
name.   And *you*, the people of the United States, are upholding *this
profanity*.   Who was it that caused God to repent and to be grieved
at his heart, that he had made *man?*   Will *you* place yourselves along-
side of that being, and against God?   All analogy says *you will!*   But
remember, that the righteous will escape—the hardened alone will
perish.

   The ways of God are *always consistent, when understood*, and always
just and reasonable.   It is a curious fact, but a fact, nevertheless, and
fully sustained by the Bible; and that fact is this: That God *never conferred*, and never *designed* to confer, any great *blessing* on the human
family, but what he *always* selects or selected a white *slaveholder* or

one of a white *slaveholding nation*, as the *medium*, by or through which *that blessing* should reach them. Why he has done so, is not material to discuss now; but the *fact*, that he *always* did so, the Bible abundantly proves. Abraham, the father of the faithful, and in whom and his seed all the families of the earth were to be blessed, is a notable instance of this truth. For Abraham owned three hundred and eighteen *slaves*. And the Saviour of the world was of a white *slaveholding nation;* and they held slaves by God's own laws, and not by theirs. And how has it been in respect of our own nation and government, the United States? A government now declared by thousands of lips, latterly, to be the best, the very best, that has ever been in the world. Who made this government? Who established it and its *noble principles?* Let us appeal to history. The first attack on British power, and the aggressions of its parliament, ever made on this continent, was made by a slaveholder, from a slave state, Patrick Henry, May 30, 1765. The first president of the first congress, that ever assembled on this continent, to consider of the affairs of the thirteen colonies, and which met in Philadelphia, September 5, 1774, was a slave owner from a slave state, Peyton Randolph. The only secretary that congress ever had, was a slave owner from a slave state, Charles Thompson. The gentleman who was chairman of the committee of the whole, on Saturday, the 8th of June, 1776, and who, on the morning of the 10th reported the resolutions, that the thirteen colonies, of right ought to be free and independent *states*, was a slaveholder from a slave state, Benjamin Harrison. The same gentlemen again, as chairman of the committee of the whole, reported the Declaration of Independence in form; and to which he affixed his signature, on Thursday, July 4, 1776. The gentleman who wrote the Declaration of Independence, was a slave owner, from a slave state, Thomas Jefferson. The gentleman who was selected to lead their armies, as commander-in-chief, and who did lead them successfully, to victory and the independence of the country, was a slave owner, from a slave state, George Washington. The gentleman who was president of the convention, to form the constitution of the United States, was a slave holder, from a slave state, George Washington. The gentleman who wrote the constitution of the United States (making it the best government ever formed on earth), was a slave owner, from a slave state, James Madison. The first president of the United States, under that constitution, and who, under God gave it strength, consistency and power before the world, was a slave owner, from a slave state, George Washington; and these were all white men and slave owners; and whatever of peace, prosperity, happiness and glory, the people of the United States have enjoyed under it, have been from the administration of the government, by presidents elected by the people, of *slave holders*, from *slave states*. Whenever the people have elected a president from a non-slaveholding state, commencing with the elder Adams, and down to Mr. Lincoln, confusion, wrangling and strife have been the order of the day, until it culminated in the greatest civil war the world has ever beheld, under the last named gentleman. Why this has been so is not in the line of our subject. We mention it as a matter of history, to confirm the Bible fact, *that God always* selects *slaveholders*, or from a *slaveholding* nation, the media through which he confers his blessings on mankind. Would it not be wisdom to heed it now?

One reflection and then we are done. The people of the United States have now thrust upon them, the question of negro equality, social, political and religious. How will they decide it? If they decide it one way, then they will make the *sixth* cause of invoking God's wrath, once again on the earth. They will begin to discover this approaching wrath: (1.) By God bringing confusion. (2.) By his breaking the government into pieces, or fragments, in which the negro will go and settle with those that favor this equality. (3.) In God pouring out the fire of his wrath, on this portion of them; but in what way, or in what form, none can tell until it comes, only that in severity it will equal in intensity and torture, the destruction of fire burning them up. (4.) The states or people that favor this equality and amalgamation of the white and black races, *God will exterminate.* To make the negro, the political, social and religious equal of the white race by *law*, by *statute* and by *constitutions*, can easily be effected in *words;* but so to elevate the negro *jure divino*, is simply *impossible.* You can not elevate a *beast* to the level of a son of God—a son of Adam and Eve—but you may depress the sons of Adam and Eve, with their *impress* of the Almighty, *down to the level of a beast.* God has made one for immortality, and the other to perish with the animals of the earth. The antediluvians once made this depression. Will the people of the United States make another, *and the last?* Yes, they will, for a large majority of the North are unbelievers in the Bible; and this paper will make a large number of their clergy deists and atheists. A man can not commit so great an offense against his race, against his country, against his God, in any other way, as to give his daughter in marriage to a negro—a *beast*—or to take one of their females for his wife. As well might he in the sight of God, wed his child to any other beast of forest or of field. This crime *can not* be expiated—it never has been expiated on earth—and from its nature never can be, and, consequently, *never was forgiven by God, and never will be.* The negro is now free. There are but two things on earth, that may be done with him now, and the people and government of this country escape destruction. One or the other *God will make you do*, or *make you accept his punishment*, as he made Babel, Sodom and Gomorrah, and the Canaanites, before you. You *must send him back to Africa* or *re-enslave him.* The former is the best, *far the best.* Now, which will my countrymen do? I do not say *fellow-citizens*, as I regard myself but as a sojourner in the land, whose every political duty is now performed by obeying *your* laws, be they good or bad— not voting, nor assisting others in making *your* laws. Will my countrymen, in deciding for themselves these questions, *remember—will they remember,* that the first law of liberty is obedience to God. Without this obedience to the great and noble principles of God, truth, righteousness and justice, there can be no liberty, no peace, no prosperity, no happiness in any earthly government—if these are sacrificed or ignored, God will overturn and keep overturning, until mankind learn his truth, justice and mercy, and conform to them.

To the people of the South, we say, *obedience* to God is better than all sacrifices. You have sacrificed all your negroes. It was *your ancestors*, that God made use of to form this noblest of all human governments—no others could do it. Do not be cast down at what has happened, and what is *yet to happen—* God will yet use you to reinstate and remodel this government, on its just and noble principles and at the *proper time.* The North *can never do it.* These are perilous times—the *impending decisions will be against you, and against God.* But keep yourselves free from *this sin*—do not by your acts, nor by your votes, in- *vite the negro equality—if it is forced upon you*, as it will be—obey the laws—remembering *that God will protect the righteous;* and that his truth, like itself, will always be consistent, and like its Author, will be always and *forever triumphant. The finger of God is in this. Trust him.* The Bible is true.

July, 1840.
December, 1866.   ARIEL.

NOTE 1. Any candid scholar, wishing to address the writer, is informed, that any letter addressed to "Ariel," care of Messrs. Payne, James & Co., Nashville, Tennessee, during this summer and fall (1867), will reach him and command his attention.

NOTE. 2. Some few kinky-headed negroes, have been found embalmed on the Nile, but the inscriptions on their sarcophagii, fully explain who they were, and how they came to be there. They were generally *negro traders* from the interior of the country, and of much later dates.

SPECULUM

FOR LOOKING INTO

THE PAMPHLET ENTITLED

"THE NEGRO:

WHAT IS HIS ETHNOLOGICAL STATUS?
IS HE THE PROGENY OF HAM? IS HE A
DESCENDANT OF ADAM AND EVE? HAS HE A
SOUL? OR IS HE A BEAST IN GOD'S NOMENCLA-
TURE? WHAT IS HIS STATUS AS FIXED BY GOD IN
CREATION? WHAT IS HIS RELATION TO THE WHITE RACE?

By ARIEL."

BY OPTICIAN.

CHARLESTON, S. C.
JOSEPH WALKER, AGT., STATIONER AND PRINTER,
NO. 3 BROAD STREET.
1867.

49

I RESIDE at a distance from Charleston, and have just learned, *since writing the following* article, that the Rev. Mr. Girardeau has recently delivered a lecture in that city, on the pamphlet "The Negro" &c., and that he took a similar view of it, to that taken by me. It seems to have been delivered while I was writing this, and I have not heard anything more of his argument, than might be inferred from this vague expression. I have never seen or heard Mr. Girardeau at any time, and have never interchanged sentiments or communicated with him on any subject. My manuscript has undergone no alteration, by addition or omission, but goes to the press as first written.

OPTICIAN.

THE NEGRO:

What is his ethnological status? Is he the proge-
ny of Ham? Is he a descendant of Adam and
Eve? Has he a soul? or is he a Beast in God's
nomenclature? What is his status as fixed by
God in creation? What is his relation to the
white race.

IT WILL not be denied, by any reader of the pamphlet
bearing the above title, that it is a remarkable production. Not more remarkable is it in regard to the position taken by the author, than to the ingenuity
displayed by him in its support. We propose to devote
a few pages to an examination of his structure, and of
the material used; in the course of which we hope we
shall do him no injustice, and yet shall be able to overthrow his work.

If we intended to write merely for the purpose of
victory in discussion, it would be our policy to represent the publication before us as one of ability. But
as we aim at no such distinction, we may be excused
for entering upon our work, without any flattering of
the pages to be reviewed. Indeed, with the view we
entertain of the merits of the publication, it would
have escaped notice, had it not been for the effect,
though it be transient, which it might produce on the
minds of some who have read it. But though some
readers might be left in the darkness into which it may
lead them, we are not backward to affirm, that the author not only did not believe in the truth of the posi-

tion he took, but did not for a moment suppose that his arguments would do more than entertain his readers with the ingenuity displayed in them. The question, then, may fairly be asked; What was his design? And such a question makes it legitimate to introduce into this paper an expression of our own opinion.

The little pamphlet appears as though it had been published in Cincinnati, (name of the publisher not given,) its author giving the curious reader (" candid scholar ") an indirect invitation to address him through a firm in Nashville, Tennessee. If we are right in our surmise as to the design of the publication, it was important that it should appear as the production of some one, who, if not a southerner, was at least one in sympathy with the south.

As far as southern sentiment is concerned, there would be no necessity to cast off the imputation, that the negro is esteemed at the south to be a " beast. " Nor do we suppose that intelligent and candid minds at the north could be made to believe that this is the estimation in which he is held by southern people.

But, suppose that, on the eve of elections, involving the question of giving the negro the right to vote, it could be made to appear that the only ground of objection to extending this privilege to him was that he is a brute. Surely the objection would be admitted to be quite as weak, as the hypothesis on which it rested.

Now, then, at such a time, a publication comes forth, in which, especially on its last pages, the author exhausts himself in showing the monstrousness of extending the right of suffrage to a " beast"—having already, as he would have it appear, fully established that the negro is a beast. What is this, but putting up a " man of straw," as the only objector to negro equality? He

does not overthrow this powerless objector himself.
O no! the design would be palpable. He does not
fear to let him stand. It is cunning to hold him up.
He is so powerful a champion, that every other may
be set aside. What is to be gained by this manœuvre?
Simply, that when a child upsets him, it may appear
that it was a very weak position which found only this
weak defender.

It will be seen then that we take "ARIEL" to be
an *advocate* of negro suffrage, who, *under the guise
of an opponent*, makes himself the champion *against*
negro suffrage. In doing so he must guard against
using such solid argument as the present ignorance
of negroes: for, had he employed this, he would
have *strengthened* the cause which he only *affected*
to support (that he might really weaken it), and
would of course have *weakened* the side which he *really
advocated*. Hence he took as the sole ground of opposition the *absurd* position, that the negro is a *beast*, and
for *that reason alone* should not be allowed to vote—
thus as a *real advocate of negro suffrage*, exposing the
opposition to so easy an overthrow.

We see on page 47 of the pamphlet, in the paragraph
beginning on the 46th page, the betrayal, that the
author wished to pass for one who sympathized with
advocates of slavery. This part of his performance is
very clumsy. Hear him. "GOD *never conferred*, and
never *designed* to *confer*, any great *blessing* on the human family, but what he *always* selects, or selected a
white *slaveholder*, or one of a white *slaveholding nation*,
as the *medium*, by or through which *that blessing* should
reach them." This needs no other comment than simply that the author must be well acquainted with all
that GOD has ever done, and with all his agents—nay
more, that he even possessed the power of penetrating

the very designs of the Almighty. If he is so saga-
cious, and all this is literally true, what does it prove
more than simply that GOD chose, and designs to
choose, one race in preference to another? It does not
follow that the *race* not chosen is a *race of beasts.* For,
by parity of reasoning, every *individual* not chosen
would be an *individual beast.* But we did not propose
at this stage of our writing, to go into the examination of his argument. We anticipated, in order to
show what seems to be the design of the publication.

And if we are right in our opinion, the author does
not care what prejudice he can create against the
white people of the south : nor does he regard the consequences of removing all moral sense from the negro,
and all idea of future accountability. After all that
he writes, he leaves the negro a human being still—
one with his human passions aroused by such an at
tack upon his humanity, and furnished with the plea
that, if the white man considers him to be but a beast,
he cannot look to him for any thing more than he
finds in beasts.

We now proceed to examine his main arguments.
We are happy to introduce our examination with the
proposition which "Ariel," our author, sets upon his
title page, that "The Bible is true." We promise not
to set at naught any portion of that volume of truth—
even such parts as "Ariel" himself employs for his
own purpose. And it will not be an exorbitant demand, to require that he also shall allow to such a
book its full force, even when we would bind him by
passages that he has used.

Notice is first taken, of the "error" "that the negro
is a descendant of Ham." He evidently conceives it to
be of vital importance, that this be proved an error;

for, (as he reasons) since the deluge was universal, all land animals were drowned by it, except such as were preserved in the ark. Hence, all races of men found on the earth, after that catastrophe, must trace their lineage to some descendant of Noah. And as Ham alone is ever claimed as the progenitor of the negro, if it can be shown that he is not, it follows that the progenitor of the negro is not to be found among the human beings that were in the ark. This is his proposition, stated as fairly as he lays it down at the length of a page or more. From this he proceeds to argue, that as he was preserved, and was not preserved as a descendant of Noah, he was preserved as a beast.

Upon this, we would observe, that the conclusiveness of his reasoning here, depends in the first place, upon the correctness of the hazardous opinion, that no son of Noah, but Ham, was the father of the negro. Now most assuredly he cannot find, among ancient commentators, one who has ever so expressed himself. And we freely admit, that our acquaintance with those of modern times, does not embrace one. Where such an opinion is put forth, it will be found to be an ingredient in some particular hypothesis, whose author desires to establish a theory in regard to some still vexed question; as for example, some advocate of slavery endeavoring to support it at every hazard, using sophistry wherever it serves better than sound reasoning. But it is evident, that only in the discussion of slavery, would it be legitimate to impugn this dogma. For ourselves, we can only say, that we have never seen that slavery had anything at stake here; and since "Ariel" announces on his first page, that *slavery* is not discussed, so much of his labor is in vain. Still, the question may be asked, what is the origin of the negro race?

Let it be asked: and let speculations be indulged in.
But speculations are not to be admitted as grounds of
argument. And all that our harper on "logic of facts"
has reached at this stage of his argument is, that since
no particular origin of the black race has been agreed
on by the learned, therefore, the negro is a beast.

If the reader would form a correct estimate of all that
"Ariel" has on this point, let him, with his Bible open
at the tenth chapter of Genesis, read what the divine
historian says about the people descended from Noah.
He will be surprised, perhaps, by the amount of information received. Not fewer than *sixty names* are
given to the descendants of Noah, exclusively of those
descendants of Arphaxad (a son of Shem,) through
whom the lineage of our LORD is traced. The cause of
truth invites the reader to this reference—it would
facilitate his investigation, and give him additional
security against being misled. The importance of it
is, that he will at a glance perceive how little occasion
there is to find any difficulty in the existing fact, that
such varieties (we choose to say) of the human race
are actually found. These sixty persons are, none of
them, further removed from Noah, than great-grand-
children. The fifth verse of the chapter, has peculiar
interest, and is highly instructive. It tells in a *general*
way, the origin of the Gentiles; and even if the negro
had been included (which in an investigation it is not
necessary to affirm or deny,) we do not conceive that
his "woolly head," his "flat nose," his "thick lips," and
we may add, his grade of intellect, either separately,
or all combined, gave him so much importance as to
entitle him to a distinct notice or record. Now, in the
order of time, the birth of all those named in this chapter, up to the fifth verse, (fourteen in number) took

place before the confusion of tongues; and only the descendants of Japheth are there named. As the descendants of Ham, and those of Shem, even omitting a large number of Shem's, far exceeded Japheth's descendants, we may set down at least, three times fourteen, or forty-two individuals existing before the confusion of tongues, from whom were derived the families and nations existing at the time of the confusion. If the heads had multiplied to such a degree at that early age, how absurd is the position that we must derive the negro from the *beasts* that were in the ark. True, the Bible does not tell us that the negro, by name, was descended from either one of Noah's sons. But does it tell us that he was descended from any one of the *beasts*? Then what is the basis of such an assumption? In reasoning from probabilities, it is a strange calculation of probabilities, that leads to the conclusion that, among seven beasts, we are more likely to find the progenitor of one animal in question, than among forty-two of the human race. Our computation in this reasoning from probabilities, leads to the conclusion, that the negro's claim to human origin is, in proportion to the charge of beastly origin, just as six to one. And it may not be said that, in this *ad hominem* argument, we took the number of beasts as it was in the ark, whereas, we took the number of men at a time when they had multiplied. This is very true. But in this kind of argument, since "Ariel" draws conclusions from *omissions* by the historian, he must abide by the omissions, when they affect prejudicially his own cause, as well as when he can employ them to the disadvantage of the cause that he opposes. Indeed, the very omission enters as an element into the calculation of probabilities.

But in order to judge what importance attaches to the historian's not giving an account of the negro in particular, it is necessary to remember that *the* end he had in view was, to lay down distinctly, *that line*, so far as it extended into his own time, in which should afterwards be found the lineage of JESUS CHRIST. A reference to the third chapter of St. Luke's Gospel, will show the lineage of CHRIST to be from Shem. The same names ("Arphaxad" &c.,) will there be found, which Moses gives in Genesis, to the line in which our LORD was to appear. With this object before him, he may be supposed to have mentioned all those sixty, who are named in this tenth chapter of Genesis, to show what lines were not to be taken in tracing the lineage of JESUS CHRIST, and at the same time, to point out with sufficient clearness, the sources, from which all the nations of the earth might afterwards be reasonably supposed to have sprung. If a guide sets out with a traveler, to conduct him to a certain place, he may call his attention to any roads that diverge from the one they are traveling, in order to caution him with regard to the future use of that road. After the traveler has reached his place of destination, the guide employed for the specific object is discharged. The traveler, however, pursues his journey, either alone or with other guides. He meets with many roads. He may not be able to get any information regarding them—whence they come, or whither they lead. Is it sound reasoning, that, since his first guide did not tell him that if he should ever extend his travels, beyond the point to which he was conducting him, he might fall in with roads which could be traced back to some point on the road they had traveled—that, because his guide did not tell him this by anticipation, therefore, those newly discovered roads had no connection with the one on which he at first set out? Is it not more like the operation of a sound mind, that the sight of these unknown roads should even call to remembrance, certain places to which his first guide had drawn his attention, where roads were pointed out diverging from the one they were traveling? If the guide had remarked, "those roads go over all the earth," the intelligent traveler would immediately infer that they were somewhere connected with those which he had just discovered. Now Moses says something very similar to this, when guiding us along the lineage of CHRIST, he digresses so far as to say of other lines: "By these, were the isles of the Gentiles divided in their lands; every one after his tongue, after their families, in their nations." (Genesis, x. 5.) The greater importance that Moses attached to Shem's descendants, so as to drop the descendants of Japheth and of Ham, beyond their grand-children, will readily be seen on referring to the eleventh chapter of Genesis. For, although he had already given the descendants of Shem to the same degree that he had carried Japheth's and Ham's, he takes up Shem's again, and carries them to Abram (*i. e.* Abraham.)

Then, as to what "Ariel" says about its being impossible that the negro should have been descended from Shem, since our LORD, who was white, was descended from him; or that he should have been descended from Japheth, since Europeans, who are white, were descended from him; for the argument to be worth anything, he must show that Shem *had no other son* than Arphaxad (from whom our LORD was descended,) and that Japheth had no other son than the one, from whom the Europeans were descended. So far from

2

his being able to prove this, Moses tells us that Shem's sons were, "Elam and Asshur, and Arphaxad, and Lud, and Aram," (Genesis, x. 22,) and that Japheth's sons were, "Gomer and Magog, and Madai and Javan, and Tubal, and Meshech, and Tiras." (v. 2.). His argument amounts to this: since all Europeans are descendants of Japheth, therefore, all Japheth's descendants are Europeans—nay, it even says, since the SAVIOUR of the world is a descendant of Shem, all Shem's descendants are saviours of the world. According to "Ariel's" logic, since all horses are animals, all animals are horses. Is this the kind of reasoning that leads to the conclusion, the negro is a beast?

Further, as the author himself speculates in his attempt to prove his position, he will concede to others, who are willing to speculate, the right to do so. And then we may meet with some who can argue as plausibly as he does for his position, that the change in skin, hair, features, &c., of the negro, took place in some particular tribe existing among the descendants of Noah subsequently to the deluge. And when it is found that after the deluge, which was universal, because of the universal degeneracy of mankind, another catastrophe occured which has every appearance of having been partial, inasmuch as the offenders were not mentioned as "man," or "all flesh," but are called "children of men," equivalent to, some families of men, there is room for speculation again. And so the conjecture, merely as such, may be thrown out, that, on that occasion, when people of one language were thrown into confusion by different languages being spoken among them, it is not a violent assumption that an accompanying change may have taken place in their skin, hair, and features—such a change at least as would give rise to a deversity no greater than we find to obtain between peoples of different languages. And there is no reason why we should limit the change to variation from white to black. It may have involved as many shades as now prevail among the different nations of the earth. This hypothesis is susceptible of plausible support, which we could easily show, if the only alternative to the position, that the negro is a beast, were that we should assign the origin of his black skin, &c. As this could not fairly be required of us, we pass from this point that the negro is not a descendant of Ham, without a word to controvert the position. It will be seen then that as "Ariel" occupied so much space in enlarging his argument about Ham, and telling rigmaroles about mummies, particularly his wonderful one which he had the rare fortune to handle, we are saved much space in passing over those pages. Still we shall not take leave of that subject yet, for it is our turn now to act on the aggressive.

We hope "Ariel" will remember his motto, "The Bible is true." It is well that we agree upon that—well that he commits himself to settle his points "by the Bible, and by concurrent history." (p. 1.) It does not help his cause, however, that in his whole argument he does not give reference to his authorities, so as to facilitate an examination of them. This might be excused in the cases where much learning on the part of his readers, and access to well assorted libraries were required to make the references available. But no such excuse can be pleaded for omitting references to the Bible, the book that is "true," and is, or may be, in the hands of every one who can read his pamphlet.

On page 19th he gives us the first intimation of what people ("beast" he would say) mentioned in the Bible, he takes to be the negro. Quoting the Prophecy of Jeremiah (ch. xiii. 23) he says, "look into your Bible,—look into contemporaneous and concurrent history—look at existing facts outside of the Bible, and running from the flood down to the present day. And hear the Prophet of GOD defiantly asks, 'can the Ethiopian change his skin, or the Leopard his spots ?' Both beasts; and when you have so looked, you will say, *true*, every 'word, *indubitably* true!" Such might be the ejaculation of one who just then for the first time had turned to these authorities. No doubt, if one should allow himself to be led along by this author, without looking to the right or the left, in other words, without considering any portions of the Bible except such as " Ariel" has adduced, he would arrive with him at the same conclusion. It is wonderful to observe how even the Bible may be impressed to serve any particular end. Nor does it require any practical christian experience to qualify a person to make such use of the Bible. For we have the instance of the Devil himself showing his adroitness in arguing— quoting more to the point we must say, than " Ariel" has done; not surpassing him, however, farther than we would expect the master to surpass the disciple. If the reader is not familiar with the occasion, let him look to the fourth chapter of St. Mathew's Gospel. He will there find the Devil quoting accurately, but misapplying the ninety first Psalm of David. This he does in the presence of the Son of GOD, actually addressing to Him the very words of the Scriptures—" He shall give his angels charge. concerning thee: and in their hands they shall bear thee up, least at any time thou dash thy foot against a stone." But he was speaking to one, who did not then for the first time learn what was to be found in Scripture; and who looked farther than the Devil would have had him to do; one who, comparing Scripture with Scripture, had not learned that the promise of GOD's protection was designed to encourage presumption. He therefore replied in words that are found in Deut. vi. 16. "It is written again, thou shall not tempt the Lord thy GOD." And we flatter ourselves that we have the knowledge of other portions of Scripture besides those with which "Ariel" would instruct us. But to confine ourselves, for the present, to the passage which he adduces to show by what appellation the negro is called in Scripture, we quote again the words of the prophet, "Can the Ethiopian change his skin, or the leopard his spots?" (Jer. xiii. 23.) In connection with this quotation, which introduces the Ethiopian and the leopard together, he exultingly adds, as if he had come to a conclusion based on the Bible, "both beasts." Here is certainly a cogent argument, if none but like subjects can be named together. It appears to us, however, that two were introduced here unnecessarily if they were of one kind; for one beas would have been enough to name. But when two animals were introduced, the introduction was clearly designed to expand the question. It may also have involved in it an *a fortiori* argument of this nature: If the Ethiopian, whose skin was not always black, but was made so some time after the era of his ancestors, cannot change his skin—if especially, the leopard cannot change the spots that have characterized his species ever since the creation, much less can ye, who have been accustomed to do evil, now do good by any natural powers of your own. There might also have been implied that *original sin* which has prevailed ever since the fall, and that which is the consequence of it, *personal evil deeds.* We fear, however, that we are indulging too far in following "Ariel's" example of speculation. And as we are not under any necessity to do so, we abstain; and will prosecute the subject of the Ethiopian in a different way.

One of "Ariel's" arguments, to prove the negro a beast from the passage last quoted, commits him for the negro's being the Ethiopian of Scripture. " The Bible is true." Well, as the negro is the Ethiopian, according to our accurate logician, and as we are happy to agree with him in this, it will not take much argumentation, from this alone, to overthrow the positions that the negro is a beast, that he has no soul. In the sixty-eighth Psalm, v. 31, we find the Prophet David saying, " Ethiopia shall soon stretch out her hands unto GOD." This surely has meaning in it, and signifies that Ethiopians shall worship GOD. But our erudite author, who generously instructs the clergy and learned men, will no doubt tell us, that this did not signify acceptable worship, but was a *profane* act; for such is the sentence passed by him on the calling on the name of the LORD, recorded in Genesis, (iv. 26.) We shall give this attention in due time. We bring it in here by anticipation, merely to meet the only evasion of this portion of Scripture. Let it pass then as a prophecy whose fulfilment is not recorded, and we shall find it necessary to search elsewhere for something to throw light upon it. And if we are carried away on into the Gospel dispensation, it will serve the cause of truth quite as well.

In the eighth chapter of Acts, is minutely recorded

an interesting incident, in which one prominent character is an Ethiopian. As he is introduced to our notice as the treasurer of *Candace*, the queen of the Ethiopians, and as Candace, according to Pliny and others, was for a long time the name of the queens of *African* Ethiopia, there is no reason to suppose that the Ethiopia here spoken of is *Asiatic* Ethiopia. Therefore, this high functionary, in all probability, was an African of the deepest dye. But as it might seem to be no great distinction that he was treasurer to a negro queen, we must find something else to give him distinction, and furnish us with some reason for believing that he had a soul, and was a human being though a black negro. God spoke to his minister Philip, through an angel, giving him the most specific instructions: "Arise and go toward the South, unto the way that goeth down from Jerusalem into Gaza, which is desert: And he arose and went." Then follows in the narrative the account of his hearing the Ethiopian read a portion of Isaiah's prophecy of Christ. Here again the Spirit gave Philip further instructions: "Go near and join thyself to this chariot." This is all very remarkable distinction to be shown to a beast, which only had charge of the treasure of a beast, the queen of beasts. But the distinction does not stop here. The beast requests Philip to come up into the chariot, and sit with him. What audacity! A beast in a chariot, presuming to request a wayfaring noble offspring of *the Adam* to sit with him. Was the beast smitten with a thunderbolt from heaven, for taking advantage of his casual elevation in a chariot, to insult a son of Adam? Let us see the conclusion. Look into your Bible, reader: "The Bible is true." You there find that Philip complied—that he even preached to the beast, that the beast made a clear profession of christianity, and was baptized by Philip, and went on his way rejoicing. Well might "Ariel" exclaim, would that I were a beast! He would then fare better, than he shall when the Queen of the South, who visited Solomon, shall rise in the judgment and condemn those who had abused greater privileges than she ever had it in her power to improve.

It would seem a work of supererogation to go any farther into the examination of this pamphlet, since its author brings himself to a conclusion the very opposite of the positions assumed. If it had been our object to encourage him in an inquiry after truth—to take him by the hand like a tottering child learning to walk, and encourage his efforts, we could very well let him alone, now that we have succeeded in showing him what he can do. But we have not altered the opinion we expressed in the first part of this article, that "Ariel" did not believe what he advanced. Influenced by this opinion, we proceed in regard for others. We are not indifferent, moreover, to the negro himself. When we find that he has been disturbed by this vile attack upon his humanity, and know how unable he is to look through its design, we would gladly furnish such of them as can read, with this contribution of our aid. He well knows that in his whole life among Southern people, he never heard such sentiments expressed as are put forth in this unprincipled pamphlet. Too many of them have, in times now gone by, enjoyed religious communion with white christians, for any considerable portion of them to be led away into the delusion, that white people of the South do not consider them to be human beings, with souls susceptible to religious influences.

"Ariel," in his disguise, carries his bad construction of
sentences so far, at times, that we are really perplexed
in arriving at his meaning. We have discovered, however, that this is the case only when he conceives the
matter to be of no importance. This applies forcibly
to his jargon about the creation. If we have come at
his meaning, it is that the noble race of man, or *the*
man, should be kept distinctly in view as referring to
Adam's descendants. But that *man* is the name which
this Adam gave to one of the beasts. This probably is
what he means, for he says (p. 24) "by such *name*
'man' the negro was known by to the flood, but not *the*
man." It would seem, either that Ariel is profoundly
ignorant in regard to the word "man," and the name
"Adam," or he designedly imposes on the ignorant
reader, or else it is one of his expedients for showing
how futile are the pretended arguments by which humanity is denied to the negro. Whichsoever it be, it is
sufficient to say for the unlearned reader, all is false
which he advances about "man," "*the* man," and
"Adam." For in the original they are all one term,
"Ish," sometimes rendered "Adam," sometimes "man,"
sometimes "the man," the propriety of the English
being the guide of the translators.

On the sixth chapter of Genesis, which speaks of the
wickedness of the world, for which the flood destroyed
its inhabitants, he says "the sons of God" were
Adam's posterity, "the daughters of men" were beasts.
There were scholars in the world before "Ariel" made
his appearance. The translators of the Bible had some
learning. The learned commentators give two interpretations of these passages, either of which was satisfactory up to the epoch of "Ariel." "Sons of God" were
great men, nobles, and rulers, who by violence, without

regard to the wishes of the lower classes, called
"daughters of men," took whom they fancied, and as
many as they chose for wives. Other interpreters
understand by "sons of God," the descendants of Seth,
who were worshipers of the true God, but now
began to degenerate by seeing and conversing with the
daughters of the ungodly race of Cain, and choosing
wives among them. Here are two natural and easy
interpretations, perfectly satisfactory, without a false
representation that because no article is used in the
term "daughters of men," it had reference to daughters
of a lower order of creation called man. What reader
of the English language would have tolerated the rendering, daughters of *the* men? In support of the interpretation that the "sons of God" were the posterity of
Seth, we may adduce one of the passages which "Ariel"
impresses into his own service, thus at one time both
dispossessing him of it and throwing light upon another
passage. The place we refer to is Gen. iv. 26—"And
to Seth, to him also there was born a son; and he
called his name Enos: then began men to call on the
name of the Lord." Now when the Bible was translated, the translators gave two renderings, the one just
quoted, and another which they placed in the margin.
The one in the margin reads thus: "men began to call
themselves by the name of the Lord." Observing that
this translation was made when there was no particular purpose to be served, it certainly has the preference
to the interpretation forced upon it by the advocate of
a private hypothesis, where there is not the shadow of
authority for it. And it is not more remarkable that
the worshipers of the true God should call themselves
after him, than that the converts under the gospel dispensation should call themselves christians, after the

name of CHRIST whom they worshipped. This they first did at Antioch, in the days of the Apostles. And it is worthy of note, that this is recorded in the same brief manner. "The disciples were called christians first in Antioch."—(Acts xi. 26.)

All that he says about the sin that brought the deluge on the earth, would be just as applicable if he had substituted for the negro race, the posterity of Cain. Indeed all his arguments that follow, in reference to the offence that caused the overthrow of Babel, all his moralizing applies equally to alliances between those who worshiped God and those who did not. So in the writings of the New Testament: "Be ye not unequally yoked together with unbelievers:"—2 Cor. vi. 14. Again, a woman after the death of her husband is allowed to be "married to whom she will; only in the Lord."—(1 Cor. vii. 29.)

It remains now only to notice how successfully the author supposes himself to have led along a reader of intelligence. "The intelligent cannot fail to discover who was the tempter in the garden of Eden,"—(p. 45.) The page that follows, to show what is so easily discovered by the intelligent, is meant for the help of those who have not so much penetration. As we fall into that class, we have availed ourselves of the proffered help. But so dull are we that we cannot perceive yet how the negro was the tempter, as "Ariel" labors to show. We will state as well as we can, one difficulty that meets us, which appears to be insuperable. The curse pronounced upon the tempter was,—"Upon thy belly shalt thou go, and dust shalt thou eat all the days of thy life." Now we find the negro to be very erect— not even a quadruped, but an erect biped. How comes this to pass? If the language is not to be interpreted literally, but means only that he should be degraded, then his degradation surely was as a beast, if he was a beast at the time. Then he would, from the time of the curse, have been found at the bottom of the scale of beasts, especially as a part of the curse was "thou art cursed above all cattle, and above every beast of the field: upon thy belly shalt thou go," &c.

But the remarkable fact that this solitary beast, the negro, is endowed with the same faculty that distinguished Adam and Eve, the faculty of speaking in their language, "Ariel" thinks must be turned to account. We are inclined to think that the miracle of a beast not gifted with this faculty being allowed to be used by the "old serpent, the devil," for his purpose, though a novelty then, has become so common that we cease to call it a miracle. No one now would think of the remarkable pamphlet which we have had under review, that it is a *miraculous* production. Yet it bears strong marks that the *old serpent*, the devil, not only uses speech, but that he has kept pace with the progress of every age, and has actually arrived at working the printing press. We have the instance of another beast on a certain occasion being employed to speak. It is found in the twenty-second chapter of Numbers, verse twenty-eighth: "The Lord opened the mouth of the ass, and she said unto Balaam, what have I done unto thee," &c. How will "Ariel" reconcile this with his assertion that the main distinction of the negro above the other beasts, is his being endowed with the faculty of human speech? Such ready wit will not be at a loss. He answers, no doubt, that Balaam was riding a negro, and that if the translators of the Bible "had recognized the simple fact, that the term *man* was the *name* bestowed on the *negro* by Adam," and that therefore the negro was a beast, they would have translated *negro* instead of " ass." But here again we cannot agree with him, for in our admiration of his motto, "The Bible is true," we must believe the truth of what St. Peter says: "The *dumb* ass, speaking with man's voice, forbad the madness of the prophet." This incident suggests one more reference to this wily production. When the author speaks so largely of GOD's never employing any agent to bless, except " one of a white *slaveholding nation*," let him remember this ass, or if, in spite of St Peter, he holds that Balaam was riding a negro, let him remember how this black negro was made a medium of blessing, in carrying Balaam where GOD designed him to go—Balaam intending to curse the people of God, for the bribe offered by Balak, but God compelling him to utter his blessing, so beautifully expressed in the twenty-fourth chapter of Numbers. Perhaps "Ariel's" design to curse the negro as a beast, may yet be overruled so as to be a blessing, as would certainly be the case if it should only stimulate white christians to renewed efforts in behalf of the blacks under their present disadvantages, so as to restore to them religious privileges, equal, at least, to those which they used to possess.

The ingenious hypothesis that the beasts of the earth must have had their peculiar federal head, in which they fell from "their primeval goodness," as the race of man fell in Adam their federal head, might have been indulged by the author, quite as well, if he had supposed that head to have been a creature of any form whatever, which, by the curse, was so metamorphosed that henceforth it was required, by its change of form to go, as the serpent does, upon its belly. Indeed, as a mere hypothesis, it finds better support in

3

that part of the curse, thou art cursed "above every beast of the field." And among assumptions we could assume that it then lost the power of speech. However, this would not have served the author's purpose. Still it appears to us as a farther obstacle to the intelligent reader's discovering that the tempter was the negro. But there is no occasion for any of these speculations, when we remember that the "Bible," which "is true," makes Adam the head of all the lower creation.

In this connection, we conclude with a reference to a blunder of "Ariel's," which betrays his sinister design, by showing that he did not believe in the position he took. Assuming that the beasts must have had a federal head in which they fell, and became subject to the calamity of the deluge, he asks, " If these had continued in their primeval goodness, wholly unconnected with Adam's sin," &c. In the line of his argument he should have said, with the *negro's* sin. He was napping here: and some might be consoled with the inference that even the devil sleeps at times, if they should not happen to consider that this appearing to sleep may be one of his strategems.

P. S.—The reader will reflect that he has not lost any thing in not having found in the above article a *formal* discussion concerning the soul of the negro. This was entirely superfluous, after having thrown off the imputation cast upon him that he is not a descendant of Adam. For, being his descendant, his possession of a soul stands in all respects on the same footing as the white man's ; and he is equally capable of worshiping God, and is equally responsible and guilty for neglecting the means within his reach, to get religious knowledge, since the same "GOD that made the world, and all things therein," "hath made of one blood all nations of men for to dwell on all the face of the earth," "that they should seek the Lord, if haply they might feel after him and find him."—Acts of the Apostles, xvii. 24, 26, 27. In this peculiar expression that the Lord was to be *sought*, even if to be found only by *feeling* after him, is very forcibly expressed the obligation to seek him under all disadvantages of ignorance. In such seeking that ignorance will be instructed, the darkness that made *feeling after God* necessary, will be replaced by light, rewarding the efforts of the diligent searcher. The words were St. Paul's to the Athenians who were so religiously inclined, that he had found them at their devotions when he entered their city; but who were so ignorant of the object of their worship that their altar was dedicated to the "Unknown God." They seemed to worship by imitation, as long as they knew no more than they did; and this worship was rewarded by the Apostle's addressing them thus: "Whom, therefore, ye ignorantly worship, him declare I unto you. GOD that made the world and all things therein," &c., as already quoted.

So then, it might be inferred, that even in the rudest condition of the negro, when the importer brought the African to America, he might have shown as much wisdom and benevolence in availing the imitative faculty of the negro by teaching him how to be religious, as he has shown his own shrewdness in setting him to work by imitation, for the white man's advantage.

THE NEGRO:

A REPLY TO ARIEL.

THE NEGRO BELONGS TO THE GENUS HOMO. — HE IS A DESCENDANT
OF ADAM AND EVE. — HE IS THE OFFSPRING OF HAM. — HE
IS NOT A BEAST, BUT A HUMAN BEING. — HE HAS AN
IMMORTAL SOUL. — HE MAY BE CIVILIZED,
ENLIGHTENED, AND CONVERTED
TO CHRISTIANITY.

BY ROBERT A. YOUNG, D.D.

"O wad some power the giftie gie us,
To see oursels as others see us!
It wad frae mony a blunder free us,
And foolish notion."—BURNS.

NASHVILLE, TENN.:
PUBLISHED BY J. W. M'FERRIN & CO., BOOKSELLERS & STATIONERS,
27 Cherry Street.
1867.

There is an association of ladies in this city engaged in supplying artificial limbs to the unfortunate Confederate soldiers. They have invited us, in the politest terms, to make this reply. The entire proceeds to be managed by themselves. After its delivery, an intelligent and enterprising book-merchant will publish it. So the stenographers present need not make very large notes.

In some respects "Ariel" is a remarkable writer. He talks about scholars, candid scholars, intelligent scholars— about Latin, Greek, and Hebrew—about versions, translations, renderings; about the Septuagint, the Vulgate, and common English Bible; ethnology, and what not. Surely, after all this array, one would suppose that he understood the right use of language, grammar, rhetoric, logic, etc.

Nay, "Ariel," you do not know the difference between "*propitiate*" and *expiate*. You do not know that a verb agrees with its subject in number and person. Your sentences sprangle about without the least unity. Sometimes your premise has no conclusion; sometimes your conclusion has no premise. When you talk natural science, it is not in the language of the books. You cannot even quote Scripture correctly. So you go. You ought never to write another "*paper*."

We are from English and German stock. No ancestor of ours ever lived north of Mason's and Dixon's Line. We have no relative on that part of the planet. We do not believe in the social equality of the Negro. We do not believe he knows how to handle a vote. We are disfranchised.

Still, we believe *the Negro is a descendant of Adam and*

Eve; that he is the progeny of Ham; that he is a human being, and has an immortal soul.

II.—ETHNOLOGICAL.

"Ariel" says on page 4, "It will be admitted by all, and contradicted by none, that we now have existing on earth *two races of men—the white and the black.*" *Varieties* would be the word used by "the learned of this age."

The Negro belongs to the class—*Mammalia;* to the order —*Bimana;* to the genus—*Homo;* to the species—*Man.* He is one of the *Varieties.*

But stop. "Ariel" is not familiar with the great naturalists of the world—Linnæus, Blumenbach, Cuvier, the two Humboldts, Owen, Pritchard, Bunsen, Lepsius, Bachman, and others. He only knows Messrs. Nott and Gliddon, *et id omne pecus.*

> " I despise this index learning,
>   That turns no student pale;
> But only holds the eel
>   Of science by the tail."

Let us take up a common Geography.* According to the form of the skull, and the color of the skin, there are *five* distinct varieties of the human species : the Caucasian, or European; the Mongolian, or Asiatic; the Indian, or American; the Negro, or African; and the Malay.

The CAUCASIANS include almost all the' nations of Europe, and their descendants in America; also the Hindoos, Per-

---

* Cornell's.

77

sians, and Arabians, in Asia, and the Abyssinians, Egyptians, and Moors, in Africa. The skin of the Caucasian is generally fair; but there is a wide difference between the color of the Caucasian of the north of Europe and him of Egypt or Abyssinia. Climate, food, manner of life, may produce this difference. The hair of this variety is generally fine and long, the skull large and beautifully shaped, the forehead full and elevated, the features regular, and the form symmetrical.

The MONGOLIANS include the Siberian tribes, the Chinese, Japanese, and Indo-Chinese nations in Asia, the Finns, Laplanders, Turks, and Hungarians, of Europe, and the Esquimaux, of North America. The skin of the Mongolian is generally of a sallow or olive tint; but there is a great difference between the white Hungarian and the dark Chinaman. Here again we see the influence of climate, food, and domestic habits in changing the color. The hair of the Mongolian is long, black, straight, and stiff; the head somewhat square, the forehead low, the cheek-bones broad and flat, the nose short, the eyes small and obliquely set.

The INDIANS include all the tribes of America except the Esquimaux. The skin of this variety is a sort of reddish brown, or copper color. But Catlin says of the Mandans of the Upper Mississippi: "There are many of these people whose complexions are as light as half-breeds; and among the women especially, *there are many whose skins are almost white*, with the most pleasing symmetry and perfection of features, with hazel, with gray, and with blue eyes." And in regard to their hair, he says that it is, generally, "as fine and as soft as silk." Humboldt informs us of *white tribes of Indians* on the Upper Oronoco. He says of them: "The individuals of the fair tribes, whom we examined, have the features, the stature, and the smooth, straight, black hair, which characterize other Indians. It would be impossible to take them for a mixed race, like the descendants of natives and Europeans." On the other hand, Dr. Morton informs us of other tribes of American Indians *that are black.* He says: "The Charruas, who are almost black, inhabit the fiftieth degree of south latitude, and the yet blacker Californians are twenty-five degrees north of the Equator." Here again, you will not fail to observe the influence of local and temporary causes in changing the complexion. The hair of the Indian is long, black, and straight; the skull small, the eyes dark and deep set, the cheek-bones high and prominent, the nose aquiline, the forehead receding, and the mouth large.

The MALAYANS include the tribes inhabiting the islands of Oceania, together with the natives of the Malay Peninsula. The skin of the Malay is tawny, or dark-brown—sometimes almost black; his hair is coarse, lank, and black; forehead low and broad, mouth large, nose short and broad, and the eyes obliquely set.

The NEGROES include all the aboriginal tribes of Africa south of Abyssinia and the Great Desert, together with those of Australia, New Guinea, and New Caledonia. The skin of the Negro is jet-black, the hair woolly, (or, as "Ariel" would say, *kinky*,) head long and narrow, forehead low, eyes large and prominent, mouth large, lips thick, nose broad and flat, cheek-bones high, and the jaws prominent.

Thus we see the Caucasians are white, the Mongolians are yellow, the Indians are copper-colored, the Malayans dark-brown, and the Negroes black—a pleasing variety of colors. *These all belong to the one great family of Man*, proving that unity in diversity and diversity in unity is the law of Nature.

This is the doctrine proclaimed by Moses, and confirmed by Paul, and maintained by the great naturalists of all ages. Learned men are greatly influenced by authorities; but we do not know that authorities will avail any thing with "Ariel" and his disciples. A man who says a crime cannot be "*propitiated*"—who does not know whether a noun of multitude conveys unity or plurality of idea—whose separate and distinct sentences are constantly strung together by the conjunction *and*—whose startling assumptions are based upon precisely nothing, except his own ignorance of a grave subject—such a man can scarcely appreciate the examinations, the researches, the learning, and conclusions of scientific men, who have grown gray with midnight study. As "Ariel" has given us the "Ethnological Status of the Negro," we will give you "Ariel's" *Status* in Zoölogy. He says: "The gorilla frequently steals the negro women and girls, and *carry* them off for wives." Dr. Bachman* says: "It should be observed that nothing is known of the gorilla but the skull; we, therefore, know nothing of either

---

* Unity of the Human Race. By John Bachman, D. D., LL. D.

the form, the outward appendages, or the color." The
Zoölogical Society ought to send straightway for "Ariel."
He could tell them all about the Animal, and the "Ethnological Status of the Negro" likewise. And yet, they tell
us, that there are men and women unlearned enough to
believe all the *tomfoolery* scattered up and down the pages
of this book.

But for the sake of our readers, we will give a few
authorities on the Unity and Varieties of the Human
Species. St. Paul says—Acts xvii. 26—"And (God) hath
made of one blood all nations of men for to dwell on all
the face of the earth, and hath determined the times before
appointed and the bounds of their habitation." Dr. Owen,
professor in the Royal College of Surgeons, who has, without a dissenting voice, been placed at the head of the list
of comparative anatomists of this or any other age, says:
"Thus in reference both to the unity of the human species,
(including the Negro variety,) and to the fact of man being
the latest, as he is the highest, of all animal forms, upon
our planet, the interpretations of God's works coincide with
what has been revealed to us, as to our origin and zoölogical relations in the world. *Man is the sole species of his
genus, the sole representative of his order.*" And this matured
conviction, we are assured, "is similar to the conclusions of
Cuvier, of the two Humboldts, of Lepsius and Bunsen,
of Pritchard, of Martin and Latham, and of the most
eminent naturalists of every country."

Dr. Bachman, who has spent his life in the study of
man and his varieties—not even excepting the learned (?)

"Ariel's" "kinky-headed negro"—thus sums up: "According to the universally received definition of Species, all the individuals in the human race are proved to be of one species, even by the admission of Prof. Agassiz himself; and the varieties, according to the same author, are induced by some modification of some native habit, such as are seen in domestic animals.

"In the number of separate bones composing the human skeleton—amounting to two hundred and forty—in the peculiar structure of the breast-bone, there being eight pieces in infancy, three in youth, and but one in old age; in the dropping out of the milk-teeth, between the sixth and fourteenth year, which are replaced by thirty-two permanent teeth, there is perfect uniformity in every variety of man. So also in the period of gestation—the number of young at a birth, generally one, very rarely two; the period of longevity, etc., the different varieties of men present a perfect similarity. They all possess those high prerogatives of man, the attributes of speech and the faculties of the mind, with capacities for transmitting any improvement to their descendants. In all there is a capacity to acquire the languages and songs of other tribes, whilst they may forget those of their forefathers. Thus whole nations have forgotten their languages, and adopted those of other nations. But no species of quadruped or biped has ever lost its native notes, and adopted the notes of another species. In all we discover the same instincts; in all, the power of conscience, the recognition of truth, and a sense of right and wrong; in all, some sentiment of religion, some recognition of a higher power; in all, the hope of immortality; in all, the idea of a happier life, and the dread of punishment beyond the grave. Positive Atheism is excluded from the creed of all nations."

Even Prof. Agassiz, the champion of one of "Ariel's" disciples, says : " I still hesitate to assign to each race an independent origin. *Man is everywhere the one identical species.*"

It never entered our mind to read "Ariel's" book until we were requested to answer it. After reading it once, we were conversing with a learned friend about it, and asked his opinion concerning an argument or two we proposed to submit in this reply. He quietly remarked: " Do you propose to *reason* with a madman ? " On reading the book carefully a second time, we must confess that we are at a loss for language to express our astonishment at any sane man who would write it, or could believe it. " Ethnological Status of the Negro," indeed ! What does he know of Zoölogy, Ethnology, or any branch of Natural Science ? If he had read any work on Hybridity, it would have saved him many a blunder. He writes along in total ignorance of the fact that a hybrid is organically incapable of propagating his race, or his kind. This most unread and unscientific of all the modern pretenders to authorship *scribbles* away about the crime that brought down the flood on the old world, that dispersed the Babel-builders, that brought destruction upon the Cities of the Plain, and exterminated the Canaanites. He fills his imaginary world with *prolific hybrids!* monsters, and Dean Swift's Yahoos, time after time; and then says, most blasphemously, that God sent flood, confusion, fire, brimstone, and the sword, to destroy the creatures from the face of the earth. He makes the offspring, produced by the "sons of God" associating with "beasts," a fertile and prolific herd, multiplying and replenishing to the third and fourth generation.

Our people generally have read "Ariel's" book—some believe it, and a few defend it. Do they not know that it cannot be true? Let us give them a delicate argument. We will touch the subject *gingerly*. For example: the genus Equus includes several species—the Ass and the Horse among the rest. In a wild state, they do not associate; domesticated, they will. What is their offspring? A *hybrid*—a *mule*—and there the breed stops. "Ariel" teaches that a white man is a descendant of Adam and Eve—Noah and his Wife. All right. He teaches that a Negro is not a descendant of Adam and Eve—that he is not the progeny of Ham—that he has no soul—that he is a *beast* in God's nomenclature. Then he does not belong to the human Species—he does not belong to the genus Homo—he does not even belong to our Order of Animals. A white man associates with a negro woman. What is the offspring? If the Negro is a beast, the issue ought to be a *hybrid*, and worse than a hybrid—a *monster*. But we know that the offspring is a fertile, prolific Mulatto. And this very test will satisfy any scientific man in the world that the Negro is a *variety* of the human *Species*.

Dr. Bachman says: "All the varieties of the human species are known to increase and multiply with each other, thus forming new varieties, which have continued to propagate from the earliest periods on record through every succeeding age up to the present time. Our neighbors of Mexico, and the mulattoes in the United States—the latter now numbering, according to the last census, 405,751—give sufficient evidence that they are far removed from the characteristic condition that belong to hybrids. In fact, such has been the blending of nations, that if the theory of the believers in the plurality of the human species (from two species to a hundred, as they cannot designate the number of species, and are all found to disagree in this particular) be true, it is evident that the *whole world* must by this time be made up of hybrids; and we in America might even tremble, lest the prediction of their admired champion, Knox, might be fulfilled, that we already evidence symptoms of premature decay, and will soon die, out and out. Very different has been the result in the production of hybrids between two species of animals or birds, however nearly allied. *No new race has ever been produced.* It is in this way that the Creator of Species asserts his prerogative in preventing a scene of confusion, and an unnatural blending together of different species in the animal world. We invite any true naturalist among the believers in the plurality of species in man, to produce a single race among animals, now existing in the world, which it can be distinctly proved has been perpetuated by the union of two distinct species. The diversities of color, and of hair or feathers, among the varieties that are known to exist in the same species of domestic quadrupeds and poultry, are also as great as are seen in the color and structure of hair in the varieties of the human family."

Our Tennessee *savant*, "Ariel," says a white man is a human being, and has a soul; that a negro is a beast, and has no soul. Suppose the white man marries a negress— will their daughter have a soul? "Ariel" says "No." Suppose this half-breed marries a white man—will their daughter have a soul? "Ariel" is in Carlyle's "center of indifference." Suppose this quadroon marries another white man — will their son have a soul? Alexandre Dumas* writes very much like *he* has a soul. "Ariel" will be forced into the "everlasting yea" after a while. Then he believes that souls are developed. Allow us to conclude this part of our reply by suggesting the Chapters for "Ariel's" next book:

1st. Vestiges of Creation.

2d. The Surface of the Earth was at first covered with Mucus.

3d. The Power of Galvanism called forth Animalculæ.

4th. These became, in successive developments, Worms, Reptiles, Fishes, aspiring Tadpoles, ambitious Frogs, and warm-blooded Animals.

5th. Baboon, Orang-outang, Gorilla, kinky-headed Negro.

6th. A Negro developed into a White man, who has a soul.

Conclusion. "Ariel" can dispense with the creative power of the Supreme Being.

---

* The great French Novelist is one-eighth Negro.

III.—IS THE NEGRO THE PROGENY OF HAM?

We quote from "Ariel" *verbatim*—please excuse his grammar: "Before proceeding with the examination of the subjects involved in the caption to this paper, we will for a moment, notice the prevailing errors, now existing in all their strength, and held by the *clergy*, and many *learned men*, to be true, which are: First. Ham's name, which they allege, in Hebrew, means black. Second. The curse denounced against him, that a servant of servants should he be unto his brethren; and that this curse was denounced against Ham, for the accidental seeing of his father Noah naked; that this curse was to do so, and did change him, so that instead of being long, straight-haired, high forehead, high nose, thin lips and white, as he then was, and like his brothers Shem and Japheth, he was from that day forth, to be kinky headed, low forehead, thick lipped, and black skinned; and that his *name*, and this *curse* effected all this."

We have read this ill-made sentence, and the pages of *balderdash* that follow, over and over again, and can think of no answer so befitting as a positive denial. We are a "clergyman" ourself; we have associated with them for twenty-five years; we read the religious periodicals of every Protestant Church; we have read hundreds of books written by the "clergy;" and yet we have never heard or read from one of them that the curse of Canaan converted his father Ham instantly into "a kinky-headed negro." It has been our fortune to know several very "learned men;" we have read a few choice works on Ethnology; we have taught Moral Philosophy; and we now defy "Ariel" to show us a single chapter, paragraph, or line, written by any true, learned naturalist, teaching that the curse of Canaan changed his father Ham from a white man into a "black-skinned negro." Come, "Ariel," you pretend to state a fact. The fact can be sustained if you have the testimony. You say this error prevails; that it exists now in all its strength; that it is held by the clergy and many learned men; that the faith of more than half the world seems to be based on it. Let us go up to the State Library in the Capitol. It contains all the standard works on Ethnology. Show us one of them expressing the opinion that Noah's curse, fulminated against Canaan, "from that day forth" changed Ham into "a thick-lipped negro." Nay, "Ariel," you have read a few catch-penny pamphlets, like your own; you have read some productions, written by wild and eccentric men, ambitious of novelty and notoriety, and forsooth you deem yourself acquainted with "the learned of the present and past ages." Suffer us to admonish you in the language of Pope:

> "A little learning is a dangerous thing :
> Drink deep, or taste not the Picrian spring :
> There shallow draughts intoxicate the brain,
> And drinking deeply sobers us again."

Noah said: "Cursed be Canaan; a servant of servants shall he be unto his brethren." Gen. ix. 25.

Noah said: "Blessed be the Lord God of Shem; and Canaan shall be his servant." Gen. ix. 26.

Again, Noah said: "God shall enlarge Japheth, and he

shall dwell in the tents of Shem, and Canaan shall be his servant." Gen. ix. 27.

These passages are prophetic, and have certainly been fulfilled. They are judicial, and the curse has been felt for ages. The children of Canaan are doomed to serve the children of Shem and Japheth, in some capacity, by the decree of their Creator. The best authority in the learned world says: "In every case the more energetic sons of Shem and Japheth have at last fallen upon the rich Hamistic territories and despoiled them. The subsequent history of Canaan shows in the strongest manner possible the fulfillment of the curse. When Israel took possession of his land, he became the *slave* of Shem. When Tyre fell before the army of Alexander, and Carthage succumbed to her Roman conquerors, he became the *slave* of Japheth."

The privilege of choosing to be free, while it was allowed to the *Hebrew* servant, was denied to the children of Canaan, as will appear from the following passage: "If thy brother be waxen poor, and fallen in decay with thee, then thou shalt relieve him; yea, though he be a stranger, or a sojourner; that he may live with thee. Take thou no usury of him, or increase; but fear thy God, that thy brother may live with thee. Thou shalt not give him thy money upon usury, nor lend him thy victuals for increase. I am the Lord your God, which brought you forth out of the land of Egypt, to give you the land of *Canaan*, and to be your God. And if thy brother that dwelleth by thee be waxen poor, and be sold unto thee, thou shalt not compel him to serve as a bond-servant; but as an hired servant, and as a

2

sojourner, he shall be with thee, and shall serve thee unto the year of jubilee; and then shall he depart from thee, both he and his children with him, and shall return unto his family, and unto the possession of his fathers shall he return. For they are my servants, which I brought forth out of the land of Egypt: they shall not be sold as bondmen. Thou shalt not rule over them with rigor, but shalt fear thy God. *Both thy bondmen and thy bondmaids, which thou shalt have, shall be of the heathen* (Canaanites) *that are round about you; of them shall ye buy bondmen and bondmaids.* Moreover, of the children of the strangers (Canaanites,) that do sojourn among you, of them shall ye buy, and of their families that are with you, which they begat in your land; and they shall be your possession. And ye shall take them as an inheritance for your children after you, to inherit them for a possession; they shall be your bondmen for ever." Lev. xxv. 35–46.

Upon this passage Dr. Rivers remarks, (Elements Moral Philosophy :)

1. That the Divine Legislator makes a clear distinction between a hired servant and a slave, between temporary bondage and perpetual, and upon the rigor which might be required in the case of perpetual bondage and which was not allowed toward the Israelite, whose bondage was but temporary, unless he chose to make it perpetual.

2. God commanded the Hebrews that all their perpetual slaves should be of the heathen that were round about them. These heathen were the descendants of *Canaan*, the very people upon whom slavery was inflicted.

3. These people were to be owned; they were to be bought as property; they were to become "chattels personal; to all intents, purposes, and constructions whatsoever."

4. These slaves were to be inherited by the posterity of their masters. "Ye shall take them as an inheritance for your children after you, to inherit them for a possession."

"Ariel" may learn from the foregoing what the opinion of "the learned of the present and past ages" is concerning the curse of Canaan.

But whence the Negro? ask the disciples of "Ariel." Where did he branch off? Before answering this question, allow us to ask a few. "Ariel" admits that the *dark-brown* Malayan is a descendant of Adam and Eve. Pray tell us, ye Solomons, where did he branch off? and from what patriarchal stem? "Ariel" says that the *dark, copper-colored* Indian belongs to the white race. (See pape 4.) And where did he branch off? You keep the Family Tree of all the offspring of Noah. "Ariel" mentions the *olive-colored* Mongolian as a descendant of Noah. How did he get his color? You observe, gentlemen, that it is an easy thing to ask questions; and that it is as difficult to account for the peculiarities of some other varieties as of your "flat-nosed negro."

But whence the Negro? The distinguished naturalists of the world—men who, like Lepsius and Bunsen, have even journeyed to the East, and examined the pictures, sculptures, and monumental records of Egypt and Assyria—men who have studied the languages of the world, so as to talk, and read, and write their way back to Noah and Adam—the

master-minds in Ethnology—have long since, and with singular unanimity, decided this question. *They have arrived
at the conclusion that the Negro Variety of the Human
Species has only been developed in the course of ages, within
the African tropics, and was derived from Egypt and Assyria.**

IV.—HISTORICAL.

"Ariel" is set for the defense of Ham and all his posterity. He writes about them as knowingly, as admiringly,
as lovingly, and as familiarly, as Thackeray does about the
various members of the celebrated Johnsonian Club. He
knows that all names in Ham's day had a meaning, a deep
significance. He says, (page 8,) "the meaning of Ham's
name in Hebrew is *sun-burnt, swarthy, dark, black*." Nevertheless, his friend Ham was white, *superlatively white*.
Shem was white and great—Japheth was whiter and greater
still; but Ham was the whitest and greatest of all, and
the father of a most wonderful posterity. This seems to
be the impression he desires to leave on the minds of
his numerous readers. Well, "Ariel" knows all about it?

---

* After finishing this sentence, we met with the learned and justly
celebrated Dr. Blackie, from the University of Edinburgh. We took his
card, and wrote the following question: "What do the Universities of
Edinburgh and Bonn teach concerning the origin of the Negro?" In
two days he presented us with the masterly paper found at the close of
this pamphlet. We know that its high authority will direct learned men
to its perusal; but we hope no one will fail to read it through and
through. It demolishes "Ariel;" though the Doctor has never read his
book.

We call upon Clio, the Muse of History, to listen. On page 13, he says: "The annals of fame do not present such an array of great names, whether in arts and sciences, and all that serves to elevate and make man noble on earth, or in the Senate, or the field, by any other race of people, as will compare with those of Ham's descendants." Again, on page 13: "It appears from his history, from *unquestioned* history, this Ham and his descendants, the long and straight-haired race, *governed* and *ruled the world* from the earliest ages after the flood, and for many centuries, and gave to it *all* the arts and sciences, manufactures and commerce, geometry, astronomy, geography, architecture, letters, painting, music, etc., etc., and that they thus governed the world, as as it were, from the flood, until they came in contact with the Roman people, and then their power was broken in a contest for the mastery of the world, at Carthage, one hundred and forty-seven years before A. D." And again, on page 15: "We have shown that Ham's descendants have led and governed the world, for twenty-three centuries after the flood to the battle of Actium; that they gave it also, the arts and sciences, manufactures and commerce, etc., etc."

Now what are the facts? Babylon was founded 2200 years B. C., and became the leading power of the world 800 years B. C., the very year the city of Carthage was founded. The Kingdom of Babylon was the first of the "Four Grand Monarchies" of the world. When King Nebuchadnezzar made a decree, it read thus: "Therefore, I make a decree, *That every people, nation, and language,* which speak any thing amiss against the God of Shadrach, Meshach, and Abednego, shall be cut in pieces, and their houses shall be made a dunghill; because there is no other God that can deliver after this sort." Dan. iii. 29. That decree does not sound like anybody was ruling the world other than Nebuchadnezzar. "Ariel" testifies, page 34, that Shem's descendants built Babylon. Well done, "Ariel!" you are correct *once*. It is also proper that we should inform you that *Astronomy* was first cultivated by the Chaldeans.

At the fall of Babylon, 600 years B. C., the Persian Empire became the leading power of the world. This was the second of the "Four Grand Monarchies" of the world. A decree from one of her kings reads thus: "Then King Darius wrote unto all people, nations, and languages, that dwell in all the earth, Peace be multiplied unto you. I make a decree," etc., etc. Dan. vi. 25. When this decree was written, the ancient kingdom of Egypt had come to an end; and it does not appear that "Mizraim's children" were exercising the trade of kingdom and lordship to any remarkable extent. The finest *manufactures* in the world are Persian.

Athens, the capital of Greece, was founded 1500 years B. C. More than 300 years B. C., the Persian Empire was subverted by Alexander the Great, and Greece became the master of the world. This was the third of the "Four Grand Monarchies." Egypt became a mere province of one of Alexander's Captains, Ptolemy. From him sprang a line of kings called the Ptolemies, who governed Egypt

for many years. The Greeks were the descendants of
Japheth. They brought the *arts* and *sciences* to greater
perfection than any other people of antiquity. In *literature*
and *architecture* they have no equals yet.

More than 700 years B. C., Rome was founded. About
100 years B. C., it ruled the world. Every son of Ham
succumbed. This was the fourth and last "Grand Mon-
archy." The Romans were Japheth's children, and led the
commerce of the world. What hero-worshiper would turn
away from the painters and sculptors, the scholars and
philosophers, the poets and historians, the architects
and orators, the statesmen and commanders of Greece
and Italy, to look among Ham's children for "great
names"?

We have made this "recitement" ("Ariel's" classical
word) from history, simply because we propose to rout the
author of "THE NEGRO" from every prominent position he
has taken. Surely he never "suspicioned" (another of his
words) that any one would reply; else he would have read
up the subject, such as it is, with more care. We recommend Rollin.

V.—HAS THE NEGRO A SOUL?

The design of "Ariel's" book is to prove that he has
none. We open it, almost at random, and quote from
page 22: "The Negro being now here on earth, and
not Adam's progeny, it follows, beyond all the reasonings of men on earth to controvert, that he was created
before Adam, and with the other beasts or cattle, and being

created *before* Adam, that like all beasts and cattle, *they have no souls.*" We quote from page 23 : "Again, we take up the monkey, and trace him likewise through his upward and advancing orders—baboon, orang-outang, and gorilla, up to the negro—another noble animal, the noblest of the beast creation." We wish "Ariel" could understand and appreciate a metaphysical argument. We would cover the remainder of our space with "inquiries concerning the intellectual powers" of the Negro. But Psychology is not in his line.

The most extensive traveler of modern times directs us never to despise the settled opinions and practices of mankind. We have arrived at them through ages of study and experience. They have grown up, like the British Constitution, by the accretions of centuries.

Negroes have been on the earth for more than three thousand years. *Everybody treats them as if they were human beings, and had souls.* We now take them at seven years of age, and educate them in our common schools, just as we do white children. This writer is not so enthusiastic for the children of Ham, as to believe they learn as readily and rapidly as the offspring of Japheth; still, they learn, and go through the "Course of Study" after a while. Give one of them time and instruction, and he would learn Ancient Languages, Modern Languages, Mathematics, Metaphysics, Natural Sciences, and English Literature, before he has done. We manage them in school as we do other children, give them the same sort of encouragement, administer the same kind of discipline, and see the same effects follow. We are certain we have met two that could write a better book than — some we have seen. Several of "Ariel's" converts say that ants and bees are *very smart* insects. That's so. Their instinct is remarkable. But they know as much at one year old as they ever can know; they know no more to-day than they did in the ark. There is no intellectual development.

Negroes have the same diseases that afflict white folks. Doctors cure them or kill them with Japheth's medicines. Knowing that the Negro's mind or soul operates mysteriously and certainly on his body, they hold out the pleasing hope of recovery to him as they do to others. If they are beasts, why are physicians so conscientious in the discharge of professional duties toward them? Would they be so conscientious in treating a horse? ("Ariel" says he is a noble animal.) When the case is dismissed, or the patient dies, we are informed that young physicians, at least, charge the Negro very much like he was a man.

The laws of every country have grown up from long experience and profound study. Negroes are everywhere responsible to the laws of the land. Beasts are not. Lawyers treat them as if they were human beings, and had souls. They prosecute them, they defend them, for the usual consideration. Among other things, we notice, they inquire into the *motives that influenced the will* in the commission of crime. What! has a beast motives to influence the will, or a will to choose the strongest motive, according to your Calvinistic or Arminian Psychology?

The Christian Church regards them as immortal beings. We were assured to-day that "Ariel" is a Methodist preacher.

We do not believe it. We were assured yesterday that he is Henry Ward Beecher. We know he is not. We were told the day before, that the substance of the book was written one hundred years ago. We think not. We have been told all along that "Ariel" is an ex-Proclaimer. We don't know. It may be, however, that once or twice in his life, he has told the Negroes that "Simon, the Canaan*ite*," was a disciple of our Lord; and that Philip baptized an *Ethiopian* Eunuch, on profession of his faith in Jesus Christ. See Matt. x. 4, Acts viii. 27.

We collect them together in Sunday-schools, read the Holy Scriptures to them, teach them to sing praises to God, and pray to him in the name of Christ; and give them catechetical instruction from books prepared for all—white and black. We usually see the same results follow. Our commission is: "Go ye into all the world, and preach the gospel to every creature." Mark xvi. 15. We build houses of worship for the Negroes, and teach them to celebrate divine service on the Lord's Day. We administer to them the Sacraments of Baptism and the Lord's Supper; and, when they die, we give them a Christian burial. We form them into classes, prayer-meetings, congregations, missions, circuits, stations, districts, quarterly conferences, and annual conferences, just as we do white people, and for the same purposes. We license colored men to preach the gospel, and when found worthy and well-qualified, they are ordained as Deacons and Elders in the Church of God. Our preachers deliver to them the facts, truths, doctrines, precepts, and promises of the gospel in the same manner as they are delivered to all the offspring of Adam and Eve; and the same results flow therefrom.

The motives and assisting influences of the gospel system are amply sufficient to produce in the Negroes the most pungent conviction for sin, and to effect their conversion to God. The Great Teacher seems to have considered the philosophy of human nature, and then placed those motives before us which would be most likely to move, restrain, alarm, and melt. Let us trace out the nice adaptation of these motives to the several properties of our being.

First. We have a delicate susceptibility of painful and happy emotions. So have the Negroes. Therefore, we teach them that misery in this life is the result of sin, and that happiness is the reward of piety.

Secondly. Another property of our nature is sympathy. Scenes of suffering and distress move and melt us. This is natural and common to every *variety* of our race. This passion is strongly appealed to by the motives of Christianity. The sorrowful life and tragical death of Jesus Christ were designed to melt us into tenderness, gratitude, and love. No theme is more effective with an audience of Negroes.

Thirdly. Another property. We have an instinctive passion for happiness and glory. This passion is regarded and appealed to by the motives of religion. Only wave a heavenly reward in view of a world of Negroes, and you produce the most intense religious excitement. Reader, bear witness.

Fourthly. The passion of fear, being an element of our

nature, is appealed to by the motives of the Christian system. The terribleness of hell, portrayed with all its fire
and fury, in the presence of a congregation of Negroes, produces the greatest consternation.*

But suppose "Ariel's" doctrine be true? What a spectacle does the venerable Church of God present! Instruct-
ing young "beasts" in the Sunday-school! baptizing "cattle" into the Christian Church! administering the Lord's
Supper to a species of "monkey"! and teaching a "noble
animal" to worship the Lord on the Christian Sabbath,
etc., etc.

Experience settles all. We have held many class-meet-
ings and love-feasts among the Negroes. Their religious
experience agrees exactly with the order of the Spirit's operations on the human heart. 1st. The light of divine truth.
2d. Conviction for sin, produced by the power of the Holy
Ghost. 3d. Repentance toward God. 4th. Faith in the
blood of Christ. 5th. Justification, regeneration, and adoption. 6th. The bliss of holiness. This is the experience
of the white man. Bear witness all ye who love the Lord
Jesus Christ in sincerity.

The whole world is made up of mind, or soul and matter.
The term Matter is a name which we apply to a certain
combination of properties, or to certain substances which
are solid, extended, and divisible, and which are known to
us only by these properties. The term Mind, in the same
manner, is a name which we apply to a certain combination

---

* Positive Theology.

of functions, or to a certain power which we feel within us, and is known to us only by these functions. Matter we know only by our senses—Mind or Soul only by our consciousness.* The profoundest philosophers write concerning the Negro's mind as they do concerning that of the White man. The Negro has all the intellectual faculties—consciousness, perception, memory, association, imagination, comparison, and pure reason. He has all the sensibilities, animal feelings, rational feelings, æsthetic emotions, and moral emotions. He has a free will, and is governed by motives. He dreams, walks in his sleep, and may become insane.† His immortality is found in those principles of his nature by which he feels upon his soul the awe of a God, and looks forward to the future with anxiety or with hope; by which he knows to distinguish truth from falsehood, and evil from good, and has forced upon him the conviction that he is a moral and responsible being. This is the power of conscience—that monitor within which raises its voice in the breast of every man—a witness for his Creator. There is thus, in the consciousness of every dark son of Ham, a deep impression of continued existence. "Ariel" may reason against it till he bewilder himself in his own sophistries; but a voice within the Negro gives the lie to his vain speculations, and pleads with authority for a life which is to come.

These are the settled opinions and practices of the world in reference to the Negro. Educators instruct him in every

---

* Dr. Abercrombie.   † *Ibid.*

department of letters—physicians administer medicines to his body and consolation to his mind—lawyers hold him responsible to every law of the land—ministers of the gospel teach him to worship God according to the Scriptures—and philosophers inquire concerning his intellectual powers. Are we all wrong? Are the opinions and practices of the five learned professions of the world to be despised? Has the whole world been in Cimmerian darkness until RABBI "ARIEL" appeared?

VI.—SCRIPTURAL.

"Ariel" teaches that the Negro is a beast—that he is older than Adam, and was the identical creature that tempted our first parents in the garden of Eden. See pages 45 and 46. The most intelligent supporters of the "Ariel" theory all agree that if we make it appear the Negro was not in the garden of Eden, the book is answered. We think so too. For if he was not *there*, then he was not one of the "men" who called "upon the name of the Lord." Gen. iv. 26. He was not the "man" whose creation "grieved the Lord at his heart." Gen. vi. 5, 6. If the Negro was not in the garden—the seducer of Eve—then it was not *association with his daughters* that brought down the flood, that confused and dispersed the builders of the Tower of Babel, that brought down fire and brimstone upon the Cities of the Plain, and caused the Lord to exterminate the Canaanites, etc., etc. If the "animal" was not in the garden, as contended for by "Ariel," then he was not in existence either to enter the ark or come out of it. *"Only argue the Negro out of Paradise,"* say they, *"and the book is obliged to go down."* Amen! say we.

The last sentence of "THE NEGRO" is this: "The Bible is true." Let us take up one. Gen. iii. 1: "Now the *serpent* was more subtile than any beast of the field which the Lord God had made." The Hebrew word translated "serpent" is *Nachash.* "Ariel" says he was a Negro. Num. xxi. 6: "And the Lord sent fiery serpents among the people, and they bit the people; and much people of Israel died." The Hebrew word rendered "serpents" here is *Nachash* in the plural. Were they Negroes? Num. xxi. 9: "And Moses made a serpent of brass, and put it upon a pole; and it came to pass, that if a serpent had bitten any man, when he beheld the serpent of brass, he lived." The Hebrew is *Nachash* again—was the brazen serpent a Negro? Job xxvi. 13: "By his Spirit he hath garnished the heavens: his hand hath formed the crooked serpent." The original is *Nachash.* Is the "crooked serpent" a "kinky-headed negro"? Eccl. x. 11: "Surely the serpent will bite without enchantment." The Hebrew here is *Nachash.* Do you suppose he is a "black-skinned negro"? Isa. xxvii. 1: "In that day the Lord with his sore and great and strong sword shall punish leviathan the piercing serpent." The "leviathan" or "serpent" here is a translation of *Nachash.* Is leviathan a Negro? Isa. lxv. 25: In allusion to Gen. iii. 14, the prophet says, "Dust shall be the serpent's meat." *Nachash* again. Surely "Ariel's" "thick-lipped negro" does not feed on dust. Amos ix. 3: "And though they be hid from my sight in the bottom of the sea, thence will I command the serpent, and he shall bite them." *Nachash* in the original. Does his "flat-nosed negro" live "in the bottom of the sea"?

We will now lay down the Hebrew Scriptures and take up the celebrated Septuagint. This is the most ancient translation of the sacred books of the Jews into Greek. It was made by order of Ptolemy Philadelphus, King of Egypt, for the Alexandrian Library, about 285 years before Christ. Dr. Clarke says: "The Septuagint translation, of all the versions of the Sacred Writings, has ever been deemed of the greatest importance by *competent* judges." Surely the learned Jews, selected for the performance of this special work, understood their own language, and the language of their royal patron. They rendered the Hebrew word *Nachash* (serpent) by the Greek word οφις *ophis*, from the beginning of the Septuagint to its close. This Greek word οφις *ophis* means a serpent, and nothing else. If the *Nachash* was a Negro, these venerable scholars would have known it.

We now appeal to the Latin Scriptures. The Vulgate is the most ancient and authoritative version of the Latin Church. This translation was made by Saint Jerome, at the command of the Pope Damascus, A. D. 384. Where the Hebrew has *Nachash*, and the Greek has οφις, the Vulgate has *serpens*—a serpent. Now if the being who tempted Adam and Eve had been a Negro, it is passing strange that no one has ever found it out until the days of polyglot "Ariel."

Finally, the common English Bible. This translation was

made in the reign of King James I., by forty-seven of the most learned linguists the English nation ever produced. Where the Hebrew has *Nachash*, the Greek *Ophis*, the Latin *serpens*, our authorized version has *serpent.*

Now, "Ariel," are you satisfied there was no Negro in the garden of Eden? If you are not, we know we can convince you. You, yourself, forgetting your new theory, say, on the sixth page of your book, "God cursed the serpent." Did you ever hear of the "*argumentum ad hominem?*"

The curse on all the parties in this sad transaction has been literally fulfilled. Gen. iii. 17, 18, 19 : "And unto Adam he said, Because thou hast hearkened unto the voice of thy wife, and hast eaten of the tree, of which I commanded thee, saying, Thou shalt not eat of it: cursed is the ground for thy sake, in sorrow shalt thou eat of it all the days of thy life; thorns also and thistles shall it bring forth to thee, and thou shalt eat the herb of the field. In the sweat of thy face shalt thou eat bread, till thou return unto the ground; for out of it wast thou taken; for dust thou art, and unto dust shalt thou return." Every fallen son and daughter of Adam, and even the inarticulate earth on which they live, will testify that this curse has been literally fulfilled. All nature is sighing, murmuring, whispering, shouting, and thundering out true and solemn testimony to this fact.

Gen. iii. 16: "And unto the woman he said, I will greatly multiply thy sorrow and thy conception; in sorrow shalt thou bring forth children; and thy desire shall be to thy husband, and he shall rule over thee." Every daughter of

3

fallen Eve is our witness that this curse has been fulfilled to the letter.

Gen. iii. 14: "And the Lord God said unto the serpent, Because thou hast done this, thou art cursed above all cattle, and above every beast of the field; *upon thy belly shalt thou go,* and dust shalt thou eat all the days of thy life." If this creature was a Negro, as "Ariel" teaches, has this curse been literally fulfilled? Is the Negro "cursed above all cattle, and above every beast of the field"? Does he travel on "all-fours," or on his "belly"? Does he eat "dust"? Every Negro, walking erect on the face of the earth, is our witness that this curse was not fulminated against him.

Who was this "serpent"? We cannot tell; but the Holy Ghost can. Rev. xii. 9, says, "That old serpent, called the devil, and Satan, which deceiveth the whole world." This is his name both in Greek and Hebrew. Again, Rev. xx. 2: "That old serpent, which is the devil, and Satan." "Ariel" says he was a Negro. If he was, here was a fine opportunity for the Holy Ghost to have informed us.

That accurate Greek scholar and learned commentator—Dr. Benson—says: "Serpents, in general, have a great deal of subtlety; but this one had an extraordinary measure of it, being either only a serpent in appearance, and in reality a fallen angel, *or the prince of fallen angels—Satan;* or a real serpent possessed and actuated by him."

Now, therefore, if the Negro was not created before Adam and Eve, if he is not a beast, if he was not the tempter of our first parents, "Ariel's" *book is false, fanatical, and of mischievous tendency.* If we have proven by the learned translators of the world that the Negro was not the tempter in Paradise, it is not necessary for us to follow him (or "Ariel") any farther, and show that it was not he who "profaned the name of the Lord," who caused God to "repent" his creation, or whose daughters assisted in bringing on the flood. It is not necessary for us to show that he neither entered the ark or came out of it, or that "amalgamation" caused the confusion and dispersion of the Babel-builders, the destruction of Sodom and Gomorrah, and the extermination of the Canaanites. WE CONSIDER THE BOOK ANSWERED.

VII.—THE END.

One paragraph more, and we dismiss this weak, wicked, and infidel publication. Repetition is a prominent feature of "Ariel's" book. He not only repeatedly disputes the word and decision of our Lord Jesus Christ concerning the unpardonable sin, (see Matt. xii. 31, 32, Mark iii. 28, 29, 30, Luke xii. 10,) but he frequently misquotes and misrepresents the Holy Ghost. Hear him: "In the laws delivered by God, to Moses, for the children of Israel, he expressly enacts and charges *'that no man having a flat nose shall approach unto his altar.'* This includes the whole Negro race, and expressly excludes them from coming to his altar for any act of worship." This statement is repeated in every form of which he was capable. He knew it would impress the vulgar mind, and be quoted more frequently than any other. But he is careful not to tell us where it may be found. *We defy him to show it.* Among the many millions who have read the twenty-first chapter of Leviticus, we suppose not one ever saw any reference to the Negro, except "Ariel," who,

> " Undisturbed by conscientious qualms,
>   Perverts the Scriptures and purloins the Psalms."

Anybody can see that the chapter alluded to has reference to the personal appearance of the *priests*, and simply forbids that any *deformed son of Aaron* should " offer the offerings of the Lord made by fire." Is the Negro a son of Aaron? "Ariel" must know that he has willfully and knowingly misinterpreted this plain passage of God's word, addressed to Aaron and his seed in the priesthood; for in the twenty-second verse it is expressly provided that this deformed son " shall eat the bread of his God, both of the most holy, and of the holy." Let us remember the language of Peter to Cornelius: " Of a truth I perceive that God is no respecter of persons; but in every nation, he that feareth him and worketh righteousness is accepted with him." "Ariel" has *deliberately* perverted the doctrine contained in this text. Let the readers and defenders of his book call to mind an old legal maxim; of daily application in all the courts, as well as in the every-day transactions of life: *"False in one thing, false in every thing."*

We take leave of "Ariel" in the last admonition of God's Holy Word: "For I testify unto every man that heareth the words of the prophecy of this book, If any man shall add unto these things, God shall add unto him the plagues written in this book. And if any man shall take away from the words of the book of this prophecy, God shall take away his part out of the book of life, and out of the holy city, and from the things which are written in this book."

DR. BLACKIE'S LETTER.

SHELBY FEMALE INSTITUTE,
NASHVILLE, TENNESSEE, SEPTEMBER 17, 1867.

ROBERT A. YOUNG, D.D., NASHVILLE—

My Dear Sir:—I have much pleasure in answering, to the best of my ability, the question propounded in your note of yesterday: "What do the Universities of Edinburgh and Bonn teach concerning the origin of the Negro?" I studied Natural History in the University of Edinburgh in the latter days of the celebrated Professor Robert Jameson; and in Bonn, under Treviranus, Budge, and Brandis. "As the twig is bent so is the tree inclined," and my subsequent study of Natural History, both in Europe and America, has naturally followed the cast in which it was originally moulded. The opinion I have been taught, and now teach, is that, as Cuvier has it—*there is but one genus, homo; and one species, homo sapiens.* Man is physically a cosmopolite. He lives among the burning sands of Africa or the frozen valleys of Grinnell Land; his family divided into tribes differing from each other in outward appearance, and each now possessing a constitutional adaptation to the climate in which they are found. Two questions concerning him have arisen: Were these tribes created separately, in the geographical centers in which we now find them, or did man receive originally in his constitution a principle of accommodation which was developed as he wandered from his first home? Had the different races distinct origins, or did man receive a peculiar susceptibility of accommodation *by* circumstances *to* circumstances? Or, is man of different species or varieties of one species?

According to the common definition, those individuals are regarded as forming a species who are capable of producing descendants, those descendants possessing the same capability likewise. Hybrids do exist, but they cannot produce offspring. All varieties of a species are capable of mixed parentage, the offspring producing continued parentage, but different species are not so capable. *E. g.*, the horse and ass, the dog and wolf, and many gardeners' varieties of plants. From this acknowledged principle in Natural Science we come to the conclusion that varieties of men must either be incapable of intermixing their stock, and thus for ever separate, or else, the contrary being the fact, they are proved to belong to the same species. As the Caucasian and Ethiopian are capable of intermixture, and their offspring are fertile, they are not hybrids, but the fact makes them of one species. Now we know that mankind, of all races, is capable of propagation by intermarriage, and has as prolific an offspring if the union be of individuals of the same race or utterly dissimilar. If there be any difference, Dr. Pritchard inclines it in favor of the latter. But supposing we could prove the existence of different species of men, we must of a certainty admit that they were of different primary ancestors, for one species cannot produce another, nor can two produce an intermediate. Still, having proved the contrary to be the case, we do not allow that we have done enough to prove the unity of man's origin. The Creator might have created separate ancestors, with the same peculiarities, identical, so as to form one species, but all occasion for the theory of separate creations is removed when the oneness of the species is proved. The only question is, whether it is possible that the immense variety found in the human race could be derived from one pair. Physiology unhesitatingly answers "Yes." Hear Müller, of Berlin: "The different varieties of species (*not excepting man*) may be accounted for by supposing the original existence of a pair of individuals of opposite sexes, belonging to the same species, and the constant action of different external modifying agencies, such as climate, upon several, or many, successive generations."

Such a position demands *facts* to sustain it.

I. *We know that varieties, similar to those of the human race, have arisen from animals of the same species.*

EXAMPLES.—1. *The Sheep.*—There is no reason for supposing that the varieties of the sheep are different species, although apparently dissimilar. In Europe even they differ in height, character of wool, character of horns, and presence of horns in both or one sex. In India and Africa they are remarkable for their long legs and hanging ears, and their long, thick tails. In Syria, the wool is more or less mixed with hair. Then we find that when transported they will lose their peculiarities, as in the case of the fat-tailed sheep of the Tartars, which, after a few generations have been fed on the dry herbage of the steppes of Siberia, become tailed like other sheep. New breeds are constantly seen among farmers. Seth Wight, in Massachusetts, had a ewe which in 1791 gave birth to a male lamb. This creature had a long body and short legs, like a Scotch terrier; and it having been observed that its build prevented it from leaping fences easily, it was proposed to propagate it. The experiment was tried with success, and the celebrated otter breed produced. Parents both of this breed invariably produce descendants with the peculiar form. 2. *The Horse.*—Here notice the different proportions of the wild horse from the most improved breeds—their larger heads, coarser tails, and crisped hair. Blumenbach says the most dissimilar human skulls bear more resemblance to each other than the long head of the Neapolitan horse does to the short skull of the Hungarian. Horses, originally domesticated, have run wild in Siberia, and now differ from the Russian breeds in their skulls, their limbs, backs, manes, hoofs, and ears. 3. *Swine.*—Hogs were introduced by the Spaniards into South America at the end of the fifteenth century, and in thirty years after hordes of wild swine infested the woods of Jamaica, and other islands, feeding on wild fruits, and resembling the wild boar, having large heads, vaulted foreheads, erect ears, and black color. Dr. Pritchard considers this as removing all doubt of the original identity of stock of the wild and domestic hog, and Blumenbach asserts that the difference of the skull of a wild hog and the English farm-yard pig is greater than that of a negro and European. Swine, too, are found in Hungary and Sweden with solid hoofs, and again in Cubagua with toes half a span long. 4. *The Cat.*—Wild in Persia and Eastern Europe, it has become domesticated in all the nations of the West, its habits and diet are altered, and the length of the intestine increased. But in the north of Scotland, when the highlands were depopulated, the cats became wild, and resuming their nocturnal and predatory habit, and carnivorous diet, the intestine returned to its original dimensions. 5. The *Cow* and the *Dog* might also be cited, did I not consider the position as sufficiently sustained.

II. *In the human species, varieties occur in one race approaching the characteristics of another.*

1. In an indiscriminate assembly of Caucasians, a number of individuals might be picked out whose faces would ally them to other races, and would exhibit the incipient types. 2. We find the frequent occurrence of Melanism as well as Albinism in Intertropical America and Java. 3. The occurrence of Albinoes, both among the white and black race, but especially among the latter, and the production by them of others similar to the parent. 4. The frequency of Albinoes in Ceylon, which are, as

a rule, not fairer than the Norwegians. Also their occurrence in tropical America, and the Indian legend that the white man is the offspring of an Albino—of course the converse of this, that the Negro is the result of Melanism, is as easily conceivable. Professor Jones, of this city, is now engaged in a series of researches which will probably throw much light on this whole subject, and prove of incalculable value to both ethnologist and biblical scholar. 5. A similar phenomenon to Albinism is the Xanthous variety, occurring among the dark-complexioned races—among negroes, both in their native places and others to which they have been transported. 6. The occurrence of *spotted* persons, which have been so often noticed, described, and figured. (See Lavater's Physiognomy.) 7. The curious facts cited by Dr. Lawrence, in regard to mixed races, in which he shows that the offspring of a black and white may be either black or white, instead of being mixed; or in some cases may be spotted. I could cite at least a dozen such cases, if space permitted. 8. The varieties thus produced have been propagated in the case of animals from the days of Jacob till now, and become permanent breeds, if the individuals constantly intermix, and none others be admitted to the breed. The Negro and the European are the two extremes of a very long gradation, and between them are innumerable intermediate stages, which differ from each other no more than individuals occasionally produced differ from the generality of the race.

III. *Very singular changes of color are known to take place after birth.* A case is mentioned in the "Philosophical Transactions," in which a Negro became perfectly white; and a few years ago a paragraph of the same nature, relating to a pilot on the Alabama River, went the round of the newspapers. A Negro at Venice is known to have become yellow; and Dr. Graves mentions a case of a child born an Albino, which gradually returned to the normal state after the third year. Such changes of color, too, are not unfrequent during pregnancy of the white female. Camper mentions the case of a French lady of rank, who gradually became brown and at last black as a negress during each pregnancy, returning to the natural color after parturition. The darkening of the areola of the nipple of the pregnant female is a familiar instance. These facts prove that, independently of solar heat, a physical change may take place, connected with the constitution, which imparts a black hue to the skin similar to that natural to the Negro.

IV. *The existence and propagation of remarkable varieties of a very wonderful kind, is a fact of importance.*

1. Of such nature is the case of Lambert, the *"porcupine man,"*

described in the "Philosophical Transactions," whose body was covered with warts like pieces of twine, about half an inch long. He had six children, every one of whom had the extraordinary peculiarity of the father. A German family was exhibited in 1802, who pretended they were members of a nearly extinct race in New Holland, who all had a series of horny excrescences on the palms of their hands—father, sons, and grandsons. 2. The peculiarity of six-fingered people running in families, has been described as far back as Pliny, (the *Sedigiti.*) Sir A. Carlisle traced one family through four generations. In 2 Sam. xxi. 20, such a case is mentioned; and in the same chapter is recorded the extraordinary stature of Ishbi-benob, Saph, and the brother of Goliath, four sons of one father. 3. Six-fingered families are not uncommon, but the case of a family at Iver is more curious. For *nine generations* they had perfect thumbs, but only the first phalanx of each finger, and no rudiment of nails; and this defect was entailed always by the women of the family. 4. Another peculiarity, now permanent and historical, is the thick upper lip of the House of Hapsburg, which is believed to have been introduced many centuries ago by intermarriage with the House of Jagellon. These varieties are mainly cited from Dr. Pritchard's "Natural History of Man," and, as he says, "they establish the fact that such deviations really take place; that varieties of structure are not always referable to ancestors and to original differences transmitted from first parents, but arise in breeds previously destitute of any such characters, and when they have once arisen become permanent in the stock." Strong presumptive evidence is thus obtained that the different families or races found, may owe their origin to similar circumstances, to the casual rise of a society, which under favorable circumstances—isolation, for example—becomes indelible in succeeding generations.

V. *The origin of the black race may be yet involved in obscurity, but there are a sufficiency of known facts to prove the probability of their having arisen from another.* I select the black, because not only you have made inquiry thereon, but because it is the most extreme variety, and his origin and claims to membership of the human family have come to be regarded as important social, political, and religious questions. Dr. Latham, who in his work divides the human race into but three varieties, says: "If we were to take three individual specimens of the human race which should exhibit the most important differences, they would, I think, be—first, a Mongolian, or a Tungus from Central or Siberian Asia; second, a Negro, from the delta of the Niger; and third, a European from France, England, or Germany. At the first view the Negro would seem to be the most unlike of the three, and perhaps he would do so after a minute and careful inquiry. Still, the characteristic and differential features of the Asiatic would be of a very remarkable kind." Understanding, then, that of the three, the African is the most peculiar, and most difficult to account for without the hypothesis of a separate creation, if I can show just cause why there is no need of resorting to the expedient of a special creation for the Negro race, it will not be required of me to show it is needed for any other variety. I have already cited facts sufficient—the changes of color, etc.—to prove the *possibility* of the Negro having sprung from another race of men. If we suppose the rise of such a variety under circumstances favorable to its propagation—isolation and compelled intermarriage, for example—all the conditions necessary for its becoming fixed are furnished. Other facts lead to the same conclusion.

1. The Arabs are of Semitic origin, and speak a Semitic language, and they have the most perfect type of the human head, but their color would rather ally them to the Ethiopic race. Silk Buckingham describes a family in the Jordan valley of pure Arab blood on both sides, who, with the exception of the father only, had crisped hair, negro features, and deep black color. A negress had never been known as wife or concubine in the family. The Arabs, remember, are pure Caucasians, but here in the burning valleys of the Jordan they are approximating another type. The Arabs in the desert between Damascus and Bassora have crisped locks, almost approaching wool. The town of Souakin, on the African shore of the Red Sea, is composed of a mixed people, first having been settled by Bedouins, or Arabs, and secondly by Turks. Burckhardt says that both these peoples have become of the darkest brown from a white stock; still preserving, however, the features of the race; and this change of color has occurred in a few centuries. Higher up the Nile are the Shegya Arabs, mentioned by the author of the "Crescent and the Cross," who are of a clear, glossy, jet-black, distinguished in all other respects from the Negroes, with whom they do not intermarry, but owe their color only to the climate, or accidental causes.

2. It is noteworthy that the Jews have assimilated in physical characters to the nations with whom they reside. They are fair in the north of Europe; English Jews have often blue eyes and flaxen hair; (I know one family intimately, the father a Greek Jew, and the mother a French Jewess, the family brought up in England, all fairer than Scotch lassies, except one dark-eyed daughter, and yet unmistakable in their origin by the nose and lips;) in Germany they are often red-bearded; in Portugal

exceedingly dark; in Malabar, and other parts of India, quite black. Mr. Catlin, too, has contended that the North American red man is of Jewish origin. Now bear in mind the rarity of the intermarriage of Jews with those of other creeds and races, and the fact is most striking. 3. The Hindoos are Caucasians, but the variety of color among them is very striking—some black as Negroes, others copper-colored, others as fair as the Turks; and this not depending upon caste, as some of the Brahmins are quite black, and some of the Pariahs comparatively white. 4. But not only in complexion do we find approximation to the Negro in the Caucasian family. The Abyssinians are known to be related to the original inhabitants of Yemen, on the opposite shores of the Arabian Gulf, and to form a branch of the great Syro-Arabian family. Notwithstanding, they are black, and are divided into two types, one of which has every peculiarity of the Bedouin, while the other is distinguished by a less acute and uniformly flattened nose, thick lips, long, sparkling eyes, and almost woolly hair. Here there is a strong approximation to the Negro type in a Semitic, and, therefore, a Caucasian tribe. 5. Dr. Pritchard (pp. 269, 270) cites it as a remarkable fact in relation to the question as to whether the Negro and other types are to be traced to one origin, that they are not separated by any distinct line of demarkation, but run into each other so that it cannot be told where one begins and another ends. The full development of Negro peculiarities is only to be found in Intertropical Africa, and there is a gradual transition from the Egyptian to the Negro character, which pass into each other by imperceptible degrees, not the result of intermixture of races—for the intermediate races are not mulattoes, or at all resembling mulattoes—they have distinguishing features, which, besides their language, mark them out as distinct races. The observations made on this matter were commenced by the scientific men of the army of the French Republic, in the Egyptian expedition, and I can prove the accuracy of their observations from the pages of Livingstone, Speke, Barth, Burton, Anderson, Baker, Du Chaillu, Wilson, and Read, with all whose writings I am familiar. 6. The differences among those admittedly Negro has its weight in the argument. The color and woolly hair are not the only characters which make them a distinctive race, but these traits are by no means constant. The frightful deformity of the "Hottentot Venus," and others of the west coast of Africa, is very different from the Negro of the West Indian colonies, whose figures often strike Europeans as extremely beautiful. The blacks from the east coast of Africa are nearly all very well made. In Du Chaillu's first, and in his last book published this spring, he describes the Fans, of the west coast, as quite a handsome people, both in feature and figure, and takes away our idea of cannibals being so terrible to behold. 7. The difficulty of supposing the African race to have risen from another is diminished by observing the effects of civilization, along with moral causes, and favorable circumstances, on physical conformation among the Negroes themselves. The fact is, the most degraded is the ugliest. The nearer the equator the uglier the tribes, and amongst the more civilized races the shape of the skull approaches to the Caucasian type. Caffres frequently approach very near the Europeans. A Caffre chief a few years ago visited England, to give evidence before the House of Commons, and it would have been hard to find a handsomer man. The late Ira Aldridge, the dramatist, was exceedingly handsome, and Frederick Douglas, of this country, is not only intelligent and shrewd in the highest degree, but handsome and regular in feature. I never saw a handsomer man on the stage than a pure South African who played Cain in the drama of "Le Paradis Perdu," in the theatre L'Ambigu Comique, in Paris, in the winter of 1856. So perfect and regular, indeed, are the Caffre features, that some ethnologists had put them in a separate branch of the human family, till Dr. Pritchard proved it to be an error. It is authoritatively stated that the third generation of our late household slaves lost much of the flattened nose, and acquired longer head and beard, while the ugliness of a field-hand is proverbial. Bosjesmen, the lowest type, perhaps, give evidence of the ugliness produced by moral degradation and external circumstances. These facts have illustrations every-where. Among the Irish, the French, the Germans, and the Spaniards, we find the same. Coarse, unwholesome diet and ill-prepared food will make the human race degenerate. All people who live miserably are ugly and ill-made. On the other hand, luxury and good living have a tendency to develop beauty, as well as long life and refinement, as we see in the aristocratic families of England. 8. The Nubians of the Nile are a striking example of a transition from the Negro to the ancient Egyptian. They have an oval countenance, curved nose, retreating chin, thick lips, scanty beard, lively eyes, frizzled, but never woolly hair, and bronzed color, and they distinguish themselves from the Negro by the softness of the skin of the palm. These people are the descendants of the Nobatæ, who were brought by the Emperor Diocletian, fifteen hundred years ago, to people the valley of the Nile, from which the Blemmyes were driven out, and in that region they have undergone a physical change. 9. The constitution of the skin is an important branch of the question now before me. Some years ago M. Flourens thought he detected in the

Negro four distinct layers between the outer cuticle and the true skin, and stated that this could not be detected in the white, while it was found in the mulatto and Indian skins. But the combined researches of modern anatomists and histologists have shown this to be false. The outer skin of white man and Negro does not consist of layers of continuous membranes at all, but of a cellular structure whose different layers are not distinguished by any definite line of separation. So that Flourens's view was based on a mistaken idea of the integument. Henle found that there are cells containing granular coloring matter in the Negro, but we find in moles and mother marks precisely the same granules of pigment, so that we must conclude the introduction of them involves no organic change in the structure of the skin of Negroes and Anglo-Saxons. 10. Another objection has been drawn from the structure of the hair. The structure of the hair of all is somewhat obscure, but Europeans are often met whose hair is nearly if not quite as crisp as that of the Negro, and among the negroes themselves there is a very great variety, tribes among them presenting every grade, from the woolly to the merely curled or even flowing variety. And in reply to the statement that the Negro's head-covering is wool and not hair, I will merely remind you that Prof. Jones is now investigating the subject, at the request of the Nashville Medical Society, and state that Dr. Pritchard most positively announces from a large series of observations, that he is "convinced that the Negro has hair properly so called and not wool." But even if he had wool, and we admitted it, it would not prove him to belong to a separate stock, for we have plenty of animals which have both wool and hair, *e. g.*, among the sheep mentioned in an early part of this letter.

The idea of the Negro race, or any portion of it, forming an intermediate link between the noble Caucasian and the ignoble gorilla or orang outang, is so thoroughly irrational as to be disposed of by a very few facts.

1. In Dr. Morton's table of measurements of six hundred crania, we find that the Negro brain is three cubic inches larger than that of the ancient Egyptian, and yet these were the foremost in the race of civilization. The brain of the Hottentot and Australian are shown to be below that of the Negro proper, but they are equal to that of the ancient Peruvians, the monuments of whose skill in art yet strike us with wonder, and the Hottentot and Australian are members of the Negro family, (of Latham,) whose physical deformity is induced by moral and circumstantial degradation. 2. The skull of the Negro is not smaller than that of the European races. 3. The spinal cord only differs with the different size of the body. 4. The cerebellum is exactly similar to that of the Euro-

pean. 5. Generally speaking, so is the cerebrum. 6. The brain is composed of the same substance. 7. The analogy to the brain of the gorilla is not greater than that of the other races. The reports of Dr. Tiedeman, the catalogue of skulls of Dr. Meigs of Philadelphia, and the appendix to Du Chaillu's last book, will sustain these facts. 8. Strip off the integuments of Venus and a Bushwoman, and the difference of the skeleton would be but slight, while there would be an impassable gulf between them and any other animal. 9. Lastly, the intelligence of the African is not the imitativeness of the monkey and parrot—it is the result of intellect and soul, and there is an accumulation of evidence to prove that the Negro possesses all human attributes.

And I may wind up in the words of Buffon : "Upon the whole, every circumstance concurs in proving that mankind are not composed of species essentially different from each other; that, on the contrary, there was originally but one species, which, after multiplying and spreading over the whole surface of the earth, has undergone changes from the influence of climate, food, mode of living, diseases, and mixture of dissimilar individuals ; that at first these changes were not so conspicuous, and produced only individual varieties ; that these varieties became afterward more specific, because they were rendered more general, more strongly marked, and more permanent by the continual action of the same causes, and that they are transmitted from generation to generation."

And now, Doctor, I believe I have fully answered your question. The origin of the Negro, as I have been taught at the great seminaries of learning of which I have the honor to be an *alumnus,* and have satisfied myself in my researches in the study, and in the two great books of Nature and of God, is the same as that of the Caucasian, and I refer confidently to the facts cited as well as to a vast number of writers, to whom my space forbids me even to allude, for support of my position. I am aware that it is a vexed question ; that some well-meaning philosophers, as well as skeptics, believe they find in it a disagreement between science and revealed truth ; but I am fully persuaded that whenever science appears at first sight to militate against the sacred record, we will find that there is something wrong in our science, and that eventually, and at no very distant date, the two will stand hand in hand, each sustaining and strengthening the other. The facts of Astronomy and Geology, ere they were rightly interpreted, long stood opposed to Theology ; and now, to what facts does the theologian more confidently turn ? Ethnology will ere long follow her sister sciences in upholding divine truth. To my mind she does so now.

I have not read the work called "The Negro," which you are engaged in refuting; but I have not the slightest doubt, from what I hear of it, that you will find the refutation an easy task; and should these remarks be of any value to you, it will afford me very sincere pleasure. *Magna est veritas et prevalebit!*

Trusting that the great Creator will endow you with sufficient light to demonstrate the great power and almighty force of truth, and to frustrate the knavish tricks of his enemies,

> I am, dear Doctor,
>
> > Most sincerely and fraternally yours,
> >
> > GEORGE S. BLACKIE, A.M., M.D., (Edin.),
> >
> > *Professor of Natural Science, etc.*

THE
ADAMIC RACE.

REPLY TO

"ARIEL," DRS. YOUNG AND BLACKIE,

ON THE NEGRO.

"THE NEGRO DOES **NOT** BELONG TO THE ADAMIC SPECIES"—"HE IS
NOT A DESCENDANT OF ADAM AND EVE"—"HE IS **NOT** THE OFF-
SPRING OF HAM"—"HE IS NOT A BEAST; HE IS A HUMAN
BEING"—"HE HAS AN IMMORTAL SOUL; **BUT NOT**
AFTER THE IMAGE OF GOD"—"AND EVERY
ATTEMPT TO CIVILIZE HIM, **AFTER OUR**
FORM, HAS RESULTED IN HIS SPEEDY
AND CERTAIN DESTRUCTION."

By M. S.

The unity of the human race is unscriptural—contrary to the laws of science,
and destructive to the welfare of every SPECIES of man.

New York:

RUSSELL BROS. PUBLISHERS,

28, 30 & 32 CENTRE STREET.

—

1868.

121

TO THE PUBLIC.

THE following criticism on the works of "Ariel," and its answer by Dr. Young, of Nashville, and Dr. Blackie, of Edinburgh, was written hurriedly by M. S., at the request of many of his friends, who are particularly interested in the subject at this time, when our National Congress is recklessly trying the experiment of forcing the negro into a state of social and political equality with the Adamic race—a policy so absurd and dangerous to the liberties of the white race, and so certainly destructive to the existence of the negro, that it savors more of the madman than the wise statesman. The same experiment was fairly tried in Jamaica, thirty-five years ago, by the English government, and, despite of every effort, was a perfect failure.

Most of the political evils of the last seven years are mainly attributable to the false doctrine of the "unity of the human race." Millions of lives have already paid the forfeit; and if persisted in, will exterminate the negro and Indian races in the United States.

REPLY

"ARIEL," DR. YOUNG AND DR. BLACKIE,

ON THE NEGRO.

THE following pages are intended to disprove the absurd doctrine of "Ariel," lately promulgated, trying to prove the negro to be a *beast*, and without a soul! Also, the answer to "Ariel's" work, by Drs. Young and Blackie, is noticed, with the hope that it will correct the many erroneous impressions relative to the *origin* of the negro and other inferior races.

> "From Afric she, the swain's sole serving maid,
> Whose face and form alike her birth betrayed;
> With woolly locks, lips tumid, sable skin,
> Wide bosom, udders flaccid, belly thin;
> Legs slender, broad and most misshapen feet,
> Chapped into chinks, and parched with solar heat!"

This is the description given by Virgil, the immortal Roman poet, two thousand years ago, and it will apply equally well to the negro of to-day. In Africa he has lived for thousands of years, in one of the finest countries on the globe, without a government, without law or order—a perfect savage; never has or ever will improve, except by contact with the superior race.

I will remark, *en passant*, that the above translation from the Latin language was made by the poet Cowper, who certainly did not *pervert it;* for Cowper, in England, like Wendell Phillips, of the United States, is (like Cæsar's wife)

125

above suspicion on the negro question. In either nation they were the forerunners of the abolition crusade, which has already *murdered two millions* of once happy creatures, by forcing them into a false position.

THE ADAMIC RACE OR SPECIES *

Includes the Egyptians, Medes, Persians, Jews, Assyrians, Circassians, Georgians, Chaldeans, Armenians, Arabs, Syrians, Afghans, Greeks, Romans, and the nations of all modern Europe, excepting some tribes in Turkey and Hungary.

This, the highest species of man, is characterized by a projecting forehead, flowing beard, long straight hair, erect position, oval features; and the most striking difference is his *unlimited mental development*, which, being after the image of God, makes him to *progress forever*. No other

* Race and species are used indiscriminately, to mean the same. Dr. Young, Cuvier, Bachman, and all the believers in the unity of the human race, use it in the sense of *variety*.

species of man possesses this faculty ; they all cease to advance at an earlier or later period. One other noticeable feature, the facial angle in the Adamic race, is from 80° to 95°, and decreases through all the species to the lowest type—the Kaffir and Hottentot varying from 63° to 67°. No other species shows the *emotions of the soul*—hence the ancient Egyptians, 3,000 years ago, characterized them as "*the blushing race.*"

THE MONGOLIAN.

This race was evidently created in Northern and Eastern Asia, where they are now mostly found, and not in Central Africa, as Dr. Van Evrie and others believe. They comprise the Chinese, Japanese, Siberia, Thibet, Tonquin, Siam, Cochin China, some of the castes in Hindostan, Ceylon, and enter into the Arab, Turkish, Syrian and Hungarian nations. Their color is olive yellow, eyes dark and oblique, black, straight hair—almost *no beard ;* the face is peculiarly constructed. The high cheek bones and broad flat space between the eyes gives the race a very striking and unmistakable appearance. Their eyes are almond-shaped—what some call *cat-eyed*—with a pyramidal head ; they are the highest type of the inferior races, and have some capacity ;

but all their monuments of art and literature are attributable, more or less, to the admixture of Adamic blood; they have not improved a whit for 2,000 years.

THE MALAY.

This species is found in the Pacific Isles and Indian Seas. Their color is a light brown; hair black and coarse, but heavy; broad thick nose, with thick lips and very large mouth, slanting and low forehead, and prominent jaws, and a ferocious, savage look; their character treacherous, and wholly incapable of civilization. In New Zealand they are evidently mixed with Adamic blood, and in some other islands the negro predominates.

All the efforts of the missionaries have proved utterly useless or unavailing; the moment they are left without restraint they lapse into idolatry and savageism. The application of *our* civilization to them has thus far been *death*.

THE AMERICAN INDIAN.

This race inhabits a vast extent of country, and with the exception of the Esquimaux, and perhaps the Toltecs, they have and do occupy the whole American continent, including the islands on the coasts and the West Indies. They are of a copper color, with high cheek bones, flat nose, black, straight hair, broad face, eyes dark, and no beard; the shape of the head is rather square, forehead low; large orbitar and nasal cavities, showing their great acuteness of sight and smell. They are like the Malays in their revengeful and uncompromising natures—they never forget an injury, nor have they any *feeling* (sense of humanity). The Toltecs, most probably, were hybrids between the Caucasian and Indian, from their higher mental capacity, as evidenced in Mexico and Central and South America, when first discovered by Cortez and Pizarro, and the magnificent remains of architectural grandeur now seen at Palenque and other places; yet they may have been a distinct species, which we consider most probable.

1*

THE ESQUIMAUX.

This peculiar race inhabits the Arctic regions of America, and appears to have been created there, and adapted to that climate as much as the elephant, lion, and alligator are fitted for a tropical climate. They are superior to the negro in the scale of being; but, like him, totally incapable of comprehending the abstruse sciences or our civilization, which, if forced on them, would destroy them in a few centuries. They have no government, law, or any conception of literature or science; the lowest and most simple mechanical arts are practised in forming a bow and arrow, a spear, or hut or tent of skins; they are all instinctively thieves, and resist all missionary innovations.

THE ETHIOPIANS

Are jet black, and form the highest type of the black races. They live in Central Africa, above the second cataract of the Nile, extending to its source and southward. In King Solomon's time the seat of their empire was in modern Abyssinia, though many learned travellers now assert that Ethiopia, in Africa, was not known until about 700 B. C., and that the prophet and king had reference to the Ethiop of Arabia, who was a dark-skinned Arab. The Ethiopian has a black, smooth skin, frizzled hair, thick lips, flat nose, large mouth, and is far superior in mental capacity to the Congo, Kaffir, or Hottentot. The Abyssinian who is now at war with England is a hybrid, from Arab and Ethiopian admixture. The Nubian enters into some of the tribes. The effects of remote miscegenation are observable on all the eastern coasts of Africa as far as Mozambique.

THE NEGRO

Race or races—for we have every evidence that when West and Central Africa is explored we shall find several distinct species of the negro. The anatomy and physiology of the Ethiopian, and the Congo and Guinea or Dahomy negro, is so marked, that many ethnologists have unhesitatingly classed them as distinct species.* They are the lowest type of the human race, with the exception of the Hottentot, and are, like the American Indian, utterly incapable of government, or any advancement in the arts or sciences, beyond that of any other imitative animal with equal physical endowments. All missionary labor has certainly been lost in that field; and, what is more to be deplored, the lives of thousands of good, pious Christians, who were instigated by the purest and best motives, were sacrificed; but all—all in vain.

* The Congo and Guinea negro, the Kaffir, the Hottentot, are *most surely distinct species;* but enough is not yet known to classify them separately.

THE ADAMIC RACE.

CHAPTER I.

HAVING examined the extraordinary treatise of "Ariel," on the negro race, and the answer to it by Dr. Young, of Nashville, Tenn., and Dr. Blackie, of Edinburgh, both works embodying some of the most absurd notions ever entertained by educated divines, we have taken the liberty of publishing the following as a reply thereto:

"Ariel" assumes, in the outset, that there are but *two species* of men—the white and the black—that the negro was created before Adam—and classes him with beasts, without a soul! He makes him to have issue by cohabiting with the gorilla, and yet acknowledges the fact (which no one denies) that he may have issue by intercourse with the Adamic race. This palpable absurdity cannot be reconciled, in any degree, for a moment. It is an established law that men and beasts cannot have issue. We know that the mulatto is the offspring of the white and negro—consequently, the negro is *human ;* but the mulatto is as essentially barren after the fourth generation as the mule, in consequence of his occupying a higher position in the scale of being, yet proving that the negro is of a different *species ;* otherwise their issue would live and produce offspring *indefinitely.* The mixing of the different tribes or *varieties* of the same species of the negro in the United States, from Western Africa, has improved the negro race. So the mixing of the different nations of Europe, being of the same species, has improved the white race : but when *different species* cohabit the offspring is essentially unlike either— is short-lived, feeble, and incapable of propagating their kind beyond the fourth generation. This is positive proof that the negro is not a *beast,* nor of the *same species* as the Adamic race.

Dr. Young, in his reply to "Ariel," certainly does not satisfactorily explain the mooted questions involved, but depends more upon ridicule and dogmatic assumptions than argument. He also perverts Bible history and ignores profane historical facts, and finally raises the shield of infidelity to protect himself. The Bible is proved conclusively to be true by the strongest collateral testimony ever adduced (as Hugh Miller says), the testimony of the "Book of Rocks," which records and preserves imperishably the evidences of the truth of that sacred volume.

In the 1st chap. of Genesis the creation of all things is recorded in a wonderfully brief and lucid manner. When the inspired writer comes to class the animal and vegetable kingdoms, he begins with the lowest orders and ascends through the different series, by regular gradation, to the highest and most complicated, until he reaches man, the masterpiece and last of God's creation, who was given government over all things on earth. Now, God rested from his labors on the seventh day, which of course is only emblematic, as he could not become tired as man doth, but to serve as a rule or guide for his creatures. Naturalists divide the animal creation into orders, classes, genera and species, and also varieties, as a sub-division of species, for the more readily comprehending and illustrating the subject, and also affording greater facilities in teaching this science. Man is classed by Linnæus and his followers as belonging to the order mammalia, class bimana, genus homo, and species man. This classification, to say the least of it, is very absurd. They place man in the same order with hogs, dogs, whales and dolphins, simply because they are all mammiferous! Dr. Van Evrie has given the world a very forcible illustration of this branch of the subject: it is that the animal creation is composed of innumerable creations, each rising above the other and resembling it, but absolutely distinct and independent—in fact, *a perfect world in itself.* This theory disposes of the notion advanced by the ancients, and still adhered to by many, of a connecting link or chain of creation ; for, while it is a perpetual series of gradation from the worm to man, there is no connection between those countless families or forms of being. All genera of animals and vegetables embody the elements of those *below* them, but some principle *above* or superior to them, which gives or embodies a *specific* difference ; yet the lowest as well as the highest is perfect in itself. Thus the negro, being the lowest type of man, embodies all the attributes and senses of the lower animals in a much greater degree than the white ; but in addition he possesses the faculty of speech and an immortal soul, which distinguishes him from the gorilla and monkey ; yet the positive and absolute *limit to his mental development* fixes him in a different sphere or *species* to the Adamic race, which has no *limit*, but is created *after the image of God.* These fixed and striking peculiarities are undeniable, and so apparent to the *senses* that there would seem to be no necessity to resort to any further proofs.

According to the opinion of distinguished Hebrew scholars, a part of the 24th verse of the 1st chap. of Gen. is not rendered, which has given rise to all the controversy and misunderstanding on the subject. In the original it reads, "The living creatures *with immortal souls*" (*naphesh chaiyah*)—*chaiyah* means "living creature"—but *naphesh* has not been translated, because all the translators of our version *believed in the unity of the human race*, like Dr. Young, Pritchard and others, and consequently suppressed or left out all the passages not conforming to that theory, to suit their prejudices. A full translation of that verse clearly defines the *origin* of the negro and Indian, and other inferior races of men, and at the same time gives them *souls*, but not after the *image of God.* Other passages would be made plausible, and in conformity to the laws of science and reason, if a just translation obtained. In chap. 4, verse 16, Cain married. Chap. 6, verses 2 to 6, also chap. 7, and many other texts, do not convey the meaning attributable to them.

"Ariel's" proofs are unanswerable, except his absurd classification of the negro, and his views on hybridity, which are as untenable and unscriptural as the theory of Drs. Young and Blackie, Bunsen, Bachman, Humboldt, Bascomb, Pritchard and others. It looks like presumption to differ with such a host of time-honored authorities, who have dictated to and ruled the world for ages on this theory; but I must say, with all due deference, that the great cause of all these misconceptions and diversity of opinion, arises from the prejudice of early education, and a holy fear, in many cases, of trenching on the validity of the Bible. From the cradle to the grave we have been taught the " unity of the human race "—we have almost universally accepted it without question.

Another cause of error arises from confounding *create* with *form*. God in the "beginning" created all things— lastly Adam and Eve. They certainly had no *bodies* yet. Their souls, their *immaterial identity*, was complete, because they were *after the image of God;* but their bodies were not *formed* until the progress of earth became *adapted to their existence in that different state.* This required countless millions of years; which is clearly proved both by geology and the Bible. In the 1st chap. of Gen. the inspired writer gives the order of the different creations, beginning with the lowest marine animals, which we *now find* in the Taconic system of rocks, or lower Silurian, in Montgomery County, North Carolina, where there is a stratum of conglomerate, composed entirely of *siliceous* corallines. These animals (the *palæotrochis* of Emmons) are found nearly 5,000 feet lower than any other fossil organism, either in Europe or any other country, and may justly be considered as the *dawn* of life on the globe, as its name indicates. No vegetable remains accompany them, to show whence they derived their support, being too fragile to be preserved; or, more probably, they subsisted on the decomposition of water and animalculæ.

In Ireland two species of zoophytes have been found in a fossil state in this same group, but nearly a mile higher up in the series. The one of which Mr. Murchison speaks, called "Oldhamia Antiqua," was considered in 1854 to be "the oldest inhabitant on earth," but must yield the palm to North Carolina.

This is a remarkable fact, and coincides so perfectly with the Mosaic account of the Creation that we must admit that it fully confirms it. Both here and in Europe we find the progress of animal life on the globe to be contemporaneous with vegetable, and were it not for the peculiarly fragile nature of the earliest plants created, we doubtless would find them to exist together in the same formation. Both were evidently formed in groups at different times, and introduced on the earth as its temperature and capacity for supporting life became suited to their natures and habits. We find *no vertebral animal remains* until we ascend sixty thousand feet above the *first sedimentary* strata or deposit of rocks, and nearly half that distance before we find *any signs of life at all!* And what is most striking, we find no *terrestrial plants* in the rocks until we pass nearly through this whole series— a thickness of ten miles—requiring millions of years for its deposition.

There was no necessity for *terrestrial vegetation*, nor could it have existed at that time. *No four-footed* animal remains are yet found—nor *man's.* We look in vain for any traces of either until we reach the old red sandstone formation, when we find the fossil remains of the *lower order of quadrupeds*, and contemporaneously, a luxuriant vegetation to support them—increasing in numbers and species through the carboniferous and tertiary systems, where we find immense numbers of the remains of the *highest order* of animals, and an increased profusion of vegetable remains, until we come to the last sedimentary rocks formed—the alluvial—and there we find the fossil remains of man, the last of *created* beings and the last of *formed* bodies! Here we are struck with the astounding coincidences between geology, or the "Book of Rocks," which is not liable to change or mistranslation, and the Mosaic history of the Creation. Why do we not find the remains of *men*, and *elephants*, *lions*, *tigers*, *horses*, *cattle*, &c., in the first sedimentary or lower groups of rocks, where we find the simple mollusk and zoophyte? Simply because they did not exist then in *bodily form*. They were *created* in the "beginning," but the earth then was too warm for any *lung-breathing* animal to live, for countless ages.

CHAPTER II.

WHEN Bonaparte invaded Egypt, he took with the army a corps of one hundred of the most distinguished *savans* of France, in all the sciences and arts, to give *éclat* to his campaigns and conquests. Near the pyramids they sunk a shaft in the alluvium of the Nile, to ascertain the length of time required for its deposition; its inundations being annual, would enable them to arrive at approximate conclusions, which were intended to invalidate the Mosaic account of the Creation. At something over one hundred feet they reached its bottom, which rested on *encrinal limestone*. They counted the strata or layers of detritus, which so nearly coincided with the biblical computation that many became converts to its truth. They raised a quantity of the rock and sent it to the museum in Paris, where it remained for years unnoticed until *geology became a science*, and some of its votaries revealed the fact that the formation whence it came was thousands of feet thick and filled with millions of *fossil remains*, which represented animal species now extinct and comparatively of recent date! But when the subject was examined by numbers of scientific geologists, in widely different countries, they arrived at the conclusion that the Bible account of the Creation was true, and that the era of man's advent on the earth in *bodily form*, to propagate their kind or species, and "multiply and replenish the earth," was not more ancient than about the time computed by the sacred writer—but not confined to the limit of Bishop Usher.

Some divines yet think there is no necessity for an indefinite time of great length for the formation of all the sedimentary strata; that they could have been formed by the Almighty in six days of our time. We grant that God could have formed all the rocks, with the fossils in them, in six days, or *six seconds;* but He never works miracles when His laws operate to produce the same effect. We contend, and solemnly believe, there is no need of a longer time than that given in the Bible to *create* all things. But the *forming* of the rocks by deposition in strata, in the bed of the sea (for the marine fossils prove it), from the metamorphic (which itself must have required an immense length of time, and during which no animal or vegetable could have lived, by reason of the earth's high temperature,) through the vast series of formations to the present time, making a thickness, exclusive of the metamorphic, of nearly eleven miles! Such a vast deposition, enclosing organic remains, must have required an immeasurable period; and when elevated by volcanic force at different times, formed those vast ranges of mountains, and plains and valleys, which now constitute our habitable world. The *tilted* or highly inclined position of the strata proves volcanic force, and the organic remains prove two-thirds of the land in the world to have once been the bed of the sea. All these facts go to prove that God *created* everything in six days, "in the beginning;" and the organic remains in the different *aged rocks* correspond with the Mosaic history, when their bodies *were formed* and placed upon the earth, or in the seas, at a time suited to their natures and habits. The distinguished Agassiz satisfactorily proves that all animals were destroyed on the earth at four different epochs; that they and vegetables were introduced in groups which were destroyed by each cataclysm, and that we are now fulfilling our destiny and biding our time when the prediction will be fulfilled, when the last trump shall sound the termination of the present epoch, and man and all other animate matter be destroyed.

The sedimentary deposits since the historic period (say 2,000 years), in Italy and other countries, in lakes, gulfs and estuaries, have not shoaled more than 600 feet, and in no instance extended outward more than 20 or 30 miles ; how long would it require, at that rate, to have formed 60,000 feet thick over an area of *fifty millions* of square miles? I admit decomposition and consequent deposition to have been much more rapid in the earlier ages of the world ; but no reasoning, except the old Italian *Romish* plea, that God could create these fossil impressions in rocks by the *plastic power of Nature*, without resorting to animal life, can satisfy us that it was done in *six days*. "Ariel" says the Bible is true ; and we say so too—geology proves it beyond a doubt.

Where we find man's remains we find also that vegetation had attained its full perfection for his support. Each group was introduced at the proper time, and everything which God *created* in " the beginning," having received *bodies* by and through which to propagate their kind and fulfill their destiny, then and not till then was the *Garden of Eden planted.* Adam and Eve's bodies having been *formed*, one from the dust of the earth and the other from human flesh, it only remained for them to obey the commands of God by propagating their species or kinds, as related in the 2d chap. of Genesis, and not as Gov. Perry says, *created them*, and the negro created in the 26th and 27th verses of 1st chap. ; which construction or interpretation would not only give the negro a soul *after the image of God*, but leave us all *without souls !* This is a more absurd doctrine than that of Em. Swedenborg, who was so much infatuated on the negro that he lost his reason. In one of his works he says : "As I was travelling along through heaven, one day, I came to the throne of God, and in the vast multitude I found the negroes occupied the *inner circle !* the Dutch, English, and other nations next in their order, and last were the Russians, who occupied the north part of heaven ! (I quote from memory.) In my travels I came to a stone church, in a kind of valley or basin, and while looking at the various worshippers arriving (the snow being about eighteen inches deep), I saw a friend and his family come up in a sledge or sleigh, drawn by four bob-tailed ponies !" The Baron was so perfectly engrossed in the subject, and so much loved the negro, that he became a monomaniac, and gave him a *heavenly position next to God.* Stevens and his confrères are determined to force them into an *earthly position above the white race,* but refuse to grant them the *inner circle* in heaven!

In the 2d chap., 5th verse : "There was *not a man* to till the ground ;" though in the 26th and 27th verses, 1st chap., Adam and Eve were both *created,* but had no bodies yet. In verse 7 he says : "And God *formed* man of the dust of the ground and breathed into his nostrils the breath of life; and man became a living soul !" Verse 8 : "And planted a garden eastward, in Eden, and there he put the *man* whom he had *formed.*"

Adam's body having received the soul which was created in the "beginning," had now an abiding place, a tabernacle in which to develop itself for good or evil, and to *multiply and replenish* the earth. Eve, who was created at the same time as Adam (ver. 26, 27), *had no body yet,* and of course they could not fulfil the commands of their Creator to *multiply and replenish the earth.* Adam went on attending his duties, by classing and naming all the animals and plants, after their kind, from the majestic cedar and palm to the "hyssop on the wall," and from the simple coralline to the noble lion, horse, and majestic mastodon—but Adam did not name himself. God called *their* name "adam" (man.) Adam had no helpmate yet, though they were *named alike, and created at the same time.* Verse 19: God formed the bodies of all animals and brought them to Adam to name

CHAPTER III.

VERSE 21: "God now formed a body for Eve from Adam's," not from the ground, but from one of his ribs, to show her dependence upon him physically, for mentally they were created *equal.* Now the creation and forming of all living beings, and all inanimate matter, being accomplished, and names given to all things, Adam and Eve took formal possession of the Garden of Eden, and began to fulfil their destinies; (the Garden of Eden evidently is metaphorical, being the earth.) "The Book of Rocks," which cannot be misconstrued, proves that all other animals were formed and put upon the earth at *different times* or epochs, as the earth's temperature became adapted to their natures. This is established by the most extensive geological developments, beyond a doubt, and coincides with the Mosaic account in every particular. Thousands of species of animals and plants lived on the earth when its temperature was so high that man could not have existed on it for an hour. They fulfilled their destiny and passed away; for they could no more live here now than we could have lived there then.

Many divines argue that this theory of internal heat is not predicated on facts, but mere assumption. In answer to this, every miner in Europe and America can testify that the temperature increases as you descend into the earth, *one degree* in about every fifty feet, which in the deepest mines is almost insupportable; the water that flows from the deep artesian wells in Charleston and in France becomes as warm as blood, and confirms the above facts. If the change was from the *sun* the temperature would *decrease* as you descend into the earth from the surface.

The assertion, also, that the earth would soon become uninhabited from cold, is disproved by numerous observations and comparisons, by scientific men, on volcanic lava, in vast masses for a series of years, from which they conclude that it would require, in all probability, millions of years for the earth's crust to cool off sufficiently to affect animals or vegetables, so as to destroy them—that it would take at *least two hundred thousand years* to lower the temperature one degree! So that it would require an immense period to make the change sufficient to cause the extinction of any group of animals or plants. Several species of both have become extinct recently (within the last two hundred years), the dodo and Madeira grape among the number. In a few more ages the buffalo will pass away.

"Ariel," as before observed, makes but two species of men (the white and negro), and yet he classes the negro with beasts, and without a soul! How he can be a beast and a human being is incomprehensible. To prove it, he says the gorilla (in Africa) frequently carries off negro women and girls into the wilderness and makes wives of them —having offspring! We have already shown this to be impossible. The sexual intercourse between human beings and beasts is without issue; but we know that the same between the Caucasian species and negro produces the *mulatto*, proving the negro to be *human*. But as the mulatto is as essentially barren as the *mule* after the fourth generation, it proves as conclusively that the negro is of a *differ-*

ent species. It is a fixed law of God that beings of different genera or families, cohabiting or mixing, will not propagate; and it is equally true that the offspring of different *species* are barren—in animals after the first, and in the human species after the fourth generation. On this subject Dr. Young advances the same absurd argument which has obtained for *three hundred* years on hybridity. He says: "The issue of the horse and the ass does not breed, but the white and negro does, consequently the white and negro are of the *same species.*" This is a *perverted* meaning of the laws of *hybridity,* and is *false* in point of fact, for the negro being of the human race, and of a higher order of being, does not come under the same laws that govern animals only in degree, for the mulatto is as perfectly and absolutely barren and incapable of propagating his kind, after the fourth generation, as the *mule;* and during that descending period he becomes more and more feeble, and soon *dies out.* The Dr.'s quotation, endorsed by Bachman, of the mulatto population of Mexico, the United States, and the Spanish American Republics, to show them to be prolific and as long lived as the white race, is very unfortunate, to say the least of it; for there is hardly a school boy who does not know that Mexico and the Spanish American (so-called) Republics have been in a perfect state of anarchy for the last fifty years, by reason of the amalgation of the races. They have no capacity for government whatever; and when one is made for them, as in Jamaica and Liberia, they utterly fail to continue it for any length of time. His statement of the longevity of the mulatto is shown, by the statistics of those countries and the United States, to be untrue. The City of Mexico, with a population of over 200,000 under Spanish rule, has dwindled down, under mongrel admixture, to less than half, and all other cities and towns in the same ratio. We might go on to adduce proofs to fill a volume. They do not increase in numbers, only by immigration. They are feeble, imbecile and short-lived, and soon *die or rot out,* as Van Evrie very justly remarks.

Sexual intercourse between the *same species*, but different "varieties" of the same family, improves the race, as shown in the United States—the negroes are far superior to the tribes in Africa whence they were taken. So, also, the admixture of the different German, Saxon, Danish and French nations with the Scots, Irish, Britons and Anglés, produced the much superior Anglo-Saxon, who now rules the world, and whose issue will continue to live and propa· gate their kind indefinitely. But the offspring from the intercourse of *different species*, as the white and negro, or Indian, *is feeble and short lived*, and *cannot propagate its kind* after the fourth generation; they are inferior to either *physically*, but *mentally* superior to the lowest cohabiting type. This is so distinctive and marked a characteristic, that no other evidence ought to be required to prove the negro a different *species* from Adam. That the mulatto is imbecile and soon *runs out* is so well established, both by British and American statistics, that I am surprised to hear such men as Drs. Young and Blackie deny it. All physiologists and physicians are acquainted with the fact that un-bridled, licentious, and indiscriminate sexual intercourse be-tween the Caucasian or Adamic species, produces the common disease known through all ages as gonorrhœa—a disease which is not fatal; but the same indiscriminate intercourse between the white and negro, or Indian, is known to generate *syphilis*, one of the most loathsome and distructive diseases known to man, and which is said to have carried off millions of Indians within half a century after the discovery of America by Columbus, and over *one million* of negroes by the army in our last civil war. The number of negresses who perished from their unbridled licentiousness was frightful.

This is certainly another very characteristic difference be-tween the negro, Indian and white, and *stamps* them as *different species*. God's laws are immutable and will not lie. "Ariel's" theory, therefore, that negroes are beasts, falls to the ground; and the same reasoning proves Drs.

2

Young and Blackie's to be utterly untenable—for, keep it in mind that there is not, and never was, or ever will be " *such a monstrosity* " *as a single species.*

CHAPTER IV.

"ARIEL'S" proofs that Ham was not the progenitor of the negro are not only strong, but incapable of successful contradiction. He also proves that Ham was *never* cursed, but Canaan—and even he was not cursed until after he had had his second son, Heth, both by a legitimate wife. Then he doubtless sinned (like some of our friends in Congress) by taking to his arms a negro, contrary to the express laws of God, who, before the flood, cursed the earth and destroyed all its inhabitants except a favored few, who had kept themselves *pure* and *holy in their generation ;* all the balance were destroyed for the accursed sin of *amalgamation,* or, in modern parlance, *miscegenation.* For this sin and idolatry it grieved God (so to speak) that he had made man—(meaning the inferior races)—"for his thoughts were evil continually."

That Ham's descendants settled Egypt no Hebrew scholar will deny ; and that they were of the Adamic race is equally well established ; but we do not pretend to say that there were no other people in that region when Misraim first made his advent ; for there is every evidence that the whole Nilotic valley was peopled. The Bible says Misraim gave his name to the country ; and we know from history that his descendants built Thebes, Memphis, and other magnificent cities—the pyramids, sphynx, and the catacombs and labyrinths, &c., which characterized them as having been far advanced in the arts and sciences. Thebes was so named to commemorate the ark.

Ham's children also settled part of India and Arabia; and his grandsons, Heth and Sidon, settled the Eastern coasts of the Mediterranean Sea, and built those memorable cities which formed the centres of commerce for ages, and finally gave rise to Carthage, whose prowess and wealth had well nigh crushed the Roman Empire in its embryo state. The name of Egypt, in the Coptic and Arabic languages, is *Mezr;* in Greek it is called *Aiguptos;* in Latin *Ægyptus*—sometimes called the land of Chimi, (the land of Ham.) Psalms, v. 23.

The Copts now in Egypt are hybrids from Mongol and Caucasian admixture. The Egyptians have not ruled their country since the battle of Actium, when Augustus Cæsar made it a Roman province. Since that century it has been governed by the Turks, who as a nation are much degenerated by miscegenating with Circassians, Georgians, Persians and Arabs; but the greatest curse on the Turk is his amalgamation with the Ethiopian, Nubian and Copt, which will soon reduce the nation to the point of extinction.

Egypt gives us the oldest relics of ancient art, which run back 3,500 years before Christ; and on the oldest monuments the black negro, the olive Mongol, and the Adamic race are sculptured and painted as perfect in type as if done yesterday ! Who can doubt the difference in the species of man when over 5,000 years exhibit him as unchangeable ?

The Hon. J. Brooks recently, in a speech delivered in Congress, said of the negro, " that *four thousand years ago* he was exactly what he is now, and what he ever will be, save as he comes in contact with the civilization of the superior race," as was the case with the slaves brought from Africa to the Southern States of America. In 200 years they were raised from savage cannibalism to an advanced scale of intelligence and moral perceptions equal to their full mental capacity—constituting them "the happiest *four millions* of negroes on the globe." But their status is now changed, and in *fifty* years they will sink into the same state of barbarism the Jamaica negroes have reached in thirty-five years, with all the fostering care of the British government, aided by a full corps of missionaries, who have labored in vain to keep them from idol worship. At this time more than half of them, either publicly or secretly, worship *snakes* or other objects equally disgusting. But to return to Mr. Brooks—he says, " The Egyptians, whose genius created the pyramids, the sphynx, the obelisk; the Carthaginians, whose soldiers under Hannibal surmounted the then horrid Alps, rolled over the Campagna of Rome and the plains of Capua; the Roman, whose arms and whose arts embraced the whole world—all have brought their civilization and their arts *before the negro race*, but all, all in vain. The church and holy foundations in Carthage, in Cyrene, in Alexandria, throughout all Egypt, and far, far up the Nile, and ascetics from Upper Egypt, clothed in the wild raiment of the Baptist, wandered forth clothed in sheep skins and goat skins, and dwelt in deserts and on mountains, in dens and in caves, to *bring the negro to Christ*, but all in vain. Pagan, savage and cannibal—even the negro in his own native home for thousands of years has *defied all civilization*, all christianity, and is only improved when in close individual contact with the superior race. It is then the negro is improved or improvable. He clings to his *gris-gris-jujus-fetishism* with as much pertinacity as he did one hundred years ago. But a wonderful imitative genius is that of the negro; it displays itself surprisingly in music and culinary arts, when associated with the white man. The negro, through his faculty of imitation, becomes in many occupations almost equal to the white man; but when left to himself—to his own guidance—as in Hayti and Jamaica, or in Africa, he returns to his barbaric tastes and serpent worship." Notwithstanding all the attempts to Christianize them in Liberia and Sierra Leone, they are worse than they were twenty years ago. It is only by the continued immigration of the more intelligent negroes of the United States, in immense numbers, that Liberia is kept from anarchy and the most revolting barbarism.

I am credibly informed that it is a very common occurrence for parties to raid into the surrounding savage tribes, within one hundred miles, and steal boys and girls, and *sell them into slavery* in their own colony, which is winked at by the officials in consequence of an *honest bribe.* Take away all Caucasian influence and stop immigration, and in fifty years Liberia will be side by side with *Dahomy and Congo*—the mass of them cannibals and snake worshippers!

That Ham's children settled Egypt no one doubts (though many affect to believe they were negroes; and Canaan's, also, were all believed to be black, in consequence of the curse). His descendants settled Tyre and Sidon. But "Ariel's" proofs are too strong to resist; all history, the unveiling of millions of mummies, and the sculptures on the temples and sarcophagii, prove the identity of the race *then* to be as distinct as *now*, and that *the ruling race was white*, and the descendants of Ham.

The miscegenation of Shem's descendants with Mongols, no doubt, gave rise to the Bedouin Arabs. and Turko-Syrian hybrids—and the same between the Arab, Turk and Ethiopian, produced the Abyssinian of the present day. The two sons of Canaan (Heth and Sidon) settled the east coast of the Mediterranean Sea, and built the cities of Tyre and Sidon, from whence King Solomon obtained much of his material for the temple, and *more* of mechanical skill and science from *Hiram Abiff.* But that they were negroes, as Dr. Young, Dr. Blackie, Bascomb, Pritchard, Humboldt and others believe, is simply absurd, untenable, *unscriptural* and *false.*

Carthage was a colony from Tyre, and "Ariel" gives an elegant extract from history, of undoubted authenticity: " That, after the battle of Zama, Carthage was invested by the Roman fleets and armies so closely that the inhabitants were reduced to the point of starvation. To obtain supplies of provisions they built ships to run the blockade, and when done, they could find no material from which to make the ropes to rig the vessels. In this emergency the noble and and patriotic ladies cut off their *fine flowing locks of hair* and brought them to the rope makers—the ropes were made, the ships were rigged, the provisions were obtained and the famishing people fed!" "Ariel" asks, "what kind of ropes do you suppose the negro's *kinky wool* would have made ?" In the name of reason and common sense, cease to profane God's name by teaching such contemptible perversions of Bible and profane historical truths, and admit that the Carthaginians were of the Adamic race, and *Hiram Abiff* belonged to the highest type of man.

Was Cleopatra a negress? The refined, delicate, beautiful and facinating Queen of Egypt a black negress ! If so, is it not passing strange and unnatural that she should have captivated and held in thrall the noble, literary, and *epicurean* Mark Antony—a descendant of Japheth? Impossible! Were all the great, the rich and noble of Egypt, negroes ? The millions of mummies lately exhumed and exposed to view " give the lie to the base slander."

Some of these mummies I have seen myself, and can testify to the truth of "Ariel's" personal observation of the cases related by him in proof of it. They were from three to four thousand years old, with fine, long, straight hair, with hands and feet of as delicate a mould as any son or daughter of Adam ; and further, a nose (as Sterne says) that would have done honor to a king; all these attributes, with every other appendage to fill up the most perfect configuration of a Caucasian body. Were they negroes? No sane man or woman, who has examined the subject *without prejudice*, believes it—no, not one.

"Ariel" also gives a very beautiful and interesting description of one of these mummies, which he assisted in unrolling or divesting of its preservative envelope. It was enclosed in a marble sarcophagus or coffin, and buried six miles east of Cairo, in Egypt. She was a daughter of the high priest of On, and an attendant on the princesses of the court of King Thotmes the 3d, who is acknowledged to be the Pharaoh who governed Egypt when Moses and Aaron brought the children of Israel from thence to the land of

Canaan. The bodies of the mummies are closely rolled or enveloped in thirty or forty folds of waxed cloth, which is otherwise chemically prepared, by the addition of creosote and carbolic acid, so as to make it not only impervious to to moisture but indestructible and incorruptible. The inner folds, he says, were made of *linen cambric,* which proved her high social position and nobility. When this was removed her hair looked as fresh and glossy as when alive ! *and from one to one and a half yards long, and very fine and straight !* Like the Carthaginians, there is no sign of the negro here in the catacombs of Egypt. " She had her face, neck and bosom, hands and feet, gilded ; her feet and hands were as delicate and small as a Broadway belle of to-day, and a perfect face and bust, that showed her Adamic origin. She had lain there *three thousand three hundred and thirty-eight years !"*

Out of the millions of mummies which have been exhumed in Egypt not a *half dozen* were *negroes ;* and they were embalmed for a specific purpose, to show kingly authority ; the date and reason for embalming them was, in every case, given on the sarcophagus. No one could be embalmed except the *ruling race* (only by especial permission) and persons of wealth and position. The very wealthy were buried in marble or granite sarcophagii, but those of ordinary means, yet what we would call wealthy, were encased in wooden coffins, with a raised lid to show the profile of the deceased, colored to life. The Egyptians were acquainted with only four colors—red, blue, green and yellow, with a mixture for a purple—they knew nothing of perspective or blending of colors for light and shade, which the Greeks invented in the days of Praxiteles, but the Egyptians surpassed all others in the *permanence* of their colors— whilst ours fade in less than a century (so of the Greek and Roman) the Egyptian is as fresh, as pure, and as unchangeable as the granite and porphyry sculptures in her temples to-day. The wooden sarcophagii were prepared by a chemical process similar to the *Robbins process* (of late invention), by expelling the moisture from the pores of the wood and then filling it with creosote and carbolic acid at a high temperature, so as to render it indestructible. We have seen them nearly 4,000 years old, and as sound as if made yesterday.

CHAPTER V.

DR. YOUNG'S labored argument to prove that "*nachash*" meant serpent in Hebrew, *ophis* in Greek, and *serpens* in Latin, is *literally* true, but certainly not applicable. It is like his quotation to prove "*Simon*" (the Canaanite) and the "*Ethiopian*" eunuch to be negroes! The Bible does not say they were negroes. Simon *was* a descendant of Canaan; but Sidon and Heth were *perfect in their generation before Canaan was cursed*. We have no Bible account of what the nature of that curse was. It could not have been for the crime of witnessing the nakedness of his grandfather (for he was not there), and we have conclusively shown that Ham, who was the offender, is not the progenitor of the negro, because all the relics of his descendants are proved positively to be of Adamic origin; but it most probably was in consequence of an express violation of the law of God in regard to keeping his *genealogy pure*, which he did not do. After the birth of Heth, his second son, we find his descendants under the curse of God everywhere. The Israelites were ordered to exterminate them, men, women and children! The order was so positive, that the Jews were severely punished for showing mercy in some instances, during the awful and indiscriminate slaughter of the doomed inhabitants.

But "Simon" was a Canaanite and a descendant of Sidon and Heth, who were of pure Adamic blood. The other children of Canaan were doubtless *mulattoes*. His sin was one of the greatest in the whole catalogue; one which brought on the destruction of all things by the flood;

and now, being perpetrated so soon after that awful and terrible chastisement, caused God to issue so seemingly barbarous an order to slay the innocent with the guilty. Yet it was done, and done to prevent temptation to evil, and to keep the race free from an unnatural admixture, which would destroy the Jewish nation and render the fulfilment of the prophecies relative to the Redeemer impossible. God is love. He is most merciful, and ever ready to bless and to save ; but beware how you transgress his commands, and *know* that some of his laws *cannot* be transgressed with impunity. Yea, there are acts which are *unpardonable*, and *miscegenation* is one of them. But to return to Dr. Young. He says the "Ethiopian" eunuch was a negro. We say that Ethiopian is here used as a *generic* term, and does not necessarily mean a negro or black man. In King Solomon's time Ethiopia was a kingdom in Arabia, and not peopled then, nor at any other time, by negroes, *but* by Arabs of the Adamic race. The Queen of Sheba was from an adjoining province. The Ethiopians of Africa are jet black, and live on the Upper Nile above the second cataract, and were never known in history until after King Solomon's time, in the year 700 B. C. Neither did the inhabitants of that day know anything of the Mongol, Malay, American Indian or Esquimaux. But if the apostle did have reference to the African Ethiopian of Solomon's time when it was a kingdom, one thousand years later, in the apostle's time, it was a conquered province, governed by Queen Candace, whose subjects were negroes, and Arabs, and Syrians. Amalgamation has nearly exterminated the Ethiopian ; long since they have lost every vestige of nationality, though a far superior race to the Guinea, Congo, Kaffre or Hottentot negro. Their jet black glossy skins, smaller feet and hands, better shaped noses, and greater mental capacity, characterize them as a distinct race. In that day we have shown that the ruling race was not the negro ; but the eunuch doubtless was an Ethiopian which "Simon" baptized, though not a negro. Dr. Young

2*

is a Tennessean; so are 270,000 negroes Tennesseans. In Georgia there are 700,000 whites and 500,000 negroes; the Reconstruction Acts of Congress have made them all Georgians!

But to return to the *serpent*. Why our common snake should be classed as the most *subtle* of all the animal creation I am at a loss to divine; nor is theré a single particle of Scripture or scientific proof to show it to be the fact, but far otherwise. The elephant, the horse, the dog, the ant, and many other animals, are far superior in instinct and intelligence or subtlety to the serpent. The impression had been made upon our infantile brain, and sticks to us, like Nessus' shirt or coat,* with a tenacity that is astonishing. In fact, half the human race lives and dies powerless to throw off the terrible, loathsome, and destructive incubus.

"The serpent was more *subtle* than any *beast* of the field which the Lord God had made." Gen., 3d chap., 1st verse. Of course, it was *not a beast* (or snake) of the field.

Adam Clarke, who certainly understood *more* languages than any of Dr. Young's authorities, says that the creature that tempted Eve was in the *form of man, and had reason and the faculty of speech!* (He thought, possibly, an orang outang or gorilla, from his prejudice of early education.) For if God did work a miracle in that case, and endow the

---

* For the benefit of such of my readers as are unacquainted with ancient mythology, I will insert the history of this inferior deity. He was a centaur (half horse and half man), who committed a shameful outrage upon Deianira, whom the demi-god Hercules had entrusted to his care. Hercules shot him with an arrow; and when Nessus was dying he gave Deianira his bloody shirt or coat, and told her if her husband wore it he would be true to her, and never more follow unlawful practices. She soon learned to her cost the virtue of it very differently from what she expected. Hercules fell in love with the Queen of Lydia and also the daughter of the King of Oechalia. His wife, in her love for and great anxiety to reclaim him and turn him from his infidelity, sent him Nessus' shirt to put on when he went to make his annual sacrifice to Jupiter—which drove him into such distraction that he raved and tried to tear it off, but it stuck so closely all his strength was unavailing, and in his distraction he threw himself upon the sacrificial pile and burned himself to ashes!

monkey with speech, he had as well endow the serpent. In the 12th chap. 9th verse of Rev., and 20th chap. 2d verse the sacred historian says, "That old serpent, called the devil and satan, which deceiveth the whole world." The writer evidently had no reference to a snake, but the *evil principle* which instigated the act. This satanic principle entered into the heart of one of the highest types of the inferior and subordinate species of the human race, who possessed the *faculty of speech* without the interposition of a miracle—most likely a Mongol of intelligence and pleasing appearance, who could converse with Eve without exciting wonder and affright, and thus seduced her to commit a transgression of the laws of God. It is not at all probable that it was the negro, the lowest and most repulsive type of man, that became the instrument in tempting Eve, as Dr. Cartwright and "Ariel" believe; yet it is certain that it was one of an inferior race, just as that same *evil principle* (the devil) now enters the hearts of mankind and prompts them to sin against God by transgressing His laws. That is the "*nachash*" that tempted Eve, and no *material identity*, but has been represented in the form of a serpent, the same as the "*sun*" was used to represent life by the Chaldeans, and worshipped as an attribute or symbol of God, and not as actually God; but in course of time the ignorant worshipped the sun, the same as the Egyptians the ox and other animals, as gods.

Dr. Young perverts the meaning of terms to suit his prejudices, just as the translators of our copy of the Bible did when they left out or suppressed the word "naphesh," in the account of the Creation, and many words and sentences explanatory of the *origin* and existence of different species, because they believed all men, of all nations, came from Adam; and as the apostle says, as quoted by Bishop Pierce, Acts, 17 chap. 26 verse, "And hath made of one blood all nations of men, for to dwell on all the face of the earth, and hath determined the times before appointed and the bounds of their habitation." In Mark, 16 chap. 15 verse, Christ

commands his apostles to go and preach the gospel to every
creature of all nations. In compliance with what they conceived to be their duty, and in accordance with their belief,
they have, from the apostolic period to the present day,
preached the gospel to many of the nations of Asia, from
China to the Pacific isles, and Hindostan, and Arabia, and
Abyssinia, and Egypt, and Guinea, and Congo, and Dahomy,
and Madagascar, and to the Bushmen and Hottentots; and
if they have ever made one of them comprehend the nature
of the gospel, we have yet to learn it. As a matter of
respect, and for some fancied advantage, they will affect to
believe anything you wish them ; but it is utterly impossible for their very finite minds to comprehend it. The efforts
of the missionaries of Europe and America, with the best
intentions, and the expenditure of millions of money, in
teaching the Hindoos the religion of Christ for more than a
century, were rendered abortive by the Punjaub war—when
the Sepoys, thinking their independence of the British
power was beyond a doubt, without a single exception, returned to their idol worship ! The same thing occurred in
Egypt, on the upper Nile, in Arabia, and nearer home, in
St. Domingo and Jamaica, where the Roman Catholics, with
their commendable zeal, and other (Protestant) denominations have expended millions of money and thousands of
lives to Christianize the negroes, and their labors have been
all in vain, for it is now an established fact that more than
half of them openly worship snakes and idols ! Look at
the Sandwich Islanders—when we were young there were
four hundred thousand of them, and, believing then in " the
unity of the human race," we contributed to evangelize and
civilize them, when lo ! after every effort was made in the
power of money and religious labor, it proved a most signal
failure—our labors and means only *murdered them*. From
four hundred thousand once happy beings there are now but
forty thousand ! We have adopted the wrong means to the
end in view ; we can never succeed by forcing the inferior
races into a false position ; it is in opposition to the laws

of God, and has destroyed millions of Indians and negroes, and will, if persisted in, destroy the whole of each of those races; whereas, if we would try a policy adapted to their limited capacity, they would increase in numbers and happily *fulfil their destiny.* The command of God to the apostles to preach the gospel to all nations and people, has no reference to the inferior races, for they never did and never will comprehend it, and, as the apostle says, "Are a law unto themselves," and will live in heaven or hell as they live a correct moral life or a sinful one here, and worship and serve the God that made them, and do his will as far as they can comprehend it; and we, as the superior species, *created after the image of God,* are commanded to govern and protect the inferior creations, and lead them in the line of life that is best suited to their happiness and well being, both here and hereafter. In all ages they have looked up to us as their superiors, and ever will.

Chapter 7, "And Noah and his family and the *living creatures* (with immortal souls) entered into the ark," &c., chap. 6, verse 2, and chap. 4, verses 15 and 16, and many others might be adduced to prove that the "living creatures with *immortal souls*" were created before Adam and Eve, and their bodies *placed on* the earth when its temperature became adapted to their habits, and that the highest type of them tempted Eve. The meaning of the sacred historian had about as much reference to a *snake* as an ass. It was the *principle of evil* (that old serpent, the *devil,*) which is here typified or characterized by *nachash.*

––––

CHAPTER VI.

THE distinguishing characteristics of the Adamic race are the color, flowing beard, facial angle, larger brain, and the most confirmatory is *unlimited mental development.* "Ariel," as before stated, makes but *two* species of men (the white and negro)—Dr. Cartwright makes but *two*—some others make *six:* the Caucasian, the Mongol, the Malay, the Esquimaux, the American Indian, and negro. We would add the Ethiopian, and make *seven,* for he is as distinct from the Congo and Guinea negro as from the Indian.*

The sculptures on the temples of Egypt exhibited the Caucasian, the Mongol and the negro as perfectly, *four thousand years ago,* as they are to day ! We agree with Dr. Cartwright, who says philosophers and divines have been contending and waiting for four thousand years for the negro's skin to turn white, and yet they wait in vain—still it remains the same; though Dr. Blackie gives an instance of a *few cases, called spotted negroes,* who are slowly changing ! We think, if they have resisted the effects of climate so long the case is rather hopeless. They never will be white, or *equal in mental capacity,* if they wait *forty thousand years.* They have lived in Canada and New England (where there is no disposition to amalgamate, as with the Spanish and Portuguese people,) over *two hundred* years, without a single shade of difference in their color or anatomical configuration, or mental capacity. They are nothing more nor less than *negroes.* Champolion, Rawlinson and others, prove positively, and to the satisfaction of any man

* Great diversity obtains in classifying the races, by different authors. Buffon divides the human race into 6 *varieties*—Polar, Tartar, Australasiatic, European, negro, and American Indian. Kant divides them into 4—white, black, copper, and olive. Hunter into 7—Metzan into 2, white and black. Viney into 3. Blumenbach into 5—Caucasian, Mongol, Malay, negro and American Indian. Desmoulins into 16 species. Barey De St. Vincent into 15, sub-divided into races. The celebrated Dr. Morton classes mankind into 22 families ; Pickering into 11 ; Jacquinot, *3 species*—Caucasian, Mongol and negro. He places the German, Celtic, Semitic and Hindoo in the Caucasian species—Chinese and American Indian together ! How arbitrary'. In Genesis the negro and all inferior races are omitted by the sacred writer, as they were always slaves in that day *where known ;* but the negro was certainly not known to the Jews until at least 700 years B. C., nor to the Greeks until a later period. There can be no question but that there are 6 distinct *species* of the negro and 2 of the Malay, one of the Mongol, 2 of the American Indian, 1 of the Esquimaux and 1 Adamic, making 12 species instead of *seven ;* but ethnologists have not as yet received sufficient facts from Australasia and interior and Southern Africa to change the classification.

or woman of unbiased mind, that the negro has not changed a whit for *four thousand years.* If so, his status and creation are established.

We would again notice the assertion of Drs. Blackie and Young that, all opportunities being equal, the capacity of the negro is equal to the white. This we positively deny. While young, they acquire a knowledge of the lower branches with some facility, but are totally and altogether incapable of mastering the abstruse sciences, the report of General Pope and his corps of school-teachers to the contrary notwithstanding. What have the Jamaica negroes done— with a rich island, fine climate, a good government furnished them by English statesmen, of undoubted ability and love for the negro—also, *fenced farms,* tools, teachers, physicians, and missionaries from every Christian church, to instruct and perfect them—national aid, in money and exemption from taxes, and every protection from fraud—endowed schools—with endless other assistance for forty-two years, and what is the result? They have decreased a *hundred thousand in number*—half of the remaining ones *worship snakes !* Their productions have fallen off more than one-half, and their farms have grown up into a wilderness, and they have become as barbarous as their African ancestors; to sum the final issue, the English government has been compelled to garrison the island with troops, and has recently taken the civil government into its own hands, to prevent complete anarchy and extermination. This is a sad commentary on negro government; and the result of a fair, full, and one-sided experiment, without any opposing obstacles in the way, upon nearly half a million of negroes, above the average scale of Africans, where soil, climate, and every other help was afforded; and above all, they were isolated from all interference from without, and yet they have relapsed, in forty-two years, into the most disgusting barbarism or fetishism ! Why is it that fanaticism will continue to conceal the true status of the negro in Jamaica, St. Domingo, Trinidad, Guiana, Liberia and Sierra Leone?

Simply because fanaticism is the child of hell! All attempts have failed to improve the negro, only by close contact with the white race; St. Domingo has been much longer under the *blessing* of a negro government, with infinitely worse results! Why? Because in Jamaica they were 'somewhat kept from downright anarchy by force—in the former they had everything their own way. Liberia would be as bad to-day, were it not for the immense number of educated negroes from the United States who emigrate there, and keep in check the tendency to original barbarism; this is so, notwithstanding the opinions and reports of interested or misled travellers. The same attempt is now being made by the United States Congress, composed of men with *less* statesmanship and *more* moral turpitude, to *mongrelize* the Southern States, and destroy four millions of negroes and as many whites.

All the monuments of antiquity are the work of the Adamic race. The Malay, Esquimaux, the American Indian, and the several species of the negro, have been a perfect blank in the world as to government, science and the arts. The Mongol or Chinese, with their varieties, have and do maintain a government (which they did not, however, originate); they have made some little advance in the arts, but most of their inventions are attributable to Shem's descendants, who penetrated into that region, and after holding most of it for ages, were either expelled or swallowed up in the *vortex of amalgamation*, like the Spanish in Mexico and the South American republics. The Toltecs and Peruvians were hybrids from the same foul sin, by intercourse between the Caucasian and Indian, at some remote period, of which we have no record or history left, except those magnificent relics of architecture found in the ruins of those ancient cities. These extensive ruins indicate the existence of a race coeval with the Egyptians, who built the pyramids, the sphynx, and the vast cities whose splendid temples, labyrinths, and crumbling columns now invest the river Nile with so much interest. The Toltecs being a higher order of hybrids than the *Mulatto*, were enabled, like the Chinese, to maintain a government, but lost most of the arts.

The Chinese being the highest grade of the inferior races, not only have the ability to continue a government, but to preserve order and cherish the arts; but they have a limit to their mental capacity so marked, that they have not advanced one iota for two thousand years! All the inferior species of the *genus homo* have a limit to their mental capacity except the Adamic, who were created after the image of God, and consequently are progressive to all eternity. What a glorious reflection! And what a transcendently glorious destiny for all who obey the commands of so great and good a God! Dr. Young and all his friends may preach the doctrine of negro equality till doomsday, and but few men and fewer women will believe it. The assertion that the doctrine is infidel is a poor argument, or rather subterfuge; the same was used by the Romish priests in Italy against Gallileo, because he said the earth revolved on its axis to produce day and night, when the Bible plainly and positively taught that "the sun riseth in the east and goeth down in the west;" they raised the same hue and cry that the Bible was in danger! It was infidel. They put him in prison and persecuted his family! How much better would it have been if they had co-operated with him in the investigations of the laws of nature, and fully determined the truth or falsity of his theory—thus science would have shed her light on the obscure pathway, brighter and brighter until the sublime developments of the nineteenth century would have burst upon the benighted minds of the clergy and philosophers of that dark age, and relieved us from the incubus which retarded the march of knowledge for ages. The clergy of this day are almost as persistently opposed to any theory which to them seems to trench on the validity of the Bible. Hugh Miller observed to a distinguished friend, just before he died, that the clergy must change their general system of studies, and adopt a course involving the requisite means to supply the increasing wants of progressive society, or be left behind in the race. We recollect the great sympathy expressed for Oliver Evans, about the beginning of this century, in consequence of his inability to obtain the means necessary to the accomplishment of his great discoveries, in the application of steam to the uses of mankind. He wished to build a steam car to run on common roads, and test other applications of that great agent which has since revolutionized the world. He begged and petitioned, and suffered every indignity for fourteen weary years, and was everywhere met by the cry of " madman and infidel," which was applied to Gallileo, and which Dr. Young applies to "Ariel." Poor Oliver! he sunk under his misfortunes and died of a broken heart—and the world lost years, perhaps ages, in consequence of his mental developments being crushed in the bud. Soon after this the immortal Fulton rose to position and took his stand on the car of progress; and, being more fortunate in pecuniary matters, he was enabled to fully develop his giant mind. He conceived the project of applying the new agent to propel vessels, and after various efforts and failures he risked all on his last attempt in this city. He built a steamboat and engine—called his numerous but doubting friends to witness his success; the steam was applied—the boat moved! The waves of the noble Hudson yielded to the magnificent embodiment, and the multitudes on board and on the shore, who had remained spell-bound, gave one loud and prolonged shout, which made the welkin ring, and *Fulton's fame and fortune were made, and he was not crazy!*

These facts prove that it is *possible* for common men to differ successfully with the learned—for nine tenths of the population of the country, and all the learned, ridiculed the idea of his success, and laughed him to scorn.

Columbus is another instance in point. All Europe was against him, and called him a madman and infidel, and but for the exalted nobility of a woman (of the Adamic race) he too would have sunk under the weight of poverty and scorn. Dr. Blackie boasts of his being an *alumnus* of the college of Bonn, in Germany—we suppose to give weight to his arguments. No one doubts the great learning and ability of the professors in that college or that of Paris, but God forbid that we should have to go to Germany or France for morals or religion.

CHAPTER VII.

WE will now give an abstract summary of the character-istic differences between the species of the *genus homo*, which are not only apparent but proved by the Bible, pro-fane history, and by science, viz:

1st. Color, and excretion of sulphuretted hydrogen, &c.

2d. Difference of facial angle—being 20° between the Caucasian and negro.

3d. Size of the brain (intellectual and animal). Differ-ence, 20 cubic inches.

4th. *Limit to mental development* in the inferior races.

5th. Bible account, confirmed by profane history and geology.

These characteristics are so palpable to the senses, so fixed and immutable, that ministers and naturalists with *one idea* may labor to all eternity to prove the "unity of the human race," yet God will hurl them back until they sink into oblivion, and leave the unprejudiced masters of the field.

We don't claim any of the *Puritan* religion of Spurgeon, Garibaldi, and hundreds of their *catspaws*, who would raise four millions of negroes by *force* to a state of *social and political equality* with the Adamic race, and thus cer-tainly destroy them. It has been left for the wonderful wisdom of this age to discover the great truth that God is ignorant of his own laws! The most striking difference between the races (apparently only) is the color, which is white in the Caucasian, olive yellow in the Mongol, dusky brown and copper-colored in the Malay, Esquimaux and American Indian, and black in the Ethiopian and negro. The jet black Ethiopian, probably, was not known to Solomon; of the negro of W., S. and E. Africa, the Indian, Esquimaux and Malay, nothing was known. The beard, next to color, is a prominent feature in the Adamic race. The inferior species have but little or *no beard;* and still another striking and peculiar difference is the excretion of sulphuretted hydrogen, nitrous and ammonical gases, which are not secreted or evolved by the Caucasian. In addition to their difference of color, facial angle, and anatomical configuration, they are *chemically* unlike, and consequently of *different species.*

In the next place, the intellectual lobe of the brain is over 20 cubic inches larger in the white man than in the negro, and proportionately less as you rise in the scale of being; whereas, the *animal* portion of the negro's brain is *larger* than the white (which coincides with our observation, and is proved by their different natures), making the cavity of their skulls to be about the same. Here Drs. Young and Blackie *pervert the truth* or facts, and with exultation produce Dr. Morton's tables of the measurement of *six hundred skulls* of whites, Malays and negroes, which is simply no proof at all, as shown above.* All *unpredjudiced* ethnologists, who have examined the *brains* of the different *species* of man, agree that the intellectual portion or lobe of the brain of the Caucasian is much larger than the Chinese (the highest type of the inferior species), and increasing in differ-

* Dr. Morton was one of the most zealous students of this or any other age, and his researches in the valley of the Nile. the Euphrates and other sections, are of the most profound importance to science. His collection of skulls embraced Egyptians, Persians, Romans, Greeks, Assyrians, Malays, negroes, Indians—in fact, all people and nations, ancient and modern, opened their sepulchral vaults and poured out their treasures into the lap of this wonderful man; but I must beg Drs. Young and Blackie to listen when I say,

ence through all the species to the lowest (the West African or Congo, Guinea and Hottentot negro), which amounts to full 20 cubic inches. The difference in the size of the skull does not so much constitute the difference in mental capacity of the different species of men as the difference in the size of the intellectual lobe of the brain. The animal portion of the brain in the negro, the Ethiopian, the Malay and American Indian, is at least 20 cubic inches greater than in the Adamic race, and hence their greater sensuality and brutish propensities, which are exhibited every day in their own country. None of those races ever produced a poet, a historian or statesman—no architect, above the fashioning of an arrow-head or ornamenting a moccasin! The integuments of the *brain* are utterly incapable of transmitting those godlike vibrations from matter to mind which obtain in the Adamic race, and stamp him as a superior being. It is no wonder these creations worshipped them in all the earlier ages; it was natural. Seeing this array of facts, we do think that all divines with *one idea*, as well as naturalists, should cease their attempts to force the negro and Indian (in spite of God) into the false position of social and political equality with the Adamic race, until, by some strange metamorphosis, his brain may become enlarged and its texture altered; which, according to Dr. Young's reasoning, *may take place*, as he says the Southern negroes, in the last century, have improved smartly in their noses !

The other and greatest difference is the limit to mental development, which is the *effect* of a *cause* shown to exist in the foregoing number. The Chinese and other Mongolian nations, or varieties of that species, being the highest type of all the inferior races, have maintained a government which

unequivocally, that Dr. Morton *did not believe* in the *unity of the human race*. He has left a voluminous collection and correspondence on the subject, which cannot be mistaken. And, by the by, I will here remark that Pritchard, after forty years of arduous labor to sustain and defend the theory, gave it up as untenable !

was most probably given them by Shem's descendants, who invaded that region about the time of Semiramis, and left a government and the arts, and those relics of antiquity which have given an undue importance to that race. Confucius, certainly, was a Caucasian—so was Atilla, Tamerlane, and other great men and warriors, whose conquests and devastations are so notable and brutal—with Ghengis Khan, who was a hybrid of Shem's and Mongol blood, showing the marked difference between the *offspring* of the *highest* type and the *lowest*. He was far superior to the *mulatto*, and possessed greater physical as well as mental power. The leaders in the late civil war are of Caucasian origin. The Mongols in China and Japan, Siam and India, possess judicial ability in proportion to the admixture of Adamic blood—they make some little advance in the arts, far more than the Malay, negro or American Indian, but necessarily have a limit beyond which they cannot go without *recreation*, which becomes more apparent through all the races.

Ministers of the church, with few exceptions, still adhere to the doctrine of the "unity of the human race," despite the floods of truthful light thrown upon the subject latterly by the developments in science. We will give an elegant extract from a late paper on the subject by Dr. Van Evrie (whose views on ethnology and the laws of hybridity are far in advance of European naturalists), who says: "The distinguished philosopher and prince of naturalists, Agassiz, claims that the human races (meaning *varieties*) were created, like all other beings, in certain zones or centres of life; but fancy them to be of the *same species*, as if the Creator had done His work so bunglingly as not only *to duplicate it*, but to endow them with ample powers of migration, never to be used!—a matter of supererogation quite as absurd as to have given us *four eyes* or a double set of senses throughout. The several human species, just as all other species in the animal world, are adapted to, and therefore were created in certain great centres of existence, and they differ from each other in their phy-

sical structure and their qualities or natures, and therefore in the purposes assigned them by the Creator, just
as clearly and absolutely as do the several species of animals that belong to a certain creation or form of being.
The physical structure—the faculties—in a word, the nature of the negro and the other inferior races, is specifically
as absolutely different from the nature of the Caucasian as
the body and nature of the crow are different from the
eagle, or the garden snake from the rattlesnake—or the
different species of the feline race; the majestic lion and
tiger, the panther and the domestic cat, all belong to the
same family or genus, but are of *distinct species;* each is a
distinct and independent creation.   Yet, notwithstanding
these plain and strongly marked distinctions, the European
naturalists and ethnologists (with few exceptions) seem utterly incapable of comprehending them ; many assent to the
American doctrine of the diverse origin of the human races
(they call them *varieties*), but really seem to have no proper conception of the *different human species.*"

Many ministers of the gospel contend that the whole system of Christianity must fall to the ground if the plurality
of the races is admitted ! This is sheer nonsense. It is a declaration, in fact, that *we must believe the interpretation, by our.
ministers, of every text and passage of Scripture, literally and
without investigation !*   This is an attempt to inaugurate the
clerical despotism of the dark ages.   When we discover,
by investigating the laws of nature, that the earth is *not fixed
and motionless in* space, we *change our opinion* of the meaning of the Scriptural text that teaches the *reverse*, and seek
to discover the reason why the inspired writer used *that
translation or those terms.*   Many passages of the Bible have
assumed a different meaning latterly, in consequence of the
wonderful discoveries in the sciences of geology, astronomy
and chemistry ; yet they all harmonize and *confirm* the
sacred record, instead of being *infidel.*

The vast array of physical facts adduced to prove the
white and negro different *species* are all patent to the *senses,*

and Scripture faith has nothing to do with it. "We cannot change these existing facts a whit by our opinion—yet some men affect to believe white to be black and black white—that a white woman, at some distant day, may have had black children (not mulattoes!") Still he must *know* it to be impossible. Solomon says: "Can the Ethiopian change his skin or the leopard his spots?" Each one is governed by the fixed laws of God, which cannot be changed but by a miracle—which we have shown is never resorted to when the ordinary laws of nature operate to produce the same effect.

The assumption, by intelligent divines, that this belief is infidel, or essential to salvation, or upholds the whole fabric of Christianity, is simply absurd.

In ancient times, authors and teachers used different methods to convey their ideas, using more metaphors, allegories and figures, to illustrate and make plain and comprehensible their unfledged ideas—like all uncultivated nations of this day. They had less help from the accretion of ages, which are preserved for the benefit of posterity, greatly lessening the labors of modern mind. The earlier authors were *self-sustaining and self-creating* (so to speak), and everywhere adapted their language to the comprehension of the people whom they addressed, hence the seeming discrepancies in some passages of Scripture. In many instances they certainly used language thus adapted to the comprehension of the uneducated, which, if taken in its literal sense, would now be looked upon as wholly inapplicable.

If physical facts be developed by scientific investigations which absolutely differ from the literal understanding of any passage of Scripture, we must not suspend our investigations, but seek to find an interpretation capable of explaining it otherwise. Languages are so diverse that it is impossible, in many cases, to convey an idea from one to another by words or signs, in consequence of their non-existence. This is shown by the missionary reports from

Asia, Africa, and among our Indians. The Indians had no word in their language to convey the idea of virtue, temperance, and a thousand other abstract principles, of which they had no conception. In the middle ages mankind accepted everything from the clergy without question—investigation, which gave such glory to the earlier ages, had almost entirely ceased; all believed in the literal declaration of Moses, that the sun and moon and stars " arose in the east and set in the west," and the earth was immovably fixed on a *firm foundation.* No one questioned it for a vast number of ages—no one dared to investigate so plain a proposition, for it seemed to need none. Years rolled on and centuries passed, when some restless spirit broke the chains of ignorance and sloth and rose above public opinion —asserted his inalienable right to investigate the *laws of the Great First Cause* that governed both mind and matter— and the result was the same that always obtains—progress —that development of the mental faculties which God commanded in our first creation, and which contradistinguishes the Adamic race from the negro, the Indian, the Malay and Chinese. Investigations went on, persecutions went on, fear of destroying the validity of the Bible were rife, and in the whirlpool of excitement and revolution science was crushed to the earth, and its advocates incarcerated in prisons and hunted down like wild beasts. But the fires of truth still burned, though slowly but nevertheless surely, until, in after ages, the controlling powers of earth became so far enlightened that they acknowledged their error, and gave the meed of praise and immortality to the noble martyrs who had perished for the benefit of their kind. Then, and not till then, they saw the principles they inculcated, instead of being infidel, only confirmed the truth of the sacred historian. When the immortal Franklin drew down the lightning from heaven by the aid of his kite, and proved it to be the same—its perfect identity with electricity—millions stood aghast, and looked upon him as a blasphemer; but he did not feel it to be so. He was only

3

carrying out God's command to fulfil his destiny, by using every means within his power to comprehend and apply the laws of nature to man's benefit. Franklin little dreamed of the vast, interminable, and astounding results of his first inception, in the benefit to mankind from the introduction of the magnetic telegraph, and its incalculable importance to commercial, social and moral good to all nations. It is the grand and god-like medium, through and by which intelligence from nation to nation and from people to people is transmitted, over the land and under the sea, in a moment of time, for thousands of miles! If Franklin had advanced the idea, in his day, so seemingly absurd and blasphemous, he would have been confined in prison as a madman; but now it is a practical fact, made to be familiar and palpable to *the senses* of the most ignorant; and the consequence is, it is received by all classes, the clergy included, as a fixed fact, and not blasphemous, or infidel even. Oh! what an inconsistent being and what a tyrant man is.

In later days, the equally strange doctrine that electricity, light, heat, and gravity are only modifications of the same principle, is being promulgated and believed, and in a few years will be generally received. This new theory teaches that all matter is composed of primitive atoms—that space, beyond the bounds of the planetary atmosphere, or suns, (which are worlds in a forming stage,)* that cannot be hab-

---

* To those of my readers who are unacquainted with geology we will append a brief description of the formation of the earth. In "the beginning" the earth was *without form and void,* and darkness was over the deep or expanse; then the *matter* of which it is composed was *invisible to human eyes,* being in what naturalists term an *atomic form;* after a time the accretion of atoms form larger bodies, called *molecules;* further aggregation forms bodies we can see, like vapor, answering to the state of our comets, which, in the middle and more recent ages, caused so much fear of destroying our world by collision—but which, if such a thing could happen, would not produce any greater effect than that much vapor or smoke!

The further aggregation of those bodies, by chemical action produced suns, like the glorious luminary that dispenses heat and light to our planet, and, after the lapse of countless millions of years, the earth became like unto our moon, which once *was without form and void.* Its changes by what we call *volcanic eruptions* break up this crust from time to time; and the lessened table while self-luminous; but like the moon, become more fitted for organic life, until, in millions of years, an atmosphere, seas and vegetation, animal life, and finally intelligent beings, *after the image of God*, will crown the whole, and be placed on them to govern and control the multifarious creations on each; as was the case on the earth "in the beginning," and until the Garden of Eden was planted, and Adam and Eve and all the animals were placed upon it. This space, in the beautiful language of Scott, of the *Atlanta Monthly*, is composed of those primitive *atoms;* by accretion these atoms form *molecules*, and by their accretion and aggregation they form larger and larger *bodies*, such as we can

temperature of the planet and surrounding space produces the further condensation of vapor; and then *it rained upon the earth, and seas and lakes and rivers were formed*. The moon has no seas nor atmosphere as yet visible to us—but we can see the volcanic fires and rocks and mountains. The high temperature acting on the broken upheaved rocky surface decomposed them; and the detrities settled on the beds of the seas and produced layers of mud or sediment one above the other, until in time they hardened into rocks again, but different from the primitive by being *stratified*, as we now find the metamorphic series—which, by subsequent volcanic action, became chrystalized and again upheaved, in the tilted condition we now find them, in the formation of our habitable ranges of elevated mountain chains, valleys and plateaus, which evidently were once the bed of the sea. Then the temperature became suited to the lowest grade of animal and vegetable life, and they were formed and put upon the earth in groups, as Prof. Agassiz and others have shown. They lived and died and were covered up in the sediment of the seas, and subsequently these strata, as before, became hardened into rocks, with the fossils in them as we now find them, increasing in numbers and genera and species for thousands of feet in thickness, when we come to the bones of *quadrupeds* and a higher order of plants to support them—rising in grade—but each family or genus independent of those below, until in the lapse of time the temperature of the earth became fitted for man, and those groups of animals and vegetables necessary to his support; and then his body was *formed*, and the *woman*, and they were placed in the garden of Eden to till it and fulfil their destiny. This regular gradation of creations we find to exist in the "Book of Rocks" in imperishable characters, and not liable to mistranslation, as we find in recording a fact in different human languages. The negroes, Central American Indians, and Malays were introduced upon the earth thousands of years before the Mongolian and Esquimaux. And lastly, God formed Adam and Eve, and placed them either in the Nilotic Valley or on the Euphrates, which is proved by those magnificent relics of architecture existing there.

see and feel, until they attain the present dimensions of planets and suns; that the planets and suns, in their revolutions around each other, through this *ether*, meet with so little resistance that it is not appreciable in millions of years; that the solar and other systems nearest to us are independent of each other only in so far that they all move around some centre; and that vast illimitable, congeries of systems, or centres of *motion*, revolve around the great central sun, which Dr. Dick sublimely calls the "Throne of God!" And yet all this matter—all these vast systems of worlds, are *moved* and kept in motion in their orbits by this one simple principle we call "*electricity*." That at every instant there is the same quantity of *motion* in the universe, and that all physical phenomena—light, heat, electricity, gravity, and chemical affinity are but *varieties of motion*—following each other by the same laws we see reigning in mechanics. These primitive *atoms* are called *ether*—their aggregation gives larger and larger *bodies*. Gravity is nothing but the action of *ethereal atoms* on *molecular matter—(the effect of a cause.)* In the *infinitely minute* we have the molecules revolving around each other, interlaced with ethereal movements, forming what we call cohesion and chemical affinities. In the *infinitely great* we have the same laws of *motion* illustrated in the rotations of suns, and the revolutions of planets around them. Throughout the whole of this system of varied aggregations we have the same laws of harmonious and rythmic motions. One definite motion bears the name of *heat*, another of *light*, a third of *electricity*, &c. All material phenomena are resolvable into modes of motion.

Molecular motion, only in the body itself, gives us the *sensation of heat;* if accelerated to a certain degree, they affect the surrounding *ether* and produce *light*. The solid metal becomes incandescent; still further accelerated, it ceases to be solid and becomes fluid—a new state of cohesion results from the accelerated movement—another increase of motion produces vapor or gas. The solid metal is no longer *visible;* the change in every stage in the metal is attributable to the increased *motion.* M. Emilie Saigey, the distinguished French savan, is the advocate and expounder of this system in Europe. Like almost all modern European philosophers, he strives to seek a cause or *material* agent in nature, independent of God, to give and continue motion to matter. He contends that electricity is a *fluid, not of any special matter but of the same ether,* whose vibrations are heat, light and actinism. In the case of electricity, the *ether* flows along the molecular matter, in the condition of *atoms and molecules* (an aggregation of the two), both being necessary to the development of *electricity.* This theory, we contend, is contrary to the laws of God, previously acknowledged to characterize electricity and govern motion. We would suggest a different explanation of these laws, advanced twenty years ago, to account for the prevalence and progress of Asiatic cholera, assuming it to be owing to a deficiency of ozone in the oxygen of the atmosphere, from electric causes, and that successful treatment was found to be predicated upon the use of such remedial agents as embodied chemical compounds, capable of supplying that deficiency in the excitability necessary to health—this, generally, can be effected by combustion of nitre, or similar substances, so as to increase the quantity of oxygen or its active principle, which is only another modification of electricity, and accounts for its disappearance from New Orleans and other cities in twenty-four hours, in August and September, when every malarious or common cause of disease was most active.

Electricity stands in the same relation to *matter* that *mind* does to the *soul* of man; each is *the effect of a cause.* The *one is the motion* of this cause (or soul of inanimate matter) through *ether,* somewhat resembling the vibrations of or waves on the surface of a placid lake, caused by the concussion of two solid bodies at different points at the same time, which vibrations pass through each other without any apparent resistance; or in the telegraph wire, which, though a solid body, transmits opposite motions or electric vibrations through immense spaces, in a manner wholly incomprehensible to a finite mind. The *other* is the effect or operation of the *soul*, acting on that universal principle which is one of the essential attributes of God, called electricity, and contradistinguished as *mind* in the highest animal creation, and exists in all animated animal organisms in a greater or less degree, giving some animals more of what we call *instinct* than others, in proportion to the more or less perfect structure of the brain. It is the larger and more perfect structure of the intellectual lobe of the brain, in the Adamic race, that characterizes them as a superior species to all others of the *genus homo*, because they are *created after the image of God*. They receive and transmit those vibrations, or the principle called *motion*, in a higher degree than any other created beings. In other words, electricity is the *soul* (so to speak) of inanimate matter, and governs and directs it in all its operations, from the germinating of the seeds of plants, and the development of the lowliest leaf and flower, to the grand and mysterious movements of countless millions of suns and worlds ! It causes the variation of the magnetic needle, and the presence or absence of ozone, as before stated, causing cholera to prevail in a more or less fatal form.

All these principles will soon be familiar to every one, and consequently man will become more and more potent in arresting disease and death; even now, with our limited knowledge, its ravages have been greatly lessened, and human suffering mitigated. Electricity, therefore, is one of the attributes of God, which gives *motion* to all matter, and preserves the harmony of the universe—gives life and existence to all animals, and gives to vegetation the power to grow and propagate its kind.

The French and German naturalists have labored long to substitute a cause of motion, independent of God. M. E. Saigey makes electricity to be a fluid, not composed of any particular matter, and yet of that same *ether* which is made of the *primitive atoms of matter !*—that this fluid, passing through *molecular matter* (duplicate atoms) creates or evolves electricity. This medley, or labored nonsense, could all be obviated by simply acknowledging the fact that all things were created by God, and governed by simple, fixed laws, which M. Saigey and others have explained clearly and forcibly to this point; and, instead of seeking a self-acting agent, independent of God, if they will admit the fact that it requires as much *omnipotence to continue the operation of the laws of nature as to create them*, then they will believe that the active agent, or principle which governs all matter, not only in its *motions* but in its *life and being*, is one of the essential attributes of God—intangible, invisible, immaterial and eternal, and that is *electricity*. Its development, to our senses, in the storm and whirlwind, where light and heat are evolved, is not apparent in the zephyr, yet it is there slumbering (seemingly only) in its vibrating cradle; and if our dull faculties could grasp its varied movements, we would observe the most intense and powerful action, far surpassing the forces required to govern suns and worlds. Electricity is the *soul of inanimate* matter (so to speak), and all the phenomena of nature are evolved in proportion to the *kind* of matter through which it passes, from *ether* and the molecule to the largest of bodies and the crudest of mediums. This accounts for the extraordinary manifestations and developments in psychology and its collateral branches, by which many men and women are led to believe it to be supernatural; the effect, in many cases, producing confirmed insanity, and in others, great disquietude and unhappiness, all of which would be remedied or prevented by simply becoming acquainted with the laws of God, and thereby fulfil their destiny. Scott, of the *Atlanta Monthly*, in his criticisms on the late French work on modern science (*La Physique Moderne*), from which we have made some extracts, evinces higher and clearer perceptions of the *cause of motion* in the universe than any writer we know.

CHAPTER VIII.

The rapid developments in the science of geology, ethnology, astronomy, geography and chemistry, of late years, have corrected and exploded a vast number of false theories, which have helped to enslave the human races for thousands of years, and in every instance confirms the validity of the sacred Scriptures. Why is it, then, that the clergy so persistently refuse to assist in the *progress* of man in this life, in conformity with the *express commands of God*, who created him in *His own image*, and told him to multiply and replenish the earth and govern and control all things, and apply them to his own proper use and benefit? All theories are now predicated on facts—fixed and immutable laws. If these tangible facts are proved to exist in the structure of the human body, and show an absolute and undeniable difference in man, we must accept them as proof of their being of different species, the same as we admit that the crow and eagle, though both birds, are of different species. The one is as plainly proved to the senses as the other, and science only confirms it—for instance, if we find the bones to differ not only in form but in chemical composition, the color of the skin, the size of the brain, the hair, the beard, the features or emotions (the negro has none), the chemical composition of the blood, the emission of sulphuretted hydrogen from all parts of the body, and lastly (though by no means least), the *limit to mental development* of all the inferior races, we must admit, from all this array of facts, that the Adamic race is a superior and absolutely distinct *species*, as proved by science and observation, and also by reason of its being created *after the image of God*, as shown in the 1st chap. Gen., 27th verse.

When we arrive at this point of our argument and investigation, we must look for some other interpretation than the present literal and (as previously shown) suppressed text of the Bible, which defines the *origin* of the negro and other inferior species of man.

The Bible clearly indicates that "Shem's" descendants settled Middle, Southern, and a part of Western Asia; "Ham's" settled part of Western Asia, Egypt, Carthage, and probably other Northern portions of Africa. "Japheth" settled the "Isles of the Gentiles," or the Northern Mediterranean coasts, as far as then known. But modern historians assume to know more, and *teach* that the Chinese, Hindoos, and other Mongolian tribes or nations are Shem's descendants! We know the Jews are of that variety; but no sane man or woman believes that the Jew, with his *illimitable* mind, and the beardless, cat-eyed, misshapen Mongol, are of the same race. Again, they say Japheth settled Europe, and that Ham is the father of the negroes! God forbid that this blasphemous theory should much longer continue as a foul blotch on the fair escutcheon of science and the church of Christ. This dogma has caused more scepticism and done more injury to all races than any other ever promulgated. The Mahomedan historians, actuated by the same prejudices, and with equal absurdity, teach that Shem's descendants peopled Eastern Asia, and were Jews, Persians, Arabs, Greeks and Romans! Here we have a medley—the Greeks and Romans were Japheth's descendants, and the Jews, Shem's. They go on to say Ham settled Southern Asia, Africa and America! Japheth, Europe (Germans, Chinese, Tartars and Turks!) It is no wonder the mass of mankind are so conflicting in opinions of the different races.

It has been conclusively shown that Ham's descendants *did settle* Egypt, and that they were *not negroes*, by reason of their having long straight hair and fine features, with small feet and hands, and flowing beards; the negroes, Indians and Chinese have little or *no beard*, and the negroes have *kinky, crisped, short wool*, instead of the graceful and crowning glory of the Caucasian's head, and are everywhere marked as a different species. The Jews are Shem's *pure, unadultera-*

3*

ted descendants, who have maintained their perfect identity for over *four thousand years!* notwithstanding they were captives in Egypt and Babylon for more than five hundred years, and time and again were enslaved by the neighboring nations; and finally, the Romans under Titus conquered them and utterly laid waste their country—scattered and sold them as slaves to all nations. Yet in despite of this servitude and unheard-of oppression for *two thousand years*, they still remain *pure in their generation*, and have resisted the seductions of amalgamation and mongrelism, which has sunk and exterminated all other conquered nations of whom we have any account. The preservation of their identity or national character, under so many and varied circumstances, for thousands of years, is altogether one of the most astonishing and inexplicable events that ever transpired, and *stamps* it as a miracle to fulfil a prophecy and a promise, and is another undeniable proof of the authenticity of the Bible. As before remarked, the Chinese have not advanced a single iota for two thousand years, either in government or the arts, which is one of the most striking proofs of a fixed law that draws the line of distinction between the *species.* The Malay, the American Indian, Esquimaux, the Ethiopian, and Guinea or Congo negro, and Hottentot, *are now* and always have been a perfect blank on the fair face of the world. They have no government (comparatively speaking), no science, no arts, no literature, and are utterly incapable of comprehending either!

Fifth, and lastly. The Bible, profane history and science, prove a difference so obvious that it is only necessary for any *unprejudiced mind* to examine the subject to be convinced. The Bible cannot be reconciled or properly understood otherwise. For instance, where did Cain get his wife? This passage cannot be reconciled if we admit the doctrine of the " unity of the human race," for Eve had no daughter as yet, and Cain was under the condemnation not only of God but his parents, and had been ignominiously expelled from their presence and country. But even if we suppose, as has frequently been contended, that he had sisters, it is hardly probable, in fact it is unnatural to suppose they would ally themselves to a murderer of their brother —a man so desperate, so dangerous—no, never; but rather he left his country and kindred, and sought consolation and companionship among the inferior races who lived in the land of Nod, on the east of Eden. From Bible testimony we conclude them to have been very numerous. That he married a negro we deny, for many reasons: the first is, that far superior beings existed, which we think we have proved. It is hardly probable he would select a negro for a companion—the lowest and most repulsive—when he could take a Mongol, whose intellectual capacity and more beautiful forms and features rendered them more congenial and desirable in his forlorn condition. If "Ariel" is correct in there being but *two species* of the human race, then Cain did marry a negro; but every argument is against it, for his descendants indicated that he married one of the highest types of the inferior races, because they were much more intelligent than the *mulatto*, and longer lived. It is natural to suppose he would affiliate with the most intelligent and fascinating. And another proof that it was not the negro, is the fact that when expelled he went *eastward*, where the Mongols have always existed to this day; and the negroes lived in Africa, *westward*, where they have ever lived. It was in Asia, among the Mongol race, that Cain got his wife.

CHAPTER IX.

"ARIEL," believing in but two species of men, says Cain married a negro. He asks who the sons of God were, mentioned in the 6th chap. Gen. If from heaven, their morals were sadly out of order. Were they angels? then it is plain they never got back to heaven—they are not on earth, for angels that sinned were cast down to hell or *drowned* by the flood; they are not the *sons* of *men* from below, nor angels, for they could not be called the *sons* of *God*. Who were they then? We answer, without fear of successful contradiction, they were the sons of Adam and Eve, thus called by preëminence. God told Adam and Eve to *multiply* and *replenish* the earth; then, it is plain, God could have no objection to their taking wives of whom they chose, *of their own race. They were expressly commanded to do so by God.* But he did object and enjoin that they should not marry the inferior species, and raise up a race of hybrids that should curse the world, and destroy all beings except a chosen few, who had abstained from these abominable crimes of amalgamation. All this discrepancy would have been prevented had the translators not rejected the rendering of the oldest manuscripts—the Chaldean, Ethiopic, Arabic, *et al*, of the Jewish or Hebrew Scriptures, in which the *sin of miscegenation* is plainly set forth. Our translators, appointed by King James, implicitly believing in the unity of the human race, also *suppressed* part of the 24th verse, 1st chap. Gen., which gives the *origin* of the *species* created before Adam; and 4th chap. ,16th to 26th verses, and 6th chap., 2d and 6th verses, and many other passages, which cannot be explained unless we adopt the plurality of the races—for Seth's first-born son (Enos) came into the world *two hundred and thirty-five years* after Adam was formed and placed on the earth—and yet our translators render this verse (4th chap. 26th verse) *"Then began men to call upon the name of the Lord."* Every biblical scholar knows that the law was given to Adam and Eve 235 years before Enos was born, and they and their families were *required to call upon the name of the Lord* and worship him, and offer sacrifices to him periodically. But now, "Ariel" says, the *negroes* began to *profane* the name of the Lord, which is doubtless the correct rendering or true meaning of the original, as it would be unmeaning to use the present translation as applied to the Adamic race, who, every day, had been in the exercise of those bounden duties. To properly understand all those passages we must admit the fact that the Bible teaches the negro and others to be distinct species of men.

The inferior races in all the early ages, and even now, look upon the Adamic race as superior beings, and regarded them before the flood as gods, and in many instances, as late as the time of Alexander the Great, they worshipped them; they will always regard them as such, until, like the Sand-wich Islanders, they become extinct, which is rapidly taking place. " Lo ! the poor Indian" is the poet's requiem on the sad and melancholy condition of the American Indian ; a few more ages and that *species of man* will have fulfilled its destiny, and be classed with the *extinct species* of the *elephant*, which once roamed over this continent in such vast numbers. And yet a few more centuries and the Malay, the Esquimaux, the Ethiopian, and the West African negro, with all their varieties, *will pass away or die out*, (from the effects of civilization,) and give place to the Adamic race. The tendency of modern civilization is destructive to them. The false philanthrophy of our legislators tends to force them into an abnormal condition, by which they adopt all of our *vices* and but few of our *virtues*. This is now shown in the whole South by the frightful mortality which exists, notwithstanding the official reports of Generals Howard and Pope to the contrary, who undoubtedly have been misled by designing men. The statistics and bills of mortality returned by the authorities of all our principal cities and towns, show that from *three to five* times as many negroes die as whites. There is one other circumstance, which has probably been noticed by more persons than myself, that in travelling the distance of a thousand miles through the South, in any direction, you will not see more than *half a dozen negro children*—infants; before the war you might have seen a hundred in the same distance. Now the negroes have few or none ; and those that do, destroy them, like the Chinese and other Asiatic and African tribes. This crime, small-pox, syphilis, drunkenness, bad shelter, bad food and *unbridled licentiousness*, has swept off at *least one and a half millions* since the year 1861 ! *What an awful reflection* for our present governors at Washington and the crowned heads of Europe, who have helped to *murder* such a vast number of ignorant human beings by a misplaced philanthropy !

I have now finished my criticism of the work of "Ariel," which embodies a great many arguments and a strong array of facts and proofs in support of the plurality of the human race. His theory of two, instead of seven or more species, is untenable, and shown to be contrary to all science. His arguments, in the main, regarding Ham's descendants, cannot be refuted. The Egyptians belonged to the Adamic race, and so did the Tyreans, Sidonians and Carthaginians. The curse of God, before the flood, no doubt, was in consequence of miscegenation and idolatry, and His curse of Canaan, after the flood, was for the same crime. But the position of Dr. Young, and a thousand other authorities, that the curse somehow fell on Ham, and made him to be the progenitor of the negro, is too futile and contemptible to be entertained for a moment.

"Ariel's" position, claiming the negro to be a *beast,* after God's nomenclature, is not only proved to be absurd but contrary to every law of hybridity and the fixed laws of God, which places him in the same class with human beings, and he is consequently human. I think I have proved to all Christians and reasonable persons, who are unprejudiced, that the negro, Indian, Ethiopian, Esquimaux, Malay and Mongol, were created *before* Adam. On this point I agree with "Ariel" and Dr. Cartwright, but where they make but *two* species I claim *seven* or more, and from their admixture came all the varieties and hybrid castes now on earth. If the 24th verse, 1st chap. Gen., had been fully translated, the inferior races would, long since, have been acknowledged as occupying their true position in the scale of being, and saved from the horrors consequent upon being forced into a false social and political state, which must inevitably terminate in their extinction, or perhaps destroy both by amalgamation. This is surely and swiftly *"rotting out"* or destroying the hybrid populations of Mexico and the Central and South American republics. In another century, if there be no immigration, they will have returned to their original savage condition—the whites and hybrids having passed away.

Again, it has been shown that Dr. Young has not answered "Ariel" and his assumption that all nations came from Adam and Eve, which is quite as absurd as that the negro is a beast, and can have issue by intercourse with human beings. Dr. Young's arguments on hybridity are positively a perversion of the truth; no doubt from the same prejudices that caused Bishop Bascomb, Baron Swedenborg and Cowper to preach a doctrine that has caused the untimely death of millions of negroes in the United States, the West Indies and other negro provinces, purely from love! It is the same to the negro and Indian as if their friends were actuated by the most diabolical motives. *It is death!*

Its baleful consequences do not stop there, but coil their slimy folds around the white race, sweeping them off by millions—all (as Cromwell says), all for the glory of God! Lord deliver us from such philanthrophy.

We must be allowed to notice the fact that both Drs. Young and Blackie frequently allude to the many distinguished men they cite, as authority which *should not be questioned.* Great names are not always positive evidence of the truth of any proposition or theory. Socrates and Plato, Thales and Demosthenes, Cicero, Justinian and Pliny, the apostles, and thousands of other distinguished men of all nations, *lived and died in total ignorance of the now simple law* that governs the heavenly bodies, and with us produces day and night! Copernicus and Gallileo *did question* this authority and posterity sustained them.

NOTE.—Dr. Young says he is from German and English stock. No ancestor of his lives north of Mason & Dixon's line. "We do not believe in the *social equality of the negro.* We are disfranchised," &c.

Why then advocate a doctrine that gives *political equality to the negro;* which invariably *forces social equality,* with all its terrible consequences?

"Ariel" says, "wo live south of Mason & Dixon's line. We have given our last vote," &c.

Now *we* also would say, with all due deference, that we were born south of Mason & Dixon's line. We are of Scotch and Norman blood; and, after laboring half a century for our common country, in developing its vast mineral resources, worth millions of dollars, we too are disfranchised. Disfranchised for trying to preserve the Constitution made by Washington, Madison, Jefferson, Adams, and a host of other patriots, with the aid of Patrick Henry, Clay, Webster, Calhoun, and the residue of a galaxy of statesmen that eclipsed all ages in wisdom and government. Disfranchised for trying to preserve this matchless Constitution! Though we have added such vast sums to the circulating medium of the nation—not by trade and exchange, but by raising it from the depths of the mines—and have advanced the arts, and added to science, yet an ignorant, uneducated negro—the lowest type of the inferior species of man—with a soul, but not after the image of God—is permitted, in fact *forced to vote, and to form a Constitution and laws to govern ten millions of intelligent, educated Christian people;* and this by the Congress of the United States of America, in the enlightened nineteenth century!

The melancholy reflection arising from the foregoing results and effects of a misplaced philanthropy, causes the friends of humanity to weep for the miseries in store for the millions of innocent creatures who must become the victims of an unnatural sympathy. The negro and Indian, as yet, are the principal sufferers. The great efforts of Catholic and other missionaries to civilize and Christianize them have totally and utterly failed—simply because they, with the best and most pious intentions, pursue a wrong course, and vainly attempt to force the laws of God to bend to their own views or interpretations. These results have been seen in so many instances, with the most frightful sufferings and death, that it is passing strange the good and the great, in our land, have not changed their policy. But fanaticism knows no bounds; in all ages it has been the same. The great national caldron is boiling and seething, and casting up mire and filth. The goddess of liberty has fled from our once happy country in affright. The scarred veteran of an hundred battles sits dejectedly upon the *wreck of liberty and a broken Constitution*, and, in a sad and plaintive voice, exclaims—

1. Why yet does vain ambition burn,
   And hope still linger o'er the urn
     Where thousands lie entombed?
   Why toil to save this feeble frame,
   Secure from danger, aloof from pain,
     To dissolution doom'd?

2. How strangely fraught with silent woe
   Are all the joys I taste below—
     How soon they fade and die!
   Thus like the meteor's sudden gleam,
   With transient glow and sickly beam
     Expiring as they fly.

3. On fate's rough sea, where storms unite
   The dauntless bosom to affright,
      The hopeless path I tread,
   But ere the port appears in sight
   The morning lowers into night,
      And all its charms are fled.

4. No anxious friend to sooth my cares;
   No gentle hand to dry the tears
      Which o'er their memory fall.
   No parent's hand to raise my head;
   Nor sisters waiting round my bed
      To hear my plaintive call.

5. A howling wilderness my home;
   A lonesome wreck my humble dome;
      Myself my only friend!
   On the wild ocean's gloomy shore,
   Where billows rise and tempests roar
      And gathering storms descend.

6. Thus like the exile doom'd to roam
   In distant lands, without a home
      Or place to lay his head;
   Whose only hope is to endure
   Until the toils of life are o'er,
      Then rest among the dead.

7. I view the pleasures once so dear,
   The objects of my youthful care,
      "How sweet their mem'ry still!"
   Each grove, each hill, each verdant height,
   Their memory glows with pure delight,
      And blooms on every hill.

8. But oh my soul, these scenes are o'er,
   Thou never can'st enjoy them more,
      Nor youth nor bliss recall.
   Then cease to mourn departed joys,
   Thy youthful plays and childish toys—
      The vernal leaf must fall.

9. Then let me triumph o'er my grief,
   And give my aching heart relief,
      Whilst hope inspires my breast;
   For sorrow's storms will soon be o'er,
   Their murm'ring sound be heard no more,
      And billows lulled to rest.

CHAPTER X.

THE Hon. Alexander H. Stephens is reported to have said recently, in a speech to his friends in Washington City, that in the event of a war of races the whites "must go under" or be exterminated, as they were in St. Domingo and Jamaica. He advised the young men to leave the country and seek a home somewhere else, and, as he was old, he would *go home and sink with the South!* This is, if true, a very unchristian, unfeeling, and unpatriotic sentiment, altogether uncharacteristic of the man, and the great statesman who has heretofore commanded the admiration of mankind. It is inconsistent with the fundamental principles of justice, law, order, and the positive and essential attributes of a good citizen. It would leave at least three millions of good people hopelessly at the mercy of anarchy and faction—people who are unable to get away, and must stay and suffer and sink under their accumulated sorrows. This is unnatural, and as a *dernier* resort most of them, driven to despair, would (as the soldiers say) die in the trenches before they would suffer such untold evils. But we hope otherwise, and *we know* that the general sentiment and feeling all through the South is decidedly favorable towards the negro; and if they could receive the coöperation of all the friends of humanity, in this and other countries, instead of the officious intermeddling of unprincipled office-seekers, who, to gain their own ends, stir up strife and bad feeling between the races, the condition of that unfortunate class would be raised in the scale of being, instead of rapidly sunk in degradation and final extinction, as in St. Domingo and other places, by forcing them into a false position. Or, in other words, whenever you compel the negro or Indian to adopt *our form* of civilization, you as certainly destroy him as you would any other animal or plant by forcing it into an abnormal state. This has been tried for three hundred years on the Indian, and from forty to eighty years on the negro, and its truth is apparent to every one who is informed on the subject. To succeed in alleviating the sufferings of that large class of humanity we must *adapt the form of civilization to their mental capacity.* Then those races will increase in population, and usefulness to themselves and to mankind, instead of decreasing in numbers and living in a state of horrible anarchy. The comparison between the Southern States and St. Domingo and Jamaica is not fair. In the former the whites are twice as numerous as the blacks—in St. Domingo there were from ten to twenty negroes to one white. There are 12,000,000 of inhabitants in the South, nearly 4,000,000 of whom are negroes. In the event of a *war of races* the disparity would be greatly increased by the vast number of the relatives of the whites in the Northern, Western and Pacific States, who would not passively look on and see their kindred exterminated; human nature is the same in all ages, and will assert itself. Hence the necessity of all Christians—all the friends of suffering humanity—all the well wishers of peace and prosperity, and all good citizens everywhere acting in concert, in harmony and promptly, to prevent so horrible a catastrophe. O, Lord God Almighty, we sincerely pray thee in mercy to move upon the hearts of our people to stay this great evil that threatens our peace and well being, and save us from sin and strife, and give us harmony, piety and humility.

To sum up what we have written we will state, first: that the negro is not a *beast*, but has a soul, but not created after the image of God; that he was created and placed upon the earth *anterior* to Adam, together with all the other inferior races, who were numerous in the valley of the Nile, as evidenced by the Mound Builders throughout Asia, and in both North and South America, when Adam and Eve were formed and placed in the garden of Eden, the last of all. Then creation was complete. This we have shown in the regular gradation of the fossiliferous rocks, formed through myriads of years, and preserving the re-

mains of animals and plants of more than one-half of all
created species that had lived and died before the advent of
the Adamic race on the earth; yet we have proved that
this does not militate against a proper interpretation of the
bible, but confirms it.

2d. We have proved that the *creation of the different
species of men*, and their advent on earth in *bodily form*,
were at very different times.

3d. We have shown that Eve was formed last of all
creatures.

4th. We have shown that Ham was not the *progenitor of
the negro;* that he was not *cursed*, and that he settled Egypt
through his descendants; yet many of Shem's progeny entered into both the government and peopling of that nation.
We have shown that the Egyptians were the earliest architects in the world, that the magnificence of their work was
far greater than that of any other people, and that the relics
of the same sculptured in porphyry and granite, marble
and quartz, 2,300 years before Christ, prove that there
were known, at that remote period, at least three distinct
species of men—the white, the olive or Mongol, and the
negro—and that the Nilotic Valley was settled by savages
before Ham's descendants entered it. We also adduce incontestible evidence that Ham's children were white, from
the exhumation of millions of mummies, all which have
long, straight hair, and fine features.

5th. We have shown that the serpent, in the form of a
snake, did not tempt Eve, and that the *Ethiopian eunuch*
was not a negro.

6th. We have fully proved the distinctive difference between the races.

7th. We have proved that the prime mover and agent in
the universe is *electricity;* that in the modern generaliza-
tion of science the European philosophers try to seek a
material agent, independent of God, to give *motion* to matter,
and keep all the worlds in their orbits, instead of frankly
acknowledging that *the spirit of God, which moved upon the*

waters in the creation, gives motion to all matter, and gives life and being to man and animals. To make this more fully understood, we will adduce a few facts to show that the *mind* and *soul* of man are different, as a majority of mankind refuse to believe. First: we will premise by stating that matter, in its ultimate or primitive form, though invisible and intangible, is still matter, which, in that state, for convenience, we call "*atomic.*" This, as before stated, by accretion and aggregation, assumes a visible form, &c.

2d. All the physical phenomena of nature are resolvable into some form of *motion.*

3d. That electricity is the universal agent which gives *motion* to all matter in the universe, of whatever form, and that *one kind or grade of motion* causes *heat;* an increased motion produces *light,* &c. Now, heat, light, gravity and chemical affinity, are *effects* of a cause; which cease to be, or *die* as soon as the cause is withdrawn. Again, the action of this agent on *animate* animal organisms develops *mind,* or what we call, for want of a better term, *instinct.* This, like heat, light, &c., *dies* as soon as the cause is removed; but its development in human animal organizations, by acting on the imperishable or immortal soul, assumes the sublime and god-like form of reason—contradistinguishing men from beasts. The soul of man, of the Adamic race, being tabernacled in a more perfect system of nerves and enlarged brain (intellectually), for the concentration of those progressive and infinite divine emanations which characterize him as of the ruling race, and the master-spirit of creation on this earth, is without limit.

NOTE.—We believe, with Prof. Agassiz, that all the different species of animals and plants were introduced upon the earth in groups, at different times, suited to their habits and natures, but that whole families were not; that the negroes and tropical Asiatics, Malays, West Indians, and Central American Indians were all introduced into those different centres or zones at one time, and long anterior to the Adamic race—the Esquimaux and Chinese, &c., at another period—but lastly, Adam and Eve were placed in the *Garden of Eden,* as the highest and last of *created* beings, and the last of *formed bodies,* singly, and not in groups, to crown the whole—as was subsequently represented in the *cap-stone* of the Great Pyramid on the Nile, in Egypt, which was *unlike* any other stone *in shape* in the vast structure, yet absolutely necessary to complete the edifice—thus, by regular gradation, the different species of the *genus homo*, from the Hottentot (but little above the ape, except in being immortal and possessing the faculty of speech) up to the Caucasian or Adamic race, who are human, like the Mongol and negro, and possess in common all his animal nature, but *specifically different, by having been created after the image and likeness of God*—this structure (the Great Pyramid) was built more than 4,000 *years ago*, when the kingdom of Egypt was populous and far advanced in science and the arts, as shown by the elegantly finished chambers and galleries and casing of that stupendous edifice. Besides, the angles of approach to the king's chamber being so exactly arranged as not only to point due north, but being inclined 30°, directed the vision to the North star! Its whole arrangements, both internal and external, are so peculiarly and mathematically exact in all their aspects, that we are compelled to admit it to have been not only a place of sepulchral rest for the great king who built it, but also an astronomical observatory. In addition to which, it differs from all other temples and pyramids built long afterwards, by being altogether free from hieroglyphic sculptures indicating their founders, and their idolatrous worship or belief. The Great Pyramid is entirely free from any trace of idolatry, and evidently built by the Adamic race; the workmen being mostly Egyptians, who had been conquered by Misrain—Ham's son—who came from Asia and entered the Valley of the Nile below where Cairo now stands, and subjugated the inhabitants as far up as the cataracts, and held the country for centuries, when Shem's descendants—the Hyksos, or Shepherd kings—conquered Ham's, and held them in bondage for ages, till they in turn were driven out and returned to Asia; after which the Jews lived there as subjects, and were expelled and came to Palestine, and built the magnificent temple at Jerusalem, corresponding (though more elegant) to the Great Pyramid. No other species of men *ever did or ever will* leave such relics of art and skill, because they have *a fixed limit* to their *mental capacity*. Thus all the known species of men were introduced on the earth in groups at three or more periods—the Hottentot being the lowest type, and the Adamic the highest.

CALIBAN:

A SEQUEL TO "ARIEL."

BY

PROSPERO.

" What have we here? A man, or a fish? He smells like a fish, a very ancient and fishlike smell. A strange fish. Were I in England now, and had this fish painted, not a holiday fool there but would give a piece of silver. There would this monster make a man ; any strange beast there makes a man. When they will not give a doit to relieve a lame beggar, they will lay out ten to see a dead Indian."—SHAKSPEARE'S *Tempest.*

New York:

PUBLISHED FOR THE PROPRIETOR.

1868.

C A L I B A N :

A S E Q U E L T O "A R I E L."

THE Bible is an inspired book, and every word
of it is true.   This proposition would never have
been disputed, if the Bible had been properly
understood.   But theologians have put into Scripture what was not to be found there, and brought
revelation into conflict with history and science.
Thus, when divines asserted that, according to
Genesis, the earth was created some six or seven
thousand years ago, that it is the centre of the
universe, and the heavens revolve around it,
geology and astronomy contradicted the assertion,
and seemed to set science at war with revelation,
until a more correct interpretation of Scripture
brought them into harmony.

It has been supposed that the different races
of mankind sprang from the same stock; whereas history and science prove the existence of
races which could not have had a common origin.
If, therefore, the Bible taught the unity of the
race, it would contradict an established fact.
But does the Bible teach this?   So far from

doing so, it records, at least, two distinct creations of human beings. *There were men upon
the earth before Adam.* For proof of this proposition, consult the book of Genesis, the only
historical authority.

In 1655, Isaac La Peyrere, a learned and pious
divine, published a work entitled *Prœadamitœ,*
in which he sought to prove that Adam was not
the first human being. The writer of this disser-
tation has tried, but without success, to obtain a
copy of it, and is, therefore, ignorant of its con-
tents.

The inspired historian records two creations,
both by the same divine Creator; the one, in his
character of ELOHIM, or GOD; and the other, in
his character of JEHOVAH, or LORD. The translators of King James have wisely distinguished the
Hebrew words by rendering one of them GOD
and the other LORD. I shall use the original,
ELOHIM and JEHOVAH.

Any one who will look into a Hebrew Lexicon, will find that ELOHIM expresses the Divinity
as all-powerful, whilst JEHOVAH designates Him
as intelligent and holy. The first creation sprang
from the omnipotence of Deity; the second was
the product of His intelligence and holiness.

Genesis, chap. 1 and 2, down to verse 6, contains ELOHIM's creation. There is also a brief
resumé of his work in chap. 5: 1-2. The creation by JEHOVAH is recorded in Gen. 2: 6-25.
ARIEL says a good deal about the use of the article in these passages, but nothing to the purpose.
It certainly gives no countenance to his singular
hypothesis that the negro is a beast, an hypothesis

at variance with Natural History and Psychology. The Hebrew article is essentially a demonstrative pronoun, and is used like the same part of speech in Greek and German, viz.: "when a definite object, one previously mentioned, or already known, or the only one of its kind, is the object of discourse." (Gesenius' Heb. Gram., § 107. Nordheimer's Heb. Gram. 2. p. 11. Winer's Idioms of the N. .T, p. 94.) This rule proves two distinct creations.

1. "ELOHIM said, 'Let us make *man.*' So ELOHIM created *the man,*" i. e., the man he resolved to make, the preadamite. *Gen.* 1 : 26–27.

2. "There was not *a man* to till the ground, and JEHOVAH ELOHIM formed *the man,* i. e:, the man for that purpose, to till the ground, the race of Adam. *Gen.* 2 : 5–🜨

The creation of the first races is recorded in *Gen.* 1 : 11–31. From this account it is evident that the material elements brought forth spontaneously everything, including man. The words are, "Let the earth bring forth grass," etc. At the bidding of the Omnipotent, forests sprang from the soil, fish and fowl from the waters, and cattle from the earth. In the same way He made man; that is, human nature at its first appearance on the globe. The ancients were right in their opinion that the aborigines of each country were earth-born, *terræ filii;* they erred only in applying it to the race of Adam.

From this account it is clear:

1. ELOHIM created the man in His own image, i.e., endowed him with *power*, a feeble image of

His own omnipotence, and gave him dominion over all other animals.

2. He appointed the race their work, to subdue the earth, to clear it of wild beasts.

3. He gave them for their subsistence the spontaneous fruits of the earth.

4. He created them "male and female." Both sexes sprang out of the earth, at once, and were independent in their origin. The woman was not, as in the second creation, taken out of the body of man. Hence, she is not his consort, but his slave.

Now, this is precisely the condition of savage life. The preadamites were wild men, fed by the bounty of nature, and waging perpetual war with wild beasts. They had no agriculture, no art, no science. The ties of domestic life were unknown. They were only one step removed from the *simiadæ*, the orang-outang and the chimpanzee.

This is precisely what the analogy of nature would suggest. Creation rises, by regular gradation, from inanimate matter, through vegetable life, sentient life, the dynasty of the reptile, of the fish, of the bird, and of the mammal, up to the dynasty of man; and this is the order related in Genesis, as is proved by Hugh Miller, in his TESTIMONY OF THE ROCKS. It is, at once, scientific and biblical. Within the limits of each class, however, there is a progressive advance from the lowest to the highest type. The human class begins with the preadamite, the lowest type. The creation of Adam, in immediate succession to the ape or the gorilla, would have involved a *saltus*, a leap unknown to nature, a departure from the order of the created universe. For, as is said by Rev. Dr. Sumner, Archbishop of Canterbury, "there is less difference between the highest brute animal and the lowest savage, than between the savage and the most improved man." (Records of Creation, 2, chap. 2. The negro is more like the chimpanzee than like the Englishman. It is remarked by Hallam: "If man was made in the image of God he was also made in the image of an ape." (Hist. Literature, 4, p. 162.) This is true only of the preadamites. The affinity of cerebral structure of the negro and of the anthropomorphous ape, is acknowledged by all great naturalists, such as Tiedemann, Cuvier, Serres, Vrolik, Gratiolet, Agassiz, Owen, Huxley.

The Bible, in its recognition of a race of human beings prior to Adam, accords with the discoveries of paleontological science. Geologists have discovered the bones of men mingled with the remains of animals, now extinct, which lived upon the earth long before the creation of Adam. The facts have been collected by Sir Charles Lyell, in his GEOLOGICAL EVIDENCES OF THE ANTIQUITY OF MAN. London, 1863. No intelligent and candid man can examine the evidence without admitting the conclusion. *Human beings, races of men, inhabited our globe long anterior to Adam.* Their skeletons are found in Europe, Asia, Africa, and even America. In the Delta of the Mississippi and on the banks of the Ohio, the cemeteries of these preadamites have been thrown open to the view of the present generation, and given evidence of their successive steps towards civilization. Geologists distinguish these by the name of the stone, the bronze, and the iron age. These primitive dwellers upon earth manufactured their spear-heads and domestic utensils, first from stone, then from bronze, and finally from iron. Their relics show that they were originally savages, and struggled, through slow degrees, after a civilization which they could never reach. However, they did the work assigned them by ELOHIM, " to subdue the earth and have dominion over the fish of the sea," etc.

Who were these preadamites? With the light of modern science the question is easily and satisfactorily answered. Naturalists are not agreed as to the races of mankind. Blumenbach makes five. (Lawrence's Lectures, p. 147.) Dr. Prichard gives seven. (Researches, 1. p. 228.) Cuvier and others distinguish only three principal divisions, the Caucasian, the Mongolian and the Nigritian; and these are sufficient. All the other races may be accounted for by the amalgamation of the original types. The preadamites were Mongols and Negroes, together with their mixed progeny. Created male and female, and in many pairs, they multiplied rapidly, exterminated the wild beasts, and replenished the earth with beings of their own species, penetrating into every land. The earth was not then divided, as subsequently, at the time of Peleg, *Gen.* 10 : 25, but formed one continent, and, therefore, presented no obstruction to their dispersion. These roving freebooters blended their blood in mongrel tribes; spread over Europe, Asia and Africa; and even penetrated into America, passing down to its Southern extremity, where they survive in their descendants, the brutal Patagonians. The cat-eyed Chinaman, the African Hottentot, the Malay, the Laplander and the Esquimaux all sprang from the primitive races of mankind. In accordance with the will of their Creator, they subsisted, at first, upon the spontaneous productions of nature; but, in the course of time, as is shown by their recently recovered remains, they began to feed upon the animals they hunted, whilst some of them acquired a relish for human flesh, and became cannibals. They make meals of the missionaries who go to them to convert them to Christianity. These savage tribes, embroiled in perpetual war, destroyed one another, and the stronger subjugated and exterminated the weaker.

The ancients seem to have attained, in some way, perhaps by tradition, a knowledge of the origin and progress of these races, which, long rejected as fabulous, is now confirmed by the disinterment of their remains. Lucretius notices the three ages, stone, bronze and iron. (De Rerum Natura, V. 1282–6.) The scholar will recall the passages in Cicero, (De Inventione, Tusc. Quæst. 1. 5,) in Juvenal, (Sat. VI, 10. XII, 57. XV, 70,) and especially the familiar lines of Horace, (Sat. I. 3, 99,)

Cum prorepserunt primis animalia terris,
Mutum et turpe pecus, glandem, etc.
1*

The error of the ancients consisted in confounding the race of Adam with the preadamites. Aristotle, deriving his observation from the
race with which he was familiar, remarks, with
more truth and justice, that civilization is the
normal state of man, that he is by nature a
political animal. Had our modern philosophers
inquired for facts instead of fabricating theories,
they would never have raised the question as to
whether humanity commenced its career in civilization or barbarism. The Caucasian never was
a savage. The other races began in barbarism,
and have never completely thrown it off. Tribes
of them occupied this continent, from the era of
Peleg down to the time of its discovery by Columbus, without becoming more than improved
savages. Even the partial civilization of the
Aztecs and Peruvians perished under the inva-
sion of their kinsmen, the Indians. The Mongolian Chinese, pent up within narrow limits, and
compelled by the necessities of an overcrowded
population to resort to agriculture and handi-
craft, and with a history that goes back far beyond the Flood, are, at this day, only semi-civil-
ized. The Negro, in his native haunts, is always
a savage ; and if reclaimed will, without the control of a superior race, speedily relapse into his
primitive condition. The negroes in the South
have already made rapid strides in that direction. Fetish worship has been revived among
them.

The creation of the Caucasian, or white race,
is recorded in *Gen.* 2 : 7–25.

Up to this period, the earth, moistened by

mists, yielded its spontaneous fruits for the support of the nomadic hunters; but no rain had fallen upon the soil, and "there was not a man to till the ground." Deity resolved to create a new race, a race of tillers of the ground, and settle them in a definite locality furnished with all the natural facilities for successful agriculture. The Adamic race began its career with agriculture, domestic life and social organization. The goal of the preadamite is the starting-point of the Caucasian.

There are certain marked peculiarities in the origin and destination of the superior race.

1. JEHOVAH "formed the man of the dust of the ground and breathed into his nostrils the breath of life." He did not spring out of the earth, but was fashioned by the plastic hands of the Creator, shaping the material into human form; and then the breath of Deity, the divine *afflatus*, was infused into him. In this way, not by the mere fiat of his Maker, he "became a living soul." The Creator intended the Caucasian to be a workman, a builder, an artist; and hence he performed the part of a divine artist in creating him.

2. The Caucasian was to be engaged in agriculture, and to be blessed with the elevating influences of that noblest of occupations. Hence, his Maker did not command the earth to bring forth grass, etc., as at the first creation, but "*planted* a garden, eastward—on the east of the preadamites—in Eden, and there he put the man whom he had formed. And out of the

ground, thus planted, made Jehovah to grow every tree," etc.

3. The Caucasian was endowed with a high æsthetic faculty, the love of the beautiful. He was to create and foster the fine arts. Hence, his primitive abode contained trees " pleasant to the sight," as well as " good for food." The savage is insensible to the charms of nature and art. The loveliness of Eden would have been wasted on the preadamites. The negro, in his native wilds, never constructs a house nor plants a rose. The Chinaman knows nothing of perspective or the effect of light and shadow in painting.

4. The Caucasian, as a tiller of the ground, was provided with the means of artificial irrigation, in showers of rain, which, collecting into lakes, or flowing in streams, could be diverted to his fields.

5. The ornaments of civilization were placed within his reach. Eden contained gold and precious stones; both of them to decorate his fair daughters, whilst gold would serve as a standard of value and a medium of exchange in the commerce which flows from agriculture. Savages only barter; the civilized man is a merchant.

6. He was to advance the sciences. Hence, the Great Teacher gave him the first lesson, by bringing to him the inferior animals—the Fauna of Eden — "to see what he would call them." This was the first classification and nomenclature in natural history. From that day to this, science has been the exclusive possession of his descendants.

7. But the loftiest distinction of the Caucasian consisted in his being made the head and repre-sentative of universal humanity. He was placed on trial for all mankind. It may be objected that Adam could not have represented the pre-adamites, who lived before him and knew noth-ing of him. But it may be objected, with equal propriety, that he could not have represented their descendants now living ; whilst all orthodox divines hold that he did represent them. The fall was retrospective as well as prospective. This doctrine, however, is the Gordian knot of theology, which human wisdom is incompetent to untie. This much may be.said, in vindication of Divine Providence, that if the Caucasian has no right to complain, much less have the Mongol and the Negro ; for they were represented by one much better qualified to stand the test than any of their progenitors. Besides, Christianity, the remedy of the fall, is designed for all races. This is affirmed by the Apostle of the Gentiles, in a part of his writings, which has greatly puz-zled his interpreters. Col. 3 : 11. His words are, *Greek, Jew, Barbarian, Scythian.* Accord-ing to his interpreters, the last term is super-fluous ; for were not these Scythians barbarians ? They certainly were the wildest of the Caucasian race; and this circumstance ought to have opened their eyes to St. Paul's meaning, which undoubt-edly is, that the gospel is to be preached not only to Jew, Greek and Scythian—the most untutored of the children of. Adam—but also to the pro-geny of the preadamite barbarians.

8. The Caucasian is, in form, color, and mental

and moral qualities, unlike the Mongolian, and the very antithesis of the Negro, who is

> " as disproportioned in his manners
> As in his shape,"

and no more resembles the white man than Caliban resembled Ferdinand, or the old hag Sycorax the beautiful Miranda.   He is a being,

> " On whose nature
> Nurture can never stick—
> And as with age, his body uglier grows,
> So his mind cankers."

Adam, in the garden, needed only one thing to complete his happiness—a wife.   But among the races already in existence, " there was not found a help-*meet* for him."   The Hebrew is *chenegdo, according to his front presence*, i. e., resembling him as one of the same race.   As JEHOVAH had shaped Adam from the dust, he formed a suitable help for him, by building a rib taken from his side into a woman.   She did not spring out of the earth, but was part of himself transformed and sublimated, " The precious porcelain of human clay."   Our first father, enraptured at the spectacle of feminine loveliness, exclaimed, " The very thing ! capital ! Bone out of my bones, and flesh out of my flesh ; this shall be called *ishah*, woman, for she was taken out of *ish*, man."   Thus, the planter became a husband, and the family organization took the place of the capricious concubinage of the other races. Happy had it been for him and our fair, sweet mother, had they retained their innocence and bliss.

The narrative of the Fall is given in the third chapter of Genesis. The tempter was the serpent, who is said to have been "more subtle than any beast of the field which JEHOVAH ELOHIM had made." Here the comparative degree is used, as is also the case in the Targum of Onkelos, the earliest and best Chaldee translation of the passage. (Riggs' Chaldee Manual, p. 93.) The tempter was more cunning than any beast of the second creation, that by JEHOVAH, these being superior in organization to those of the first creation. He surpassed all brutes in intelligence; and, therefore, was not himself a brute. What was he? Unquestionably, one of the preadamites, the only human beings prior to Adam. True, he is called a serpent; and this has puzzled the commentators. Dr. Adam Clarke, pressed by the difficulties of the case, is driven to the supposition that he was an ape or ourang-outang, in which he came very near the truth. The tempter was a preadamite, perhaps a negro; and he is denominated a serpent, by a common figure of speech, just as a vile man is called a reptile, brute, a dog, etc. The Hebrew verb, from which the appellation is derived, signifies, according to Gesenius, "to utter a low, hissing sound, to whisper, especially of the whispering or muttering of sorcerers." It presents a vivid picture of an African medicineman, or conjurer, with his "grey dissimulation," whispering his diabolical temptation into the ear of unsuspecting Eve. That the tempter was a preadamite is evident from his name for Deity, "Yea, hath ELOHIM said." He knew nothing of JEHOVAH. The first false step taken by Eve was her recognition and repetition of his title of Deity. "ELOHIM hath said." In this, she virtually renounced JEHOVAH and forfeited his protection. She fell, and became the occasion of her husband's fall. But, although fallen, they were not utterly degraded. "They knew that they were naked," and, with the modesty of their race, " they sewed fig-leaves together, and made themselves aprons." Whilst the preadamites have always been shameless in their nudity, the Caucasian covers his person. It is the unanimous testimony of travelers that the negro, even the female, appears perfectly naked, without any sense of indecorum.

The existence of so absurd a form of superstition as Ophiolatry, or Serpent-worship, has excited special wonder. It assumes two forms, and is traceable to two different sources. The savage adores the serpent, in honor of his illustrious progenitor and his exploits in the garden of Eden ; the Caucasian, blending mythology with history, has received his system from the tradition of the brazen serpent, which Moses erected, as a type of our Saviour. The antagonism between the seed of the woman and the seed of the serpent, originated in Eden, and is irreconcilable. The experience of centuries has only exasperated it. The negroes of the South, in their ingratitude and insolent demeanor, leagued with the vilest white Trinculos, who batten on the miseries of the people, and " steal

by line and level," are ready, at their behest, to
brain their former kind master,

> " Or with a log,
> Batter his skull, or paunch him with a stake,
> Or cut his weazand with the knife."

In view of all this, well may the Southerner
exclaim,

> " Abhorred slave,
> Which any print of goodness will not take,
> Being capable of all ill. I pitied thee,
> Took pains to make thee speak, taught thee each hour
> One thing or other : when thou didst not, savage,
> Know thine own meaning, but would'st gabble like
> A thing most brutish, I endowed their purposes
> With words that made them known. But thy vile race,
> Though thou did'st learn, had that in 't which good natures
> Could not abide to be with."

The first-born of Adam and Eve was Cain.
His pious mother recognized in him " a man
from JEHOVAH." Her fatal experience was well
suited to impress her with a horror of " a man
from ELOHIM." As she caressed her infant boy,
her heart warmed to him, as the image of his
father and the image of JEHOVAH. Next, Abel
was born. The sons adhered to the civilized
vocation of the father, but with a division of
labor. " Abel was a keeper of sheep, but Cain
was a tiller of the ground." *Gen.* 4: 2. The
cultivation of the soil and the breeding of cattle
are the chief care of the intelligent farmer.

" And in process of time, it came to pass that
Cain brought of the fruit of the ground an offering unto JEHOVAH. And Abel brought of the
firstlings of his flock." Abel's offering was
accepted, whilst Cain's was rejected. Why was

this? Each of the brothers brought the avails of his own occupation; but Cain's offering of fruit was the oblation of a preadamite, recognizing only ELOHIM, the Omnipotent, whilst Abel's acknowledged JEHOVAH, the Holy One, whom fallen man could not approach, except through the medium of sacrifice. He thus confessed himself a sinner; and, by faith in the Atonement, "offered a more excellent sacrifice than Cain."

The sequel of the narrative would seem to warrant the inference that Cain was contaminated by intercourse with the barbarians around him; for he evinced the possession of their murderous spirit by slaying his brother. The penalty inflicted upon the fratricide is worthy of notice. Having indulged the temper of a savage, he was doomed to dwell among them. "When thou tillest the ground, it shall not henceforth yield unto thee her strength: a fugitive and a vagabond shalt thou be in the earth." The import of this malediction evidently is, that he should no longer be an agriculturist; but must become a savage, eking out his subsistence from the precarious bounty of nature. "And Cain went out from the presence of JEHOVAH, and dwelt in the land of Nod." As it is impossible to escape the presence of the Omnipresent, the expression must mean that he was exiled from the race created by JEHOVAH and enjoying His special protection.

This narrative proves, beyond question, the existence of human beings prior to Adam; for the murderer exclaimed, "every one that find-

eth me shall kill me." Whom had he to fear?
Abel was dead; and his parents would not harm
him. It may be supposed that his apprehen-
sions were only the creation of an excited imagination, conjuring up the spectres which always
haunt the guilty; but it is added, " JEHOVAH set
a mark upon Cain, lest any finding him should
kill him," which proves that there were men who
might slay him. Cain's fears were groundless.
The preadamites, flattered by the visit of a
white man, welcomed the felon, and gave him a
wife; just as the negroes of the South caress
the recreant whites, who, because repudiated by
their own race as contemptible villains, have
gone among the freedmen, for the purpose of ac-
quiring wealth or political importance.

The history of which the above is an epitome,
illustrates a fundamental principle of the divine
government — the purity of race. The Lord
would not permit Adam to marry a Mongol or
Negro. He cursed the first murderer by imposing such a wife upon him. *Miscegenation is a
crime against nature*, an unlawful attempt to set
aside the ordinance of Heaven, and reverse the
wise and beneficent order of creation. It is sin,
and the penalty of sin.

The mongrel posterity of Cain blended the
occupations of civilization with the pursuits of
savage life. He himself " builded a city," with
the hope of habituating his family to domestic,
social and civic manners; but it could have been
nothing more than a rude collection of wig-
wams. Jabal devoted himself to a sort of pas-
toral life; Jubel cultivated music, and amused

his leisure with the composition of war songs and corn-dances, whilst Tubal-Cain set up a forge for the manufacture of weapons of bronze and iron. This dutiful son presented to his father Lamech, the first polygamist, a sword; and the first use he made of the weapon was to try its temper upon a young preadamite. In his exultation over his exploit, he boasted that the vengeance threatened against the slayer of Cain was a trifle compared to that which he would inflict upon his assailants. The very temper of the insolent savage breathes in his defiant appeal to his squaws. Herder calls it "The Lay of the Sword." It sounds very much like an Indian war song:

> "A man have I slain for his wound to me,
> Even a young man, for hurting me;
> If Cain was to be avenged seven-fold,
> Truly Lamech seventy and seven-fold.

The reputation of these hybrid races became so infamous that, as early as the time of Enos, the grandson of Adam, the Caucasians assumed a distinctive appellation. *Gen.* 4 : 26. "Then began men to call upon the name of the Lord." The literal rendering of the Hebrew is: "A beginning was made for calling by the name of JEHOVAH." This is sanctioned by Piscator, Diodati, Le Clerc, Bishop Patrick, and other learned men, and is adopted by Kitto, Biblical Cyclopedia, ii., p. 425. Its meaning is this: the posterity of Adam, in consequence of the awful increase of wickedness, assumed the appellation of Jehovahites, or SONS OF ELOHIM—not his slaves, as the preadamites had proven themselves to be.

"Ariel" is correct in viewing the deluge as JE-
HOVAH's declaration against miscegenation ; but
mistakes the nature of the offence. The crime
which occasioned that catastrophe, was not the
copulation of men with beasts, but the *intermixture of the races of men.* "The sons of God [Cau-
casians] saw the daughters of-men, [preadamites,
or, more probably, the hybrid Cainites,] that
they were fair, and they took them wives of all
which they chose." The Adamites were ensnared by these lascivious women, mulattoes and
quadroons. The offspring of these alliances
were prodigies of wickedness, the perpetrators
of gigantic crimes, and filled the earth with violence. To preserve the purity of Caucasian
blood, JEHOVAH swept these mongrels from the
earth, and saved Noah and his family, the only
unadulterated Caucasians then living. Ariel supposes that the negro went into the ark, along
with the other beasts. But the negroes were
never in the ark; nor did they perish in the
Flood. The only persons destroyed were the
mulattoes, the mongrel progeny sprung from the
amalgamation of the Caucasian and the Cainite.
The Mongolians and Nigritians, together with
the hybrid races caused by their intermixture,
had not committed the crime of which the Deluge
was the divinely appointed avenger—the crime
of blending the blood of Adam with that of the
preadamite. The Flood was only partial, limited
to the portion of the earth's surface inhabited
by the culprits. The notion of a universal flood
has been abandoned by all intelligent theolo-

gians. The Bible does not teach it, and science utterly ignores it.

The race thus rescued by JEHOVAH was elevated to higher privileges and blessings. "I will not again curse the ground any more for man's sake." The primitive malediction resting on the soil was removed. "That old curse," says Bishop Sherlock (On Prophecy, p. 89), "was fully executed in the flood ; in consequence of which discharge from the curse, a new blessing is immediately pronounced upon the earth." To Cain, the earth, saturated with his brother's blood, was cursed with barrenness; to Adam, it yielded reluctantly and scantily; but Noah and his sons inherited a new world, and, ever since, agriculture has been the most pleasant, healthy and remunerative of all vocations. It is the favorite pursuit of the Caucasian race. and the main spring of their opulence and prosperity.

The first production of the "new earth," was the wine-producing grape, the noblest of fruits, which "cheereth God and man." *Judges* 9 : 13. The farmer, now, had "*corn and wine,*" the Scripture epitome of all temporal blessings. "Noah planted a vineyard, and drank of the wine, and was drunken." Fanatics are shocked at the conduct of the patriarch; but the Bible does not censure him. On the contrary, upon awaking from the torpor of vinous inebriation, he was filled with the spirit of prophecy, and predicted the fortunes of his sons, in which, he signified his reproval of Ham's unfilial demeanor, by disclosing to him the degradation awaiting his son Canaan. The common explanation of this affair is preposterous. It is said that Noah cursed Canaan, because of the conduct of Ham. Strange justice this, to punish one man for the sin of another—the child, for the crime of the parent. But Noah did not curse Canaan; he merely predicted the curse which was to fall upon him—a curse which has been repeatedly fulfilled in the subjugation of his descendants by the posterity of Shem and Japhet. Remark that this was the subjection of the white to the white. It was reserved for the *Radicals of this country*, in their fiendish malignity, *to subject the white man to the negro.*

After the Flood, the discrimination between JEHOVAH and ELOHIM, as also between the sons of God and men, became less important; and hence these terms are not used with the precision which is observed in the earlier chapters of Genesis. The race of Noah went forth to their mission, under the protection of JEHOVAH-ELO-HIM; and, as the only men worthy of the name, the subsequent accounts are restricted chiefly to them. Inspired history is the history of the Caucasian. It contains a genealogical table of Noah's descendants, with the countries to which they migrated. There is not the slightest evidence that any of them were colored people. They are, and always have been, white. The Ethiopians, or Cushites, as the Bible terms them, were not blacks. As to Canaan, the effort to identify his posterity with the negro is utterly absurd. Dr. Hickok justly remarks: "It is not probable that distinctions of race at all took their rise in the three sons of Noah." (Empirical Psychology, p. 43.) History and science demonstrate the contrary. These distinctions existed long before the Flood.

The Caucasians scattered over the earth, driving the inferior races before them, and gradually took possession of its fairest portions. At the era of Peleg, the fourth in descent from Shem, "the earth was divided." *Gen.* 10 : 25. This was "an occurrence in physical geography, an earthquake, which produced a vast chasm, separating two considerable parts of the earth, in or near the district inhabited by man." (Kitto, Bibl. Cyclop. 2, p. 393.) The event recorded was, doubtless, the disruption of the globe into two continents, by which the preadamites, who had wandered to America, were cut off from the Caucasians, and intercourse between the two suspended, until the discovery of this continent, where Europeans found the descendants of the original emigrants, and began to press upon and exterminate them. At a very early period, anterior to the dawn of profane history, the Caucasians drove the negro into Africa, and pursued him to the edge of the Great Desert, which he crossed, and concealed himself in Southern Africa, where he has subsisted, an unmitigated barbarian, to the present time. The Rev. T. J. Bowen, 1856, and Mr. S. W. Baker, 1866, describe him, as he is in his native haunts, the lowest type of humanity.

The advocates of the Unity of the Race insist upon the assertion of the apostle Paul, *Acts* 17 : 24, "God has made of one blood all nations of men." This is literally true; and the only wonder is, how St. Paul came to know it; for it is a very recent discovery, which could be made only by the microscope. Prof. Lehrmann says: "The blood globules are distinguished by peculiarities of form and size in every animal *genus*. The corpuscules of the blood of many of the mammalia can be individually detected and distinguished from that of man." (Physiological Chemistry, 2, p. 156; Kölliker, Histologie Humaine, Paris, 1856.) Sameness of blood does not prove identity of species, but only of genus. The different races, or species, of mankind are all made of one blood; just as the lion, the tiger, and the cat are made of one blood; and as the dog and the wolf are of one blood. But the blood of one genus differs from that of others. Men are of one blood, but of different species. Let the skeptic inform us, if he can, where St. Paul got this knowledge of a fact unknown to Aristotle and Pliny.

Naturalists have been greatly perplexed with the doctrine of species, and some of them, in their attempts to define it, have fallen into the fallacy of the *argumentum in circulo*, making fecundity the test of species, and species the measure of fecundity. The argument, which they derive from the analogy of other animals, fails in an essential particular—the absence of reason. In virtue of this special endowment, man possesses more vital force, and is, therefore, capable of wider and more varied propagation. The wolf and the dog produce a hybrid offspring; but the offspring is not prolific. Now, a sound logic arguing from analogy, would con

2

clude that, as man is superior to the brute, he
must possess a superior power of propagation,
and the species may intermix beyond any assign-
able limits. Hence, mongrelism, which is limited
in the different species of brutes, as the wolf and
the dog, the horse and the ass, extends, in man,
throughout all generations. There are only
three original types, or species, but several hundred varieties. The pure Caucasian stands
alone, in his character and his achievements.
Within a short period after the Flood, he had
already founded vast empires, built magnificent
cities, and erected the pyramids of Egypt, the
temples of India, and the gorgeous palaces which
Layard and Rawlinson have exhumed from the
mounds of Assyria. All history, chronology,
art, science, and all literature worthy of the
name, are his.

"Ariel's" hypothesis that the Canaanites were
a mongrel people, is highly probable, if not absolutely certain; although his reasons for it are
destitute of force. He mistakes a mere gentili-
tial or patronymic termination, *ite*, for the designation of a cross between a man and a beast.
But the hypothesis is amply supported by the
facts of the case. The patriarchs were averse to
all matrimonial connection with the Canaanites;
and no reason can be given for it but the impu-
rity of their blood. Abraham charged his servant: "Thou shalt not take a wife unto my son
of the daughters of the Canaanites, but thou
shalt go unto my country and unto my kindred."
In what respect were the Canaanites not the
kindred of Abraham, since they had come from

a common ancestor, except that they had become debased by amalgamation and were mongrels? For the same reason, Esau's connection
with a woman of that race was "a grief of mind
to Isaac and Rebekah," *Gen.* 26 : 35 ; and Isaac
charged his son Jacob : "Thou shalt not take a
wife of the daughters of Canaan." But the clear-
est evidence of the fact is found in a very singular circumstance related in *Gen.* 34. Schechem, a young Canaanite prince, had cohabited
with Dinah, a daughter of Jacob. He was really
devoted to her, and asked her in marriage, prof-
fering her father and brethren any amount of
" dowry and gift." This was certainly a fair and
even generous offer; but the brothers of the
girl, so far from accepting it, devised a scheme
of terrible vengeance, which resulted in the extermination of the whole tribe. The affair looks
like the vengeance of white men exasperated
beyond control by their sister's pollution by a
mulatto; and this is its most natural explanation.

Jacob might well have addressed to Schechem
the language with which Prospero rebuked the
monster Caliban :

> "Thou most lying knave,
> Whom stripes may move, not kindness; I have used thee,
> Filth as thou art, with human care; and lodged thee
> In mine own cell, till thou didst seek to violate
> The honor of my child."

The Stephanos of the age, inebriated by fanaticism, have emancipated the negroes, and the
liberated brutes, wild with joy, are dancing and
crying out:

> " Ban, Ban, Ca-Caliban
> Has a new master :—Get a new man.
> Freedom, hey-day! hey-day, freedom, freedom!"

But when the deluded victim of drunken
philanthropy regains his senses, he will exclaim,

> " What a thrice-double ass
> Was I, to take this drunkard for a God,
> And worship the dull fool."

There is another point, in which "Ariel" has
approached, and yet perverted, the truth. He
affirms that the law in *Levit.* 21 : 18, which excludes from the priesthood one " that hath a flat
nose," was intended to exclude the negro from
divine worship. The regulation refers exclusively to the priesthood, into which no negro
could enter, because it was limited to the posterity of Aaron. Nevertheless, the exception is
very significant ; for it proves that if an Aaron-
ite was so unfortunate as to have the *blemish* of
a flat nose, that point of resemblance to the
negro would interdict his "approach to offer the
bread of his God." It is an indirect but powerful testimony against the negro, whose very
similitude the God of Israel abhorred.

It is unnecessary to pursue the Biblical argument further. In it, Heaven's protest against
admixture of race, the contamination of Caucasian by inferior blood, is as plain as if traced
in letters of fire, like the " handwriting on the
wall." Our own country affords the most recent
illustration of the primitive and unrepealed law.
It has been said that the institution of slavery
was wrong, and God punished the people of the

South for sustaining it. This is rank fanaticism and falsehood. Nothing can be clearer than that slavery was not only tolerated, but sanctioned, by Abraham, Moses, our Saviour and his Apostles, and by the whole Christian Church, down to a very recent period. This was proved, some years ago, by that learned prelate, Dr. England, Roman Catholic Bishop of Charleston, S. C., in his LETTERS TO THE HON. JOHN FORSYTH, and, more recently, by the late revered Bishop Hopkins, of Vermont. Southern slavery involved no violation of any law, human or divine; and it was the best condition for the negro. He can live with the white man, only as his slave. The South sinned; and the South has suffered, in consequence; but her crime was not slavery, but amalgamation. Boston, New York and Philadelphia were, and are yet, more licentious than Charleston, Mobile and New Orleans; but, in the former cities, illicit intercourse was confined to the same race; whilst the sexual commerce of the latter was debased by miscegenation. The men of the South are, in many respects, a noble race; but they tolerated among them a crime which Divine Justice never passes by. They contaminated their blood by admixture with the lowest type of humanity. For this, they have been punished—most significantly—by subjection to the accomplices of their crime. God has permitted unprincipled politicians, vile and wicked men, the basest that the world has ever seen, to inflict this penalty upon them. So, He permitted the Pharisees to murder our Saviour; but took vengeance on

them for the crime. The Radicals are the
flail of Deity. They offered themselves for the
service, and have been accepted. Ruled by
self-interest and goaded by rancorous hate, they
have perpetrated a crime of colossal magnitude;
and, in subjecting the Caucasian to the Negro—
the highest type of humanity to the lowest—
they have turned traitors to their race, their
religion and their God. Never before has the
world beheld such criminals; never such a retri-
bution as awaits them.

> "Lingering perdition (worse than any death
> Can be at once) shall step by step attend
> Them and their ways."

They have exalted the ignorant and brutal
negro to be the civil and political master of the
South, the legislator and the ruler of white men,
their wives and daughters. They have thrust
him into the jury-box, the magistracy, the Common Council; forced the white into disgusting
contact with him in all public conveyances; and
filled all places with the noisomeness of his filthy
odor, the "ancient and fish-like smell" of the
monster. This, and more than this, with cool
and calculating ferocity, have they done. These
cruelties heaped upon the countrymen and
kinsmen of Washington, Jefferson and Jackson! History will be searched in vain for
a parallel to the deep, inexpiable wrong inflicted by the Radicals upon our brethren of
the South.

> "It were a torment,
> To lay upon the damned."

The vengeance of JEHOVAH, the guardian of our race, will pursue those miscreants, and will vouchsafe neither peace nor union to our unhappy country, until they are hurled from office, stript of the power they have abused, and trampled in the dust by the people, whose confidence they have betrayed, whose honor they have stained. This fair land of ours is the heritage of the Caucasian, the Western home of the German, the Briton, the Irishman; in short, of all in whose veins beat the proud pulsations of "earth's best blood." It is a WHITE MAN's country. The Caucasian, after occupying and embellishing the fairest seats of the Old World, has reared a mighty Republic on this continent, from whose western shore, he looks over the Pacific, to the primitive cradle of his race. This is his possession. The negro is an intruder here, an alien and a foreigner, a vagabond, as all his fathers were—and this great Commonwealth will never achieve its destiny, so long as the negro is allowed to vote, or to exercise any political right or privilege whatever.

To subject the Caucasian to the Negro is a higher crime against nature than to place the negro under the ape or the baboon; and nothing can equal its atrocity. It is "the sum of all villanies, a league with death and a covenant with hell." The doom of the felons, who have perpetrated this foul iniquity, this *crimen lœsœ majestatis* against the noblest type of humanity, has already been pronounced by the American People. Outraged justice and insulted virtue cry out against them,

> Never pray more, abandon all remorse,
> On horror's head horrors accumulate,
> Do deeds to make heaven weep, all earth amazed ;
> *For nothing cans't thou to damnation add*
> GREATER THAN THAT.

A REPLY

TO

ARIEL.

BY HARRISON BERRY,
A Full Blooded Cushite.

MACON, GEO.:
AMERICAN UNION BOOK AND JOB OFFICE PRINT.
MDIIILXIX.

PREFACE.

When, in the course of Human Events, it becomes necessary to reply to a work, a saying, or an idea put forth, there are two distinct courses to be pursued. The first is, in replying to an eulogistic work upon the merits of an act of high commendation, the progress and prosperity of Nations, or the intellectual capacity of a race; all of which is an easy undertaking, for the theme itself, flows in a natural channel of liberal perceptions, which constitutes it a pleasant theme for all right minded men to write upon.

But the second is not so pleasant; for where the actions of men, the progress of Nations, the intelligence of a race, (its Humanity questioned,) is assailed with opprobrious epithets, the task is not so easy to reply to illiberal conclusions, calumnious slanders, and infidelitrous slang, as it would be if it was unconnected with such revolting and unjust ideas. Under these considerations, I sincerely hope and earnestly beg the reader to criticise with all due allowance any misapplied conclusion brought to bear upon the following reply to "Ariel."

Hoping that I have asked no more than the reader will be willing to grant, I present the work to the public, and I do most especially present it to the colored man for his perusal, hoping that he may find it a Lever Power put into his hands to tear down that hitherto impregnable wall of ideas built by that monster, the Great Slave Power, that God had created the Negro inferior to the White Man; consequently he is born the White Man's servant.

To Ariel I apologize for any antagonistic representations I may have made in my reply, earnestly requesting him at the same time, never to suffer the Devil to get such a controling influence over him again, as to cause him to write such slanders against my Race, assuring the learned gentleman that if he does, I shall reply to him again, with all my ability, so help me God.　　　　　　　　　　　　　　　　　HARRISON BERRY.

224

REPLY TO ARIEL.

I now take up my pen to confute a hypothesis that for malignancy, arrogance, and misanthropy of the colored man, is undoubtedly without a parallel in the annals of History—Ancient, Modern, or Periodical. I wish it distinctly understood that I do not intend to follow Ariel through his labyrinth course of what he would like to have the world believe is historical facts, and Scriptural certainties, for his arrogant perception and imbecility of conclusion is so apparent that I doubt not, a ten year old boy, who had read his Bible a quarter through, and Parley's juvenile Geography, could refute the argument. I do not mean by this assertion that the gentleman is unlearned, for he claims to be the most learned of all the learned, and to have a much clearer perception of the creation than did Moses, or in fact God ; for he says on the 46th page of his pamphlet, that if the serpent who beguiled Eve was not the Negro, but a serpent and talked to Eve by the miraculous power from God, and after that was again turned into a serpent, then it follows beyond contradiction, that God is the immediate and direct author or cause of sin. The whole of Ariel's pamphlet abuses with such just absurdity and hyperbolical cant as his conclusion is that God was the author of sin. Such a flagrant and badly concepted idea of God's being the author of sin, would naturally exclude his doctrine of the progeny of the Negro. Even had the pamphlet been written with more consistency in other parts, for a man who sets himself up as the only true expounder of the Scriptures, and the commentator thereof, shows conclusively that he is either an imbecile or else working in the interest of a diabolical faction, as I expect to show before I have done with him, and as he has proved to be doing in the latter part of his book. The gentleman set out by making the Scriptures commetaries, and the general received opinion of philosophers and historical writers subservient to his slave oligarchical views, notwithstanding the gentleman's enedavors to wash his hands in an anti-political basin in the commencement; but if you follow him through, you will readily see the whole foundation of his fabrication is built upon the flimsy and slippery ground of a justifiable pretext of enslaving the Negro. He commences by saying the Biblical interpretation, and the general received opinion of historical writers, together with the out-side concurrent opinions are false and untrue. This I consider a pretty bold assertion—pretty strong talk; but not quite so strong as to say that "if the Negro was not the serpent, God is the author of sin." The gentleman next sallies around and strikes logic, as to be seen on the 3d page, 29th line, beginning with the 12th word in Ariel, and makes one man shoot another down with a gun without anybody's seeing him put the ball in, for the ball was found in the man's body, and how could it have gotten there unless it was shot from that very gun, and put into the gun? No one else could have had the gun with a ball in it, for that would not be logic. And the gentleman says that is the strongest evidence of what is true of any testimony that can be offered. The gentleman having got his logic fixed up, he next sets sail in his little dilapidated and flimsy bark, and we next find him in Italy, italicising the word "man," when speaking of the Negro. The next trip he makes is around the whole world and examines the hair, forehead, nose, lips and skin of every man, and comes to the conclusion that there are but two races of men on this earth, or in fact but one, for the gentleman says the Negro is a beast, and dares and defies the learned world to put their finger on a single page of history showing the Negro to have ever done anything more than a beast could do. The only difference is, he considers the Negro the ridge-pole of the brute creation. I suppose that the gentleman would be willing to acknowledge that the Negro has, and can do something more than a rabbit; but I have no idea that the gentleman would think of acknowledging the Negro to be superior to the newfoundland dog. The next place we find this most learned Ariel is in the garden of Eden, fixing up God's nomenclature of the creation. He gets the creation of animals separated into six parcels, but not with any disparagement to anybody ; but just before the learned Ariel gets ready to set sail again, he deals out a tremenduous blow to the clergy, and learned men of the former and present age. Then sails off to the outside of the garden, where Adam had been driven for suffering the beast (Negro) to fool him and Eve. Tells us what God meant by cursing ; stating that it don't kink anybody's hair, nor flatten noses, nor anything of that kind. This done he takes Noah's family and settles them just where he pleases, securing good comfortable homes of course, some in the isles of the Gentiles, some in the plains of Shimar. One he carried away down the river Nile, and settled him in Egypt; but in passing through the country, the learned gentleman shows that he is not altogether so good an explorer as Dr. Livingstone, or he would have discovered on his rout that Ethiopia was settled before Egypt, and that the Egyptians borrowed their arts and sciences, together with architecture, embalming, and hieroglyphic inscription from the best authority that can now be brought to light from the kinky headed, flat nosed Negroes. This I am willing to join issues with the gentleman on, and defy him to contradict it. Ariel next sails over into Judea to learn the Hebrew language, to find out the reason that Ham was named Ham and not Shem or Japheth. I hope he will find out before he gets ready to set sail again. But here I shall learn him for the present to study Hebrew. Perhaps when he leaves, he can tell whether Ham's name means black or white.

I will now view the gentleman's claims for asserting the Negro is not the progeny of Adam ; that he was created before Adam, and Eve, and consequently is not the descendant of Noah's family, and if not the descendant of Noah's family, he cannot be the progeny of Adam, and if not the progeny of Adam, he must undoubtedly be a beast, and if a beast, he has no soul. These are the points to be looked into before we can show up the real cause of Ariel's writing such an outrageous book on the Negro's inferiority. I shall only notice the most cardinal points, as I consider the other unworthy the notice of a school boy.

Ariel says, and says it emphatically too, that the Negro is a beast and has no soul; he does not seem to leave the reader in any doubt of that fact whatever. But if we take into consideration his wantonness in scriptural points, we can very readily see his fallacy in quoting history, and outside concurrent facts, which he has promised to prove his hypothesis by. It is too apparent to be doubted that the whole fabrication is founded on the interest of the great diabolical slave power, making the enslavement of the Negro justifiable on the hypothesis of his being a beast; taking for his authority, the scripture where God give Adam dominion over all the beasts of the field.

Well, let us now view his claims on his ideas of the Negro's being a beast without a soul. We read in the first chapter of Genesis, 26th verse, that God said let us make man in our image; read on to the 27th verse, and it says, so God created man in his own image; in the image of God, created he him; male and female, created he them. But Ariel says (24th page 39th line) that Adam gave the name to man; this we know to be untrue, for Adam was not created when God spoke of creating man, which goes to show that man was named before he was created. But the weakest part of Ariel's hypothesis on this point, is that he says Adam was named Adam by God, and that Adam gave name to man, setting aside the 26th and 27th verses, where God had given the name "man" before Adam was created; but the most funny part of Ariel's views on this point is where he says, (or intimates) that as God named Adam, the whole of the white race is named Adam too, fogetting (that is, if he ever knew it,) that the name Adam, is a proper noun; whereas, the name man, is a common noun. I think Ariel had better examine his grammar again. But in his ardor to heap up disgrace upon the Negro, he has forgotten all sense of decency or decorum in writing. The point Ariel is endeavoring to make is simply this: he knows that unless he can disprove the Negro's being the progeny of Adam, he cannot cut him off from Noah's family, and if he suffers him to remain in that family, he cannot extricate him from Ham's, and that if he leaves him in Ham's family, both ancient and modern history, will confirm the Negro's being the first in the arts and sciences; hence the ardency of Ariel's endeavors to cut the Negro off from the progeny of Adam; but I shall take

228

the *learned* gentleman on his own ground, and show him that notwithstanding all his fallacious endeavors to disgrace and degrade the Negro, he (the Negro) has proved himself the white man's superior; for Ariel says the serpent was the negro who begiled Eve, which brought death and destruction upon the whole *White Race.* It would not do to say the whole of mankind, for Ariel tells us that the Negro is a beast and has no soul; consequently, he is not included in the destruction, and that this destruction could only be arrested by the penalty of death. This could not be accomplished by the death of any one, save the very son of God himself. Now, if the kinky headed, low foreheaded, flat nose, thick lipped, black skined Negro was so much smarter than Adam and Eve, so much so as to cause them to disobey the God who had not only created them, but whose power was sufficient to speak this world into being, does it not look like the one kinky headed Negro had more sense than the straight haired, high foreheaded, sharp nosed, thin lipped, white skin, Adam and his wife had?

I should be pleased to have Ariel explain to me how the Negro serpent knew the result of Adam and Eve's eating the forbidden fruit? How did that inferior, wooly headed, low foreheaded, flat nosed, thick-lipped, black skin beast of a Negro, know that if Adam and Eve eat of that tree they would become at once wise as Gods—knowing good and evil? What sort of a Negro beast is this, with no more soul than a rat, who knows the secretsof that Being who, by pointing his finger at that luminary yonder, could burst it into atoms in the twinkling of an eye? What! do you say that that all powerful Being would take a no-soul beast Negro into his place of abode and reveal to him those inestimable secrets, which I doubt whether Angels knew or not? I tell you, Ariel, the Negro must be a great no-soul beast. Perhaps, Ariel, I can help you out a little by supposing it to have been the beast of Daniel, or the Revelations. I do not know as that will help you much for we have no account of either one of these beings, having kinky heads, or being flat nosed Negroes.

Well, Ariel, a few more words on this subject: and what I have to say now is this, if the no soul Negro had so much more sense than the white Adam as to control and lead him into that

2

fatal error of bringing death upon the whole of his posterity, it does look to me as if he must have been Adam's superior by far; and if he is the same Negro now that he was before the flood, as you verily say he is, it follows in the natural channel of events, that his race is superior to Adam's race to-day, as he has always shown himself to be by your own predictions; for you say that when mankind multiplied on the earth, that Adam's sons looked upon the daughters of the Beast, (negroes;) but where the Scriptures say the daughters of men were fair, you get out of that by quoting Hebrew. The word fair don't suit your purposes in this place; but if it had been said of the sons of God, there would have been no use of quoting Hebrew to have found out what the word *fair* meant. The massing of the sons of God with the daughters of men, you say, was the whole cause of the destruction of the world; and you also say that it grieved God that he had made the beast, (negro,) though God has said no such a thing. God said it grieved him that he had made man—the very same man he spoke of before he made Adam, of course; but Ariel has here the kinky-headed, low forehead, flat nose, thick-lip, black skin Negro to fool Adam again, into the fatal error of suffering his sons to marry their beastly daughters, which Ariel says was the prime cause of the flood. I tell you, Ariel, these beast Negroes seem to be pretty sharp fellows, don't they? But perhaps these sons of God were not Adam's posterity; for you say that God named Adam, and Adam named man; so, as man is frequently mentioned before the flood, and as Adam's sons was called something else, it is hard to find out what become of Adam's family. You say Adam was the name God gave to the white races. We can very easily find the beast man, (Negro;) for his name—man—is all through the Scriptures; but God only knows what ever become of poor Adam's family, for we have never heard him spoken of only in the singular number, and as we know the name—Adam—to be a proper noun, we know that it will not do to apply a proper noun to a race of men. I am at a loss to know what become of Adam's family. Oh! what fallacy, what fallacy! Would to God you had written with a little more consistency. But, it may be that God would not favor you with much consistency in laying such an untrue construction on his holy Scriptures. I think it very likely that you was led by that wicked serpent—beast—Negro, who has no soul. My honest opinion is that no other spirit other than that actuated you in writing that calumnious book against the Colored Race.

But, sir, I promised to show by your own hypothesis, the Negro's superiority over the White Races; and this brings us down to Noah's family. The sacred historians tells us that after the waters of the flood abated, Noah and his family came out of the ark and planted a vineyard, raised grapes, made wine and Noah got drunk. While in this condition, wallowing about over the floor of his tent, he by some means became naked, and Ham, one of his sons, happened to pass by, saw his father's nakedness and went and told his other two brothers. The two modest and obedient boys took a garment, and after spreading it over their shoulders, they then, for decency's sake, walked backwards and spread it over their father. But when Noah awoke from his wine, he knew what had taken place, and that Ham had seen his nakedness, and instead of covering him up had gone and told his brothers; showing, no doubt, a haughty disposition in not doing so; which, I think, is the most probable cause, for it does not seem reasonable that for his son's accidentally seeing his nakedness, should have awakened so much displeasure on the part of Noah. Be that as it may, he cursed Ham's youngest son Canaan; telling him that he should be a servant in the tents of his two uncles, and his cousins. This was the whole of the curse of Ham's family, and that was fulfilled when Joshua crossed the Jordan and conquered the Canaanite's Nation. But Ariel says their destruction was not on account of the curse pronounced on Canaan by Noah, but wholly and solely on account of their suffering those beast-Negroes to fool them into amalgamation with them. These beast-Negroes had some time before that fooled Nimrod, the first Monarch we have any account of, into that wicked undertaking of building a tower whose top was to reach unto the Heaven. Ariel says the reason they wanted to build such a tower was because they knew that God had destroyed the world once on account of their amalgamating with Adam's Race. So as they had commenced the same old practice, and to guard against their destruction by another flood, they fooled Nimrod into the building of a tower for their preservation in case of another flood. I tell you, Ariel, these beasts (no soul Negroes) fooled the White sons of Adam and Noah, just whenever they pleased; for don't you see these beast (Negroes) fooled Nimrod and made him take all the responsibility on himself? We have no account of the no soul Negroes having anything to do with it in the sacred writs, it is all put on Nimrod.

Now, Ariel, we have shown by your own commentations, that the Negro has fooled Adam's Race twice, and Noah's twice; three of those times the circumstances were of such grave magnitude that, to regulate, and set things right, the immediate descension of God upon the earth was absolutely necessary to arrest their progress. These Negroes must be smarter than the white souled races, for they first fooled Adam and Eve, and fooled their posterity into amalgamation, which, Ariel says was the cause of God's destroying the world with water; 3d the fooling of Nimrod to build the Tower of Babel, and 4th, the fooling of the Canaanites into amalgamation again; causing their utter destruction by the white races. If Ariel will not acknowledge their management to be superior to Adam's and Noah's posterities, I am at a loss to know what superiority means. But Ariel seems to be at a loss to know how it is that the Negro has kinky hair, low foreheads, flat nose, thick lips and black skin; while the other race has straight hair, high foreheads, sharp nose, thin lips and white skin. I can readily answer that question, by calling the gentleman's attention to his ignorance, or dishonesty, in asserting that there is but two races of mankind in existence. That is one of the weakest points in his conglomeration of diabolical slang. For everybody knows there are five different and distinct races of mankind; so much so, that they can be designated wherever they are found on the globe: North, South, East or West. Their heads, eyes, noses, mouths, cheek-bones, and chins, differ materially one from another; and even their long straight hair, which Ariel boasts so much over, of the ladies of Carthage, cutting off and making ship rope of, are different to a considerable extent, in some of these respective races. And if the straightness of the hair of man is an inevitable sign of his intellect, the Chinese and the Indians stand first in the ranks of intelligence, for the White skin Caucasian has a much stubborner, and frizzlier hair than the other two Nations named above. Had I the time and space, I would insert here what Mr. Chambers says of the five Races of mankind, in his work entitled "Information for the Pœple," the first Vol. 60th to 76th page; but I have no idea that Ariel will receive the gentleman's physical history as true, for he commenced by calling the whole learned world fools for not believing as he does; though we know the physical difference of the human Races are so apparent that none who have eyes, and not blinded by prejudice, can doubt its truthfulness. The question I now wish to ask Ariel is, why could not the colored Race differ from the white, as well as the brown, yellow and red? The gentleman gets out of that by saying those swarthy fellows are sun burnt. I do not think that will fit the case, for who would dare think of the sun's burning a Laplander or an Esquimaux Indian? That doctrine will not suit the case in this particular point. So, I do not know what he will do to extricate himself. Perhaps he will say they got sunburnt before they went there, and all the snow and ice in the country, could not wash it out. I know not what conclusion the learned gentleman will come to, nor do I care; I only reserve the right of requesting the gentleman, that if in the course of his life he feels that dreadful and deplorable disease (monomania) coming on him again, please do not suffer it to embrace the subject matter of the Negro Race.

I have now gone with Ariel as far as I can on that subject. I will quote and insert a part of the travels of Her Brittanic Majesty's Exploring Agents up the Nile, some years ago. I here urge upon the reader a very strict request to note what he says of black, the Negro, and Ethiopia. I do this because I shall afterwards quote some of the Prophets, where the word Ethiopia will occur in several places; I therefore wish the reader to keep in mind that wherever he sees the word "Ethiopia," it means the Negro, or Black Race. We read in the 11th Vol. 485th page of Chambers's Information for the People, the following:

"Few travelers proceed farther up the Nile than Phileo, as the journey through Nubia is less safe or agreeable than that within the Egyptian Territory; yet without a visit to the Nubian valley of the Nile, which extends to near the head branches of a river in Abyssinia, much of the ancient grandeur, of this part of the world will remain unexplored. Nubia which is at present a Turkish province, subject to the Pasha of Egypt, is frequently called by the name Ethiopia from the black complexion of whose inhabitants the term Ethiopian, came in early times to signify one who is black, or a Negro. This country of Nubia, or Ethiopia, is understood by some Historians, to have enjoyed a degree of civilization and refinement in arts at a date even earlier than Egypt; and till the present day it possesses Pyramids and other monuments of architectural skill as wonderful in the eyes of the traveler as those in the lower divisions of the Nile. One of the latest travelers who penetrated to this inner Ethiopian region was Mr. G. A. Hoskins, who in 1835 published a large volume descriptive of his journey. At about the 17th degree of North Latitude he reached Meroe; an Island formed by the forking of two upper branches of the Nile. This Island is between three and four hundred miles long, and contains several distinct groups of pyramidal structures, of extraordinary magnificence, but greatly damaged by the hands of Barbarians; also, some traces of the remains of the city of Meroe, once the capital of Ethiopia. Never, says Mr. Hoskins, were my feeling more ardently excited than in approaching, after so tedious a journey, to this magnificent Necropolis. The pyramids in the distance announced their importance, but I was gratified beyond my most sanguine expectation when I found myself in the midst of them. The pyramids of Gizeh are magnificent and wonderful from their stupenduous magnitude; but for picturesque effect, and elegance of architectural design, I infinitely prefer those of Meroe. I expected to find few such remains here, and certainly nothing so imposing, so interesting as these sepulchres, doubtless, of the Kings and Queens of Ethiopia. I stood for some time lost in admiration. From every point of view I saw magnificent groupes —pyramids rising behind pyramids, while the dilapidated state of many did not render them less interesting, though less beautiful, as works of art. I easily restored them in my imagination; and these effects of the ravages of time, carried back my thoughts to more distant ages. The Porticoes on the East side of each pyramid soon attracted my attention, and I passed eagerly from one to the other, delighted to find, in several of them, monuments of sculpture and hieroglyphics, which, few as they are, have, I trust, given us the assurance of the locality, and will, I hope, throw some light upon the mythology and arts of the Ethiopians. There are the remains and traces of eighty of these pyramids; they consist chiefly of three groups; the principal and most imposing at which I arrived first, is situated on a hill, two miles and a half from the river, commanding an extensive view of the plain. There are thirty-one pyramids in this group, of which the plans of twenty-three may be traced; while to the South-east is another group of thirteen, in some degree of preservation. There are three other groupes, two consisting of two pyramids each, and the other six. And at 5,600 feet to West of the chief group may be traced the remains of twenty-five pyramids, but almost buried."

After mentioning the appearance and minor details of these remarkable structures, this author continues:

"I have carefully described this interesting and magnificent cemetery; but how shall I attempt to express the feelings of the traveler on treading such hallowed ground? One who in passionate admiration for the arts, had visited the chief galleries of Europe, gazed upon the breathing image of divinity, in Apollo of the Vatican, or the deep expression of the most poetical of statues, the Dying Gladiator of the Capitol; who had beheld and felt the pictorial creation of a Rapheal and a Carregio, and with delight contemplated Grecian, Roman and modern sculpture, could not be unmoved on finding himself on the site of the very metropolis where those arts had their origin. The traveler who has seen the architectual antiquities of Rome, and has admired the magnificent use that Nation has made of the arch, making it the chief ornaments of their Baths, Palaces and Temples, would be further interested at finding here the origin of that discovery. These emotions would be felt with peculiar force by one who, like myself, had been fortunate enough to trace art through her earliest creation, from the splendid Gothic edifices of the North, to the ruins of the eternal city; from Rome to Magna Grecia; from the magnificent Temples of Neptune at Paestum, tot he still purer antiquities of Sicily, particularly at Girgenti, where nature and art seem to have vied with each other. From that interesting island, to the Morae and the city of Mineva, where the knowledge of the arts shown in the most genial soil, produced the perfection of elegance, chastness and magnificence. But the seeds of knowledge of the Greeks were derived from Egypt; and the Egyptians received their civilization from the Ethiopians and from Morae, where I am now writing, the beautiful sepulchres of that city affords satisfactory evidence of the correctness of the Historical records. Where a taste for the arts had reached to such perfection, we may rest assured that other intellectual pursuits were not neglected, nor the

science entirely unknown. Now, however, her schools are forever closed, without a vestige of them remaining. Of the houses of her philosophers, not a stone rests upon another; and
where civilization and learning once reigned, ignorance and barbarism have resumed the sway. These pyramids are of sandstone; and the quaries of which are in the range of hills to the
East. The stone is rather softer than the Egyptian, which added
to the great antiquity, may account for the very dilapidated state
of most of these ruins, and also for the sculptures and hieroglyphics being so defaced."

So much for Ethiopia, the land of the Negroes; but perhaps
Ariel will not consent to this country ever being settled by Negroes, for the account is given by a learned traveler, which Ariel has already denounced in the first of his book. However, as
the gentleman has quoted Historians to prove his doctrine,
where it suits his case, he must, if consistent, admit other testimony, whether it suits his case or not; or he will be traveling
on the line of inconsistancy. This the gentleman denies being,
so I will take him on the ground he claims to be his strong
forte, which is the Scriptures.

But before entering upon that topic, I shall endeavor to set
before the reader a few plain facts, not to be disputed, and which
I hope he will keep in mind and not lose sight of. The facts are
these; we have shown in the above insertion, that the Ancient
term Ethiopia · means the Negro, or black man; consequently,
wherever we find the word Ethiopian in the Holy writ, it undoubtedly means the Negro Race. The next question of importance I wish the reader to observe, is whether the sacred
writers in refering to, or in speaking of the Ethiopians, allege
any disgrace or degradation different to that of other Nations
for like offences. I defy the combined world together with
Ariel and all his coadjutors and colleagues, to show in one
single instance where the prophets, Christ, or the Apostles
spoke, or even hinted, in any of their writings, that the Ethiopians were inferior to the other Nations in any shape, form, or
fashion. In vain may we hunt; but it can never be found in
that Holy book, and the God of Heaven be thanked for it.

I will now endeavor to point out a few passages, or rather
chapters of Scriptures, for the reader to examine for himself.

The impression I wish to make on the minds of the public, is that all Nations are of the same progenitor, and stand before God in a similar relation to that of brothers to a father. A very striking illustration corroborative of this view is shown in the family of Jacob; for although he loved Joseph better than his other children, it does not seem that that peculiar love had anything to do with the blessings imparted to, and bestowed on the other children when he became to die. Just so with God; he set apart the children of Israel, through whom to promulgate his gospel; but it does not exclude them from the same obligations to obey and serve God which was incumbent upon all other Nations. We are all commanded to love and serve God and to give him all the glory. It seems that the sins most abhorrent with God was the worship of Idols; though Ariel says, either ignorantly, or hypocritically, that the greatest sin with God is the beast-Negroes marrying white people. As I do not consider that assertion worthy of notice, I will not give it any attention in this place. What I wish the reader to pay particular attention to in the scriptures I point out in this place is, that God punishes all disobedient and idolatrous Nations alike, according to the magnitude of their sins, regardless of their color, hair, nose, lips, forehead, or any other physical appearances.

We read in Isaiah, XXVII chapter, that God's chastisement differs from his judgment; showing conclusively that God punishes Nations in some instances whom he does not destroy.

Again, in the XXXIII chapter, God's judgment against the enemies of the church, shows that they must be spoiled even should it take treacherous dealings to counteract treacherous dealing.

Again, in the XXXVII chapter, 9th verse: Here we see king Tirhakah, of Ethiopia. Here comes one of Ariel's beast Kings to make war with Hezekiah; but not one word is said about his being a beast, but is spoken of just like all other Kings and Nations are.

Again, in the XLIII chapter, 3d verse, Egypt and Ethiopia and Sheba. Here all three of the Nations are spoken of in a collateral point of view. Not one word is said of the beasthood of Ethiopia, nor of her inferiority. I think if Ariel will

3

examine the XLIV chapter, 24th, and 25th verses, he will see what God does to just such arrogant creatures as he is.

Again, the XLV chapter, 14th and 15th verses, we find Egyptians, Ethiopians and Sabeans, all taken captive and put in chains by the conqueror, but not one word is said about the Ethiopians being beasts or inferior.

Now, let us hear what Jeremiah has to say. Jeremiah XLIII chapter, from the 10th to the 15th verses, you will see the destruction brought on Egypt for her idolatry.

Again, we read in the XLIV chapter, by reading the whole you will see the destruction of Judah, Jerusalem and other Nations, kingdoms and cities for their idolatry.

Again, in the XLVI chapter, in prophesying of the overthrow of Pharaoh's Army on the Euphrates, he speaks of the Ethopian together with the Lydians and Libyans, in 9th verse, as being mighty men, and not as mighty beasts.

Again, in the XLVII chapter. Read the whole chapter, you will see the destruction of the Philistines, all for their wickedness.

The next, see the XLVIII chapter. The destruction of Moab for her contempt of God.

See the next XLIX chapter, and the judgment of the Ammonites, an almost utter destruction, with a partial promise of being restored; but in the very next chapter, the Lth, we see Babylon is to be destroyed, and the third verse says, both man and beast shall depart. Now I do not see how Ariel will defend that line, for he says that the word man means the beast-Negro, being given by Adam, who named beast and man. But, Ariel, I want to know how come that cojunction—"and"—between the name man and beast. That, I would think, a pretty hard question for you to answer.

We next examine the LI chapter, and see the judgment against Babylon, in revenge for Israel. Zedakiah rebels, and Jerusalem is besieged and taken.

We will now point out a few chapters in Ezekiel: XXV, 10th and 15th verses, we see again man and beast cut off, and in the XXVIII chapter the judgment of Tyrus for his pride; again in the XXIX chapter, the destruction of Egypt cut off man and beast; 10th verse, they will be smitten from the borders of Egypt to Ethiopia; see XXX, whole chapter, the XXXI and XXXII chapters and 13th verse, in last chapter you will see that the beasts have hoofs, but men have feet. I am unable to say what Ariel will do with this, for he says the Negro is a beast, and here the prophet says the beast has hoofs, and I have never heard of a Negro having hoofs, and I know I have never seen one in all my travels; so Ariel either contradicts the scriptures or else the scriptures contradict him. Which one of the two are right, I will leave the reader to judge for himself. I have pointed out these passages of scripture to show the credulous dupes of Ariel that the degraded position in which the colored man is now found, is not the result of his being naturally inferior, as Ariel is endeavoring to make appear, but to the contrary, for his forefather's sins, as you see in scripture pointed out above, was visited upon all other Nations for theirs. This, Ariel could have seen had he not been blinded with prejudice, or else an ignoramus, I care not which; for the former makes him a bad man, and the latter too weak to set post for the lamp carriers to go by.

I will now see if Josephus knew anything about where Ham's posterity settled. 1 will give his own words for testimony. He says in the first volume of his History; the VI chapter, 21st page, in speaking of Noah's sons and their settlement, in these words as follows:

"The children of Ham possessed the land from Syria and Amanus, and the mountains of Libanus; seizing upon all that was on its sea coast, and as far as the ocean, and keeping as their own; some, indeed, of its names are utterly vanished away; others of them being changed, and another sound given them, are hardly to be discovered; yet a few there are which have kept their denominations entire; for of the four sons of Ham, time has not at all hurt the name of Chus, (Cush) for the Ethiopians over whom he reigned, are even at this day both by themselves, and all men in Asia called Chusites, (Cushites) the memory also of the Mesraites are preserved in their name, for all we who inhabit this country of Judea, call Egypt "Mestre" and the Egyptians, "Mestreans." Phut, also, was the founder of Libya; and called the inhabitants Phutites from himself. There is also a river in the country of the Moors which bears that name;

whence it is that we may see the greatest part of the Grecian Historiographers mentions that river, and the adjoining country, by the appellation of Phut, but the name it has now has been by change given it from one of the sons of Mestriam, who was called Lybyos. We will inform you presently what has been the occasion, why it has been called Africa also."

Now, Ariel, what do you think of Josephus's account of Ham's sons? He says Cush reigned over Ethiopia, and Josephus says that down to his day, (which was some forty years after Christ) they were called both by themselves and all men in Asia Cushites. This account of Josephus's corroborate exactly with Mr. Hoskins's account stated above. Now, learned Ariel, you recollect Mr. Hoskins said that the word Ethiopian meant one who was black, a Negro. This proves the Negro to be the Ethiopian, and the Ethiopian to be the descendant of Cush, the son of Ham, the son of Noah. Now, Ariel, you said that if the Negro was the descendent of Noah, he ought to be received and treated as a brother. I being a full blooded Negro, would like to offer you my hand, but I doubt very capitally whether Ariel will ever be heard of again.

As for the opinion of Ariel in regard to God's knowing Ham's posterity would be scandalized by the Negro's being called his children, is too weak to be argued. To think of a man's endeavoring to prevent the real intention of God in endowing the Egyptians with the knowledge of embalming the dead, hieroglyphics, sculpture and architectural skill, for the lone purpose of showing posterity that Ham's children was not Negroes, is too absurd to be entertained for a moment.

Now, Ariel, let us suppose a case: Suppose I was to write a book descriptive of a country that abounded with all the arts and sciences, such as hieroglyphics, Pyramids, architecture, sculpture, and the art of embalming the dead, and you were to become so excited over the account, that you could not be satisfied without going to that country to see those magnificent structures; but on reaching that country, you could find none of those magnificent pyramids and temples, which I had so beautifully described, in my book. What do you think would be your conclusion of the authenticity of that book? Would you not think the whole of it was a fabricated falsehood? I believe you would. And do you not think it to be as likely that God, in order to prove the truthfulness of the scripture in that early age of the world when there was no prophets appointed to describe the actions of men, should move and actuate those Nations who was foremost in the arts and sciences, to leave a tangible and perceptible sign whereby the truths of his Bible should be substantiated and verified? Yes, indeed, these structures, of Egypt and Ethiopia was no doubt erected to leave a lasting and enduring testimony of the truthfulness of the scriptures leaving no gap down whereby the sceptic, infidel, nor the atheist, could come in to contradict the verity of his revealed word. Now, Ariel, I think the above conclusion is a sufficient refutation to your diabolical scheme.

The next point to be considered, is Ariel's positive assertion that the Negro is a beast and has no soul. This assertion is so bold and so groundless, that it is hardly worth while to offer a refutation; for all ten year old boys know it to be without sense, or foundation. But to please Ariel, I will touch him in one or two tender places to see if he will bear spurring. Ariel says, and says it emphatically too, that the Negro is a beast, and has no soul. And that the greatest sin that the white races are capable of committing, are amalgamation with the beast-Negro. I have neither time nor space to waste with such tom-fools, and shall content myself with citing Ariel to a few cases only, for if we were to attempt to go into details on this subject it would place Ariel in such an imbecile position that I fear the adherents to his doctrine would become alarmed at their situation. But to the subject. Ariel says the whole cause of the destruction of the antideluvians were in consequence of their amalgamation with the beast-Negroes. Now, as we have proved the Ethiopians were termed Negroes, we can find out how it operated by the scriptural accounts, for we read in Numbers, the *XII* chapter, from the first to the fourth verse, that Moses married an Ethiopian woman. I would like to be informed by Ariel, if it is probable that a man after God's own heart; a man into whose hands he had committed the destiny of his chosen people; and who he had appeared to in a bush of fire, and talked to, face to face ; and who he called upon the mount, keeping him there forty days and nights, teaching him the divine oracles of Revelations, writing it down on two tablets of stone, and delivered it to him to explain and promulgate to his chosen people for an everlasting law and guidance for them. Would he have, is it likely, committed this important charge into a man's hands and custody, who had not only lain with a beast, but had married her? thereby laying the foundation of prostitution, when he was to deliver to the people himself, God's protestation against man's laying with the beast? And, friend Ariel, will you be so kind as to tell me how much soul Moses' children had? Or, will you tell me how much soul the mulattoes of this country have? Or, if a mulatto marries a white person, how much soul will their children have? Or, if a mulatto marries a Negro, how much soul will their children have? I see no use in arguing such unfounded and silly conclusions, for if the Negro has no soul, the Prophets who prophecied of the conversion of the Ethiopians, knew nothing of it; and if man set apart by God, who had received their instructions from Heaven, knew nothing of the Negro's being a beast, and having no soul, how in the name of common sense came Ariel to find it out?

Well, Ariel, let us try the other point. You say that the white people of this country, who encourages the beast-Negro to call upon the name of God, are committing a very great and almost unpardonable sin. If you will take up the New Testament and read the VIII chapter of the Acts of the Apostles, commencing at the 26th verse, you will see where an Angel from Heaven told Philip to go and preach the gospel to one of those beast-Ethiopian-Negroes; and that is not all, for so intent was the spirit to have the gospel preached to the Ethiopian eunuch, that it went with Philip and told him when to join himself to the chariot, which command Philip obeyed, and preached Christ, and him crucified; after which the spirit took him away, so that the eunuch saw him no more. Thank God, there the gospel was preached to one beast-Ethiopian-Negro. And if an Angel came, or was sent from Heaven to command the apostle to preach to one beast-Negro, I do not think our white clergy need have any fears about preaching the gospel to the beast-Ethiopians of the United States, notwithstanding Ariel's remonstrance against it.

Now, Ariel, you had better read and study for yourself, before you branch out so far on the weak and rotten limbs of your great preceptor Agassiz, the wonderful discoverer of the age— the great professor of a college.

Now, sir, if the Negro is a separate, and distinct race of mankind, as your preceptor Agassiz pretends he is, and which, if true, would place him with the beast creation as you say he is, I would like to know how it is that the mixing of the two races come to be so prolific? Hybrids do exist, but I have yet to learn of their propagation; whereas, the mixing of white and black races produces the most prolific race of man, as well as the most handsome that we have among us; for I do believe the mixed blood on the colored side, will not fall short of two-thirds of the whole black population of the United States. Knowing the mule to be a hybrid, we know it is brought forth by the generation of the Horse and Ass; but who ever knew a mule to propagate? This goes to prove that the Horse and Ass are of different species of quadreped beast. But the white mixing with the colored Race, produces quite a handsome and intelligent people; the most prolific we have among us. This ought to convince Ariel that we are the progeny of Adam and the descendents of Noah.

Now, Ariel, you ask the question why does the Negro differ from the other Race, which you are pleased to term the white Race? I can readily answer that question. It is because you have been so dishonest and unfaithful in your demonstration, in regard to the number of different Races of mankind; for if you had confined yourself to the plain and emphatic teaching of the learned world, that there are five different Races of mankind, you would have had no trouble in solving that question; for it is as plain as the stars of Heaven, that there are five Races of mankind, differing in complexion, in the shape of the head, in eyes, nose, mouth, jaws, hair, and to a great extent in statue.

Now we read in the Holy writ, that the iniquities of the fathers are visited upon the children unto the third and fourth generation, whether it be deformity of the nose, lips, hair, head, or whether it be prostitution of character; or whether it means a political curse, or a non-progress in religious prosperity, or an enslavement of their children, we are unable to say; but one thing we do know, and that is, Ezekiel says: the father's eating sour grapes, the children's teeth are set on edge. Now, friend Ariel, let us bring things nearer home. The rules I expect to lay down here admits of some exceptions, but in a general sense of the word, I hold are good; for I know they are correct generally speaking.

If you will go to the cradle and take two boys, (brothers,) you may shut your eyes and take choice; the one you will raise up from the cradle with all the care possible, clothing him well with the best kind of garments, and giving to him the most nutrious food, and compel him to take care of himself, giving him a good education, the consequence will be, when grown, you will have a fine looking, erect, nice, trim muscled young man, with regular features, with smooth tender skin, and fine smooth and silken hair.

Whereas, the other you suffer to run at random, bare-headed, bare-footed, and half naked, and before he is able, put him to work, and by the time he is ten or twelve years old, put him to ploughing, hoeing and malling rails, and the result will be that when he has attained to his fortieth year, you have a rough skin, wrinkled face, large, broad feet and hands, coarse and rough hair, the head not so well developed, the muscles hard, and the spine somewhat curved. Follow the two brothers to the fourth generation, their offspring living successively as their forefathers had, and that, too, in different climates, and I will show you two young Nations, looking like anybody else but brother's children. You may go into a company of a thousand men, and you can pick out very nearly every aristocratic family from the poorer classes, who have had to labor hard all their lives. I have been a pretty close observer all my life, and have noticed the slaves brought from Virginia, who were raised up more tenderly for the slave market, have more erect forms, and more regular features than does those raised on the Southern Cotton, Rice, and Sugar plantations, where they were put to work much sooner, and less care taken of their raising. Thus you will find those born and bred on those large farms, looking like a different tribe of people, entirely; their deformities are more apparent, both in feature and in body; but the most striking illustration of this fact is in some of the European Nations; there, where the aristocrats and common people are kept as distinct as if they were two different Races of mankind, the dissimilarity has become so apparent that the aristocrats seize that as a sacred right to prevent the intermixing of the common laborers with the aristocrats; and, indeed, the very same spirit has got a pretty strong foothold in some of the United States; but this country, having a Republican form of government, they are compelled to give it a different name here; whereas, it is called a difference of blood. Now, Ariel, if you will take up your map and examine it thoroughly, and then take history and read it carefully, you will find that on some of the African Islands, settled by the Portugese some centuries ago, that they have by the heat of the tropics, coarse and common living, become much deformed in their features, and have black skin and kinky hair.

Now, sir, if you will examine the accounts of the Missionaries sent to Africa, some of whom traveled through the country and preached to the natives for many years, and of whose authority no sane man will doubt, you will see that there are tribes in Africa as beautiful as you are; and I do hope, possessed of a little more charity. These Missionaries say there are tribes of a very low type; but they are generally found near the Equator, or on the banks of the Niger river. And if you will allow me to use the expression, I can find as many tribes of a low type among the much boasted Caucasian family, as you can among the African family. By following your family to India, we find some as black as tar, and their features not so very regular either. You also claim the Abyssinians as a tribe of your Race, who inhabit the head waters of the Nile; and I tell you Ariel, some of them have awful thick lips and kinky hair too. I am only speaking of those the learnd world calls Caucasians, for if I were to take your doctrine, that all except the beast-Negro belongs to the white family, I could find some hard cases among the Indian tribes, I tell you.

Ariel, I do not think you can be a Southern raised man, for

4

if you were you would certainly know the difference between the servants raised in the yard, and about the house, and the one put to work on a plantation. You may take two brothers or sisters, one you will raise up about the house, with a great deal of care, giving him or her fine and nutritious food, while you send the other to the farm, feeding him on coarse and scanty food, the continuance of which, for two generations, will produce two distinct looking families, in form, features, color of skin, and softness of hair and muscles. This, all Southerners who have been used to slaves know to be true. Now while I admit there are differences in the features of children, I at the same time am compelled to dissent from the opinion so prevalent that the Negro is a distinct and separate Race of mankind, any more so than the Mongolian, Malay, or Indians are a separate Race from the Caucasian, or White Race. I hold that the tropical heat of Africa, the coarse diet they use, together with every species of heathen depravity, has degraded the African Nation more than any natural cause that can be brought to bear on the subject.

I am now compelled to advert to a subject, (and that reluctantly too,) which I hoped, when I commenced reading your book, I should have nothing to do with. I mean politics. For you promised in the first of your book that it was not a political cause by which you were actuated; you had not voted, nor taken any part in politics for years, and therefore you was not actuated by any subserviency; but such I find is not the case. After you have done with vilifying the Negro Race, with your hypothetical slang, you wind up by saying, as the Negro is a beast, he ought, of right, either to be sent to Africa, or be enslaved again. This, Ariel, is too audacious to be borne with. You also assert that slaveholders have added more honor and dignity to the Constitution and the Congressional body, than any class of men; and you undertake to prove it by referring to Washington, Jefferson, Henry and others. While I hold in my bosom the very highest respect for these time honored fathers, I am at the same time unwilling to yield to that hypothesis, that a man must be a slaveholder to constitute him an honorable, dignified gentleman. This doctrine, if it proves anything, proves too much; for it excludes all others who have never been the owners of slaves. Well, Ariel, you are quite a genius indeed.

I have no disposition whatever to persecute the late slave-holders. I certainly have no bad feelings towards any man for using an inheritance left him by his parents; let it be money, lands or slaves, so long as he uses it within the bounds of justice and equity; but I am not prepared to believe that slavery in it-self, is right; nor do I believe it honorable to be a slave-owner. Nevertheless, I cannot go as far against the slave-owner as Ariel goes in his argument, for I know there are men who have been slave-owners that are as high-toned gentleman as any I have ever made the acquaintance of. Therefore, it is not the owner of slaves alone I expect to write against, but the great aristocrat-ic slave power. I care not whether a man has ever owned a slave or not, if he belongs to, and is a co-worker of that power; I hold he is a worse enemy to the ex-slave than many of those who had formerly owned them. It is not the man who has owned slaves who is his worst enemy, but rather the man who gives his whole influence in support of that diabolical aristocrat-ic slave power. There is the whole sin of the affair. It has done more to degrade and keep the colored man down than all the slave-holders put together. Do not understand me to ex-empt the slave-holders, for they all, at one time, belonged to this aristocratic slave power, though their excuse for a co-opera-tion with it was a much better one than those who were not pe-cuniarily concerned, for we all know to touch a man's pocket is touching his heart; so I am not prepared to say that there are no high-toned, philanthropic and humane gentlemen among the ex-slave-holders, as Ariel is disposed to say there were none who did not own slaves; for about twenty years ago when the de-mon slave power had risen to such an alarming extent that it took control of the legislative acts, and defied the whole world to disobey its mandates, it forced the legislatures to make laws prohibiting the slave buying himself. Hon. Robert Toombs assisted a poor slave who had, by hard work and strict economy, acquired money enough to purchase himself, wife, and one child, in getting up a petition, setting forth the facts of his good char-

acter, honesty, and peculiar right to that privilege, had it presented to the Hon. G. W. Crawford, who was then Governor of
Georgia, and procured his consent to the legality of the purchase, and assisted him in getting off to a free State, upon which
the legality was based.   In this case we see a gentleman who
owned a hundred or two slaves, voluntarily, and without remu-
neration, helping a poor slave off, who he had every reason to
believe was his just right; and I have been credibly informed
that the Hon. A. H. Stephens was so lenient to his slaves that
he could not restrain those who were not disposed to do right.
I have also been informed that Hon. B. H. Hill was a very lenient master; also, Hon. Joseph E. Brown, I have been told by
one of his ex-slaves, was a very lenient master.   There are
many more, had I the time and space to mention them.   But all
these men, as a matter of course, were strong auxilaries to the
aristocratic slave power.   Now, as I said above, I have no bad
feelings towards any man for owning slaves, so long as he treated them in a humane and lenient manner, but I do object to that
diabolical slave power which held the exclusive right to deal
out to the tyrant the privilege to treat his slave like a brute.
These are some of the troubles of the great slave power.   While
such men as I have mentioned above, treated their slaves with
humanity and leniency, they at the same time lent all their
strength, energy, and power to that diabolical monster, which
knew no man but its adherents, nor recognized any proceedings
not sanctioned by its tribunal, receiving appeals from none other.   This is the power I propose to attack, for it has lain every
obstruction and hinderance in the path of the colored Race that
has ever been placed there, by pretending that the Negroes are
inferior to all other Nations; courting for its text the sacred
writ where it speaks of Canaan being cursed for his father Ham's
laughing at his father Noah's nakedness.   Notwithstanding the
curse was visited on the Canaanites, when Joshua conquered
those Nations, and notwithstanding the curse was not delivered
against any of Ham's posterity, other than Canaan's, a large
number of clergymen have given their implicit credence to the
doctrine that Ham's posterity was doomed to perpetual servitude.

In 1442 the Portugese commenced the importation of Africans from the western shores of Africa, to St. Domingo ; one of the West India Islands, and such was the thirst for gain, that the English, French and Spaniards engaged at once, after having received the approval and encouragement of the Bishop of St. Domingo, which held that the enslavement of Ham's posterity was a scriptural command, and it was but doing the will of God to enslave them.

Now, after receiving this commission, the slave traders were turned loose with two commissions; one from Heaven, but the other from Hell. The Bible in one hand, and manacles in the other. Vessels were soon fitted up and loaded with rum and red handkerchiefs to seduce the coast Chiefs, thus giving them encouragement to make war upon their neighboring tribes to secure more slaves, to buy more rum. And where the coast Chiefs were unable to subjugate their neighbors, a sufficient quantity of rum was furnished to induce them to surrender their obstinacy, after which it would be an easy matter to engage them in the same nefarious traffic. Having secured their concurrence, the next thing to be done was to induce them to use their influence to engage their neighboring tribes in the same business, and when that failed a resort to arms was the consequence, and hence the frequent wars of Africa, which have kept back the efficacy of the Missionary work, and has driven civilization from the shores of Africa. After they had stretched their lever from Europe and America to Africa, and had placed their hands upon the beam, all they had to do then was to move the beam, and the whole of the coast tribes were thrown into a tumult, and this made capital for the announcement that the Negro was incapable of self-government, and from whence came the God-sent right to enslave them.

Ariel, I have now given a meagre synopsis of the effect the slave power has had in keeping the African tribes in a state of hethenism. We will now return to the shores of the United States, and see what it has done there. In the first place, it proscribed the Negro ; put him in the cotton field and forbid his leaving there without the conset of the overseer, who was given absolute control over him, and who had no further interest in

him than to press all the labor from him he was able to perform
for one year, to enable the overseer to make a big crop, to get a
big name, to get big wages somewhere else the next year.
Under these circumstances, it is not to be supposed that a man
who had no interest in the slave, longer than one year, and
whose future success was based upon the number of bales of
cotton raised by those slaves, should treat them like he would
his own property ; this reputation of being a good farmer was
worth more to him than an other man's slaves were, and if driving the slaves late and early, at the top of their speed, would
secure it, success with them was a certainty ; there was no use in
telling the planters that he had servants capable of attending to,
and carrying on his business for that was out of their power,
unless the master lived on the premises himself, for the slave
power had already told the legislatures that the Negroes must
be kept under the white man all the time, or he would get in-
surrectionary notions in his head. So it matters not how lenient
the master wished to treat his servants, he was forbidden the
privilege on account of this power's mandates. Under this
rule I ask the question what chance had the master to offer any
encouragement to his slave to become honorable ? Or what advantage was it to him to teach his slave anything more than to
obey the overseer, and to be struck with awe whenever he saw
him the least displeased ? As a matter of course, the slave became more careless and unconcerned about anything, other than
what he was bid to do, which offered a favorable pretext for the
slave power to say the Negro would not work without a master.
This, together with the non-observance of his marriage, has been
the main-spring of the degraded and demoralized condition in
which the ex-slave is now found. I will now leave this part of
the subject, and see what it has done to the government. This
aristocratic slave power went into Congress, the Executive, and
the Supreme Court, and threw fire-brands into each department ;
it told the members that if they did no give it their support
they should never be elected again. It told the President he
must recommend its support in his messages, or it would damn
him politically forever. It told the Supreme Court that if it
did not decide in its favor, it would instigate Congress to throw

it overboard, from which cause the decision in the Dred Scott case, that there was property in man, sprang. And this aristocratic slave power is the prime cause of the colored people in the Northern States not being entitled to suffrage. At the first sight, it looks strange to see a people who were born and bred in free States, give this support to such a diabolical scheme; but when we consider the whole subject thoroughly, it is not a hard problem to solve. Unless the power could have engaged the strongest support in the Northern States it would have been impossible for it to have held its own in the South, the colored people being free in the North, and in some instances found in a very poor and degraded condition, was one of the strongest evidences this side of Africa, of the Negro's inferiority; hence, keeping him down was the great paramount object of the slave power North. In order to accomplish this, he was proscribed, denied the right of suffrage, and whenever a white man could be found to work he could get nothing to do; rejected, hated, scorned, and driven from pillow to post, he would, as a natural consequence, (unless he be the most superior Race of mankind on earth) become discouraged, without a dollar, no home, nor friends to look to for help. These are a few of the hardships the colored people have had to contend with, instigated and kept in circulation by that aristocratic slave power North. And all this was done to prove the Negro's inferiority. It is just like condemning a man without giving him a hearing. This power soon found its way into the Legislative Halls of a majority of the Northern States, where it persuaded the members to make laws to keep the Negroes in a menial condition; and where law failed to bring him down low enough, prejudice was introduced, and every white man, woman and child, who refused to fall down and do homage to the monster, was cut off and cast into the abyss of degradation; the effects of which could be seen a few years ago in the city of New York, when a white man was seen shaking hands and talking with a Negro on the side-walk, they could be seen sneering all around at the sight, and this too, in the Metropolis of the United States.

Now, when all the machineries were put into working operation, the demon is next found in the editorial sanctum, giving

orders to the editors to fight that little God sent veteran group
of men who had opposed it all the time; teaching and interpreting the preamble of the declaration that all men are created
equal, &c., and until that doctrine was observed, there could be
no permanent peace in the United States, for a house divided
against itself could not stand, and that they knew their cause
was right, for it harmonized with the teachings of God, the
Prophets, Christ and the Apostles. This was the little band the
demon placed its heaviest siege guns to play upon, and these
guns were the Whig and Democratic editors of the North.
They were told that if they did not fight and kill that band of
veterans, their papers should never cross Mason and Dixon's
line again, and it was too true for a joke, for no paper which
did not advocate its doctrines could be circulated in the Southern
States, nor could a man come South and advocate any other.
This was a great free government, where a man was not allowed
to go to one section and express his disapprobation of its in-
stitutions. That looks like freedom of speech and the press.
It was an untramelled right with the advocates of the great
slave power, for they could go North and condemn any policy
or institution they pleased.

But to the working of this power again : After issuing their
commands to the editors, it strikes commerce and the manufac-
tories; it tells the proprietors of the factories that unless they
give their own and laborer's support to the power, they should
loose the investment of their money. They tell the laborer that
unless he votes for the power he will be thrown out of employ-
ment, for cotton cannot be raised without slave labor. They tell
the merchants that if they don't give it their support they will stop
trading with them and open the Southern ports and import their
own goods from Europe. After setting in order these function-
aries North, it sent a Messenger South to tell the clergy how to
preach to the slaves. Tell them, says he, that they are an inferior Race; made so by God, expressly to serve the white man,
and that if he resist the will of his master, he will be damned in
that awful Hell where there is weeping, wailing and gnashing
of teeth, and from whence there is no return; and in order
to prevent the slaves reading the Bible and interpreting for

themselves, laws were passed prohibiting them being taught to read the Bible, or any other book. All this being done to keep the Negro down and in ignorance, it was an easy matter to impose upon the weak and credulous the natural inferiority of the Negro.

This is the power that caused George M. Dallas, while Minister to France, to refuse giving a passport to a colored man there from the United States to return home; stating that he was not authorized to grant passports to any but American citizens, and as he was not a citizen, he could not do it. This is the power which caused J. J. Crittenden to say in a speech delivered during the war, that he had rather see the last one of Kentucky's sons brought home a corpse, than for them to be degraded fighting by the side of Negroes. This is the power which caused the Convention at Montgomery, in 1861, to incorporate in its constitution that they held as a sacred truth that the Negro was inferior to the white man, and that his true and legitimate status was servitude. This was the power which caused the Confederate Congress at Richmond, after incorporating the slaves in the Confederate army, to say in the fifth section : "provided nothing herein shall be so construed as to impair the relations existing between master and slave." Great God ! Force a man to undergo all the hardships, facing the point of the bayonet, and the mouth of the cannon, to keep himself, wife and children in slavery ! This is the power which caused Andrew Johnson, a short time ago, to say in his message to Congress, that the Negro Nation had shown itself less capable of self-government than any Nation. Here we find it in the Executive Chair, that had taken an oath to execute the laws and carry out the principles of the Constitution. Ariel, this is a great monster, for it is the first thing I ever knew to be of more importance than money. That it is so can be easily proven, for when the Emancipation Proclamation was issued, the Northern slave power urged the South to accept it, but when the time come to citizenise the ex-slaves they held up their hands and exclaimed: "Great God ! we can never degrade ourselves by making citizens of Negroes." And to prevent the Negroes having suffrage, they are perfectly willing to disfranchise a great number of ignorant whites to

5

keep the Negroes out. This is not because they consider the
Negro so inferior; it is done with the same view that aristocratic
England had, in disfranchising her poor classes, to keep a subordinate and unprivileged, inferior class to do the bidding, and
be the menials of the rich. They are willing to conglomerate
the illiterate whites with the colored, because they well know
that to take the ballot out of the hands of the ignorant whites
and withhold it from the colored, will place them in a condition
which would prevent either one from voting for a general free
school system, and being unable to pay for an education, the
consequences are that this generation, and the next, and next to
it, and God only knows how many more, would grow up in ignorance and poverty, until it would become a proverb that the
Negroes were an inferior Race, and the poor whites of low
blood, as the poor whites are now called in Virginia. Under
the influence of this power, the late war was commenced and
fought until it saw it could no longer fight, expecting to renew
it in the Halls of Congress. But I hope it can never get the
hold it has had there again. Though if chicanery and duplicity
will carry them there, they will be sure to go, for they are now
endeavoring to saddle their old hobby horse, (Democracy,)
though the old animal is very lean and weak, too much so, I
think, to make the trip ; but if giving him different kinds of
medicine will bring the old fellow up, I think he must come, for
sometimes they give him Conservatism ; other times the Constitution, and others the white man's government; of course, all in
opposition to the beast-Negro. Ariel, you see what that power
has done for you, for it has driven you into infidelity. Though
I believe you are about as consistent as the other part of your
dupes are, for you say if it can be proven that the Negro is the
descendant of Ham, he ought to be offered the right hand of fel-
lowship, whereas the others say he is, and deny that concession.
I think you will have to come over on the Negro's side, for it has
been proven that the Negro is a descendent of Ham; but I would
like to have you send a substitute, if it is convenient, for we
would like to have a man with a somewhat larger heart, and a
little more brains, if you please. Ariel, your's is the last effort
of the great diabolical aristocratic slave power ; if you fail in

this, you are done; and I think you must certainly fail, or else the scriptures must be revealed again to fit your doltish slang.

Ariel, this is the reason the Southern States connot Reconstruct; the men who followed Generals Lee, Longstreet, Johnson, and others so faithfully through the four years' war, would have done the same in political matters had it not been for that infernal slave power in the Northern States; for when the people were getting ripe for reconstruction through the advice of their reputed leaders, you raised the Democratic whoop which caused some of your disappointed and disaffected demagogues to blow their horns which collected a few of your adherents, which collection they were pleased to call the rallying of the Democratic forces. Had the South not been encouraged by your slave power adulation of its reactions, its people would long since have been prepared to reconstruct on the broad basis of equal rights to all men. But the Devil, who has led and controled that power so long, would not suffer such an equitable adjustment to be made, it was an easy matter to prevent it after he got a foothold in the Executive.

My learned sir, suffer me to inform you that there is not, nor can there be a law or constitution in a Republic that can legitimately proscribe its citizens who are compelled to pay taxes and shoulder arms and fight for the Republic. No sir, with this view before the framers of the Constitution, knowing that colored men had helped to save the Republic, they were careful not to put in one single word about color, African or Negro; expecting, no doubt, that so soon as those who owned slaves at the time, were remunerated, they would set them free, as the illustrious George Washington did in his will, when they arrived at the age of man and womanhood. If this were not their intention, why did they so particularly refrain mentioning the words Negro, African or color? Is this the way your Democratic faction expects to hoodwink the people and make them believe the Constitution says what it does not? Can you find in the Constitution where it says the colored man is proscribed? Can you find anywhere in that instrument where it says Africans are not citizens of the United States? No, indeed, you cannot find it there. Nevertheless, your diabolical faction claims to be (with Andrew

Johnson at your head) the only constitutional party in the Union.
The whole sum and substance of your interpretation is found in
one or two clauses of the Constitution, where it speaks of persons held to service.   Does those clauses name any particular
Race of American citizens except the Indians ?   If the framers
had intended the Africans should be excluded from citizenship,
why not speak of it as in the case of the Indians ?   The reason
they were not termed citizens was because they were not taxed.
Does it not look reasonable that if the fathers had intended the
colored Race disfranchised they would have exempted them
from taxation as they did the Indians ?   We well know there
were numbers of free persons of color in the United States at
that time.   Why were they not set apart as a non-taxable people, as were Indians, if the framers did not consider them citizens ?   Now, my dear sir, if you want the Constitution to control
the African's rights, here's at you.   Carry it out with all its
bearings, and we ask for no more.   In regard to the inferiority
of the African Race, I have only to say that there are, as a matter of course, some tribes of a much lower type than others,
but not more so than is found in other families.   Take for instance, the Caucasian family.   You commence with the English,
French and Germans.   All you have to do is to run it down until you strike the East Indians and Abyssians, and you will find
some of the tribes pretty low down in the scale of humanity.
You next take the Mongolian and run them down from the Chinese, Turks and Tartars to the Esquimaux, and Laps, and you
will find some of the lowest and most degraded people in the
known world.   Now, Ariel, if you can show that the colored
woman does not conceive and bear children, as does the white
woman ; if her children are not helpless babes when born, as is
the white woman's ; and if they both do not bring them into
this world with the same pains that God told the woman she
should bring them forth with, I will admit your hypothetical
slang has a little consistency, but not until then.

If you are not too jubilant over the Negroes who were hung
up to the lamp posts in New York City, in 1863, by, and under
the auspices of your infernal slave power party, perhaps you
will read this essay carefully.

ARIEL'S REPLY

TO THE

REV. JOHN A. SEISS, D. D., OF PHILADELPHIA;

ALSO, HIS REPLY TO

THE SCIENTIFIC GEOLOGIST AND OTHER LEARNED MEN,

IN THEIR ATTACKS ON

The Credibility of the Mosaic Account of the Creation

AND OF THE FLOOD.

Price, 50 Cents.

Sent by Mail to any address, on receipt of the money.

NASHVILLE, TENNESSEE:

PRINTED AND STEREOTYPED BY "THE AMERICAN" PRINTING COMPANY.

1876.

EXPLANATORY.

ARIEL's last work on the status of the negro made its appearance in May, 1872. Like its predecessor it created a most profound sensation. Great was the anxiety to learn whether it was unanswerable, and if not, who would answer it (or what periodicals or newspapers would), or venture to review its startling positions. At the first, it seemed as if Ariel would be overwhelmed with opponents.

Many indications were given privately, as well as from the pulpit and press, that answers would be forthcoming which would entirely demolish Ariel in his strange, and apparently immovable Biblical statement of facts.

But no answer appeared; many denunciations of him and his views were put forth. These called forth many letters to Ariel, inquiring of him what competent Biblical scholar to whom application could be made personally, for a candid review and reply to his startling works. Although having no personal acquaintance with Dr. Seiss, yet having read some of his works, and being impressed by them that he was not only a scholar, but had exhibited traits of fairness in all his discussions of Biblical questions, he was recommended. But we cautioned them at the same time not to expect too much from him, as it was almost impossible for any man to rise above the prejudices of his early education, to be able to examine candidly any documents which assailed his faith in the truth of propositions which had not before been questioned. But on this point, Dr. Seiss had shown much freedom from educational prejudices. He was applied to, and agreed to examine and review Ariel's works. Ariel was informed that the review would make its appearance in the *Prophetic Times*, of which paper Dr. Seiss was one of the editors, in July or August, 1872. Ariel wrote for a copy or copies to be sent him three several times, but failed to get any response. We do not think Dr. Seiss is in the slightest degree responsible for these failures. Irregularities somewhere occasioned a delay of about five months before we got a copy; and then we were indebted for it to a friend in Delaware. This accounts for the delay in writing.

But the cause of delay in its publication was the following: Considerable anxiety was manifested by many of Ariel's friends that the publication of his reply should be made in one of the large Northern cities. Correspondence to this end was then opened, and copies of Ariel's works forwarded for examination. There was no difficulty in getting publishers to undertake it, but all of them declined to put their name or their *imprint* upon the works, alleging as a reason therefor, that the works uprooted the received opinion of the world, *politically* and *religiously*, in regard to the negro; and that, although the works had been examined by some of the ablest scholars in Europe and America, and by them pronounced unanswerable by any believer in the truth of God's Word, yet they were afraid it would injure their business if the work appeared with their name on it as publishers. They did not doubt there would be a great demand for the works. Ariel at once decided that men whose moral cowardice was so great that they were *afraid* for their names to stand beside the truth, and that truth God's truth, that Ariel would not stand beside them to aid them in making money to fill their pockets. In reaching this decision Ariel may have been wrong, as this commercial age measures the value of everything by dollars and cents. But he does not think so. This explains why the publication has been delayed until this time.

ARIEL'S REPLY

TO REV. JOHN A. SEISS, D. D., OF PHILADELPHIA.

Ariel's first publication on the *status* of the negro as fixed by God, first made its appearance before the public in September, 1867. His second work, in continuation of the same subject, made its appearance in May, 1872. These works severally created a great sensation among all classes of readers. Their Biblical array of facts, showing that the negro was created by God a beast, as the slave-servant of *ha* Adhom, and so designated by God, when He installed *ha* Adhom in the Garden of Eden, as lord and master over this world and his dominion, extending over everything that lived and moved on earth ; that this array of Biblical facts were so terribly destructive of the theory previously existing, that the negro was the product of Noah's curse on Ham, or that of his grandson Canaan, as to make the desire intense that they should be answered, if Biblically untrue, or indorsed by all competent scholars as true, and in accordance with the Word of God.

The answers called forth by the first publication did not fill the public expectation. Denunciations were plenty, and the arguments were few. A number of gentlemen, distinguished for pulpit oratory, and noted for Biblical learning, made the effort to crush Ariel and his positions. Their labors are also before the public, with Ariel's answers thereto, and can be found in his work of May, 1872. The eagerness of the public mind to have a more complete and perfect answer continued unabated, and which the publication of May, 1872, seemed rather to whet into keener anxiety and to awaken the hope that some good Hebrew scholar, well versed in the Bible, would take up Ariel's works on the negro, and review them with fairness and

261

candor. Immediately after the second publication made
its appearance, a number of literary and religious journals
made promises in response to this public anxiety that
Ariel should be reviewed, his arguments answered, and his
positions uprooted fairly, fully, and completely. Ariel's
works were readily and gratuitously furnished to all such
papers as proposed to review him.

In the meantime Ariel's works had been put by various
gentlemen before some of the ablest scholars in the United
States, and many copies sent to Europe for the purpose of
eliciting the opinions and judgment of the ablest Hebrew
scholars. The result of these investigations, so far as
we are informed, substantially sustained Ariel throughout.
Whether it was this, or the result of their own second
sober thought, which prevented the promised replies being
made, is left with the reader to decide for himself. So it
was, however, that no reply was made to Ariel, unless
strong denunciations can be called a reply. Many of the
clergy, however, and leading men of the different denominations, cautioned their members against reading Ariel's
works, as dangerous. This state of things brought about
a correspondence with Ariel from many gentlemen North
and South, asking of him the names of the best Hebrew
scholars in the United States to whom they could apply
for information touching the various Biblical points made
in his works. In answer to these we furnished the names
of some six or eight of the best scholars known to us, and
among them was that of the Rev. John A. Seiss, D. D., of
Philadelphia. In our replies to such inquiries, we expressed our anxiety to have some competent Hebrew
scholar to criticise our translation from the Hebrew of certain portions of the Bible, which we had given in Ariel.
If we were right, we wished to be sustained ; and if wrong,
we wished our errors pointed out that we might correct
them, and do it as publicly as we had put them forth. We
did not wish to be wrong, or lead others into error by our
writings.

It seems from the letter published by Dr. Seiss in his
review of Ariel, that he had been addressed on the subject
of answering Ariel, and had agreed to review it through
the columns of the *Prophetic Times,* of which periodical
he was the editor; and in which he was assisted by the
following named gentlemen as assistant editors: Rev.

Richard Newton, D. D., of Philadelphia, Episcopalian; Rev. John Forsyth, D. D., of Newburg, N. Y., Dutch Reformed; Rev. E. E. Reinke, Moravian; Rev. Robert Adair, of Philadelphia, New School Presbyterian; Rev. William Newton, Episcopalian; Rev. L. C. Baker, of Camden, N. J., Old School Presbyterian; Rev. B. B. Leacock, Episcopalian; Rev. Samuel Laird, of Pittsburgh, Pa., Lutheran. Besides the assistance of these learned divines, it may be well for us to add that Dr. Seiss is the author of several learned critical works on the Old and New Testament, showing great linguistic knowledge, which have placed him in the front rank of Biblical scholars. We felt highly gratified when we learned that so distinguished a scholar, aided by so many men of learning, was about to review Ariel.

It will be well for the reader to look at the fearful array that is on the one side in favor of the accepted opinion of the world for centuries past, that the negro is a descendant of *ha Adhom* and Eve, and therefore the full equal brother of all the white race; that the negro's color and the other personal peculiarities that now distinguish him, were the results of Noah's curse of Ham.

The letter which Dr. Seiss publishes as the one that induced him to reply to Ariel, and review his works, is as follows:

" July 17, 1872.

" We send you a copy of a work on the '*Status of the Negro*,' by 'Ariel.' It has produced a great sensation wherever read, in this country and Europe. His Biblical array of facts are startling, his reasoning and logical deductions upset all the previous views of Catholics and Protestants regarding the black man; placing him along with the beasts, endowed, however, with speech, and placed by God at the head of the beast creation to fill a certain station in reference to the white man by God. This work has never been *answered* by any one in the five years it has now been before the public. It has been *denounced* in the strongest and most unscrupulous language, which has only added to its strength, by a single practical admission that its array of Biblical facts, and the logical deductions therefrom, could not be successfully met, and therefore, denunciations and sarcasm alone could be used to ward off its powerful blows. This work has recently received new life by the appearance of another work by the same writer on the same subject, much extended and intensely fortified by a great accumulation of Biblical facts, drawn from Hebrew words, evidently and plainly *mistranslated* in our authorized version of the Bible, which are truly startling; accompanied by a review of his reviewers which bears evidence of the writer possessing a mind of rare strength, and an amount of cultivation and learning but seldom found even among our best scholars; and which throws his reviewers so far into the shade as leaves them but as pigmies beside a giant. We send you this work also. The positions he has taken in the two works has been so fully and powerfully sustained, that all of our most learned scholars in and out of the pulpit, in this region, have generally given it up, and now concede that the works are *unanswerable* by any intelligent believer in the Bible. His positions are Biblically taken, and the conclusions the most startling ever presented since the Christian era, and startling from (not his) but the Bible language used by the inspired writers, presenting in bold relief the facts that the negro or black-*man* is *only a beast*—in fact, the 'tempter, the dragon, that old serpent, which is the devil.' Greatly as this must challenge our credulity, yet, when we read his Bible array of proofs, and his criticism of the Hebrew, and the translations in our Bible, this incredulity is startled into convictions, and *forced* on our minds, of their absolute truth.

"It should be answered (not damned,) but answered *fair and full if it can be answered;* and if it cannot be answered from the word of God, its truth should be accepted by all our pulpits, and a new departure had. In this view it is that we, at the request of many of the most intelligent Christians, and many of our most learned men in and out of the pulpit, send you by this mail copies of each of his works, requesting you to carefully read them, and express through the columns of the *Prophetic Times* your candid opinions of the works; and that you make (if you differ with him) a candid, full, and fair examination of his main points. The people *wish you to do this.* Since you have been at the head of *The Prophetic Times,* you have built up a reputation for learning and fairness that secures great deference to everything you say. We therefore hope you will gratify numerous friends and Christians by complying with our request."

The foregoing letter presents fairly and plainly what the writer desired at the hands of Dr. Seiss, or any other scholar. How far Dr. Seiss has filled the expectations, and satisfied the public mind on these grave points, the reader must decide for himself, after he has read our response.

We wish our readers to bear in mind the exact issues between Ariel and the commonly received opinion; which are these:

THE QUESTIONS AT ISSUE STATED.

1st. That the negro is a lineal descendant of *ha Adhom* and Eve. This Ariel denies.

2nd. That the negro was made or produced with all of his peculiarities of color and person, by the curse which they say Noah hurled at his son Ham, or at Ham's children, Kush and Canaan. This also Ariel denies.

3rd. That the negro is our full equal brother. This Ariel also denies.

4th. That the negro is a proper subject of salvation by the Gospel of Jesus Christ, and may have eternal life beyond the grave. This Ariel denies also. On the other hand Ariel affirms that the negro, when created by God, was a beast, the head of the beast creation, and endowed by God with the organs of speech, that he might fulfil the more readily the duties of his station as slave (*Ebhodh*), servant to *ha Adhom* and Eve.

His duty was to obey *ha Adhom;* all things then being good, consequently *ha Adhom* could give no command but what was good. That the negro by his own conduct in lying to Eve made himself the tempter, the dragon, that old serpent, which is the devil. That he had mortal life, and God declared that he would put enmity between him and the woman; and between his seed and her seed. That God has not only overthrown and destroyed, heretofore, every nation on earth that recognized whites, blacks, and mulattoes as equals—nay, that he has gone further; he has exterminated without exception all the old nations of the

1*

world that recognized this equality; viz: Egypt, Chaldee, Babylonia, Assyria, Media, Persia, Greece, Rome. The present inhabitants of none of these can run their history back at the present day to the time when these States were in their grandeur and glory. That every civilized nation now on earth, and every Christian society on the globe, have, at the bidding of the negro, who is himself the tempter, the dragon, that old serpent, which is the devil, and the arch-fiend of God and of man; and such has been the adroitness of his conduct that he has united all earthly political and religious powers in his behalf to elevate and put himself forward, while but few sustain our Lord Jesus Christ.

We would like to enquire whether or not Dr. Seiss comprehended the extent and magnitude of the questions at issue? If he did, there was a condescension to little matters unworthy of himself and the gravity of the questions at issue. We greatly regretted and felt deeply humiliated when we observed, as the first of his Hebrew criticism, his exception to our orthography in spelling the Hebrew words *Ish, Adhom, ha Adhom,* &c., &c., even if we were wrong; but being right, as we know we are, we felt humiliated, that a man of his reputation would, under the circumstances, which he knows well, regarding the Hebrew language, that so worthy a man and distinguished a scholar as Dr. Seiss would descend to such trifles. The celebrated John Randolph, of Virginia, is reported to have said that the most learned man and ablest debater in Congress was from Connecticut, and invariably spelled the word Congress with a K.

HEBREW ORTHOGRAPHY.

Dr. Seiss well knows that the orthography, in our Hebrew Bibles, of all that date as far back as 1820, differs in many words from those of anterior date; and that those of the last few years, and which are published in the United States, are intentionally made to differ more widely from the ancient correct Hebrew orthography. His exceptions are taken on account of these latter Hebrew publications. Dr. Seiss knows that there is a movement on foot among the learned D. D.'s of Europe, and of this country, to make a new Bible, or such a translation of the old one as will harmonize with the truths of science, as they choose to call it. This clique, or party, want to change not only the orthography, but also the words and the very meaning thereof which they had when spoken by God. We therefore do not sympathize with the movement, or fraternize with any of its abettors or advocates. But besides this, it is well known to Dr. Seiss as a scholar, that the orthography of the various editions of the Hebrew Bible differs in many words. This was known to him as a Hebrew scholar, but not known to his English readers, and his only object, as it seems to us from the manner in which he noticed our orthography of the Hebrew words *Ish, Adhom, ha Adhom,* &c., was for the purpose of creating a suspicion in the minds of his readers regarding our knowledge of the Hebrew.

This was uncandid, and as a scholar he should have advised his readers that such differences existed. For example, Dr. Adam Clark and Alexander Campbell, writing years one after the other, and each quoting from the same editions of the Hebrew Bible of Buxtorf, and of Grotius, they write the Hebrew word for *slave*-servant *Gehved,* while Dr. Seiss writes it *Evod,* and Augusti Hahn writes it *Ebhodh.* Mr. Hahn's edition of the Hebrew Bible is pronounced by the ablest critics of Europe to be the best extant, in which opinion we concur, not even excepting the modern editions printed in this country, with their " *improved* (?) text," as spelled by Dr. Seiss. We can readily understand why he wishes to change the orthography of *Adhom* to the spelling that he uses, viz: *hā-āhdahm.*

Dr. Seiss has accepted as true the commonly received opinion among the learned, that Adam's name was derived from *Adhamah,* red earth or ground; as Josephus says, that Adam was made of red earth, " for such earth is virgin earth," as though Josephus was such a fool as not to know that all earth is *virgin* earth until used, whether red or black. Dr. Seiss, therefore, says in his review, that the first man and the first woman were red, and this orthography of his is intended to favor that derivation of Adam's name, and causes him to assert that " he knows from God and from His Word that the first pair was a red man and a red woman."

Now, reader, the question before us is, is this statement of

Dr. Seiss true? Dr. Seiss says it is, and we say it is not. How shall we decide this to your satisfaction, so as not to leave a doubt in your mind? Can it be so decided? We say yes, in the most positive manner, and by God's authority.

Dr. Seiss tells us that Adam was made out of this red *earth* (*adhamah*.) This is the commonly received opinion of the learned of this day. But, reader, how shall we prove to you, so you can know it positively to be erroneous? Plainly thus: by turning to the 7th verse, of the second chapter of Genesis, where God tells us in his own language how he made *ha Adhom*, and what he made him out of. In King James's translation it reads thus, " and the Lord God formed the man of the dust *Gnapher.*" Now, reader, which will you believe? God says he made him of *Gnapher*. Dr. Seiss and the learned contradict the Almighty, and say that He made him of *Adhamah*. God says it was *Gnapher;* the learned say that God was mistaken, and that it was *Adhamah*. It is no excuse or defense for the learned to say that the *dust* was from " red ground," for if God had intended to convey the idea that he had made *ha Adhom* out of red ground, he would have used the word *Adhamah*, and not the word *Gnapher*. He expressly says that He *made* him of *Gnapher*, the dust of the ground. But we may be told that this dust was red. This is but an assertion of the learned, without one particle of proof in, or outside, of God's Word, for there are many, and all shades of colors in the earth, from purest white to the blackest shade. Nor must we forget that we have *red* wheat, the dust of which is certainly not red, but white.

But this is not all. Those who may read our other work, " The White Man" (not yet published) will see that the word God, wherever it occurs in the first chapter of Genesis, is from the Hebrew word *Elohim*, which is plural, and is used in this plural form wherever it occurs in our Bibles, with but a single exception, and that exception is when our Saviour used it on the cross just before he expired, when he said *Eloi*, and is the only place where it occurs in the singular.

Those who may read, as we have said, our other work, " The White Man," will see a full, plain, simple, and intelligent explanation why the term *Elohim*, plural in its form, was applied, and properly applied, to the Almighty

Creator of the heavens and of the earth, and that singular form of expression used by the Deity himself, when he said, let *us* make man, and which, when read, will serve to explain the origin of Adam's name.

There is one other word used by God which is also singular and plural, and which is also applied to God, viz: *Adonai*, which is in the singular, and *Adonim*, which is its plural. It is from the latter that Adam's name is derived. *ha Adhom* is expressly declared by name to be the Son of God. And no intelligent man, possessed of any sensibility, can allow his mind to imagine for one moment that a child of heaven could be named after the earth which is to be burned up. The earth which was cursed by God, his father, could not, and did not originate Adam's name. His name, like himself, was of heavenly and divine origin, which the word *Adonim*, while applied to the Deity, yet covers His son *Adhom*. The name, therefore, of Adam, is derived, not from *Adhamah*, but from *Adonim*.

Dr. Seiss cannot but see the injustice done to himself, not to say anything of that done to Ariel, by his withholding from his readers the knowledge that this variety in the orthography of the Hebrew has long existed. Nor can he be unaware of the advantage which one student of God's Word, who sits down at the feet of the Almighty, to learn from his lips what he has said, and what he meant by what he did say, has over another student who sits down to learn from the Word of God whether what he has learned in his theological school is true or not.

Ariel has a particular *penchant* for, and delight in, the Hebrew language, which was the language of our illustrious father, *ha Adhom*, and of our beautiful mother, *ha Chavah*. It was the language of Eden, nay, it was the language of Heaven and the language of God, as certain and sure as we know that a father always teaches to his son the language which he himself speaks; that it was still the language of Heaven more than four thousand years afterwards, we have plain and positive evidence in the New Testament. Hence our delight in trying to understand the language first spoken by God our Father, to his children on earth, and our regret that our amiable brother, Dr. Seiss, should so far have forgotten himself and done such injustice to the Word of God, our Father. We are, however, still glad that he has noticed the He-

brew contained in Ariel,.even in the way in which he has
done it, as the sequel of this reply will show that God's
truth (not Ariel's talent or learning) cannot be overthrown
by even the splendid talent and learning of John A.
Seiss, D. D., backed by his able assistants.   And we trust
he will become an advocate of that truth that he now assails and does so many things against.

Reader, this subject can be understood, and what God
has said and done can be comprehended by the dullest intellect, if the man is only candid and honest with himself,
and content and satisfied with what God has said and done
in regard to it and the negro.

QUESTION OF THE STATUS OF THE NEGRO.

Now, reader, let us see if you and Ariel cannot know
exactly what God has said and did in fixing the *status* of
the negro when he created him, in this our reply to Dr.
Seiss.   We will first settle the position of some words
used in the original Hebrew which were never comprehended nor translated by King James's translators, nor
any of our learned commentators, since that translation
was made; or if comprehended by any, they have never
noticed them.   We will try and do this in a way that any
man, black or white, can understand, whether he knows a
letter of Hebrew or not: and in a way that they shall
know positively and unequivocally exactly, what God has
said and done in the premises.   It will be admitted by all
persons that every father has the right to name his own
son.   This will not be contested by any one.   And certainly none will contest God's right to name His own Son.
But whether this right is contested or not, God has certainly asserted His right to bestow a name on His Son,
and He has called Him *Adhom, ha Adhom.*   None but
Omniscience alone could have selected these terms or
names, for they cannot be translated into any other lan
guage that ever was spoken on earth, for the following plai
simple reason: For they are both *masculine* and *feminine*
at one and the same time—they are also both singular and
plural.   Now how would a scholar go about translating
this name into any language on earth ?   If he should translate it *man*, as King James's translators have done, the

translation would be false, for that term has its *feminine* in *woman*. This is so plain that any person can see it. There must then have been a reason with God why He selected that name.   To learn this reason, we enquire, what right have we to call a being of Divine origin *man*, or by any name other than the one bestowed on him by God, *his Father?* Clearly, we have none. We will admit here that the divine writers adopted the various aliases which, in the lapse of ages, became current among men. As proof of this, look at the various terms by which the children of Abraham at different times have been designated, and to the various terms applied to the tempter. But in all cases the aliases always refer to the original term.   There is another term of great importance, which has not been understood in all the force it originally had: that term is *wife* in English, in Hebrew, *ishshah*. This term has no plural, nor can one be made for it or put to it. The word translated *wives* is translated from a totally different word, and is *nashim* and comes from *nashi*, the female negro. God never instituted marriage relations between any beings on earth except a male *ha Adhom* and a female *Adhom*; and never intended him to have but one wife, *ishshah*, as our Saviour plainly declares in Matthew, when commenting on this first marriage.   We will add here that the translation of King James, which says, and they twain *shall* be one flesh, is incorrect—it should be for they *are* one flesh, which is in perfect accordance with the fact of Eve being taken from the body of *ha Adhom*.   With these facts before our mind, let us move to the next great step, when God installed His Son, *ha Adhom*, in his dominion over the earth, and everything that lived and moved in it.   Eden was to be his dwelling place.   God installed him lord and ruler before he separated Eve from his body, intending to show, thereby, in this unmistakable manner, that God did not intend for woman to have anything to do with the government, the ruling, or the laws of earth, or dominion over it in the slightest degree.   Women's rights, as now talked about, has no authority from God, nor foundation in his word.   King James's translation of this reads thus: "And the Lord God took man and put him into the Garden of Eden, to dress it and to keep it." This is a bad translation and does not express the ideas contained in the original.   It should read thus: "And the

Lord God took *ha Adhom* and placed him in the Garden of Eden, to be his dwelling place, and commanded him to keep it in order by his slave (*Ebhodh*)." This Hebrew word Dr. Seiss chooses to write as though it was spelled *Evod*. It is the Hebrew word for slave, as a chattel, and does not mean anything but *slave*. It is the same word that Noah used when he cursed his grandson Canaan, saying: "a servant of servants," or as it should be properly translated, a slave of slaves, should he be. Now, reader, we shall have some use for your common sense. It is plain from the whole narration given by Moses, that God did not intend either *ha Adhom* or Eve to labor or do any labor. The state of innocence and goodness in which God created them, joined to the language used by God in all the affirmative commands given them, expressly forbid the idea that they were to labor. Labor, therefore, was a consequence of their disobedience in eating the forbidden fruit, and was one of the chastisements which God inflicted upon them for their transgression afterward. This position cannot be contested by any candid man or woman. Now for a few facts of narration: The Lord God had planted a garden, and when it was in full bearing and perfection he took His Son, *ha Adhom*, into it, to install him in it as his dwelling place, and as lord and ruler over everything that lived or moved. Now, these logical facts plainly teach that, things planted had to grow, and in time would thereby reach perfection. It was in this full perfection when God introduced *ha Adhom* into it, for he expressly stated to him that he might eat of the fruit of all the trees in the garden except the fruit of the tree of the knowledge of good and the knowledge of evil. It is plain from this statement that the garden had grown to perfection, and the things that had thus grown would continue to grow, and would require labor to dress them and keep them in order. This the logic of facts plainly teaches us. Now who was to do this labor? It is plain that *ha Adhom* was not to do it, as the duty of laboring was not put upon him by God until after he fell. The reader will bear in mind that in this installation of *ha Adhom* in his dominion by God, that necessarily the slave that had to do this labor must be present and hear and understand the commands given by God, and that it was God's direction that *ha Adhom* was to keep this garden in order by him, his slave, as *ha Adhom* might direct. In this order God not only directly gave *ha Adhom* dominion in and over the negro, but it is also plain that he had this right of dominion and rule, as God had created him to rule all that he had made.

The Hebrew word *Ebhodh* (slave), indicates the *being* and the service to be performed, just as a man owning a slave whose name is George, the word slave attached indicates and describes the service. It was this service as a slave that *ha Adhom* was to command (George) and direct in keeping the garden in order. But have we any other facts to sustain this interpretation? Yes: it will be remembered that this installation of *ha Adhom* as lord and ruler of all, took place before Eve was separated from his body. That God said the tempter was a beast and that he then talked, are both plainly stated. The logic of these facts plainly teaches us that the tempter knew Eve was not present when God installed *ha Adhom* in the Garden of Eden, for he introduces his conversation to Eve in a way that proves this. He says: God doth not permit you to eat of the fruit of all the trees in the garden. How did he know this? How could he have known it except by being present himself with *ha Adhom*, where he heard the command of God prohibiting the use of the fruit of one tree. The manner of his introducing this conversation with Eve, proves that he had previously heard what God had said to *ha Adhom* and that Eve was not present thereat. He was a beast, and so declared by God when he said that he was more subtle than *all the beasts the Lord God had made.* From this statement there can be no retreat, nor any doubt in the minds of any believer in the Bible on the points, viz:

1st. That the tempter was a beast.

2nd. That he then talked.

These two points must be conceded by all candid believers in God's Word.

The next point to which we advance, is that of the interview after the fall. The Divine Record limits the number present to God, to *ha Adhom*, to Eve, and to the tempter. The three latter were then all the beings on earth that *then talked,* and that belonged to the creation. No other beings but these did then talk. This none will contest. God commenced the interview to which we refer, by enquiring of *ha Adhom* why he had done this, and received his answer. He next made a similar enquiry of

Eve, (his wife,) and received her answer. He next proceeded to the tempter. He made no enquiry of him, but at once denounced him: "Cursed art thou above all cattle, and above every beast of the field, and above every creeping thing—of things, that go upon their belly, and eat from off the dust, all the days of their life." We have written the curse against the tempter as it was originally spoken, and which King James's translators could have seen, and should have corrected, had they compared the facts and collated their copy with other manuscripts.

Now, we have this evidence before our minds, that the tempter did speak, for he voluntarily had a conversation with Eve, and next, God did talk with him when He sentenced him, and which he would not have done if the tempter could not talk. This establishes the fact that the tempter, whatever he might be, did then talk, although a beast. The next part of the sentence which God denounced against the tempter is: "I (God) will put enmity between you and the woman; and between your seed and her seed; and it shall bruise thy head, and thou shall bruise his heel." Now, the tempter is plainly declared by God to be a beast. It is equally plain and clear that he was to eat, live, and die. That he was to have "children," between whom and the children of the woman, God put enmity, a knowledge of which enmity would be perpetuated from generation to generation by talking. It is plain that *ha Adhom* and Eve were the tempted persons, and that they were white, all creation attests. And they are of this earth and of this creation. Who are or is the other party? There is but one answer that can, in truth, be given to this question, and that answer is, that the tempter is the black-man, the negro, and this will be made so plain in this document before we get through, that not even a negro can be found on earth, that will doubt that it is God's exact truth. None shall doubt it, except religious and political politicians; they will make their *lips* say they don't believe it, but the power of God's truth will make their hearts give the lie to what their lips say.

The logic of facts plainly teaches all men (and here we include the negro) that such a being, or slave, was necessary to *ha Adhom's* position, and that the being or slave thus created by God "was good, very good," for the station he was to fill, and as the *Ebhodh* (slave) to *ha Adhom* and Eve,

for *ha Adhom* could give no order or command for him
to obey, but what was good, he himself being, in God's
language, good, very good. The negro, the tempter, by
his own acts, left the station in which God had created
and assigned him; and although he caused the fall of our
first parents, and the loss of Eden to our first parents,
yet God did not denounce death upon him, but has reserved him in chains of blackness, (his skin being black,
is a chain that cannot be broken or taken off, and in this
blackness or darkness, God says He has reserved him,) unto the judgment of the great day.

There are two places is which the Hebrew word *Ebhodh*
(slave) occur in the Scriptures previous to the fall of *ha Adhom.* One we have already referred to as occurring in the
verse giving an account of *ha Adhom's* installation in the
Garden of Eden, as the lord and ruler of this world, and
so made by God; and which we have before referred to
that God had directed *ha Adhom* to keep the garden in order
by his slave *Ebhodh,* but which Dr. Seiss had written as
though it was spelled *Evod.* In this change of orthograhy
he seems to emulate the celebrated and Rev. C. J. Bunsen,
D. D. and L. L. D., who, although a pulpit divine, yet he
rejects the book of Genesis, and, in order to get around
Moses' account of the flood and his three sons Shem, Ham
and Japheth, and invents for these three brothers more
changes in their names, and of the orthography by which
he spelled them, than could be effected by a dozen came-
leons in the changes they could produce in their own color.
There is one other place where the term slave (*Ebhodh*)
occurs while *ha Adhom* was in a state of innocence before he
fell, and that is found in the latter part of the 5th verse of
the 2nd chapter of Genesis; and in King James's translation it reads thus: "And there was no man to till the
ground, for the Lord God had not caused it to rain upon
the earth." In our previous work on the negro, we have
written out the Hebrew in full, using the English alpha-
bet for that purpose; for a more unjust and improper translation could hardly be made. *Ha Adhom's* name is expressly
used, and he is directed by God, not to put or make his
slave (*Ebhodh*) till the ground, for the Lord God had not
then caused it to rain upon the earth. But a mist went
up that watered the whole surface of the ground.

Any person can see that this translation is in strict ac-

275

cordance with the facts, as the earth spontaneously produced everything that God's creatures required; and continued to do so until the Flood, when the foundations of the Great Deep were broken up, and the present high mountains, now on the earth, were then thrown up, and which caused the earth to be thrown from its perpendicularity to its own center, causing it, from that day to this, to oscillate 23½ degrees north of the Equator to 23½ degrees south, thereby producing *Winter* and *Summer*, making seed-time and harvest a necessity, and then rendering it necessary for the ground to be tilled to produce in summer what was necessary to be eaten in winter. All of which had been previously spontaneously produced, and Noah became the first husbandman on earth; and which was after the Flood, when he planted a vineyard. It can be demonstrated with mathematical certainty, that it never rained before the Flood; and that the climate before the Flood was equal from center to circumference, and that there were no such mountains as those we now have. The reader is referred to our work on "The White Man" for a full explanation of all these points, Biblically sustained.

From this explanation, the reader can see that our translation of the part of the 5th verse, why *ha Adhom* was not to direct his slave to till the ground, is in perfect accordance with the fact that it spontaneously produced everything until the Flood brought about winter and summer. Yet, in the face of these plain facts, Dr. Seiss asserts positively that the proper translation of the word *Ebhodh* (slave) referred to *ha Adhom*, that he was to be in the one case, the slave of the garden, and in the other place, he was to be the slave of the earth. If these translations were true, then it follows that God, instead of creating *ha Adhom*, his son, lord and ruler, that he actually made him a slave. We leave it to the reader to call such a translation by what name he pleases.

But we have said that the *status* of the negro, as fixed by God in creation, and what he made himself afterwards, to be, by his temptation and lying to our illustrious parents, can be made so plain that even a negro shall not doubt it, nor any one else who has eyes to see, and has not lost his five senses.

God said to Moses, on one occasion, while he was with him on the Mount: "See thou make all things according to the pattern shown thee in the Mount." In the creating of this world, God himself made all things after a uniform pattern, and under a uniform law. The first thing that he created that had life, it was *inanimate life*, grasses, sprouting herbage, fruit bearing trees, and everything that grew from the bosom of earth. The *law* under which he created everything that thus grew from the face of the earth, and which law was to control and govern each variety through all time, was that each thing or product should produce its own kind, in its own image, and after its own likeness. This was the law that was to govern, and which still governs, all inanimate life.

The next advance in the order of creation is to animated life; the lowest order of which is fishes or marine animals. Their's being of the lowest order is shown from the fact that they breathed water, which is but condensed air, while the higher orders of animal life breathed air—this air is breathed by all mortals.

Ha Adhom, being the son of God, breathed light; his life being breathed into his nostrils by God his Father, he continued to breathe light until the moment of his transgression, when he ceased to breathe it, fell, and then breathed this atmosphere which all mortals breathe, and died when he was nine hundred and thirty years old. The command of God was "that the waters bring forth creatures having living souls." The Hebrew words for which are *Naphesh Chaiyiah*, which are the exact words which King James's translators have rendered living soul, in regard to *ha Adhom* when God breathed into his nostrils the breath of life. Everything that has animated life, from the lowest stage of existence up to the highest, all, *all* have *souls*.

The command was for the waters to bring forth abundantly fishes, fowls and birds of the air, that fly in the midst of Heaven. The same uniform law is continued here for animated existence that started with inanimated life, and reiterated according to the original pattern, that each thing should produce its own kind, in its own image, and after its own likeness, and which law governed then and still governs in the vast numerous varieties still to be found among fowls, birds, fishes and other water products, and which still controls and produces each kind, in its own image, and after its likeness, with unerring certainty.

We advance again to the still higher order of animated

life. The command of God is to the earth: "To bring
forth cattle, and creeping things, and beasts of the field,
having *living souls* (*Naphesh Chaiyiah*). The same law is
again reiterated, the pattern of which God started with
inanimate life, that each thing should produce its own
kind, in its own image, and after its own likeness. This
was the law of their creation, and continues to be the law
under which God created and placed them.

All is now created except one being, and that one being is
God's son, *ha Adhom*. We now ask the reader to note the
change in the phraseology, now that the son of God, *ha Adhom*, is to be brought forward. The word translated God in
the singular throughout the 1st chapter of Genesis, is in
the plural form, *Elohim*, and this term is properly in the
plural form, and should never have been translated at all,
and certainly should never have been translated in the
singular.

The term in its plural form covers all the attributes of
the Deity; by each separate one, the different things of
creation were brought into being, and which we thus explain,
so that any reader can understand it. For example: The
power or attribute of God that brought forth grass, was one
power or attribute of God, and the power or attribute that
brought the horse into being to eat it, is another attribute
or power of God, but different from that which produced
the grass, and both are of one God.

With this little explanation before us, we now call
attention to the first point in the change of the phraseology. In every phrase in this chapter where anything is
created or made, the word is *Elohim*, "created or made or
said." In all these places the word is *Elohim*, but in the
26th verse it is: "And *Elohim* said, let us make *Adhom*." This term *us* is in contra to the individual and
separate powers or attributes of God, and covers the whole
of them. All the powers, or attributes of perfection, pertaining to God, are needed to produce his son. This all
can know, and all can understand, who will think for a
moment, and let their common sense guide their thoughts,
and direct their decision. This is one peculiarity to be
noted by the change in the phraseology. The second peculiarity, to which we invite attention, is this: All animated
beings, as well as all inanimate life, has God's uniform
law put over them, *after* they were created, that they

should produce their own kind, in their own image, and after their own likeness; while in regard to *ha Adhom* the phraseology refers alone to the Deity, its phraseology being, "let us make man in our own image, and after our own likeness."

All the brutes, animals and beasts, creeping things and birds, fowls and fishes, all being of mortal life, could have no antetype in the eternal world, and, therefore, the order or law was given after their creation, to produce their own kind, in their own image.

The thing must exist before a likeness or shadow can be produced from it. God always existing, was, therefore, at once the antetype as well as the father and God of *ha Adhom*. *Ha Adhom* being then in the image and likeness of God, was likewise under that same law, according to the pattern required, to produce his own kind, in his own image, and after his own likeness.

This law started with inanimate life, and we have seen it advance from that to that of the lowest stage of animated existence, and passing thence to the highest, concentrates itself on God alone. Now, reader, does not every variety belonging to inanimate life continue under this law and produce their own kind, in their own image, and after their own likeness, to this day? Yes. For example, we have before us three trees, the Elm, the Ash, the Oak; they have continued to produce their own kind, in their own image, from the time of their creation to the present moment. And this is true of all other parts or portions of inanimate life, from the time of creation to the present.

Amalgamation was clearly foreseen by God, our Creator, for, in one of his laws, delivered to the children of Israel by Moses, was, that they should not plant their gardens with divers seeds, lest they amalgamate and thereby become corrupt. Thus it is plain, that God knew from the beginning that amalgamation could take place, even in inanimate nature, and, therefore, guarded against it by his law.

But we know that no amalgamation of any kind can take place without its being obvious to the sight, and to all our common sense, that it is a violation of God's order of creation. We have seen cucumbers, gourds and tomatoes all growing from one stalk, at one and the same time. But there was not the slightest difficulty in detecting it.

Now we ask the question, is there anything on earth that is commanded to produce its own kind, in its own image, and after its own likeness, that cannot do it? No. *Ha Adhom*, the white "man," is commanded. to produce his own kind, in his own image, and after his own likeness; and did he not accomplish it in his first born son, Cain? Yes. Did he not accomplish it with regard to his sons, Abel and Seth, also? Yes. And cannot a white man still produce his own kind, in his own image, and after his own likeness still? Most certainly he can. Cannot a black man, who is likewise commanded to produce his own kind, in his own image, and after his own likeness, do so? Yes. But can a white man and a negro woman produce their own kind, in their own image, and after their own likeness? No; they can produce something, but it is not in the likeness or image of either the white or the negro. This is plain to sight and senses, and shows unequivocally that they are of a totally different order of creation. Nor can the negro produce with a white woman, a being in his own image and after his own likeness. That the product is a clear and positive violation of God's law, can be seen with the naked eye, for the product is not in the image or likeness of either the black or white.

It is not in the power of either white or black to violate God's law of creation in regard to themselves; nor any other law of creation, without its being palpably seen and known at the time. And that this knowledge of its being a violation of God's law, God has ordained it to be co-extensive with the race.

The horse can produce his own kind, in his own image, and after his own likeness, and can continue to do so until the end of time. He can also produce by a cross with the ass, something, but it is neither in the likeness or image of the one or the other. We cannot violate God's law, nor any of his laws of creation, without its being plain to the eye that we have done so. The product of the white and the black is neither white nor black, but is a mulatto. The term by which the mulatto is distinguished in Hebrew is *Enosh*, and means one that is incurably afflicted in his skin, in its color, being produced by neither the one nor the other. The incurability does not refer to sickness, but to something implanted in the skin that cannot be removed.

We have now settled, by God's authority, in a manner that cannot be shaken by all the learning on earth, that the whites, the pure whites, descendants from *ha Adhom* and Eve, are God's children, and as distinct from the blacks as a child of God can be from a beast, and in a way that does not leave a quiver of a doubt in the mind of any negro on earth, who recognizes the Bible as the Word of God, and has five senses.

There remains now but one other point to be shown, and that is, that the negro is a beast, and was so created, and so remains to this day. This can be made as plainly and as palpably true in the divine language as we have just shown with divine authority, that the whites can produce their own kind to the end of time; and that the negroes or blacks can also produce their own kind, so long as they exist or remain on earth; and that the whites, by amalgamation with the blacks, produces a mulatto, a being that is not in the image or likeness of either the white or the black—this is plainly proven by divine authority. And by the same divine authority it will be now equally plainly shown that the negro is a beast, and was originally created a beast and endowed with speech to be the slave of *ha Adhom*. St. Paul expressly declares, "that all flesh is not the same flesh; that there is one flesh of men (*ha Adhom*), another of *beasts*, another of *birds*, and another of *fishes*." Now, from what we have seen, and this plain declaration of St. Paul, that there are but four kinds of flesh, and we know that the negro's flesh is neither that of fish or birds, and God has settled that it is not that of *ha Adhom*, it follows, with irresistible and crushing force, that the negro is a beast, and his flesh beast flesh.

This explains what was put before Peter, when the great sheet was let down from Heaven before him, knit at the four corners, and filled with all manner of *four*-footed beasts, and a voice came from Heaven saying unto him, "arise, Peter, slay (kill) and eat." Why say in the divine language of Heaven, *four-footed*, but for the fact that God knew that there was a two-footed beast, which should not be killed and eaten? These facts settle beyond the equivocation of a doubt, by divine authority, that the negro is a

2

beast, and not a human being, although endowed by God with speech and five senses, like *ha Adhom*.

WHAT GOD CALLS THE SOUL.

We might end here our reply to Dr. Seiss, but we think it better for the benefit of our readers to take up another branch of this subject, bearing directly on the points at issue, and which is as little understood by all religious parties, Roman Catholics and Protestants, as that of the *status* of the negro as fixed by God, viz : That of *the soul*. The reader will have seen already, that the term living soul God has applied as belonging equally to fishes, fowls, birds, cattle, and creeping things, and beasts of the field, as well as to his son *ha Adhom*. The Hebrew words for living souls are *Naphesh Chaiyiah*, and they occur in the 20th, 21st, 24th, and 29th verses of the first chapter of Genesis, as well as in the 7th verse of the second chapter, but are translated in neither of these places but in the last. *Ha Adhom* alone is made to possess a living soul by King James's translators. Why they omitted or declined to translate these identical words in the other places, we will leave for the reader to decide. One thing is certain, the idea or ideas entertained by Roman Catholics and Protestants, of what *the soul* is, is certainly not the idea, nor what God calls, the soul ; nor is it for want of clearness and precision in God's language that made this confusion.

If people would be content to believe God, and knew what He said, and that He meant what He said, and would put God's ideas in the translation which He put into the original Hebrew, all could readily and easily understand Him. But so long as we take the liberty of changing God's words at will, and substituting other words in place of those used by God, or of arbitrarily putting such meaning as suits our ideas of what God should have said, we must forever be in darkness and confusion in understanding the blessed Word of our Heavenly Father. Our learned men are alone responsible for the confusion and infidelity that has, and is now, overspreading the world with the drapery of death. The reader need not be told by us that the present received opinion of all the religious world is, that the *mind* is the soul of man, and is that part of him that does not die when the body dies, that it is his rational, his reasoning faculties, the mind, that survives the body and is the soul of man. Any of our readers can satisfy himself that this is the accepted idea of *the soul* of all religious parties, by taking up any of our large dictionaries and examining these words. It is the Pagan idea of the soul, as given in all their Lexicons, but it is not what God calls the soul. The Hebrew word *Naphesh* is the term by which God designates the soul, and the Hebrew word *chaiyiah* is the word by which God designates *life*. God in his laws expressly prohibits the *eating of blood*, and gives as his reason to Moses why he did so, " that the blood is the *soul of the flesh*." He uses the word *Naphesh*, and which King James's translators have translated life, as though God had used the word *Chaiyiah*, making it to read in our Bible that " the blood is the life of the flesh."

The reader will see that by accepting what God calls the soul, he can readily understand why God applied the terms *Naphesh Chaiyiah*, " living soul," to all animated beings, from *ha Adhom* down through beasts, cattle, creeping things, fowls, birds, and down to fishes, and that it is through the blood specially fitted that all the different varieties of fishes, birds, creeping things, cattle and beasts, are kept up and preserved, and that it is in this way, also, that all the varieties of species or kinds are kept up in inanimate nature through the medium of their sap, which is the same to them that blood is to the flesh. Every competent physician or surgeon knows, and can tell you, that the first start of animal life, whether in man or beast, is from a small speck of blood, which grows and enlarges, until the heart is formed in the child or other being, and when it reaches a certain stage or point, it then can move, showing thereby that it has some kind of existence or life.

This existence or life, it derives from its parents, and which God calls *Naphesh*, the soul; and the moment it is born, it then breathes, and has *Chaiyiah*, " life," and which life it derives, not from its parents, but from God. Oh ! the wisdom, the goodness, the wonderful wisdom of God, our Father, in thus connecting all his creatures directly with himself. We now can understand the beauty and strength of that expression of St. Paul, at Athens, that God is not very far from any of us; that we might feel after him, if, peradventure, we might find him; for it is in him we live, and move, and have our being. But, reader, this wisdom cannot be learned in all the theological schools on earth, but can be learned alone by us, His children, sitting down at the feet of our Father, and our God, and learn it alone from His word as it fell from His Almighty lips. But this wisdom does not stop here. In the order of his creation it yet goes further. We ask what is the *life* of the soul? And how can we know it, and know it with positive and absolute certainty? We answer, that it is the air we breathe, for God has placed the lungs within our body, that for every pulsation of our heart, we must breathe to give *life to the blood,* and if we fail to breathe, we instantly die.

In the case of *ha Adhom,* his blood, which was the soul of his flesh, received its life directly from God's breath, (not this air), directly from God himself. *Ha Adhom* never breathed this air until he fell. He then became mortal, and breathed this air, and died when he was nine hundred and thirty years old. We may be asked what it was that *ha Adhom* breathed before he fell? We answer— no, not we, but God answers—that it was light. How do we know this, and can we know it with unerring certainty? Yes, we can. St. John says: "In the beginning was the Word, and the Word was with God, and the Word was God. The same was in the beginning with God. By it all things were made that are made, and without it nothing was made that is made. In it was *light,* and the light was *the life* of man," (*ha Adhom*), just as this air is the *life* of all mortals. This light he breathed until he fell. God made a special place, which in King James's translation is called the firmament, to hold the air which his mortal creatures should breathe; while God, who is Light, is everywhere, and which Light *ha Adhom,* as His son, breathed. Light being the first thing presented in the order of creation, and used by immortals only, while the firmament contained the air which is the life of all mortals.

Let us now return to the word soul, and take up God's declaration that *the soul of the flesh is the blood.* God commanded all things that had life, inanimate life and animated life, in all their separate varieties, for each to produce their own kind, in their own image, and after their own likeness. *Ha Adhom* was so commanded, and being

himself created in the image and likeness of God, did so
obey, and we are expressly told that his sons were in his
own image, and after his own likeness. His descendants
continue to this day. Now the soul of a white man,
which is his blood, cannot produce anything but whites under God's law; while it is true that he can, by amalgamation with a negro, produce a being, but it is not in his
image, nor in his likeness; for it is impossible, *impossible*
to violate God's law or order of creation, without its being
palpably known to sight, and senses, the moment the creature is born. And this evidence runs *pari passu* from the
beginning to the close of the world.

The soul of a negro, which is his blood, can produce
nothing but negroes, just as the blood of a white man,
which is his soul, can produce only whites or white children. The soul of a black bear, which is his blood, can
only produce black bears. The soul of a horse, which is
his blood, can only produce horses. The soul of a peacock, which is his blood, can only produce peafowls. If
it were possible otherwise, how many bipeds of the *genus
homo* would soon have the peacock's gaudy plumage trans-
ferred to their own tails, if we are to judge of the delight
with which some men like to have a long or short string
of titles appended as a tail to their own names, as if the
worth was in the tail, and not in the other end, where
their head is. Can the soul of a fish, which is its blood,
produce a peacock or goslins, one with feathers and the
other having scales. We see the same positive law running through and governing every tree of the forest, every
herb of the field, and every rose of the garden, with un-
changing force and power; and we ask, in view of these
facts, can any white man, who respects his own senses, believe that the negro is his flesh and blood. Nay, we go
further, and ask can there be found on earth a single
negro, that does not know, after reading this, that God had
created him a beast, had made him a slave to *ha Adhom*,
in which he was " good, very good," but by his lying *made
himself* the tempter, the dragon, that old serpent, which is
the devil, reserved in chains of blackness, unto the judgment of the great day.

But we are not through yet with all that we have to say
about the soul. Do not be surprised, reader, at our telling
you that the blood, which is the soul of your flesh, is

intelligent. But it is so, as you will readily see in a moment.

The Psalmist says we are fearfully, and wonderfully made. Reader, look at that small drop of embryotic blood; see how it goes to work, and first forms the heart, and sets it to beating; see it forming the veins, arteries, nerves, ligaments, cartilages, bones, flesh, skin, brains, etc., of the whole body, and see with what perfection every part of it is adjusted to the functions intended, and never making a single mistake, and endowing it with all the senses, and sensibilities necessary to a perfect being. When it reaches a certain maturity, it is endowed with motion, and shortly after its state is changed, and it becomes an inhabitant of this world, but its careful intelligence is immediately seen in its new state of existence. It increases in stature and weight just in proportion as its strength is developed. In the meantime, however, by accident the artery of the upper arm is injured, and several inches has been cut off, the forearm would perish, if not again supplied with blood, the soul goes at once to work and makes a new one, which supplies the hand and arm with blood. Again, the leg or arm is broken; now, although the soul cannot put the bones together, yet it can mend them like a good blacksmith; and when the body has reached a certain stature in height, the soul stops its further progress in that direction.

Now if intelligence did not guide, it would still keep on growing, the new artery would be unmade, and the broken bones unmended. It is that tie that connects mortality with spiritual existence, but is not that part of man that does not die when the body dies. But, on the contrary, it is obvious to the thought of every intelligent man, that it must be the first part that dies; as its life is the air that is breathed. In the case of persons hung this is shown to be true, for the body shows symptoms of life long after breathing has ceased.

On the other, and last branch of this subject, the soul, as held by pagans and Christians, that it is the *mind*, or rational faculties, or reasoning powers, that do not die when the body dies, and is the soul of man, and lives beyond the grave, it can be briefly answered, and leave not a quiver of doubt in the mind of any intelligent man and candid reader.

1st. It is by the mind that we know right from wrong, good from evil, and all this we arrived at through crime, sin against God. But our Saviour settles the question in a way that no Christian can possibly except to. It is recorded in the Gospel of St. Matthew, that on being asked which is the greatest commandment, he replied: "Thou shalt love the Lord thy God with all thy heart, and with all thy soul, and with all thy *mind*, and with all thy strength." Plainly showing that our Saviour knew that the soul was one thing, and the mind another, and should never have been confounded.

But some will say, that the negro is only an inferior species below the white man, and therefore has an interest in Christ's death, and is the subject of future salvation. Let us look at it. Christ was the second Adam. It was Adam's race that fell. It was Adam's blood which was in the veins of our Saviour. It was Adam's race that was to be regenerated and redeemed. If there are any other races that fell, and are to be redeemed, God's Word gives no account of them. The negro is plainly shown to be a beast, by God's Word, and by God's Law. And we have no account that God ever had any intention of raising a single beast from death, or from the earth to heaven. Nor is there the slightest allusion in God's Word that the negro is to be an exception among the beasts for salvation of any kind. On the contrary, the very first one that was created on earth was cursed by God. And everything cursed of God is to be burned up. He cursed the tempter, and our Saviour plainly declares of the wicked of *ha Adhom's* race, depart from me, ye cursed, into everlasting fire, prepared, not for white men, but prepared for the devil and his angels.

God cursed the earth, and we are plainly told that it is to be burned up. So, as the head of the race (negro) was cursed of God, it is not possible that one of them could be saved, even if they were not beasts. And if one beast be saved, why not all? And in what way could the Saviour's blood be applied for the salvation of a beast. We must not be surprised nor misled by those who tell us that the negro has faith, that they believe on the Lord Jesus Christ, and, therefore, will be saved.

Our Saviour tells us the same thing of them in his day, that the devils believe and tremble. Our Saviour uses the term devils in its plural form, and in which form it applies to the negroes, and not to that old gentleman in the singular, as now preached from our modern pulpits, who is represented, if not omnipotent, to be omnipresent, and in the heart of every person on earth at one and the same time. And St. Paul expressly declares "that the carnal (or beastly) mind is not subject to the law of God; and neither, indeed, can it be."

We might very well stop our reply to Dr. Seiss again at this point, inasmuch as the whole ground upon which his argument, and that of every other man in favor of negro equality with God's children, the whites, is completely swept away by the language of God and by his laws, when creating the world. But we do not intend to let a vestage remain; no, not even a pin-hook, on which a single doubt can be hung, regarding the *status* of the negro as fixed by God, nor the position in which God placed his children, the whites.

EXAMINATION OF DR. SEISS'S HEBREW.

As Dr. Seiss has favored us with some Hebrew, and Hebrew criticism, we desire to pay our particular respects to him in this line, least it be thought that there was something in *his* Hebrew of power and importance, that we wished to avoid.

We are always delighted to meet with a gentleman who can instruct us in this beautiful language—it was the language of our illustrious father *ha Adhom*, and of our beautiful mother, *ha Chavah*—it was the language of Eden, the language of Heaven, and of God then; it was the language of heaven more than four thousand years afterwards, and is its language still. We are no admirer of Dr. Seiss's *improved* text; nor do we call all changes improvements, as many of these modern alterations are erroneous, and based on false ideas, and, unfortunately, our poor brothers and sisters, whose education is limited to the English, these alterations are all in the interests of infidelity and atheism.

We will refer our readers here to what we have elsewhere said concerning the variety of orthography of Hebrew words in different Hebrew Bibles, as containing a full answer to Dr. Seiss's criticism upon our manner of spelling Hebrew words. We will now notice his criticism, and our use of the Hebrew word *Ish*, as designating the negro, and which Dr. Seiss spells *Eesh*.

Dr. Seiss, like all other scholars trained in theological schools, does not dare to think for himself, if the thought be outside of his theological training. In such case, as in this instance, if God's Word presents a different idea, it must be passed by and overlooked, and the theology of the schools substituted for God's truth. To enable the reader to fully comprehend us, we will re-state here what we had partially stated in the work which Dr. Seiss was reviewing, explanatory of the duties which *ha Adhom* was under to God as a "man," and all other duties or things he might do, or his necessities might require him to do. As *Adhom, ha Adhom,* he had certain duties to perform to God; but as a husband, his duties were to his wife; as a father, his duties were to his children, and so of every other position that he could be called to fill on earth, whatever they might be. In filling these duties, and which pertained to every calling, he is called *Ish;* that being the name by which the negro, who was the head of the beast creation, and under service to *ha Adhom,* was designated, and the service that he was to perform was that of *ebhodh,* a slave.

Now, in regard to *ha Adhom,* when Eve was brought to him, King James's translation says " she is bone of my bone, and flesh of my flesh; she shall be called woman," *Ishshah,* wife, " for she was taken out of man," *Ish,* husband. King James's translation is grossly erroneous, and which any person can see, whether they are scholars or not. It was a *wife* which God intended to make as an help meet for *ha Adhom,* and she was taken out of his own person. Every wife must necessarily be a woman, but it does not follow that every woman is a wife, and, therefore, King James's translation grossly misleads the reader where it says she shall be called *woman* instead of wife, as it should be; and when it says she was taken out of man, it should be husband, as the term is *Ish,* which is masculine, and has its feminine in *Ishshah.* Every one knows that Eve was taken from *ha Adhom's* body, but as *ha Adhom* said she was taken from *Ish,* Dr. Seiss should have explained why *ha Adhom* used this term instead of his own

2*

name, so that his readers could have understood that the
term *Ish* designated the white man, in any duties, labors,
or callings of a purely earthly nature, whatever they might
be.   And we instance the case of Esau, a hunter, Jacob, a
herdsman, and Noah a just man, all of whom are called
Ish, in these several senses or callings.

Now, had Dr. Seiss given our explanation, his readers
could have understood in every instance, which he has referred to in the Divine Writings, just as we do.   This was
a duty which his candor, as a scholar, and his honesty as
a man, owed alike to his readers, to himself, and to Ariel,
if he would not misrepresent Ariel's views.   And had he
have given it, it would have saved some of his readers
from being misled.   Any person can readily imagine the
thousand and one things that *ha Adhom* and Eve might do
without its being thought religious service to God; for
example they might, in the garden, be engaged in throwing roses at each other, and here the term *Ish* would apply
to him, while the term *ha Adhom* would not.   And this
explains why he said she was taken out of *Ish*.

In addition to this explanation, Dr. Seiss should also
have added some historical information for the benefit of
his readers, if he were simply anxious to correct Ariel's
mistakes, and set the Word of God truly before them.
The point of history to which we here refer, cannot be
otherwise than well known to him.   It is this: On the
first promulgation of the Gospel, it was in the Greek language.   Not many of the first Christians could read the
Hebrew of the Old Testament, and had to use the Septuagint version, made for Ptolomy Philadlphus, two hundred
and sixty-four years B. C.

To this version the first Christians had to resort for all
their knowledge of the Old Testament.   The Jews had
rejected Jesus of Nazareth as the Messiah, and cordially
despised the Christians as his followers, and, knowing that
the Christians could not read the Hebrew of the Old Testament, multiplied copies of this Septuagint version, in
which they took the liberty of altering the texts in every
way they could to make the Christians appear ridiculous.
To such an extent was this hatred carried, that they
altered the text of their own MSS. until most of the MSS.
in Asia Minor, where the Gospel was first preached, were
tampered with and altered.

Among other points, we notice one alteration to which we specially refer, and that is this: The first Christians did not preach to negroes or mulattoes; nor did they baptize any; nor did they ever establish a church of such. This point will be made so plain before we get through with this reply, that Dr. Seiss himself will not question or doubt it.

These interpolations and changes made in the Septuagint became so extensive as to cause that version to be rejected, by both Jews and Christians, before the close of the second century. The want of a correct version of the Old Testament, for the use of the early Christians, caused Origen, a learned Christian, to compile his celebrated Hexapla, in which he inserted, in parallel columns, the Hebrew and five of the best copies of the Septuagint that he could get. Only a portion of this has descended to our times.

Many fragments of the mutillated copies of the Septuagint have come down to us, showing the outrages that had been perpetrated in making them. Origen died A. D. 253. These interpolations and alterations made in the Hebrew MSS. justly excited the fears of the honest Jews, for the purity of their own divine writings, and caused them to make an effort to restore them to their original charcter. They brought their labors to an end about the year A. D. 300.

In these amended MSS. they added some punctuation marks, and some vowel pointings; the Hebrew of Moses and the Prophets was written originally without either punctuation marks or vowels. It was discovered, however, that all the interpolations and changes had not been corrected; and which the Jews attempted to correct about A. D. 500. This also proved faulty on comparing and collating with the oldest MSS. of other countries, and resulted in the production of the present text, in the early part of the eighth century. It is the text now used, and is now called the Masoretic text; and is the same from which our Bible was translated by King James's translators.

Notwithstanding this great care on the part of the Jews to restore their divine writings to their original purity, yet it is not unreasonable that they should have overlooked some of the changed words, in different places, and thus errors escaped correction. Nor is it unreasonable to suppose that they made mistakes both in the punctuation and in the vowel pointings, which they made full and complete in the Masoretic text.

We do not know whether Dr. Seiss's attention had been directed to these points or not; if it had, he would have discovered, like ourselves, a number of places where these errors had not been corrected. A knowledge of the histories we have referred to must have been known to Dr. Seiss; but it seems that the idea never occurred to him that some of these errors had been overlooked by the Jews themselves, to say nothing of the power that punctuation exerts in determining the sense of a sentence, nor the value imparted to a word when correctly spelled, over erroneous spelling.

Dr. Seiss quotes from the Old Testament, against Ariel, two of those errors of statement which the Jews left uncorrected, and which will serve us for illustrating the facts which we have asserted respecting those errors, and, at the same time, to correct Dr. Seiss, and set him right. The first one to which we shall call attention in Dr. Seiss's review of Ariel, is where he quotes the dispute that arose between the herdsmen of Abraham and the herdsmen of Lot. Dr. Seiss quotes Abraham as saying to Lot, "Let there be no dispute between us, for we be (*enoshim*) brethren." The point that the Doctor was trying to make against Ariel, was, that Ariel had said that *Enosh*, of which *enoshim* is the plural, meant mulatto, the first cross of white and black; and, therefore, that Abraham and Lot were both mulattoes. The difficulty that enveloped Dr. Seiss on this point, is that which commonly attend the minds of such critics as are anxious to avail themselves of even an error to sustain their theory, even though that theory be false. Now the value of this quotation made by Dr. Seiss is to be found in the fact (if fact it be) that the word *enoshim* means *brethren*, for if it does not mean brethren, it is of no value, and should not have been cited.

Now, my dear old brother Seiss, (for if you are a pure white descendant of *ha Adhom* and Eve, then indeed you are my brother, and entitled to all the affections that a brother's heart can give,) we ask you in all kindness to state, as a scholar, whether the word *enoshim* means *brethren*, or not? It no more means brethren than it does owls or eagles. This shows one example where the Jews have themselves failed to correct one of the errors we have referred to.

Had the proper correction been made, it would have presented Abraham as saying, "We be rulers, (for God gave this earth and the dominion of it to *ha Adhom* and his children,) you command your servants (slaves) and they will obey *you*, and I will command my servants (slaves) and they will obey me, and there will be no dispute between you and me."

Is it not a duty, Dr. Seiss, that you and other learned men owe to your unlearned brothers and sisters, to point out these inaccuracies, and put the language just as God used it, before them? Is not this a duty that you and other learned men owe to God to do so? There is no difficulty in ascertaining the precise words that ought to be used to enable the reader to comprehend and know for himself, exactly what God did say, where these mistakes occur.

The next case that we will note, as stated by Dr. Seiss, is that where, in King James's translation, it is said, "the sons of God saw the daughters of men, that they were fair, and took them wives of all they choose." Ariel had said that the word translated *men* here did not mean or refer to those of *ha Adhom's* race, but were negroes or mulattoes. Ariel at the same time admitted that in the Hebrew text, from which the translation was made, the words were *ha Adhom*, but which he stated was thus inserted through mistake, by the copyist who made the manuscript, but did not give any reason for saying it was a mistake, hoping that some scholar would, like Dr. Seiss, take up the point, and discuss it. This is another of those uncorrected errors, to which we have referred.

God gave to Esau Mt. Edom, as a dwelling-place. Esau had two mulatto wives; and their children, as well as those of Cain, are called in Hebrew *beni ha Edomi Ebhodh ha adhamah*, the sons of red slaves of the earth.

Now, Dr. Seiss knows very well, as a scholar, that the words Edom and Adam are spelled exactly alike in Hebrew, and that it is the vowel pointing alone that makes the one Adam and the other Edom; and this vowel pointing has been added long since the Christian Era, and did not belong to the Hebrew originally. But Dr. Seiss, or any other Hebrew scholar, can be at no loss in deciding that

293

it was not the white man that is referred to in this place, the moment their attention is called to it.

Our Saviour, in commenting on the first marriage, plainly states the matter in such a way that God did not intend that *ha Adhom* should have but one wife; for the Hebrew term *Ishshah*, by which she is designated wife, has no plural. God saw proper in the selection of that term, to place it beyond every possibility for *ha Adhom* even to imagine that he was to have more than one wife. Connect this fact with another one of very significant importance, and which fact is, that God never established marriage relations between any beings on earth except *ha Adhom* and Eve. That no marriage, with God's authority, can ever take place, except between a male *ha Adhom* and a female *ha Adhom*. The word that is here translated *wives* is *nashim*, which is the plural of *nashi*, which describes the female negro. This is sustained by the hieroglyphic paintings dating anterior to the flood, and running back to a time when *ha Adhom* was alive on the earth. In these pictures a negro woman is painted representing her to be on her hands and knees, generally, though not always, with a rope doubled and in a noose around her neck, the two ends being held by a man. The hieroglyphics accompanying this painting spell the Hebrew word *nashi*, of which *nashim* is the plural, and is the word translated *wives* in the place referred to by Dr. Seiss. Had Dr. Seiss's attention been previously called to a critical examination of this subject, as we have stated it, he would doubtless have concurred with us that the word wives did not refer to the daughters of *ha Adhom* and Eve, and that the word men, occurring in the phrase, daughters of *men*, should have been pointed to spell *Edomi* and not *ha Adhom*.

The reader will perceive that we have referred to the hieroglyphic language and paintings that were existing before the flood, to illustrate a certain fact in regard to what Dr. Seiss had quoted, from a part of the 6th chapter of Genesis, where it is said, "the sons of God saw that the *daughters of men* were fair, and they took them *wives* of all they choose," to show that the word *nashim*, translated wives, did not refer to the daughters of *ha Adhom* and Eve for reasons given. But it was singular that hieroglyphics, paintings, and language of the date named, should sustain the same fact; it is, to say the least, very remarkable. We did not refer to either the hieroglyphic paintings and language, for the purpose of proving anything to be found in God's Word; or to prove the truth of anything said or done by God, *for we never refer to any man, nor to any man's opinion, to prove what God said or did was true; we never could think of debasing, or degrading of God, our Almighty Father, by referring to any man and his opinions, or to any works of man, to prove what God had said or done to be true.*

We could not so degrade our Almighty Creator, as to think or believe for one moment, that it was in the power of any man, writer or preacher, in or out of the pulpit, *to give a credibility to God,* which God's own Word and works carry with them, beyond all human power to strengthen. Our reference, therefore, to these hieroglyphics, was not to prove anything contained in God's Word, but to show a harmony between them and our statement of a mere matter of fact which had been referred to in God's Word. We will here add that there are some very strange matters connecting the hieroglyphic writings and paintings of Bible history, as far back as the curse of Cain, and which have been strangely overlooked by our Egyptian archeologists, and many divines, to which a full reference and explanation will be made in our work on The White Man.

CREDIBILITY OF THE BOOK OF GENESIS.

While on the subject of historical references, we will add to them what may be deemed a full answer to "scientific geologists" and their attack upon Moses' account of the creation and of the flood. Although the discussion which this involves is not legitimate to the discussion of the *status* of the negro, yet, as the Book of Genesis, containing Moses' account of the creation, and of the flood, which involves that of the negro, and which, if the whole book is false, the account of the negro's creation must also be false.

The Book of Genesis has been assailed in every imaginable manner, that the extremes of atheism and infidelity could devise, countenanced on the other side by corrupt Christianity, that is willing to accept Moses as a law-giver, divinely inspired by God, to lead out his people from bondage, and deliver them divine laws at Mt. Sinai, but in all other matters entirely ignorant, knowing nothing scientifically.

Professor Agassiz, of Cambridge University, Massachusetts, in his opening address to the College, expressly said that he did not wish any person to attend his lectures who believed in either the historical truth or Divine inspiration of the Book of Genesis. He was highly applauded at the time for uttering this sentiment. That Rev. Mr. Prichard, D. D., author of a large work on the races, rejects Moses' chronology—rejects his genealogy and his account of the Flood. The Rev. Mr. Davidson, D. D., rejects Moses' account of the creation of the world—that in six days God created the heavens and the earth—as unscientific and false. He, with Bishop Colenzo, reject the account of the Flood, and allege that the cubical dimensions of the Ark were wholly inadequate to receive what was said Noah put into it. They further assert, to show their contempt for the Book of Genesis, that it was a physical impossibility for such a flood to have taken place as is described by Moses, for all the waters on the earth or under it, or contained in the air, condensed into water, could not produce a flood that would cover the highest mountain fifteen cubits and upwards—Himalaya for example. That the Rev. C. J. Bunsen, D. D., LL. D., with Max Müller and others, deny that Moses ever wrote the Book of Genesis,—don't know who wrote it—but assert that it was written in the time of Solomon, and certainly not earlier than the days of David.

We give the foregoing as samples of the growing discredit which scientific men are throwing on the Book of Genesis, and now accepted by the pulpit orators of the leading denominations of the Christian religion, all over the land, in this country as well as in Europe. To these we will add that we saw, not long since, a newspaper statement to the effect that a letter had been addressed to the Archbishop of Canterbury, requesting him to head the movement for a new Bible, or translation, that shall be in conformity with the truths and discoveries of science, and particularly referring to the science of Geology.

The reader can see from this formidable array, attacking the historical truth and Divine inspiration of the Book of

Genesis, that if well founded, the religion of Jesus Christ is likewise unfounded, and without Divine authority. For it so happens that our Lord and Saviour, Jesus Christ, has quoted from the Book of Genesis, throughout, in different parts, from beginning to end. Did our Saviour endorse an impostor and his imposition? If the book is false, and not of Divine authority, then he has so endorsed the impostor and his impositions. And so have all the Jewish Prophets; and so, likewise, have all the Evangelists and Apostles of our Lord and Saviour, Jesus Christ, done the same. And the Christian religion falls to the ground, and man's brightest hopes are blasted forever. But, reader, we will see, directly, that the Book of Genesis is true, and that neither Jewish Prophets, nor Apostles, nor the Son of God, were mistaken when they endorsed it as of Divine origin.

What we shall say in regard to the contest involved, affecting the credibility of Moses, divides itself into two parts: First, his account of the creation, and second, his account of the Flood.

Geologists except to his account of the creation, on the score that it was impossible for it to be true, that in six days God made the heavens and the earth. They say that according to the laws of nature, as developed by the science of geology, it would take many hundreds of thousands of years, if not millions of years, to form this earth. As to the number of years it would thus take to form the earth, they are by no means agreed among themselves. For example, one thinks it might be done in ten or eleven thousand years, while others, equally or more learned, assert that, according to the laws of nature, it would require at least two hundred millions of years to make or form red sand stone, and, therefore, for Moses to assert that both heaven and earth were made in six days, cannot be true in any sense, and must, therefore, be totally false.

Now, reader, we take the ground that Moses' statement is literally true—that God did make the heavens and earth in six days. And we mean to be understood, that they were just such days as we have now, of twenty-four hours each. Reader, do not be astonished to see how easily and how effectually this great error will be forever crushed, and dissipated, and leave not a vestige behind. These

gentlemen were so intent in fastening falsehood on Moses,
that they seem never to have thought that they themselves
were wrong, when they took Moses' account of the creation of the *earth* for an account of the creation of the
globe.

Moses' account of the creation of the earth, *arrets,* the
Hebrew word used by Moses, is limited in its meaning,
and is the only word, and that of soul, in the account of
the creation, to which God himself has affixed the meaning; and He has so fixed the meaning of this Hebrew
word, *arrets,* that it is not possible for any candid scholar
to be mistaken about it. God plainly tells us that he said,
"Let the waters be gathered together unto one place, and
let the *dry land* appear; and God called the dry land
earth," and in the fifth verse, of the second chapter, he
says: "There went up a mist that watered the whole surface of the *ground.*"

Now, reader, we put it to your common sense, could
you, with these three before you—dry land, earth, and
ground—imagine for a single moment that red sand
stone, or any other stone, constituted either the one
or the other? Look at Our Saviour's solution of it;
he said: "A sower went forth to sow, and some seed
fell on stony ground, and sprang up, and immediately withered, for it had not much earth;" but a little
too much stone. It would be a singular account if the
Hebrew term *arrets* should mean rocks, and minerals, which
are found in the globe, and if this were so we should
have no earth. On the other hand, Moses was describing
the skin of the globe. As we have elsewhere shown,
God makes everything after a pattern, and this globe,
which had been heated to an incandenscent state, and then
drowned out by that great deep, mentioned in the second
verse, (over which God's spirit moved,) the *foundations* of
which deep God broke up, when he drowned the world by
a flood in the days of Noah. Now this earth, which was
to make the skin of the globe, was held in solution,
curdled up, muddied up, in this great deep, over which
God's spirit moved; for it was to be endowed, not only
with life in itself, but with power to impart life to all that
God had ordained should grow from its bosom. And
where was it to get this life, and power to impart life, but
from God's spirit alone, and which spirit God then placed

on the face of the waters, and has not removed it thence from that day to this.

Not one single thing which geologists pretend to show, can be found in this earth, which Moses is describing, that antedates for one hour the existence of this earth, as given by Moses. Red sand stone, and other geological formations, minerals, &c., &c., all belong to this globe in its anterior existence, before the new skin, called the earth, was put upon it, as described by Moses. When God made the globe, of which red sand stone forms a part, he never told *ha Adhom* nor Moses, and neither you nor I, reader, and, I am equally sure, that he never told any geologist, when he did make it. It is, doubtless, just as old as many of the stars and planets, by which it is surrounded. And no intelligent man, whether scientific or not, would willingly subject himself to the ridicule that would inevitably follow the attempt of any man, to give the ages of the different stars and planets. Of the age of this, our *globe*, or when it was made, Moses has not written one word, but has confined his account to the earth, and when it was made; and which, as before said, is but the skin of the globe. The earth has life, and has the power also to impart that life to everything that grows from its surface; and everything that grows from its surface has *life*, but it is inanimate life. But each separate kind, or variety, is, like the globe, covered with its bark or skin; and so it is equally true of all animated existences, from *ha Adhom* down through beasts and creeping things, and fowls, down to fishes, each, and all, are likewise covered with their skin. And it was of this skin (*errats*), then newly put around the globe, that Moses described as being made in the six days, when God created the heavens and the earth. The Hebrew word for globe is *tavel* and not *errats*.

For some cause or crime, God had burned up the previous heavens and earth, just as he intends to burn up the present heavens and earth, and make new ones, as he has plainly told us. And when the new heavens and new earth are created, we may have some future Moses to tell us when, and how it was done. Our geologists appear to be greatly at a loss to know what constituted the light of the first, the second, and the third days of creation, as the light of the sun did not present itself until the fourth day. We can see no difficulty in comprehending this, if we will be content with what Moses has said. The reader will perceive from the language of the second verse, that darkness was upon the face of the deep which invested the globe, and that this darkness existed before anything was created. We are also divinely told that God is light, and in Him is no darkness at all; that he dwells in light inaccessible, or which cannot be approached by mortal eyesight, and that it requires special action, or the exercise of a divine attribute of the Almighty, to make it visible to mortals. For example: When Moses came down from the mount, his face shone with a resplendent effulgence of light, so great, that the children of Israel could not look upon his face, and he had to put a veil over it while delivering the law. A second instance occurs in the case of the transfiguration of our Saviour, when Moses and Elias appeared with him. A third instance occurs in the case of Saul of Tarsus, when jouneying from Jerusalem to Damascus, and when about twelve miles from the latter city, when on the top of a high rounded hill, he says that at mid-day, "Oh, King, suddenly there was a light from heaven above the brightness of the sun, that shone round about us, and when we had all fallen to the ground," &c., &c. The effect on Saul was such, that he was blind for three days, and then was restored only by the interposition of Divine power.

While it is perfectly true that God is everywhere, and fills immensity with his presence, yet he choses to make himself thus visible only on such occasions as require it. We can, therefore, readily understand why the first thing commanded in the beginning of this creation—why God said, " let there be light."

The first word in the Hebrew Bible is *Bereshith*, beginning. This word beginning indicates a time when, and a place where; and the words, "let there be light," shows the first movement of the Almighty Creator. This light was stationary over that beginning point. The globe, although surrounded and covered by the deep, continued to revolve on its own axis, as it had always done, and yet continues to do; and consequently divided that light from the darkness, just as the light is now divided from the darkness, making day and night every twenty-four hours, just as we have it now. The first light was from God direct, the second was from the sun. The first light is the breath of immortality, for St. John tells us that the light was the life of man, *ha Adhom.* The second light was from the sun, which eliminated from the face of the deep this air, or atmosphere, which is the life or breath of all mortal beings, and without which they could not live a moment. The first light is co-extensive with God, who is everywhere, and like eternal life, is endless. While on the other hand, the life, or breath of mortals, is limited to what King James's translators call the firmament, in Hebrew, *rakia*, but means that space from the surface of the earth up to what, in common parlance, we call the sky, or as high as animated life can exist therein.

The reader has now before him the boundary, so to speak, of immortality, and also the boundary of mortality, the breath of one is light, and that of the other is this air, or atmosphere. God furnished the one by breathing into *ha Adhom's* nostrils, while that of the other is breathed from this atmosphere. The reader will find this subject fully elaborated in "The White Man," and made so plain, that any candid man or woman can understand it.

Our reason for calling attention to it, in this, our reply to Dr. Seiss, is, that as the geologists have called in question the truth of the Book of Genesis, and the credibility of Moses' account of the creation, we felt that it was due to our readers to state this much of it, that they might understand what Moses has said, and at the same time see the errors which the geologists, and other learned and scientific gentlemen, have run into. And we fear, from what Dr. Seiss has said about the "*improved text*" of the Hebrew, that he partakes of their infidelity regarding Moses' cosmogony, and would not correct him by showing their mistakes. That a man can be honest and sincere in his mistakes, we have no doubt, as St. Paul furnishes an eminent example in his own person and conduct. But that we are correct in our description of the abode or kingdom of immortality and eternal life, we have but to call before the mind of the reader St. John's description of the future abode of the righteous beyond the grave. In that description St. John tells us that "they have no need of the sun, nor of the moon, nor of the stars, nor of a candle to give light therein; for the Lord God, and the Lamb, are the light thereof." He also expressly tells us, that "there is *no sea there*," for if so, there would be air or atmosphere there, and which is breathed alone by mortals, and not by immortals.

THE TRUTH OF MOSES' ACCOUNT OF THE FLOOD.

Just here, and on this point, the credibility of Moses, we will add a few remarks touching the credibility of his account of the flood, as follows: Our learned geologists and others tell us that it is impossible that his account of the flood can be true, for if all the water on the earth, and under the earth, and if all the water contained in the air, was condensed into water, it could not then make such a flood as Moses has described, covering the highest mountains, Himalaya, &c., fifteen cubits and upwards.

We have already shown the great mistake committed by geologists, when they supposed that Moses meant the globe, when he used the word earth. And a similar mistake in understanding Moses seems to afflict them in regard to his account of the destruction of the world by the flood. What world was it that Moses was describing the destruction of? Was it the world as it existed from *ha Adhom* to Noah ? Or was it the world after the flood ? If the latter, then Moses never wrote anything about it, as it is evident he could not, and would not overlook these high mountains. What a pity that these good and learned men should thus distress themselves about that which has no existence in fact, except in their own misconception of what Moses was writing about. If such reasoners would think a little before they ventured to assert a fact, on which to build a theory, they would not be so often wrecked, as they now are, in such shallow water. And, in this instance, they ought to have learned from their own theory, that no such mountains as the Himalaya, Alps, nor even Ararat, could have existed previous to the flood. For in all their works these geologists have established the fact, that this globe had been once in an incandescent state, heated with a melting heat; and in this they are doubtless correct, as that heated condition must necessarily precede the present condition of the earth, and must have been extinguished before the present earth was spread around it, as the new skin of the globe.

Now Moses accounts for this extinguishment by telling

302

us in the second verse, first chapter of Genesis, (as badly translated by King James,) that the earth was without form and void, and that darkness dwelt upon the face of the deep, showing how this great heat, or fire, had been extinguished; and it is the foundations of this deep, meaning the body of the globe thus covered with this water, that God broke up when he brought the flood upon the world. But another point which these geologists have presented, but about which they could not have thought for one moment, intelligently, or they would not have committed the blunder which they have committed, in supposing that such mountains as the Himalaya, or Alps, could have existed before the flood. And that point is this: That the *globe* was at some time anterior to the formation of the earth as we now see it, heated to a heat that melted it, and reduced to a fluid form more or less, by that intense heat. This being shown to be true by their own investigations, and known to be true by Divine Revelation, which declares that, " that which is to be has already been ;" and that it further declares that the present Heaven, and the present Earth, are to be burned up. Their own theory then, the result of their own investigations, shows that the globe was once in an incandescent state.

Now the point that they have overlooked, for the want of intelligent thought, is this: What form could the globe take, while in this fluid state, while revolving on its own axis, and gradually cooling down? Does not every person know, that as the globe now revolves on its own axis, that it must always have done so from the moment it was launched into existence by its Almighty Creator? Does not every intelligent person know positively, and without a doubt, that it must take the form, or shape, of a *perfect* globe, and which it was in the beginning? Most unequivocally it must have done so. This can be verified now by any one, who will take the trouble to visit a shot tower, and witness the perfect globe formed by the melted lead; each shot revolving on its own axis, as it is cooling and falling. With this fact before them, these geologists could never have imagined that this globe, which they now call the earth, could have been of the form that it now is. Impossible that it could be so; and that its present shape must have been given to it, changing it from its perfect globe form to its present shape. Now

Moses' account of its first shape is in perfect accordance
with every fact which he has stated in connection with human and animal existence from the time of its creation,
until the flood, when its present shape was, by that terrible
event, given to it. As a perfect globe, it revolved upon
its own axis, perpendicular to its own centre. This must
necessarily have been so. The globe, now called the earth,
from its outer skin, revolving perpendicularly to its own
centre, must have given a climate equal from centre to circumference. This explains how *ha Adhom* and Eve, who
Moses tells us were both naked, could multiply and fill the
earth. That this position is true, is further sustained
by the fact, that the earth produced, spontaneously, everything that was necessary for the maintenance of *man*, and
beast, and which it could not do, if the climate of the
earth had been in the beginning such as we know it to be
now. Nor would God have given such command to *ha
Adhom* to multiply and fill the earth, as it would have
been impossible, physically impossible, for him to have
obeyed him, if our climate was then what it now is; nor
could the earth produce, spontaneously, what was necessary
for *man* and animal to live upon, as the food of *man* was
restricted to the fruit of the earth, and the seed or grain
of the earth, and that of beast and animals, to its grass
and herbage.

This proves that the climate of this primeval world
was uniform and equal from centre to circumference; for
without this, these things could not be produced spontaneously. The climate of the globe must, therefore, have been
one perpetual spring and summer. And had King James's
translators done themselves, or the Word of the Almighty,
justice, in translating the 5th verse, of the 2nd chapter of
Genesis, where they say, " and there was no man to till the
ground, for the Lord God had not then caused it to rain upon
the earth; but a mist went up that watered the whole surface
of the ground," they would have rendered it thus : That *ha
Adhom* was not to direct, or command, his slave (*Ebhodh*)
to till the ground, for the Lord God had not then caused it
to rain upon the earth; but a mist went up that watered
the whole surface of the ground. This shows two facts:
First. How the earth was watered in its primeval condition, by which all things were spontaneously made to
grow; and, secondly, that it never rained upon the earth

until the flood. And this latter fact is proven to be true, with mathematical exactness, by the sign of the rainbow given by God to Noah, that he would no more destroy the world by a flood; and we know that the rainbow is alone produced by rain, or when it rains. We are further assured of the correctness of this reasoning, by a knowledge of the fact that God makes all things perfect, adapting everything to the purposes for which it was created, and adapting the circumstances by which he surrounded them to that condition. In that condition everything was "good, very good." *Ha Adhom* and Eve were created naked, and in that condition could obey all the commands God had given them. But after their fall their condition was altered, and to meet the requirements of this changed condition, God himself then clothed them.

What are we to understand from the words used by God to *ha Adhom* after his fall, that in the sweat of his face he should eat his bread; and that when he tilled the ground it should not *henceforth* yield unto him its strength? What are we to understand from this language? Does it not plainly teach us that the earth, previously to his fall, had spontaneously produced everything necessary to his well being. This is obviously and plainly the intent and meaning, sustained, as it is, by the whole of Moses' narration of the Creation. The labor of *ha Adhom*, and his tilling of the ground in his primeval condition, are not once named. But, on the contrary, it is expressly stated by God, when he installed *ha Adhom* in the Garden of Eden, that he was not even to keep the garden in order by his own labor, but was commanded by God, to have that done by his *slave* (*Ebhodh*). And in the 5th verse of the 2nd chapter, *ha Adhom* is told not to direct his slave to till the ground, for the Lord God had not yet caused it to rain upon the earth. Convincing and satisfactory as this statement must be to every candid believer in the Bible, that its truth cannot be questioned, yet it is not all the testimony presented by physical facts, and these facts noted by Moses in his account of the Flood. The first one is the sign of the covenant made by God with Noah, that he would no more destroy the earth by a flood, the rainbow. Now, if it had rained previously to the Flood, the rainbow would have been seen, and, therefore, it could be no *sign* that God would not again destroy the earth by a

3

flood.   But in addition to this, we are told, in King
James's translation, that, after the Flood, Noah "*began to be
an husbandman*," and planted a vineyard.   The proper
rendering of the Hebrew, in this place, and as it is sustained by all the facts contained in our previous reasoning,
of the condition of the earth previous to the Flood, that
it should be rendered into English thus : *That Noah began
husbandry or tillage of the earth.*   But why was it left for
Noah to begin this tillage?   Plainly, because God had
said to *ha Adhom*, (meaning his whole posterity,) " in the
sweat of thy face, shalt thou eat bread until thou return
unto the dust from whence thou wast taken."   To enforce
this condition, Winter was absolutely necessary to be introduced by an organic law of God, compelling man to
labor in Summer, and to produce that, by the sweat of his
brow, which he was to live on in Winter.   Thus, whether
in Winter or Summer, his bread was the product of the
sweat of his face.

But the question arises here, that as the climate of all
the earth previous to the Flood was equal from centre to
circumference, how was Winter introduced?   Moses plainly
tells us that at the Flood the foundations of the great
deep were broken up, (referring to that deep spoken of
in the 2nd verse, 1st chapter of Genesis); when the great
mountains that now cover the face of the earth were
thrown up; as we have conclusively shown that no such
mountains could have existed before the Flood.   And by
the throwing up of these mountains the earth was thrown
from its perpendicularity to its own centre, and made to
oscillate $23\frac{1}{2}$ degrees north and $23\frac{1}{2}$ degrees south of the
Equinoctial line.   This oscillation of 47 degrees exactly
causes Winter and Summer.   And which God told Noah
then, that Winter and Summer, seed-time and harvest,
should continue.   How any sensible, common sense thinking man, seeing and knowing that such are the exact physical facts as they now exist, can have a single doubt about
the correctness of Moses' account of the Flood, is to us
astonishing.

But besides this, after the fall, God told Eve, *ha Chevah*,
that he would " greatly multiply her *conception*."   Now, he
had previously told them, *ha Adhom* and *ha Chevah*, to
multiply and *fill the earth.*   Now, where was this multiplied conception to be placed, unless the earth's surface

was enlarged from the water to receive it?   By the breaking up of the foundations of the great deep, the mountains that now cover our earth were then thrown up, causing, in the first place, the confining of the water into deeper and narrower channels, by which more of the earth's surface was exposed to receive this multiplied conception; and producing, secondly, the oscillation of the earth before referred to, and thereby producing Winter and Summer. That this flood did take place, and the present mountains were then thrown up, we have abundant evidence furnished by the tops of some of these highest mountains, which contain the remains of the denizens of the great deep, in bones and fossil remains, showing the crest of the mountain to have been once the bottom of the ocean.

But there is another curious fact in this: That there was found in northern Siberia, about one hundred years ago, immense deposits of elephants' tusks, which have been worked ever since, producing so much ivory that they have obtained the name of "ivory quarries"—they are still worked.   It is well-known that the elephant could not exist in a climate so cold as that of Siberia, or any part of it.   Now the question is, how did they get there?   This can only be accounted for by taking Moses' account as true, that the primeval conditon of the earth's climate, previous to the Flood, was equal from centre to circumference.   The elephants could then naturally be found there.   And as it is known that their habits are gregarious, the Flood found them in droves, and so drowned them. This is the rational solution of the question how they came there.

There remains now but two other objections to examine, made by the learned, against Moses' account of the Flood, being universal, covering the whole globe.   The first is that the Flood was only partial, being a high rise of either the Nile or the Euphrates, as they claim, of which Noah was previously advised, and built him a raft for the saving of himself and family, and flocks.   The answer to this is plain and simple.   If Noah had been *advised* beforehand of a coming rise in the river, in time to build such a raft, that same power could have told him where to go without being disturbed by the water.   But, secondly, a high rise of any river produces swift currents, and either the Nile or Euphrates, would have carried him out to sea with his raft. How could he have gotten back? But again: Noah was directed to take birds into the Ark. Could not these have flown to any part of the earth if left uncovered, had the Flood been partial? There is no rational or plain commonsense way of accounting for the phenomena exhibited by and now found on the earth, but by taking Moses' account of the Creation and of the Flood to be true. In Moses' account he has stated every fact necessary to enable any intelligent person that will think and reason, taken in connection with existing facts, which we now know to be true, and by which we comprehend and know with positive certainty, that his account must be inspired truth.

The position of the earth, as herein stated, before and after the Flood, any person can demonstrate who will go to the trouble of making a proper globe of equal density, that will sink half-way in water. On this globe let him draw the equinoctial line, then place the globe in water, and he will see that it is equi-distant from the equinoctial line to the water on each side, showing that it stands perpendicular to its own centre. Now, let him add to the globe the different ranges of mountains now on the earth, and then place the globe back into the water, and he will see by the equinoctial line that the globe is then canted from its perpendicularity to its own centre, exhibiting the exact position which the earth now fills. And if made with mathematical exactness, and of materials of the same density, and the mountains arranged with geographical exactness also, it will exhibit the earth as now occupying the position assigned it by astronomers, and the sun's course, in the earth's annual revolution, would cut the equinoctial line at the exact point that it now does.

For the benefit of such of our Christian readers whose learning is limited to the English language, we add the following citicism on the 2nd verse, 1st chapter of Genesis, as it will aid them in understanding the Mosaic account of the Creation. The part of the verse which we intend citicising, stands thus in King James's translation: "The earth was without form and void." Now, reader, that you may comprehend that this translation is grossly improper, we have only to ask you to think for a moment who it was that was making this revelation, of when and how God had created the heavens and the earth. The divine

record plainly tell you that all animated beings that were
brought into existence before Adam, consisted of beasts,
cattle, creeping things, birds and fishes. Now, it is plain
to your common sense that none of these could have told
Adam when and how God created the heavens and the
earth. The logic of these facts plainly teaches us that it
was God himself, telling to his son Adam when and how
all things were created. Could not God speak plainly,
and did he not intend that his son should understand him?
Certainly he did. Now then, we ask again, what idea
could Adam form of a thing that had *no form*, or what
idea he could have of a material substance that was *void?*
It is clear that he could have no idea of either, and that
if God had used Hebrew words that represented what is
covered by the English words, "without form and void,"
that neither Adam or Moses could comprehend what was
said. The Hebrew words thus mistranslated are *tohu* and
bahu, and should have been translated thus: "The earth was
masculine and feminine," this being the literal meaning of
these words. But how can we make our English readers
know that this translation is correct? Plainly thus:
Everything that grows from the bosom of the earth, trees,
shrubbery, grasses, &c., have life, but it is inanimate life;
and each of them have their seed *in it self*, and consequently both masculine and feminine. The earth has life
in itself, this life is also inanimate, and renders the earth
both masculine and feminine; for there must of necessity
be both a male and a female to *produce* anything. Adam
himself was both masculine and feminine when he was
created, and in one place the word earth is used to represent Adam, where Cain says that "thou has this day driven
me out from the face of the earth," meaning from the face
of his father. From this we learn another fact, viz. That
inanimate life has no feeling. Our bones have life, but
no feeling. God thereby teaches us that when we cut and
burn wood, that we inflict no pain.

Reader, please excuse this long digression, rendered absolutely necessary, in our estimation, in this day, when
Moses' authority, as a divine writer, is not only scouted,
but the whole Book of Genesis is not only attempted to be
put aside, but to be rejected as an imposition. We therefore
thought it a duty to thus extend our reply to Dr. Seiss, in

defense of that precious Book of God, for when as first written in Hebrew, *it was the Word of God.*

WE RETURN TO DR. SEISS'S REVIEW.

We again take up Dr. Seiss's review of Ariel. We were glad when we heard that so fine a scholar, and such an amiable gentleman, agreed to review Ariel. It was our earnest desire to have Ariel reviewed by a competent scholar; especially did we desire our Hebrew criticised. Although we could not see how it could be assailed, and the conclusions arrived at set aside, yet we were anxious to know what the first scholars of the land could say about it. We were anxious not to be mistaken ourselves, or be the instrumenal in leading others into error. We had privately consulted some of the ablest Hebrew scholars, who indorsed both our translations and our conclusions.

Dr. Seiss's reputation as a scholar was world-wide. The only drawback against him was whether he could rise above the prejudices of his early education and theological teachings. Could he reach the point above these prejudices, and be guided alone by God's Word; or would he be guided by the erroneous prejudices of his early teachings? How he has succeeded, the reader will perceive, after reading this, our reply.

His first criticism is on Ariel's use of the Hebrew words *ha Adhom,* the meaning of which is *the Adhom* (Adam). He does not except to the meaning, but does to the orthography that we use, which we have previously explained, and we still adhere to our spelling of that name. He also excepts to our emphasizing these words in the manner in which we did. We could not then, nor now, do otherwise.

The question at issue with Dr. Seiss and Ariel was, on whom did God originally confer immortality and eternal life? Dr. Seiss and his friends contend that he conferred it upon whites, blacks and mulattoes of every shade. Ariel denied this, and said it was limited to the pure descendants of *ha Adhom* and *ha Chavah* (Adam and Eve); and that the blacks were beasts, and that neither they nor their mulatto descendants had any claim or title to eternal life. We referred to the fact that after the first use of the term, *Adhom,* occurring in Genesis, 1st chapter and

26th verse, that ever afterwards God himself, when speaking of him, always called him *ha Adhom*. We followed the language of God himself, and if what we said was giving emphasis to these words, the reader can see that it was by God's authority, for he so invariably called him after the first time.

The only place where Dr. Seiss quotes the word against Ariel, with any plausibility of his being right and Ariel wrong, is in the 6th chapter of Genesis, where King James's translation says: "The sons of God saw the daughters of men, and took them wives," etc. Here we readily admit that the Hebrew words *ha Adhom*, are used in the text from which our Bible is translated. But we have shown, in these pages, so clearly and so plainly, that this was an error of the copyist, in copying the Hebrew MS., that even Dr. Seiss, or any other Hebrew scholar, will not doubt but that we are correct; and that the proper words to be there are *ha Edomi*, and not *ha Adhom; Edom* and *Adhom* being spelled exactly alike in Hebrew; and it is the vowel pointings alone that make the one *Adam* and the other *Edom*. We refer the reader to what we have said before with perfect confidence that no man will doubt our correctness.

But let us return, to see if we can learn what being it is on whom God has conferred immortality, with power of endless life beyond the grave. Dr. Seiss, and all Roman Catholics, and all Protestants, accept the 7th verse of the 2nd chapter of Genesis, as describing both the being on whom the immortality was conferred, and what it is of man that does not die when the body dies, which, in King James's translation, is called a living soul. This term *soul* is defined by them as being the *mind*, the rational faculties, as the reader can see by consulting the English, the French, the German, the Spanish, the Italian and the Latin dictionaries and lexicons.

Now, we readily admit ourselves that the 7th verse of the 2nd chapter does describe the being on whom God did confer immortality, that might pass into eternal life; and what it is that thus connects him with eternal life. But while we accept this verse, it must be distinctly understood, that it is as it appears in the original Hebrew, and not as it stands in King James's translation. As it stands in King James's translation it reads thus: "And the Lord

God formed man of the dust of the ground, and breathed into his nostrils the breath of life; and man became a living soul." Will any man of candor, having a knowledge of the Hebrew language, *dare* to say this is a correct translation of the original? We use the emphatic word *dare*, not in an offensive sense, but to arouse the attention of God's children to this the most important verse, to them, that can be found in the Bible. We will answer for Dr. Seiss, that he will not dare to do it; although he will abuse Ariel for making God's Word appear in English in the exact ideas contained in the Hebrew words. Nay, there are plenty of men to be found who will not only defend the translation of this verse, but every other false translation found in either the Old or the New Testament, as these false translations aid in keeping up the present religious parties and strife. There is not an honest Hebrew scholar on earth that will say that this verse is even fairly translated, or that the ideas of the original are correctly given. But, on the contrary, we will say that it is intentionally falsely translated.

If there is a Hebrew Bible or MS. now on earth, which contains the Hebrew word *Chaiyah*, which is the word for life, we have never seen it or heard of it. On the contrary, the word thus translated *life*, in this verse, is in every Hebrew Bible or MS. *Chaiyim*, which means *lives*, plural; and every person, whether knowing a word of Hebrew or not, must know that it should be in the plural, if he believes there is another life beyond the grave. It is on this account that we have said that the translation of this verse was intentionally made false; for, as before said, there is not a Hebrew Bible or MS. on earth but what has it plural, so far as has been yet known. Why our learned men, in the pulpit and out of it, and our Bible Societies, continue to publish the Bible with this false translation in it, we leave to our readers to decide.

But there is another Hebrew word in this verse which King James's translators have not translated at all; it is *Nishmath*. It stands in the orignal thus: "God breathed into his nostrils *Nishmath Chaiyim*"—the spirit of lives—conveying the idea of a *spirit life* from God, by which he was connected with eternal life; and the *soul life*, by which he was connected with earth; and *body life*, for even our bones have life; all of which was breathed into his nostrils by God himself, fitting him for mortal and immortal life.

But this is not all of our objection to King James's translation of this verse. Our next objection to their translation is positive and decided, for reasons that will appear directly, which are, that they have used the word *man* in their translation of the Hebrew words *ha Adhom,* which we have shown before cannot be translated by the word *man;* for *ha Adhom* is plainly declared to be the son of God, and the word *man,* as now understood, cannot be applied to him. The reader will remember Dr. Seiss's objection to our use and special application of these Hebrew words, *ha Adhom,* but the reader can see why we were thus particular in our application of these words.

All Roman Catholics and Protestants preach from their pulpits and say, that there was a being, or some being, on whom he did confer two lives, an earthly, and a life beyond the grave—we say, three lives. Now, reader, on whom did he confer these? Can any being tell us but God himself? Certainly not. And this 7th verse of the 2nd chapter tells us on whom he did confer them. It reads thus: "And the Lord God formed *ha Adhom,* out of (*Gnapher*) the dust of the ground; and breathed into his nostrils *Nishmath Chaiyim*—the spirit of lives—and *ha Adhom* became a living creature, possessed of *more* that *la Naphesh Chaiyah,* possessed of *more* than a living soul— God having expressly declared, as we have shown, that the *soul* of the flesh is the blood.

We will now show the reader why we were thus particular in our application of the words *ha Adhom.* He can see in the above that it was on this being alone that God did confer three lives. Now, wherever the words *Adhom* or *ha Adhom,* occur, designating the white man, and on whom God conferred these three lives, King James's translators have translated them by the word *man;* and wherever the word *Ish,* the plural of which is *Ishim,* designating the black man, occur; they translate these also by the words *man* and *men;* and wherever the word *Enosh,* the plural of which is *Enoshim,* designating the mulatto, the first cross between the whites and blacks, occur, they also translate by the words *man* or *men;* and wherever the word *Anshey,* the plural of which is *Anshim,* occur, designating the further cross of the whites with mulattoes, they

3*

also translate by the words *man* or *men*. Now, we respectfully ask every candid man or woman on earth, unskilled in the Hebrew, how could they understand or comprehend, on reading King James's translation of these terms, which of them designated the being on whom God conferred immortality and eternal life, or to which of them they referred; as they have used one and the same word, *man*, in every instance. God has plainly said he conferred it upon *ha Adhom*, and which designation includes alone the white man and which cannot be translated into any language on earth. That the term *man*, as now used and understood, cannot be applied to the son of God, except as an alias, like the terms Jew, Israelite, is applied to the Hebrew children of Abraham. But, like all aliases, refers back to the original for the exact idea or being referred to.

If God has conferred upon either the blacks or the mulattoes immortality and eternal life, let it be shown in God's Word in the same plain language that God uses when He conferred it on *ha Adhom*. If this cannot be done, as we know it cannot be, it will not do to assert or claim that they obtained this immortality by being the descendants of *ha Adhom;* for every person can positively see and know—even all negroes and mulattoes can see and know—that this assertion is false. For God commanded each being to produce their own kind, in their own image, and after their own likeness. We know that a white man and a white woman can do this; and we also know that a black man and a black woman can produce in their image, and after their likeness. But when it is attempted, by amalgamation, the product is not in the image or likeness of either the one or the other; and by which each are made to see and know that what they have done is in direct violation of God's law.

It was *ha Adhom* that fell. It was *ha Adhom* that lost his immortality; and which immortality Jesus of Nazareth, the son of Mary, came to restore, and by which we could have eternal life beyond the grave. He came four thousand years after the fall; the genealogy had been kept with perfect exactness from *ha Adhom* to Mary; and St. Paul says of him that "he was the *express image of God's person.*" That he was white none can doubt, nor does doubt; and God's command to *ha Adhom* was, that as he (*ha Adhom*) had been created in the image and likeness of God,

314

that he (*ha Adhom*) should produce his own kind, in his own image, and after his own likeness, also.   But St. Paul further tells us that "all flesh is not the same flesh ; there is one flesh of (*ha Adhom*) *man,* and another of *beasts,* and another of birds, and another of fishes;" and he also tells us that "the mind of a beast, the carnal mind, is not subject to the law of God, neither indeed can it be."   If, with these facts before the mind, any can be found, either black or white, to assert that the negro, or black man, is anything but a beast, has a perversity of intellect, and a disregard of moral truth below that of ignorance made drunk.

In regard to the accepted idea, that it is the mind of man that is the soul, and does not die when the body dies, it is sufficient answer simply to repeat what our Lord Jesus Christ said: " Thou shalt love the Lord thy God with all thy *heart,* and with all thy *soul,* and with all thy *mind,* and with all thy *strength.*"   It is plain that he did not hold the mind as being of *first* importance, nor the soul either; but he did regard the heart as being first in importance in bowing before God our Father.

If Dr. Seiss had done himself justice, and had treated Ariel with fairness, he might have saved himself the trouble of writing and printing, with his long line of references, all that he has said against Ariel in his criticism on the Hebrew word *Ish,* which he spells *eesh.*   For Ariel had expressly stated that the duties of *ha Adhom* were of two kinds ; first, to his Father and his God, as His son, and in the performance of these, which brought him in direct contact with his Father, he is called *ha Adhom;* and in the second, commencing with his being made an husband, he is called *Ish,* the feminine of which is *Ishshah,* wife. Here commenced his family, personal, *earthly* duties, callings, or pursuits.   As an husband, he called himself *Ish,* although God had named him *ha Adhom,* as His son. His duties as a son any person can see, were different from his duties as an husband.   The one was to God, the other to his wife; and in the performance of these duties, growing out of the family relations, he, and no other, could act and perform them.   God made the discrimination by his laws of what he required at *ha Adhom's* hands.   All other things or actions, the service of which was performed by *ha Adhom,* pertained alone to his earthly relations, and which he might or might not do just as he choose. In the performance of these services, duties or callings, whatever they might be, he called himself *Ish*, because *Ish* being the name he had bestowed upon the negro, and which had been given to him as a slave servant, and, being the head of the beast creation and *under rule to ha Adhom*, he called himself *Ish*, as he was under rule, as an husband, to his wife. Not that the word *Ish* describes the service or duties which, as an husband, he had to perform, but describes the relationship out of which his duties as an husband grew, and these were duties that he owed to his wife, and not to his creator, as none but himself could discharge them. To make this matter so plain that none can misunderstand it, we say: We have the word horse. It describes an animal well known. You see that horse plowing. Does the word horse describe the work he is performing? Certainly not, although under the law of his creation it was a part of his duties. Just so with the word *Ish*, but God took care to designate by the word *Ebhodh*, which means slave, the kind of service, and all service that *ha Adhom* should require to be performed by him, who proved himself to be the tempter, the negro, whose head, which contained his intellect, *ha Adhom* should bruise; or compel to do what he directed, and which would force *ha Adhom* to follow after him, to see that he did do that which he was commanded, and this is called the bruising of *ha Adhom's* heel, and which the negro compelled him to do. This is still true, as every one knows, who have managed and controlled negroes to this day. The term *Ish*, as we have here applied it to *ha Adhom*, is applied by the divine writers not only to *ha Adhom*, but to Noah, to Moses, and to our Lord Jesus Christ, and to many others, but always in the sense in which we presented it, where whites are referred to. Our Saviour, when he came into the world, was under earthly rule, which he recognized. The Hebrew term *Ish*, as the reader will perceive, applies to *ha Adhom* in everything, and in whatever position, duty, calling, station, or pursuit in life, other than his duty and obedience to God; in this latter, he is *ha Adhom*. The term *Ish*, in the above sense, refers to everything of a purely earthly nature, that *ha Adhom* might wish to do, but not in things connecting him personally with God, his Father. The negro was the head of the mortal creation and was a beast, and so made

316

by God when he created him, but endowed by God with speech, that he might the more quickly comprehend *ha Adhom*, and give him the ready obedience which his orders required.

The position taken, by what is termed the religious world, that it is the *mind,* the reasoning faculties which constitutes the soul, and does not die when the body dies, has led to the adoption of certain text-books, on moral science in our colleges and theological schools, in which is asserted the same idea.   Dr. Abercrombie, for example, says: " The world is composed of mind or soul and matter.   Matter we know by our senses, and mind or soul, by our consciousness."   Reader, can there be anything more untenable than the averments, contained in the above sentence?   Matter, it says, we know by our senses ; mind, or soul, by our consciousness?   Now strip a man of his five senses, and where is his consciousness? he is but like a tree, insensible and unconscious?   But we had a purpose in introducing this, to show that whether we call the mind or reasoning faculties the soul or not, still it cannot be that part of man that lives beyond the grave, that does not die when the body dies.   The ideas embodied by Dr. Abercrombie, and accepted as true by learned divines, must have been adopted without thought.   For without the five senses, it is impossible for any being to reason at all; and it is their aggregated and combined powers that constitutes, or makes the mind.   They are natural to the human body, or being.   Now, if the senses produce the mind in man, that which is to live forever, we would have our mortal bodies to produce something that was immortal, and which would ignore that axion in logic, which says a stream cannot rise higher than its fountain head; for this exhibits mortality producing immortality. And, therefore, any person can see, that will think, that it is impossible for the mind to be that part of man that does not die with the body.   What is the mind?   Is it not that faculty or power, by which we arrive at the conclusion to ascertain whether a thing is right or wrong, or that it is good or evil?   Now, reader, how did we reach this power?   Was it not through crime, through disobedience to God, in eating of the forbidden fruit of the tree of the knowledge of good, and the knowledge of evil?   Would God consecrate to eternal life

that which man obtained by sin and crime?   We think
not.

THE SIZE OF THE ARK, AND ITS CONTENTS.

The reader will excuse us for turning back to look at
the size of the Ark, which our learned men in their parlance, demonstrated as utterly incapable of containing all
the animals, birds, &c., &c., which Moses say went into it.
The Bunsens, the Müllers, the Davidsons, the Colenzos, all
of whom are D. D.'s, and with a thousand others in this
country and in Europe, have set down with slate and pencil in hand, and figured out the cubical capacity of the
Ark; and demonstrated, to their own satisfaction, at least,
the impossibility for the Ark to have held all that is said to
have been contained in it by Moses.   In other words, demonstrated that Moses was not to be believed.   Yet these
gentlemen hold on to their pulpits, and preach the Gospel,
whose founder had endorsed Moses as true.   We would like to
give these gentlemen, or any of them, a sum in arithmetic
from the New Testament, as they are so handy with slate
and pencil in proving a part of the Bible false.   It is this:
At a certain time Our Saviour retired to the mountains,
and the place was desert.   The people found him out; and
there gathered unto him about four thousand men, besides
women and children.   The latter would make, added to the
first, at least ten thousand persons that were with him in
this desert place.   They had been with him three days; and
He would not send them away hungered, least they faint by
the way.   He therefore told his Disciples to set something
before the people to eat.   They told him there were but
seven loaves and two fishes that belonged to two boys;
but what, they asked, are these among so many?   The
people were made to sit down, and the loaves and the
fishes were broken, and divided among them; and after
they had all eaten, they took up twelve basketsfull of the
fragments.

Now, Bishop Colenzo, with your able assistants, please
come forward, and with your slate and pencil, and figure
up the size of these loaves, allowing a pound to each person.   There were but seven loaves.   Each loaf would
have had to contain about seven and one half barrels of

flour to feed such a multitude. Now Bishop Colenzo, with his other Rev. D. D.'s, come forward and demonstrates that there was not in all that part of the country, nor in all Asia Minor, a bake-oven large enough (just like the Ark) to bake one of these loaves; and even if there were, there was not a cart in all Palestine large enough to haul one of these loaves up into the mountains, to this desert place; much less could one small boy, a lad, carry the whole of them himself in his satchel. The same objection that is applied by these learned gentlemen, showing the Ark to be too small, to receive what is said to have been contained in it by Moses, applies with equal force to every bake-oven in Palestine, that they, too, were too small to bake any such loaves; and we will admit, with all other intelligent persons, that a small lad could not possibly carry seven such loaves in his satchel, each loaf composed of about seven and a half barrels of flour. Such a lad, nor any grown man, since the days of Samson, could carry any one of them, even a short distance, much less to carry seven of them a long distance into the mountains, unto a desert place. If these gentlemen's reasoning have any force, as to the size of the Ark, and its incompetency to hold, from its smallness of size, what Moses has said was put into it, the same reasoning applies with equal force to these loaves, and the size of the oven in which they could be baked. Then we ask a question of our readers, why do these gentlemen continue to preach " *the Gospel* " as true? and yet, upon precisely the same evidence, the same *kind* of evidence, they reject Moses and the Book of Genesis as true, although the latter has been hallowed for nearly thirty-five centuries. We wonder if their salaries as preachers has anything to do in accepting one as true, and denouncing the other as false? This we will leave our readers to decide, as their best judgment may determine. It is a great misfortune to our race for us to know that learned men, *religious* men, and doctors of divinity, can be found on earth, who will advocate any set of opinions that may be required for *money.* This is a misfortune, and has led to the breaking up of Christianity into sects and parties; and has led to the inquiry, whether or not the Christianity taught by them is not a failure. This may be true, and if not true now, it

will prove a failure; but the Christianity of our Lord
Jesus Christ will never prove a failure.

RESUMPTION OF DR. SEISS' REVIEW.

We now resume our reply to Dr. Seiss' strictures on
Ariel.   It is easy to be seen, by any Hebrew scholar, why
Dr. Seiss favors the "improved orthography" of certain
Hebrew words.   Ariel had said that the first man was
white.   This Dr. Seiss disputes, and says, on page 136–7,
thus: "Ariel says Adam was a white man. Well, perhaps
he knows; but the Bible nowhere tells us so.   On the contrary, he who made him, and saw him every day he
lived, called him by a name significant of another color
altogether.   Josephus, who knew a little Hebrew, says
Adam in the Hebrew tongue signifies *one that is red*, * *
*   And whatever may be embraced in the name God applied to our first parents, a *red* or *earthly* color is insepara-
bly included.   *   *   *   At any rate, *the Bible* gives us a
red man and a *red woman* to start with, and that it is easy
to see how bleaching influences on the one side, and
browning influences on the other, that it is not remarkable
that their posterity in certain localities should be *characteristically dark* and *black,* and in some other localities and
climates should be *characteristically* fair and white."
We have quoted you fairly and now reply to you thus:
Our orthography of the Hebrew is from Augusti Hahn's
Hebrew Bible, regarded by all scholars, in Europe and
America, as the best and most correct edition of the Hebrew Bible extant, until about forty or forty-five years
ago, when learned scientific gentlemen, aided by the
atheists of France and Germany, attacked the credibility
of Moses' account of the creation; asserting that the
science of geology had developed the fact, that it was impossible for Moses' account to be true, that in six days
God had made the heavens and the earth; for, that by the
laws of nature governing the creation of matter, it would
require many ten thousands of years to form red sand
stone, etc.   In arriving at this conclusion, the French and
German assailants of Moses' account assumed the word
earth, to mean the *globe.*   They were replied to by a number of learned men of the Church of England, who, un-

fortunately, in their replies admitted, or at least did not
contest the fact, that the word earth did not mean the
globe. If this error of the learned atheist had been then
corrected, and the word earth limited to its true meaning,
that it was only the skin of the globe, and not the globe
itself, it would have saved the Christian world from the
doubt and infidelity that has since overspread it ; producing the impression in many honest minds that Moses was
mistaken. This produced the further attack upon Moses'
account of the flood, thus spreading the virus of doubt
and infidelity, until, as we have seen, many learned, in and
out of the pulpit, have concluded to reject the Book of
Genesis as historically true, and without divine inspiration ; while others, like Dr. Seiss, think that a new Bible
should be made, or a new translation made where language and statements shall be in accord, as they say, with
the truths of science. To this we squarely demur, for
there is not a man living on earth, who can successfully
attack the truth of Moses' account of the creation. It
never has yet been done, and never will be done, while an
intelligent believer in God's Word lives on earth.

The change in the orthography of some Hebrew words,
and a "*revised*" meaning given to them, and some others,
can be alone for the purpose of enabling conscientious, but
ignorant, men—men ignorant of God's Word, and of the
meaning he put upon his words, when he spoke them, but
otherwise *learned* in the estimation of the world—to enable
them to swing the corners, and still hold on to their pulpits as Christian preachers. Dr. Seiss quotes from Josephus, who, he says, was a learned man and knew some
Hebrew. Josephus wrote the antiquities of the Jews, and
other books about the Jews. Now does it not seem strange
to you, reader, that these books, written by Josephus about
the Jews, who were themselves Hebrews, that he should
write neither of them in the Hebrew language, but wrote
all of them in the Greek language. Now it seems strange,
that if Josephus understood the Hebrew, that he did not
write these works in the Hebrew language. It is historically well known, that he wrote these works shortly after
the fall of Jerusalem, and just in the infancy of preaching
the Gospel of Jesus Christ ; and that in a few years after
his death his works became so interpolated, and corrupted
by infidel Jews, Pagans, and professed Christians, that

C2

were they universally rejected. It is only in late years they have been received. But how much of what is now known, as the works of Josephus, was written by him is unknown; especially in all those parts that covers the controversies between Jews and Pagans, and between Jews and Pagans on the one side, and Christians on the other, the statements are so evidently corrupted, that none can receive them as true; nor can any one accept his works now *as true*, without rejecting the truth of many parts of the Old Testament. And if Josephus ever said, that the word Adam means one that is red, in the Hebrew language, the statement is false; for the word Adam does not mean any such thing, and Dr. Seiss must know it.

Dr. Seiss says: " At any rate *the Bible* gives us a *red man* and a *red woman* to start with." He also says, " on the contrary, He who made him, and saw him every day he lived, called him by a name significant of another color altogether than of white." Now, Dr. Seiss, we have a question to ask you: Did you ever see a Hebrew manuscript, or a Hebrew Bible on earth that gives, as you say, a " red man and a red woman to begin with ?" You know you have never seen such, as it cannot be found in any Hebrew manuscript or Bible, and is, therefore, an assumption of yours, without due reflection. Nay, we will go further and say, that it cannot be found in any translation of the Bible, in either the Spanish, the French, the German, the Russian, the Italian, or Latin languages, and we are certain that the idea is not given in our English Bible. The idea of *red*, associated with the name of *ha Adhom* comes from the mistake which our learned men have made in supposing that God made *ha Adhom* from *Adhamah* (the ground), for God plainly tells us that he made him of *gnapher* (the dust) of (*adhamah*) the ground. God's words are: And the Lord God formed *ha Adhom* of *gnapher*, (the dust) of (*Adhamah*) the ground. Now, Doctor, we have a grain, called *red* wheat, would you say that a loaf made of its dust, that the loaf was *red*, because it was made out of red wheat? We think you would not. And we think you will, on mature reflection, change your opinion that *ha Adhom's* name was derived from the ground (*adhamah*.)

Ha Adhom was the son of God, and it is unreasonable to suppose that God would call His Son's name from anything out of heaven, His own dwelling place; and it is equally unreasonable, that the all wise God would call his name after that which He himself cursed—for He cursed the earth, the ground; and all that is cursed by God is to be burned up. It is, therefore, unreasonable, if not impossible, to believe that God would call His Son, who He made immortal, after anything that he would burn up under his curse. On the other hand, it is equally plain that He gave His Son his name from *Adonim*, the plural of *Adonai*, one of the Hebrew terms or names by which God called himself. Reader, is it not reasonable that God would thus call His Son after one of His own names, rather than that of the ground on which His creatures walk? We think so, and therefore have no hesitation in saying that *ha Adhom's* name is from *Adonim*.

The term, or name, *Elohim*, is that by which God made himself known, while he was creating the heavens and the earth, and is plural, (mistranslated in our Bibles in the singular God) and being plural when he created *ha Adhom*, He said, "Let *us* make *Adhom* in our own image, and after our own likeness." This word *Adonim* is also plural, and must be the term from whence the name of His Son is derived; as it is one of the names by which His Father was called, both *Elohim* and *Adonim* being plural. It is, therefore, plain to every reader, and we trust also to Dr. Seiss, that God did not call His Son by a name that designated any other than white, and white alone. How could he do so, as he expressly tells us that He created *ha Adhom* in His own image, and after His own likeness, and commanded *ha Adhom* to produce his own kind, in his own image, and after his own likeness; and which commandment, or law of creation, God extended to all other animated beings, and even to inanimate things, that they, too, should produce their own kind, in their own image, and after their own likeness.

It was *ha Adhom* that fell, and all his progeny bearing his image and likeness, are with him, alone the subjects of redemption through Christ our Saviour. *Ha Adhom* was in the image of God, and his children bore His image, and St. Paul says of our Saviour that, "He was the express image of God's person." That He was white, of the tribe of Judah, of the line and lineage of David, a son of Abraham, a descendant of *ha Adhom*, who was the Son

323

of God, none will dare dispute. That his mother, Mary, was of the same tribe and descent, is equally indisputable. Now, suppose the *niggar* (we use the Hebrew orthography, representing by that word the black man) had been in any way related to the white race, how, we ask, was the *niggar* to be connected by blood with the Son of God, and what would have been the consequence? God would have had, from the necessities of the case, to have selected a *niggar* wench, to be the Mother of our Lord Jesus Christ, with her kinkey head, low forehead, flat nose, kidney lips, gizzard foot and black skin, and that would have produced a mulatto. Was the Saviour of the world a mulatto? The veriest devil that ever lived on earth, from the day of the catastrophe at the Garden of Eden, down to the present time, dare not assert it. We know that negroes now produce their own kind in their own image, and that the whites also do the same. But if either amalgamate with the other, the being produced is not in the likeness or image of either, but is a mulatto, showing palpably to the eyesight and all the senses of each, that both of them have violated God's commandment and order of creation. Reader, do you believe that God ever did, or would violate one of His commandments? Those who believe, say, or teach, that the negro is the equal of the white, must first believe that God himself is a transgressor of His own laws.

But, suppose we admit it to be true, as Dr. Seiss has said, that our first parents were a red man and a red woman, how does that help the Doctor in his argument with the negro? God's commandment is still the same, that each should produce their own kind, in their own image and likeness, and if they did so all of *ha Adhom's* race would be red men and red women still. This only increases the Doctor's difficulty, for he would now have to account for the existence of both whites and blacks. The Doctor's argument of the bleaching influences of time in certain localities, and its browning influences in others, producing whites in the one case and blacks in the other, vanishes like the baseless fabric of a vision, on the asking of a single question, thus: Did you, Dr. Seiss, ever know or hear of a place that if negroes went there they were bleached into white men and women; their kinkey heads changed to long beautiful hair; their flat noses raised up; their kidney lips transformed to beauty, and their gizzard feet made into feet like the whites? If there is such a place on earth or ever was, and if you will only point it out, every negro on earth would soon be there. Such arguments, Doctor,—excuse us for saying it—are but childish follies; for you must know that no such place exists on earth, and neither you, nor any one else, have ever heard of negroes turning to white men and white women since the world began, nor on the other hand, of white men and women turning to negroes.

Dr. Seiss, why do you and other learned clergymen continue to insist that God did make *ha Adhom* out of *adhamah,* (the ground) when God has so plainly stated that He made him of *gnapher,* thus grossly contradicting the Almighty? If He had made him of *adhamah* it was just as easy, and would make as good sense to have said so. God is too wise to err, and too good to mislead, and he always uses the exact word to express the exact idea that he intends to convey. And this case is evidence of the truth of what we say, and, therefore, He used the word *gnapher* and not the word *adhamah.* Now, Dr. Seiss, if the term from which *ha Adhom's* name is derived was meant to indicate his color, producing, as you say, a "red man and a red woman to begin with," then it logically follows that his name, constituted out of this word, must mean, in itself, that *ha Adhom* was *red,* for it is an axiom in logic that, that which is in the constituent, which, in this case, is in the word *adhamah,* must also be in that which is constituted out of it, viz: *ha Adhom.*

Now, Dr. Seiss, we appeal to your candor as a scholar, does the name *ha Adhom* mean *red,* or a red man in any sense? You know it does not; and this fact should have convinced you that his name was not derived from *adhamah,* (red ground,) but from *Adonim,* one of the names of God his Father. The meaning of *ha Adhom's* name is, as you well know, *the blood,* "the *man,*" in Hebrew; and it is the same meaning in Chaldea and in the Arabic, the first two languages that sprung out of the Hebrew. And this is in perfect accordance with what God had said, that the soul of the flesh is the blood. The soul of *ha Adhom's* flesh being his blood, and the *life* of his soul being God's breath, breathed into his nostrils, he was commanded to produce his own kind, in his own image, as he was himself thus made in the image of God. And as it was his blood, made by God himself, the soul of his flesh, it was by this blood alone, that he could produce his own kind, in obeying God's commandment. The soul of the negro being his blood, and the life of his soul, the air or atmosphere, he to is commanded to produce his own kind, in his own image, and which he does by his own blood, specially ordained by God to produce nothing but negroes or black men.

Of this latter fact you have had occular proof in your own city of Philadelphia, within the past few months, and which was published in many, if not all, your papers. It was this: A black man, a negro, had the flesh torn by a musket shot from the side of his face, exposing his mouth. The wound was so large that the edges could not be drawn together. His physician told him that by cutting a piece of flesh from his (the negro's) arm, and inserting it in the wound, that it would grow and cover the place completely. The negro consented to the operation, which was successfully performed. As an experiment of curiosity, the doctor cut a piece of flesh out of his own arm, about the size of a dime, and inserted that also. It did grow; and the white spot was plainly seen. But now what followed? In the course of a few months after, the soul of the negro's flesh being his blood, knew that this white flesh was not of its production, and did not belong to the black man, went to work and covered it with veins, and, in the course of a few months, turned it as black as the negro. Thus proving, by occular demonstration, that the soul of the flesh is the blood; and by this ordainment of God, every species and variety of animals, creeping things, and fowls, and birds, and fishes are kept up by the specific blood appointed by God to each of them.

DR. SEISS'S CHALLANGE ACCEPTED.

The next point which Dr. Seiss presents is a challenge to Ariel. Ariel had said that he defied all Roman Catholics and all Protestants, of every name, to show a single instance wherein either our Saviour or his apostles or evangelists had ever preached to or baptised a negro or mulatto, or had ever established a church of such on earth.

Dr Seiss, without denying the truth of this, proposes to offset it by the following rejoinder: " We defy all the doctors on this earth now living to point out a *single* instance between the covers of the New Testament, in which a negro or mulatto was ever rejected from hearing the Gospel, or from baptism and church membership, because he was a *negro* or mulatto, or in which an opportunity to preach the Gospel to one was not embraced. Will Ariel accept the challange?"

The foregoing is the language of Dr. Seiss's challenge. Reader, look at it. Is it possible that no clergyman of any religious sect on earth can or will act fairly? We expected better things of Dr. Seiss. It is not our fault if we take him as he presents himself. He asks us to prove a negative—a thing never expected to be done nor required to be done in any law court on earth. But feeling himself driven to the wall, he could do no better—and better would it have been for him not to have made such a demand, and then in his boastful language to ask, "does Ariel accept the challenge?" Does not every man know that an affirmative can be proven, and that the *onus probandi* lays on him who says a certain thing was done; and not on another to prove that it was not done.

But, notwithstanding this unfairness on the part of Dr. Seiss, we accept his challenge, and will, with God's help, show to every reasonable and candid mind that there were certain persons or creatures to whom the Gospel was forbidden to be preached; and that there was another, who, hearing the Gospel preached, believed, and was baptised; but when it was found out that a certain thing beset him, he was expelled from the church, and not from any bad conduct on his part. Should we succeed in this, and we will by God's help, will you, Dr. Seiss, then become an advocate of the truth that you have labored so earnestly to destroy? We would be happy to know that you would do so. The case is plainly stated in New Testament language thus: Jesus, after his resurrection, spake unto his disciples, saying, "All power and authority is given unto me in heaven and on earth, go ye, therefore, and teach all *nations*, baptising them," &c. And St. Mark says thus: "Go ye into all the world, and preach the Gospel to every *creature*," &c. The world is composed of nations, and nations are composed of individuals or creatures. All things *named* by God are directly responsible to God. *Adhom, ha Adhom*, was the first creature, and God named him; hence his direct responsibility to God. To this being, or person, *God gave the whole of this earth, and the dominion thereof.* Nations are composed of individuals—God *named them goim,* (nations.) Now it is an axiom in logic, that that which is in the *constituent,* (*ha Adhom,*) must also be in the *constituted,* (*goim*) nations. Nations, according to St. Matthew, must be taught; and the creatures of each *nation* hear the Gospel preached to them, according to St. Mark; and that which *he called the Gospel,* St. Luke defines to be, "that repentance and remission of sins should be preached in His name among all *nations,* beginning at Jerusalem." It will be seen by the reader that our Saviour's instructions, as recorded by St. Matthew, was for them to go and "teach all *nations;*" and that of St. Luke, is that the Gospel should be "preached among all *nations;*" and St. Mark says, to "preach the Gospel to every *creature;*" and St. Paul says that "of one blood God hath made all *nations,*" referring to the fact that Eve was taken out of the body of *ha Adhom;* and God himself, when He divided the earth into seventy nations, among the descendants of Noah, is particular to trace the genealogy of each back to Noah, and from Noah back to *ha Adhom* and Eve, the beginning of that *one blood,* and He divinely called these seventy nations, *goim* in Hebrew. That these were all whites, and lineal descendants of *ha Adhom* and Eve, no candid person can or will doubt. *Ha Adhom* and Eve alone fell, and it was to redeem them and their children that the Saviour of the world was manifested in the flesh, being himself a lineal descendant of *ha Adhom* and Eve on the side of his mother Mary; God himself being his Father. After his resurrection from the dead, he said to his disciples: "All authority and power in heaven, and in earth are now given unto me, go ye, therefore, and teach all *nations,*" &c.

We are thus particular, reader, that you may know to whom the Gospel was to be preached. With this statement before us, we now reply to Dr. Seiss's challenge. In the execution of this commission to His disciples, Paul and Silas were preaching the Gospel in Asia, in the region of Phrygia and Galatia, preaching the Gospel very successfully, they were *forbidden* of the Holy Spirit to preach the Gospel in the adjoining parts of Asia. They then went to Mysia, and from thence they assayed to go into Bythinia, "but the *Holy* Spirit suffered them not." Now, Dr. Seiss, we have the words of our Saviour commissioning His disciples to go into all the world, and teach all nations; to preach the Gospel to every creature, saying that all authority and power in heaven and in earth are committed to Him; and in the execution of their mission, so to preach the Gospel, Paul and Silas are forbidden of the Holy Spirit to preach the Gospel in certain parts of the world—certain parts of Asia. Would the Holy Spirit thus contradict our Saviour, and contravene his commandment to his Apostles, if the regions referred to had been occupied by whites, the children of *ha Adhom* and Eve? Most assuredly the Holy Spirit would have done no such thing. And contemporaneous history shows the regions referred to were occupied by blacks, by negroes, as the reason why the Holy Spirit forbade them to preach the Gospel in those parts. For if the region had been uninhabited, neither Paul and Silas could have had any motive to go there, to visit it. This will be a sufficient answer to that part of Dr. Seiss's challenge respecting the refusal of the Gospel being preached to negroes and mulattoes. We now take up the second part of his challenge.

The Evangelist, Phillip, went to Samaria and preached the Gospel, which the Samaritans hearing, believed, and were baptised, both men and women. Among those that attended Phillip's preaching, and wondering at the signs and miracles performed, was one Simon, a Magician, of whom it is said, he also believed and was baptised. (The reader will remember that our Saviour had said that the devils believe and tremble.) Now when the Apostles at Jerusalem heard that Samaria had received the Gospel, they sent down unto them Peter and John, to pray for them, that they might receive the gift of the Holy Spirit. And when they had come unto them, and prayed for them, the Holy Spirit fell upon them. And when Simon saw that he was left out, he put his hand in his pocket, and took out money to buy from Peter the like gift. To which Peter answered: "Thy money perish with *thee*, as thou hath thought the gift of God could be bought with money." Just at this time, it would seem, the Apostle's attention was rivited on the man's face, and discovered he

4

was a mulatto, and he said: "Thou hath neither part nor
lot in this matter; for I perceive that thou art in the gall
of bitterness, and bond of iniquity." Peter here used the
exact language that Moses had used in the 32nd chapter
of Deuteronomy, when speaking of the mulattoes. In the
language of St. Peter, "thou hast neither part nor lot in
this matter." This was the last of Simon and his church
privileges.

Dr. Seiss, you know that the Holy Spirit could not,
would not, and did not, contradict our Saviour's commands
to his Apostles. An instance somewhat similar occurs in
the Old Testament, where the commands of a Prophet
contravenes a moral law of God, but arises from the bad
translation of our Bible. It is this: God had commanded
a man to love his wife, and the wife to love her husband;
and that they should love their children, and bring them
up in the nurture and instruction of the Lord. Now, on
the return of the Jews from their captivity in Babylon to
Jerusalem, Nehemiah and Ezra not only commanded certain Jews to put away their wives and children, but made
them swear upon the altar that they would do so; for, as
King James's translation has it, their wives "were of
strange flesh;" they were negroes or mulattoes, and the
the translation would have been exactly correct to say,
they were of beasts' flesh. This explanation removes the
contradiction of God's moral law, justifies the action of
the Prophets, in what they required.

In regard to what Dr. Seiss has said in his exegesis
of Genesis VI, 1-2, respecting the sons of God that saw the
daughters of *men* that they were *"fair,"* and took them
wives of all they choose, we refer the reader to what we
have previously said on this point, and now add: That
the word translated fair, in Hebrew is *tovoth*, does not
mean light or fair complexion; the Hebrew word for fair
complexion is *yapha*. But, besides this difference, Dr.
Seiss seems to have overlooked the fact that God had
given, in the preceding chapter, the genealogy of *ha Adhom* down to Noah; and in the 6th chapter commences a
statement about the daughters of *men* as contradistinguished from the sons of God whose genealogy had just
been given, and who are now stated to have *corrupted*
themselves, by taking wives of these daughters of men;
and which corruption precipitated the Flood that destroyed

the world. It was an amalgamation by the sons of God with negroes and mulattoes—beasts. We add also one remark on Dr. Seiss's criticism about the Hebrew word *Ish.* Dr. Seiss has, perhaps, unintentionally done himself and Ariel great injustice in his criticism on the use of this word *Ish.* Ariel had thought his statements so plain about the word *Ish,* and its application to the whites, that none could misundertand him. He still thinks so, and is surprised at the mistakes and misrepresentation of Ariel on this point by Dr. Seiss. We thought it a matter so plain, and that it was understood by every person, the difference between a man's religious duties which connected him directly with God, and to perform which required all his heart, all his soul, all his mind, and all his strength, in sincere obediance to God; and the common everyday duties and obligations and transactions that were of a mere earthly nature, everyday affairs and business, whether political or otherwise, and which he might do or let alone, as he chose. This we thought was so apparent to every one, that we could not be misunderstood when we applied the word *ha Adhom,* as God does to *ha Adhom* from the beginning, as covering his duties to God, his Father; and that the term or name *Ish* is applied to him in all earthly things, that he might do or not do as he chose. It applies to him in every station, civil or political, social or otherwise, whatever they might be, and which he might do or let alone, as matters pertaining alone to this earth. For example: Our Saviour attended a marriage in Cana, of Gallilee. This he could do or let alone without violating any duty to God. This every one can see and know to be true, and in this sense, Ariel had said that God in His divine Word had so applied the term *Ish* to the white man. The reason why the term *Ish* is divinely applied to the whites is that the negro, being the head of the beast creation, and all beasts, creeping and moving things, were made by God to be slaves, to or servants to, His son *ha Adhom,* and all the service that they could render him, being of an earthly character only, *ha Adhom* while using them for his earthly gratifications or pleasure, might do as he wished, that, as the negro is the head of the beast creation, and as all beasts were made for *ha Adham's* earthly pleasure, he, as controller and director, is called *Ish,* as that head and for whom these pleasures were to be gratified, all of which belong to the animals and earthly enjoyments of earth, and as such, *ha Adhom* is called *Ish*. We have met the Doctor's challenge, corrected his exegesis of Genesis VI, 1-2; and explained the injustice he has done Ariel and himself about the use of the word *Ish*.

WHO BUILT THE TOWER OF BABEL.

But the next point which Dr. Seiss makes against Ariel is, that Ariel asserted that the builders of the Tower of Babel, were not white men, but were negroes and mulattoes. To this Dr. Seiss dissents, and declares that they are the descendants of *ha Adhom*. Dr. Seiss would not said so, nor can any other intelligent man that will think for a moment, on all the facts and circumstances connected therewith, and as stated in the Bible. God had certainly a purpose to accomplish in confounding their language, of which their being unable to understand each other was one part of it, but not all. Ariel had said on page 33 of his first work, after quoting the exact language which God had used on the occasion: that there was more in this language than appeared upon the surface, or that would catch the mind of a superficial reader of God's Word; but that he would not stop then to examine it. Dr. Seiss's attack on this part of Ariel's works now furnishes the occasion to do so. We will illustrate what we meant when we said there was more in God's language, used on that occasion, than appeared upon the surface, or to a superficial reader of God's Word, by an incident that occurred in New York, in the summer of 1869, and then published in the New York papers. It is this: A gentleman had a copy of the Bible translated by the Rev. John Elliot into the Indian language of the Indians, that lived in that part of Massachusetts, immediately around Tremont, now Boston. This translation the Rev. Mr. Elliot had commenced in 1646, and on its completion it was printed in England in 1663. The kind hearted Mr. Elliot had his sympathies so aroused in behalf of the savage Indians, that he determined to furnish them with the word of life, in their own language. To this end he commenced the study of their language at Roxbury, in 1638, and completed the study, making himself master of the language by 1646, when he commenced the translation. He translated from our English Bible, into the Indian language. He tells us that the vocabulary of the Indians consisted of eighty-six words. The usual number of words belonging to the native Indian languages, at that time, ranged from sixty-five to one hundred and eight words; that, into which he translated had eighty-six. It was a copy of this Bible in the Indian language, that the gentleman, on the occasion referred to, proposed to present to the New York Historical Society; only three other copies were known to be extant. The gentleman addressed a letter to the President of the New York Historical Society, expressing his intention to present it, and asking that a day be appointed for the purpose. This was done. At the time appointed there was assembled a number of learned divines, judges, and learned professors of different colleges. The speech of the gentleman who presented it, was followed by a number of others from the learned gentlemen, all highly complimentary of the Rev. John Elliot, extolling his kindness of heart, his philanthropy, and his benevolence, that caused him to spend his life in trying to teach the poor Indian the way of salvation; they called him the apostle to the Indians.

Now, reader, we have the facts before us, on which we would call your attention. God's Holy spirit required the Hebrew language, consisting of six thousand and four hundred words, to express what is contained in the law of Moses, in the Prophets, and in the Psalms of the Old Testament containing his law and will. Our Saviour and his Apostles required the Greek language, consisting of seventeen thousand words, for the Holy Spirit to express the Gospel in the New Testament. Now these gentlemen, unthoughtedly believed, and from their speeches would have you and I believe, that the Rev. John Elliot had accomplished with eighty-six words all that which God's Holy Spirit had required so many thousands of words to express God's will in. Impossible! Suppose Ariel had been present, and had asked the learned gentlemen, if either of them could express in eighty-six words *all that is contained in the Old and New Testaments?* what answer could be given to the question in truth? Every one must know that the only answer that could be given, would be that it was an impossibility.

This, however, is but the preface to what was covered by God's language, referred to. The vocabularies of the various negro languages, range from fifteen words, that of the Bosjamins being the lowest, up to thirty-five words, and in one or two instances, as high as sixty-three words. We now call our readers attention to the fact stated in the Bible, that at the beginning of the building of the Tower of Babel, that all the world was then of one speech or language; and there is abundant evidence furnished by the Old Testament that, that one speech, one language was the Hebrew; for we know that this was the language of the Garden of Eden, and is the language of heaven, and is still the language of heaven, as it is so recorded in the New Testament.

Now for the purpose, the grand remaining purpose of Almighty God, in confounding the language of this mixed crew of Babel builders, of blacks and mulattoes, under the leadership of Nimrod, will now be presented. The reader will bear in mind the fact, that this confounding of language, was done directly by God himself; and we will see directly, that it was limited to, and extended alone to the blacks and mulattoes; and was intended by God to prevent their having a knowledge of his will and laws. Now, reader, for the proof this, which is patent on its face to every intelligent man or woman, now on earth, and belongs to the white race, thus: We take the Bosjamins for example. God smashed his vocabulary down to twelve, or at most fifteen words. Would God hold him responsible for violations of his laws, which God himself have rendered impossible for him to know, through the very language which he had thus forced upon him by his own omnipotent power? The very asking of the question carries with it its own answer. And what is true of the Bosjamins, is equally and absolutely true of every other tribe of negroes; and of every class of nationality of mulattoes, or tribes of colored people now on earth. The Chinese language has but four hundred and fifty words; that of the Japanese, about one hundred and ten words less; and into neither of these can God's Word be translated; much less can it be translated into languages of fewer words. The man who says he can translate God's Word into the Chinese or Japanese languages, is simply asserting that he can do that which God's Holy Spirit could not do, and did not do.

The next point—that this confounding of languages was limited to, and included only the blacks and mixed races is equally clear, to any mind that will think. We believe that we shall be able to make our dear old brother, Dr. Seiss, to see and know that it did not include the whites. God himself gave the first language that was spoken on earth to *ha Adhom;* that language was the Hebrew, as can be easily proven to any believer in God's Word. It was a perfect language, and like everything else from God, must be perfect, and capable of expressing everything that is necessary to the glory of God, and happiness of man on earth and in heaven. This language consists of about six thousand and four hundred words, and was given to *ha Adhom,* who was certainly white. Now, Dr. Seiss, we will make you answer the question, which will forever settle the fact that the language of the whites was not included, or intended to be included in the confounding at Babel. That question is a plain one, which every one can understand, and understanding it, will know, without a quiver of a doubt, that it did not include the whites. And that question is: Can you, Dr. Seiss, or any other man on earth, whether learned or unlearned, can you now point your finger to a single white nation, now on earth, whose language consists of less than six thousand and four hundred words? You cannot do it. This you and all intelligent persons know is true. While on the other hand, you cannot point to a single tribe of negroes, or any "nationality" of them, or of the mixed blood or mulatto races, the vocabulary of whose language contains more words than we have stated. Now do not mistake yourself, nor commit the blunder that because you can take a negro, and soon learn him to speak any language now spoken by the whites—we say you must not commit the blunder by supposing that through *this medium,* God intended His Word to reach them, for that would be making their salvation (if there were any for them) to depend, not upon themselves, but upon others. God, in making the negro a beast, and the head of the beast creation, endowed him with speech, and made him the slave servant (*ebhodh*) of *ha Adhom,* and by which he could readily understand and obey the commands given; and in this station, and for this purpose, "he was good, very good," and *ha Adhom* could give no command but what was good.   By his own act, and at his own volition, he made himself the tempter, the dragon, that old serpent, which is the devil.

Would it not be well for our Bible societies to look a little more closely after those to whom God's word should be sent?   It might save a vast amount of money, and the lives of a great many deluded missionaries.

Dr. Seiss's translation of the 15th verse of the second chapter of Genesis, where the Hebrew word for slave occurs, but is not translated by King James's translators, admits the existence of the word in the original Hebrew, but now, strange to say, he changes its orthography from *ebhodh* to "*evod*" in the first place, and then in the next place, with the most astounding composure, translates the verse to mean that, *ha Adhom* was created *to be the slave of the garden*.   He next translates the latter part of the 5th verse of the second chapter of Genesis, where King James's translators also skip, and do not translate the Hebrew word for slave, and puts it thus: "And there was no man to till the ground."   Here, again, Dr. Seiss admits the existence of the Hebrew word for slave, and again changes the orthography, and makes this wonderful translation that, *ha Adhom* was to be *the slave of the earth*, or was *the slave of the earth*.   By this kind of translation, every one can see, that Dr. Seiss would contradict our Saviour to his face, and tell him that he knew nothing about the matter, when he said that the Sabbath was made for man, and not man for the Sabbath.   We are pained to notice such trifling with God's Word, by a man of the character and standing of Dr. Seiss.   He surely must have been imbibing a glass or two of the wine of a certain lady in Babylon.   The reader is referred to pages 134 and 135 of Dr. Seiss's pamphlet, for these wonderful translations. Ariel has, in this and in his previous works, given the correct translation of these verses.

DR. SEISS'S ENQUIRY: DID ADAM HAVE SLAVES IN THE GARDEN OF EDEN.

Dr. Seiss's next enquiry: Did *ha Adhom* have slaves,

black slaves, negro slaves? This is a most strange question to be put by a doctor of divinity. Reader, do you think he ever could have read the Bible in any language, to *know* what is said? If he had so read it, does he not know that God installed *ha Adhom* lord and master over everything on earth, and that he was thus placed by God over the negro, is plainly declared in His Word, and demonstrated in this work to be so plainly true, that any person, black or white, that believes the Bible to be God's Word, and has capacity enough to know that two and two make four, can neither mistake or doubt its truth.

The Doctor next asks: Can any one point out in the New Testament, where the *Lord's Supper* was ever *administered* to women? It is plain, from his asking this question, that he does not believe that it can be done. This only proves to us that our modern clergymen, as we have said, seem never to have read the Bible to know what it said. Our Lord Jesus, on the night in which he was betrayed, instituted the Supper, and said to his Diciples: "Do this in rememberance of me; for as often as you eat this bread and drink this cup, you do show forth the Lord's death till he comes." After his resurrection from the dead, he told his Diciples to preach the Gospel among all nations, baptising them, &c., and to teach the baptised "to observe all things whatsoever I have commanded you." Now, the Samaritans, hearing and believing, were baptized, both men and *women*. The Lord did command the Lord's Supper to be observed; he did command his Disciples to observe all things that he had commanded them. Does not the case of the Samaritan women, Dr. Seiss, fully and squarely answer your question that women partook of the supper? It surely does.

The Doctor says, on page 138, that "the Bible calls the tempter *nachash*, but never applies this word to a black or white man; all translators render it *serpent*. But Ariel says this is incorrect—a mere copy of Ptolomy's Scribes in making the Septuagint, who knew no better, and it really refers to (or means) the negro. If so, then we must read: Moses cast down his rod on the ground, and it became a negro, &c. * * * Shall we accept *such nonsense* for God's Word?" Whose nonsense is it, Doctor Seiss? It is certainly not Ariel's, for you can find no such word or meaning, line or sentence, in all of Ariel's works, from

4*

beginning to end.   Ariel never said that the Hebrew word *nachash* was negro, or meant negro ; on the contrary, he plainly asserted that it described the *mind*, and was the mind; that it was applicable to *ha Adhom*, and to every being, from him down to fishes that had five senses, for the *mind* is the product of the five senses, and when they are absent there can be no *mind* or reasoning faculties. It is other declarations of God's Word that fastens it on the negro, that he was the being whose reasoning faculties, or mind, that led Eve into the temptation.   Dr. Seiss can certainly distinguish between the mind and the being possessing it.

The word " vicious" is alike applicable to the horse, and to the serpent, under some circumstances, but because of this, will Dr. Seiss say that the *word* " vicious " describes either the horse or the serpent? Surely he will not.   All beasts and animals have mind—reasoning faculties.   Ariel gave the meaning of *nachash*, which it had at the time it was used, and criticised the other meanings which have since been *added to it by learned men*, in which Ariel showed that it was impossible that the word " serpent " could, in any sense, be the meaning of. the word *nachash;* that it was not the Hebrew word for serpent, that the Hebrew language, like all other languages, had its own word for serpent, and that word was *saraph*, and had it been a serpent in reality, the divine writer would have used that word in that place; for Moses certainly used it when the Hebrews were bitten in the wilderness by fiery serpents—*saraph meophesh*.   If Ariel were wrong in the meaning he gave to *nachash*, and in his criticisms, why did not you, Dr. Seiss, attack his statements and show what the true meaning of the word was, and the errors of his criticisms.   Dr. Seiss's failure to do this proves that Ariel was correct, and that Dr. Seiss could not successfully assail the one or the other, but chose rather to rely on misrepresentation of Ariel, and that he must have done it intentionally.   If we are wrong in this conviction, we shall be most happy to be corrected by him.   But his other misrepresentations of Ariel, viz: on the use of the word *Ish*, and on the use of the word *Enoshim*, which he said meant *brethren*, when he knows, as a Hebrew scholar, that it no more means brethren than it means owls or bats, and that it was evidently introduced into the manuscript by an error of the copyist.

What Abraham said to Lot, on the occasion, as shown by the manuscript, was that we be "rulers." The plain idea of Abraham was, God gave the earth and dominion over it to *ha Adhom*, and his children. "You command your servants, and they will obey you; and I will command mine, and they will obey me; and there will be no strife between you and me, for we be rulers." And your forced translation, Dr. Seiss, not to call it by a harder name, of a part of the 5th verse, 2nd chapter of Genesis, where you make *ha Adhom* the *slave of the earth;* and of that part of the 15th verse, of the same chapter, where you make *ha Adhom the slave of the garden*, and you do this in the face of the fact, which you well know, that *ha Adhom* was not to labor, much less to be the slave of the earth or garden, for you well know that God did not require him to labor until after his fall. But you were forced, by Ariel's translation and reasoning on these two verses, to admit that a slave, or slaves, did exist before the fall, and which King James's translators refuse to translate. You even changed the orthography of the word slave to *Evod* from *Ebhodh*. Why you did so, you may explain, or not, if you will. These things, taken together, compel us to fear that they were intentionally done, and against your better knowledge as a scholar.

If we have done Dr. Seiss injustice in arriving at this conviction, we ask him to forgive us, for we would not intentionally do him or any other *being* on earth, the least injustice. Our object in writing is to know and put forth what God has said, for it is God's Word alone that will stand, and what He said is alone that which we are interested in. Man's words, in this case, are of no value. The negro has his five senses, as all other beasts and animals have, and these constitute their mind, and which direct them how to protect themselves, and supply their wants and gratify their passions. It is this, and this alone, that governs all beasts and animals. But while *ha Adhom* had these appetites and passions, yet he was to be governed, not by them, but by every word that proceedeth out of the mouth of God, directing him how to use them, as our Saviour has plainly stated in His own temptation in the wilderness. When the divine writers speak of a snake or a serpent they invariably use the word *saraph*, and not the word *nachash*. Copyists have sometimes put *nachash* in their manuscript by mistake, where it is plain, from the context, that *saraph* was intended.

THE ENMITY PUT BY GOD BETWEEN THE TEMPTER AND HIS CHILDREN, AND EVE AND HER CHILDREN.

The next point that Dr. Seiss introduces, is that of the enmity which God said he would put between the tempter and the woman, and between her seed and his seed. Dr. Seiss's remarks on this point quite astonish us. That there was a temptation, a tempter, and the tempted, none doubt. That the tempted were *ha Adhom* and Eve, and that the tempter talked, and that he was to have children (seed), and that he was to die as other beasts and animals, is equally plain. Now who, or what, is now on earth that talks, has children, and dies, that could be the tempter except the negro? For *ha Adhom* and his children are plainly shown, from God's Word, to be white. Yet, in the face of these facts, Dr. Seiss enquires "if the *enmity* put by God between the tempter and the woman, and his *seed* and her *seed*, where then has this enmity been all the while, if Ariel's views be true, and the negro be the tempter," and says: "Ariel may call it what he pleases, *a story of enmity*, but it is very like a story of marvellous *love*, quite equal to that of whites and whites." Reader, is not this strange reasoning? Did not God say that he would put enmity between them? This *quasi* contradiction of the Almighty, by Dr. Seiss, in his assertion that it looks, on the contrary, like a "story of marvellous love," which places him in a position that no lover of God should occupy.

Is there no enmity between sin and a man's eternal happiness, placed by God, because man loves sin and rolls it under his tongue as a sweet morsel? Is there no enmity between whisky and the drunkard, and his present and eternal welfare, because he loves it? Do not all our temptations to sin arise out of our love of wrong doing, even when we gratify our most excited passions? Why did God destroy the world by a flood? Was it not because of the antediluvians' love of corruption and wickedness? And will you say, Dr. Seiss, that there was no enmity between this corruption and wickedness and their everlasting welfare, that brought this destruction upon them? Will you say there was no enmity between the wickedness and corruption of the people of Sodom and Gomorrah and their best welfare, and for which God burnt them up, and sunk these cities more than thirteen hundred feet beneath the slimy asphaltites? Or did, and will you say that the Almighty God drowned the world, burnt up Sodom and Gomorrah, and its inhabitants, and sunk the ground upon which these cities stood, beneath the salt and slimy asphaltites, *merely* because he was "*mad*," and not because of the love of the antediluvians, and of the Sodomites, for wickedness and corruption? *Their love* for this wickedness and corruption was not the cause, but it was the wickedness and corruption itself, then practiced by the people, that brought on these destructions? You, Dr. Seiss, dare not say to the contrary. And yet, in your above interrogations you have palpably made a *quasi* contradiction of the Almighty, that *he did not* put enmity between the tempter (the negro) and the woman, and his seed and her seed. We ask you, Dr. Seiss, if you do not believe that God did actually put this enmity between them, or are we to understand you as believing that He put nothing but this "marvellous love," of which you speak? Are we to understand you, and did you intend for your readers to so understand you, that God put no such enmity, and that the Almighty was mistaken and put no such enmity whatever, but, on the contrary, established "marvellous love" between them? Please explain yourself to your readers, if you can.

We do not think it necessary to notice the Doctor's criticism on the name *Enosh*, which means one that is degraded, that is incurably afflicted in his skin, in the color, (not like jaundice that medicine can cure) but which can neither be washed out, cured, or rubbed out; subject to all maladies, and when death ensues, without the hope of a resurrection hereafter. Such was Cain's first born. The other name, *Enoch*, means one that is dedicated, and devoted to God. Now it is impossible but what the latter applies to the whites; and that the former must apply to Cain's first born, whose mother was a negress.

ARIEL'S REPLY TO

THE MEN BEGAN TO CALL, &C.

The next point of Dr. Seiss's that we shall notice, is his translation of the latter part of the last verse, of the fourth chapter of Genesis, where it is said in King James's trans-lation that, "Then men began to call upon the name of the Lord." On this Dr. Seiss remarks as follows: "We read in Genesis IV. 26, in connection with the birth of a grandson of Adam who his father called by a name that Ariel says designates a mulatto. Did Seth call his son's name *Enoch*? or is it a slip of the pen of the transcriber of the manuscript." Evidently the latter.

The Doctor's criticism on "Then men began to call on the name of the Lord," and his own translation of how it should read, after excepting Ariel's translation, he goes on to say, "unfortunately for Ariel's exactness, the original does not say ' men ' at all, whether whites or blacks. The literal Hebrew is *impersonal*." Thank you, Doctor, for calling my attention to the *fact* that it is *impersonal;* for neither *negro* or *mulatto* are regarded as persons, any more than cattle, or sheep, or horses. He says, on page 139, " two explanations present themselves; either, that up to the time of the birth of Seth's son, mankind had not called upon God by that remarkable name, *Jehovah*, and only *then* began to conduct their devotions with reference to this name. * * * That it was only now that man-kind began to have convocations for *public worship*." And he says: "We are inclined to accept both, and hence read: 'Then it was began to call (assemblies for public worship, and to worship and preach) on the name of Jehovah.'"

Reader that is his translation; what do you think of it? Ariel had translated the exact *idea* contained in it, thus: "Then men began to profane the Lord by calling on His name," and that the Jews translated it thus: "Then men began to profane the name of the Lord." He says: " *To profane* is nowhere among the meaning." The Jews put their translation in ten words; and Ariel put his in twelve words; and Dr. Seiss in *nineteen*, and complains of Ariel that profane is not among the meanings. Will you be kind enough, Dr. Seiss, to tell us where you find the original for " assemblies or convocations of the people," for worship, or calling on this remarkable name

342

Jehovah? Who was to do this calling, and who was to constitute these assemblies, and convocations of the people when called? There was then living *ha Adhom*, and Seth, and Seth's little baby; for Cain had been banished after the killing of his brother Abel? If Seth did the calling, then *ha Adhom* constituted the *assemblies and the convocations of the people*, and if *ha Adhom* did the calling, then Seth constituted, with the women, these august assemblies of the people.

Reader, what a terrible and destructive engine is the logic of facts in destroying false meanings, false reasoning, and false translations, and false assertions of human contrivance, when attempted to be brought to bear against God's truth. Here we have before us this able scholar and most amiable man, so weighed down with the dogmas of theological schools, as to be unable to proceed a single step in his translation without contradicting the Almighty and His Word, and the inevitable fact, which the logic of their statements must prove to have existed. Dr. Seiss says: "Then it was that the people began to call *public* assemblies, and to *preach* on the name of *Jehovah*." Now who constituted these public assemblies, and who was it that did the preaching? and where do you find, in this verse, the Hebrew for public, and for preach or preaching, and for the words assemblies and convocations? You know it cannot be done. You do not seem even to know that the word *Jehovah* is a term God never applied to himself personally—it describes relationship, and is not one of the names by which He chose to reveal himself to the world. Had you read God's Word with the least respect for Him, and regard for His holy name, that from the meaning of this word *Jehovah*, that God never did, and never could, have applied it to himself. It is the term, or name, applied, or bestowed, by the Jews in substitution of the real name of God, the immediate and *unpronounceable* name by human lips; and which the Jews assert was lost, and if ever found, and pronounced, it would be the signal for the annihilation of the universe. This Jewish figment had its origin directly after the death of Solomon; and is based upon God's declaration to Moses, when he said: "I did not make myself known to Abraham by my name, *Jehovah*, but by my name *El Shaddai*, (God Almighty.") The Jews taking it for granted, that Abraham, their father, was so great a man, that God would certainly have communicated it to him, unless it had been lost or withdrawn from the world on the fall of *ha Adhom,* they had the name carefully erased from the manuscripts of Moses, and inserted the name, or term, *Jehovah* in its place. The meaning of this term, shows that God never could have applied it to himself, as one of His names; its meaning is a being, or relationship, that once existed, but does not now exist, but shall hereafter exist. The true name is not lost, nor will the universe be destroyed when it is pronounced by human lips, for Ariel has often pronounced it. It will appear in the " White Man," when that book makes its appearance.

CHRIST PREACHING TO THE SPIRITS IN PRISON.

The Doctor's next point that we shall examine says: " That Christ being put to death *in the flesh,* but quickened by the Spirit, * * * went and preached unto the spirits in prison, which sometimes were disobedient, when once the long suffering of God waited in the days of Noah, while the Ark was preparing. If we are to interpret this literally of the underworld, then sure mulattoes must have had ' *souls*' to be alive yet, at the time of *Christ's death,* and Ariel is mistaken." Dr. Seiss, God has plainly declared, that " the *soul* that sineth shall die"—now you tell us that the " souls" of these mulattoes, that were drowned in the flood were *alive* at the time of Christ's death, and ergo, *still alive.* Which are we to believe, God or Dr. Seiss? Which do you believe, Doctor? " And any interpretation given as to *how* the preaching was done that these same *mulattoes* were regarded *by Christ,* as proper subjects to whom to preach and minister, and hence again not beasts without *souls.*"

In all this Dr. Seiss has committed two very grave errors, or he would not have made the quotation from the New Testament, or the comments upon it which he has. The first of these errors, is that he has confounded the word *soul* and the word *spirit* as the equivalents of each other, and meaning the same. This mistake is common to all clergymen, especially if he has been educated in a theological seminary or college. With all such educated men, they seem to overlook that the Divine Writers speak of body, *soul*, and *spirit*. The distinction is plainly kept up in the Old Testament in the Hebrew language, and are never confounded; and the same distinction is kept up in the Greek language, in the New Testament. In the Hebrew language the word for soul is *Naphesh*, which we have previously explained, that it is the *blood* which is the *soul* of the flesh, as is expressly declared by God himself. The Hebrew word for *spirit* is *Ruach*, which we have also explained. These words differ in their meaning, as widely as they do in their orthography. In the Greek of the New Testament, the word for soul is *Psyche*; while that for spirit is *Pneuma*, and have the same meaning of the Hebrew words. Dr. Seiss's quotation shows that Christ preached to the *spirits*." He then says that these mulattoes who were drowned in the flood, must have had souls, to be alive at the time of Christ's crucifixion. Not only does he confound soul and spirit as meaning one and the same, but would, as it seems from his language, have us believe that all that lived before the flood, and were drowned in it were, mulattoes. This is another very grave mistake of Dr. Sciss. The Saviour never preached to either the soul or spirit of a mulatto or negro, any more than that of horses; for each have souls alike. But the Doctor seems to forget, that the divine writer furnishes us the exact geneology of *ha Adhom* down to Noah; and it was to the *spirits* of these that Christ preached. They had all died without receiving the promises, and hence was regarded as being in the darkness of a prison; for life and immortality are brought to light through the Gospel, by the resurrection of Jesus Christ from the dead. It was this good news that Christ preached to the spirits in prison, and who were the genuine descendants of *ha Adhom* and Eve. Had King James's translators done justice to the seventh verse, of the second chapter of Genesis, or to themselves, Dr. Sciss would not have been led into these grave errors. Why he did not correct the translation himself, is a matter of surprise. A part of that verse stands thus in the original: "And God breathed into his nostrils *nishmath Chaiyim*." Why our translators saw proper to slur over, in the manner they have, this most important verse to *ha Adhom's* race, is to us unaccountable.

This word *nishmath* is not translated at all. Had it been

D2

translated it would have read: God breathed into his nostrils the spirit of lives. Three lives, viz: 1. Spirit life. 2. Soul life. 3. Body life. Now can we make our readers comprehend, with absolute certainty, the exact truth of these three lives? We think we can make it plain to any candid person, male or female, whether they know a word of Hebrew or not, that God did bestow these three lives upon *ha Adhom*. And in such a way that they shall not doubt it. The first, "*spirit life*," which is life eternal. About this there can be no dispute. The second, "*soul life*." God says the soul of the flesh is the blood; and the life of the soul is the breath that God then breathed into him—and *ha Adhom* ever after breathed light until he fell, as St. John tells us in the first chapter of his Gospel, when speaking of *ha Adhom's* creation says: "In it (the word) was light, and the light was the life of man, (*ha Adhom*,) just as this atmosphere is the life of all mortals, beasts, and animals, and is the life of their souls by breathing it. Of this there can be no doubt. The next is body life. Has not the body of every person this body life, so palpably existing that he can neither question it or doubt it. Why his very bones have life. If they did not they would never grow together after being broken. It is inanimate life, such as we see in trees, etc. Negroes, mulattoes, and all beasts, down to fishes of the sea, have the two last, but not the first. And consequently, when God breathed into *ha Adhom's* nostrils he became a living creature, possessed of *more* than soul life—*la naphesh Chaiyiah*.

WHO PIERCED OUR SAVIOUR ON THE CROSS.

The next point which Dr. Seiss brings up and assails is, that where Ariel said that the Roman soldiers, who were the executioners of our Lord, were mulattoes. He does not question the correctness of our interpretation of that part of God's Word, showing this to be true, but says substantially: "That Ariel must be wrong, for our Saviour prayed for their forgiveness, and that a time was coming that, not only every eye should see him, but they that pierced him should look upon him." The mistake of the Doctor here is, that he applies our Saviour's prayer to, and applies the words that they that pierced him, and shall look upon him, to his *executioners*, instead of applying it to the Jews and their rulers, who had it done. These executioners had nothing to do with his trial or condemnation, they but simply obeyed the mandate, which they were bound to do, of those who were in authority over them, and who had tried and condemned him. It was those rulers whose judgment caused him to be nailed to the cross and to be pierced. And it is these who shall look upon him, and for whose forgiveness our Saviour prayed.

This is so plain that we feel a hope, that Dr. Seiss, without thought, wrote what he has said on this point. To illustrate more strongly the correctness of this view, we present the following incident of the late war. A general had been stationed in a certain town, some of the people of which had done something, one night, that annoyed him. In his exasperation, next morning, he ordered a file of soldiers to go out and arrest the first ten men they found, and bring them before him. It so happened that the first ten men they met with, were countrymen coming into town from the country, with marketing to sell, who were arrested, and taken before the infuriated general, who immediately ordered them shot. And they were shot. Now, Dr. Seiss, who is responsible for the death of these men? The innocent soldiers who obeyed the order, as they were bound to do? or the infuriated general who commanded it to be done? Your answer to this question, Dr. Seiss, will show your error, in regard to the Roman soldiers, who were the executioners of our Saviour.

The Doctor seems to think that because the Syro-Phœnician woman, whose daughter our Saviour had healed, had *faith*, that, therefore, she was a subject of salvation, even if Ariel was correct in saying that she was a mulatto. Does not the Doctor know that devils have *faith*, and in divine language are said to "believe and tremble?" That Simon, the Sorcerer, who was also a mulatto, believed and was baptised, but as soon as it was found that he was a mulatto, he was expelled, and told that he had neither part nor lot in this matter.

We wonder what good, reading the Bible does clergymen? They seem to note nothing except it builds up some one of their dogmas. Look at what Dr. Seiss has said about the soul, and then look at what St. Stephen says, at the moment of his death, when the Jews were stoning him. Did he pray that the Lord Jesus would receive his *soul?* No; but he prayed, "Lord Jesus receive my spirit." Was he mistaken, Dr. Seiss? Which do you believe was mistaken, reader, Dr. Seiss or St. Stephen.

Dr. Seiss, we have now traveled through your reply to Ariel. We could have closed our remarks without taking up your criticisms on Ariel's Hebrew; for you were so completely prostrated by the Biblical facts stated in the former part of this reply, as to render any attention to your Hebrew criticisms entirely unnecessary. But we did not intend to leave you a pin's point to stand upon, nor a pin hook to hang a doubt upon. We, therefore, took them up *seriatim*, more for the purpose of showing you your errors, with a hope that you might become, as you can be, an able advocate of *God's truth*. Will you still allow us to indulge in this hope? If, in this our reply to you, Dr. Seiss, we have used a single word, or written a single line, to give offense or hurt your feelings, we ask you to forgive us, and to consider the word or line as not written.

Reader, whoever you are, male or female, and whether you be white or black or mulatto, know *you must bow* to the Word of the Almighty. You, nor any other being, nor all beings besides on earth, cannot change one jot or one tittle of what he has said, nor of what he has commanded. All shall submit to it; whether willing or unwillingly. Our plain duty then, is to know what he said, and obey what he commanded.

Reader, we are on the eve of the greatest revolution, politically, religiously and socially, that ever afflicted the inhabitants of this earth. All nations, since the world began, that have admitted the political, religious and social equality of the negroes and mulattoes with whites, God has not only obliterated their nationality, but exterminated their people. The people of the United States have recognized this equality. Your fate is before you. Look! The first of nations whose fate you are following is Egypt; the seond, Chaldee; the third, Phoenicia; the fourth, Assyria; the fifth, Medo-Persia. We do not mention in this list of ancients, the smaller nationalities, nor that of the Jews, for reasons that will be apparent to the reader. But even the later nations, the Greeks and Latins, God has exterminated, leaving just enough to point, like their ruined cities, to the grave of their nationalities, which says to you and I, here they once lived.

The same causes are now draping the nationalities of Europe in the vestments of the grave, from the loom of death. Look for example at France. In the beginning of this century, under the guidance of one unequaled in the annals of fame as a warrior—that proud eagle who built his nest of tumbled Empires, and who, by his genius, raised France to the highest pinnacle of grandeur. Where is France now? Will our rulers take warning? No. Will the men in high places take warning? No. Will your Congress take warning? No. Will your Governors and Legislatures of the different States take warning? No. Will your Eclesiastical bodies take warning and reform? No. Will the Roman Catholics reform? No. Will the Episcopalians reform? No. Will the Presbyterians reform? No. Will the Methodists reform? No. Will the Baptists reform? No. Will the Congregationalists reform? No. Will the Cumberland Presbyterians and on down to Mormons reform? No. Will the Jews reform and become obedient to God? No. All these political government and eclesiastical bodies, the rulers of which will never allow their people to lay aside their own additions to God's Word, nor will political rulers allow their people to enjoy their rights that God conferred upon them.

But we may be asked, why we think none of these organizations will never reform? To this we reply: that the Biblical facts, stated by God, show first, that from the fall of Adam, everything declined. A new start was made at the Flood, which also declined until Moses, when a new start was again made, continuing a short time, when they commenced declining by the traditions and additions of the Jews, until overwhelmed, and a new start made by Christianity, and which continued pure a short time, when it began to be corrupted by man. Yet, notwithstanding these religious denominations all take the Bible as the Word of God, yet, when we read that book from cover to cover, we cannot find the name of a single religious denomination now on earth in it, which is our second reason why no reformation can take place.

Then who is to move in this matter; in this approching crisis? We answer, none but those that are of that class who gladly receive our blessed Saviour, the *common people;* and of whom our Saviour said to John's disciples: "Go tell John (in prison) that the poor have the Gospel preached unto them." The common people must take this in their own hands, if they would escape the pending calamity; and in doing which they must be guided alone in their words and actions by God's Word. The leaders and the rulers of the people will never do it. They are now, as they were in the days of our Saviour, opposed to the simple truth, more or less as God spoke it, and command- ed it to be obeyed.

In conclusion, we address ourselves to our friend and brother, Dr. Seiss, as a scholar, and as one that believes in the truth of God's revelation; and now ask him as a scholar, if he does not know that the 1st, 2nd, 20th, 21st, 24th and 29th verses of the 1st chapter of Genesis are gross mistranslations; and that wherever the words *God* or *Heaven* appear in this chapter, that they are false translations. That the 5th, 7th, 15th, 17th verses of the 2nd chapter of Genesis are also gross mistranslations, and some of the former, as well as these, must have been in- tentional mistranslations by King James's translators. That what God said to Cain, before he killed his brother, commencing with the words "why art thou wroth," is also grossly mistranslated. That where it is said by Cain, after God cursed him, "thou ha t this day driven me out from the face of the *earth;*" and yet in a few verses after, that Cain went into the *land* of *Nod,* and took him a "*wife;*" this contradiction, you well know, should not exist. That the first part of the 3rd chapter of Genesis, is a gross mistranslation and perversion. That the mar- riage ceremony between *ha Adhom* and Eve is misstated and mistranslated; as any one can see by looking at our Saviour's comments on it as recorded in the Gospels. That the last verse of the 4th chapter of Genesis is also mistranslated. That the 1st, 2nd and 4th verses of the 6th chapter of Genesis, mistakes and mistranslations are found, consequently, what God's original Word said is not understood. That it is a gross mistake to translate the words *Adhom, ha Adhom*, by the word man at all; and that it is still a grosser mistake of King James's translators to translate the words *Ish, Enosh* and *Anshey* by the same word *man*, as they have done. These are but few of the instances of mistranslations occurring in the Old Testament, without referring to omissions and additions made by copyists of MSS. plainly to be seen and detected by any scholar.

We will now refer to a few in the New Testament. We commence with the 1st verse of the 4th chapter of Matthew, which King James's translators makes it to say: "Then was Jesus led of the Spirit into the wilderness, *to be* tempted of the devil." Does not every one know that it is impossible that God or His Holy Spirit could do so? What would you think of a father or mother that would voluntarily send their son or daughter to a house of ill-fame, to be tempted forty days and forty nights by what they might see and hear there? The idea is horrible; yet here we have it stated that our Saviour was led, not to a house of ill-fame, but to the very devil himself; and this statement is made, in the face of the Divine Record, that says God tempteth no man. That these same translators represent our Saviour as saying: "If I bear witness of myself, my witness is *not true*." Would He say anything about himself that was not true? You know He would not. Again, they represent Him, a few chapters after, as saying "though I bear record of myself, yet my record *is true*." Would the Saviour thus contradict himself? You know he would not. Again, they represent our Saviour as crucified along with two *other* thieves, or malefactors. Was our Saviour a thief or malefactor? You know he was not. Let these instances suffice for our purposes. Ariel has given the correct translation to many of these, in this and his other writings.

In the work which he is preparing for publication, he will, with God's aid and assistance, give in "The White Man," the correct translations of these and many others, which are now stumbling blocks in the way of honest minds, in comprehending what God *said*, and correct the omissions and additions which have been improperly made to God's Word. Our dear brother, Dr. Seiss, you can aid and assist us by your great learning and talents, if you will.   Will you let your poor, blind brother Ariel have your assistance?   God grant it.

To that class of common people, who gladly receive our Saviour, and who are now on earth, God says to you: "Come out from her My people; come out from them, and be you separated from them, and I will receive you, sayeth the Lord."   So mote it be.

ARIEL'S REPLY

TO

Dr. John A. Seiss, D.D.,

OF PHILADELPHIA,

This is Ariel's reply to the Rev. John A. Seiss, D. D. of Philadelphia; also containing his reply to the scientific geologist, and other learned men, in their attacks on the credibility of the Mosaic account of the creation and the flood.

It is a fact, well known to he public, that Ariel has never published a single letter from any of his numerous correspondence endorsing the correctness of his works regarding the biblical status of the negro. He now seemingly departs from this line by publishing the one below. His reason for doing so is found in the fact that the letter was not addressed to him, and was brought about by some gentlemen asking the privilege of showing his manuscript reply to Dr. Seiss, as they had learned it was written, though not published. Some of these gentlemen had been instrumental in getting Dr. Seiss to review Ariel's work, and having seen his review, desired to put Ariel's answer before one of the best Hebrew scholars for his examination and opinion. This request was granted by Ariel on condition that he would examine it as a scholar and give his opinion of it without favor or fear. After his examination of it he returned the following reply:

"GENTLEMEN: I have examined Ariel's reply to Dr. Seiss and the learned geologist, and say that his Hebrew is correct and his translations correct.

"That his reply to the scientific geologists in their attack upon the Mosaic account of the creation and the flood, is full and crushing, and sustains the exact truths of the Mosaic accounts of those two events. The work should be published immediately, and should be endorsed by all the clergy of all the different denominations, and spread broadcast over all the land, for that every lover of God's Word would want a copy wherever Christianity is known."

Orders may be sent to B. H. Payne, agent for Ariel, or to the American Publishing Co., Nashville, Tenn.

Price fifty cents per copy. One-third off to those that order by the hundred copies or more. Agents wanted everywhere.

NOW NEARLY READY FOR THE PRESS,

"THE WHITE MAN:"

"That he is the Son of God, and he alone can have Endless Life."

Showing 1. That God's Word is literally true, that in six days, of twenty-four hours each, He did make the heavens and earth, and "all the hosts of them." 2. That Moses' account of the creation, the fall of man, and the destruction of the earth by a flood are LITERALLY TRUE, and will be made to appear so to every intelligent, candid man and woman. 3. That when God spoke to man, he intended to be understood literally as we understand the speech of each other. 4. That when God's Word is properly translated, there is no difficulty in understanding it. 5. That when thus translated, no such unphilosophical and absurd sentences as "that the earth (a material substance) was without FORM and VOID," and "that in the day thou eatest thereof thou shalt surely die," and that the word "soul," as used and described in God's language is totally different from the ideas of Roman Catholics and Protestants as now held by them, and that the Roman Catholics and Protestants are equally mistaken in understanding the word "sacrifice." God's idea on both these words differ ENTIRELY from the received views of the present age, as will be seen by an examination of their translations. 6. That the Hebrew manuscripts from which our translation of the Old Testament is made, has many additions, transpositions and omissions in them, made by the copyist, which should have been corrected, and can be easily and satisfactorily corrected by comparing and collating text with the other manuscript and versions, without leaving a shadow of doubt as to what should be the true reading. 7. That the Hebrew of Moses and the prophets was written without PUNCTUATION marks, and these have, since the Christian era, been supplied by learned Jews, as late as the eighth century, and however honestly done, no candid man could expect them to punctuate so as to contradict their faith in rejecting Jesus of Nazareth as the Messiah. 8. In many leading Hebrew words, meaning have been added in our Lexicons from the Greek and Latin languages, and still more recently in editions published in the United States, which did not belong to those words when used by the divine writers, for these languages, and especially the English, had no existence or either of them for more than thirty centuries after the events of the Garden of Eden. 9. An examination of the "Septuagint" version and its history clearly shows how the word NACHASH, in the third chapter of Genesis, came to be translated SERPENT, and which is NOT the proper translation of that word. 10. That God's laws were given ALONE to the WHITE MAN, and never intended by him to be translated into any of the languages of the black or mixed races. 11. That the mixed bloods die out—become MULES—in the fifth white consecutive cross. 12. That God never created a mulatto or mule in this earth. 13. That God made two separations of the sons of Adam: First, from the blacks or negroes, when he divided and gave the earth to the whites alone; second, from the mulattoes in the family of Isaac, as both are plainly stated in His Word. 14. That the day called "the judgment of the great day" must not be confounded with the "Resurrection;" there are two of the former, first, that of the black man or negro; second, that of the white man, and between these there is a space of a "a little season," over one thousand years, and both take place on this earth before it is burned up. 15. The lake of fire is to be on this earth, and into which "death and hell" (HADES) are to be cast, which is the second death. 16. The BEAST, the false prophet, the devil and satan, and all the wicked are cast into this lake of fire burning with brimstone, before the new heaven and earth are brought into existence, as the future abode of the righteous. 17. The plain meaning of the words at the time they were used by the divine writers, literally understood, forces the conviction on every candid man of the truth of these propositions. 18. The great error made by the learned in translating, by one word, MAN, the various Hebrew words by which the white man, the negro and the mulattoes are designated is most grossly wrong, and perverts God's Word. 19. That the received idea by all Christians, that the mind, the reasoning faculties in man, is the "soul," and never dies, is wrong and grossly false, and is entertained from no want of clearness and precision in the Hebrew language in describing what God calls the "Soul." The mind, held in common by the white man and the negro, God cursed in the latter, but not in the former. The various names of the Diety explained, and why given or bestowed, &c.

This will make a work of about 500 pages, and will be furnished to Booksellers and others, as soon as published, on application to

B. H. PAYNE, Nashville. Tenn.

355

SOURCES

THE "ARIEL" CONTROVERSY

Ariel. [Buckner H. Payne] *The Negro: What Is His Ethnological Status? Is He the Progeny of Ham? Is He a Descendant of Adam and Eve? Has He a Soul? Or Is He a Beast in God's Nomenclature? What Is His Status as Fixed by God in Creation? What Is His Relation to the White Race?*. Second Edition. Cincinnati: n.p., 1867. (Courtesy of Garland Publishing)

Optician. *Speculum for Looking Into the Pamphlet Entitled "The Negro: What Is His Ethnological Status? Is He the Progeny of Ham? Is He a Descendant of Adam and Eve? Has He a Soul? Or Is He a Beast in God's Nomenclature? What Is His Status as Fixed by God in Creation? What Is His Relation to the White Race? By Ariel."* Charleston: Joseph Walker, 1867. (Courtesy of Duke University Library)

Young, Robert A. *The Negro: A Reply to Ariel. The Negro Belongs to the Genus Homo. He Is a Descendant of Adam and Eve. He Is the Offspring of Ham. He Is Not a Beast, But a Human Being. He Has an Immortal Soul. He May Be Civilized, Enlightened, and Converted to Christianity.* Nashville: J.W. M'Ferrin & Co., 1867. (Courtesy of the Library of Congress)

M.S. *The Adamic Race. Reply to "Ariel." Drs. Young and Blackie, on the Negro. "The Negro Does Not Belong to the Adamic Species"—"He Is Not a Descendant of Adam and Eve"—"He Is Not the Offspring of Ham"—"He Is Not a Beast; He Is a Human Being"—"He Has an Immortal Soul; But Not After the Image of God"—"And Every Attempt to Civilize Him, After Our Form, Has Resulted in His Speedy and Certain Destruction."* New York: Russell Bros., 1868. (Courtesy of Duke University Library)

Prospero. *Caliban. A Sequel to "Ariel."* New York: n.p., 1868. (Courtesy of Yale University Library)

Berry, Harrison. *A Reply to Ariel.* Macon: American Union Book and Job Office Print, 1869. (Courtesy of University of Georgia Library)

357

[Buckner H. Payne] *Ariel's Reply to the Rev. John A. Seiss, D.D., of Philadelphia; Also, His Reply to the Scientific Geologist and Other Learned Men, in Their Attacks on the Credibility of the Mosaic Account of the Creation and of the Flood.* Nashville: "The American" Printing Company, 1876. (Courtesy of the Library of Congress)

CONTENTS OF SERIES

Other Books by John David Smith

Window on the War: Frances Dallam Peter's Lexington Civil War Diary, with William Cooper, Jr. (1976)

Black Slavery in the Americas: An Interdisciplinary Bibliography, 1865–1980 (2 vols., 1982)

An Old Creed for the New South: Proslavery Ideology and Historiography, 1865–1918 (1985; reprint edition, 1991)

Dictionary of Afro-American Slavery, with Randall M. Miller (1988)

Ulrich Bonnell Phillips: A Southern Historian and His Critics, with John C. Inscoe (1990)